THE ART OF
SOUTH
AMERICAN
COOKING

ALSO BY FELIPE ROJAS-LOMBARDI

—

Soups, Beautiful Soups
Game Cookery Recipes
The A to Z No-Cook Cookbook

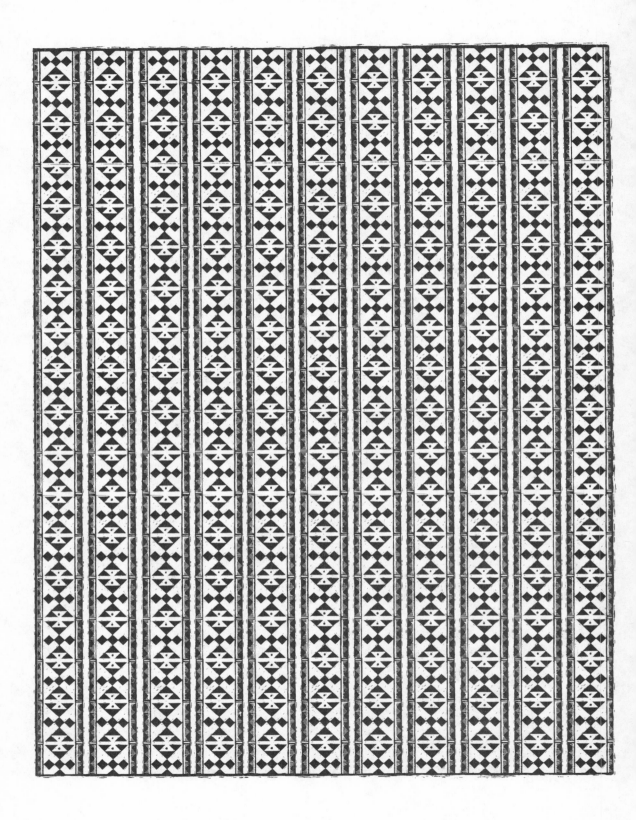

THE ART OF SOUTH AMERICAN COOKING

Felipe Rojas-Lombardi

HarperCollins*Publishers*

The author thanks Rosemarie Aldin, Gregory Dawson, and Susan Derecskey.

FIRST EDITION

DESIGNED BY JOEL AVIROM

Border Design by Jim Cozza

LIBRARY OF CONGRESS CATALOGING-IN-PUBLICATION DATA

Rojas-Lombardi, Felipe.
    The art of South American cooking / Felipe Rojas-Lombardi.
—1st ed.
        p.   cm.
    Includes index.
    ISBN 0-06-016425-5
    1. Cookery, Latin American.   2. Cookery—South America.
I. Title.
TX716.A1R65   1991
641.58—dc20
                                                            90-56395

    98 97 96   DT/RRD 10 9 8 7 6 5

To Tim Johnson, partner, mentor, friend

CONTENTS

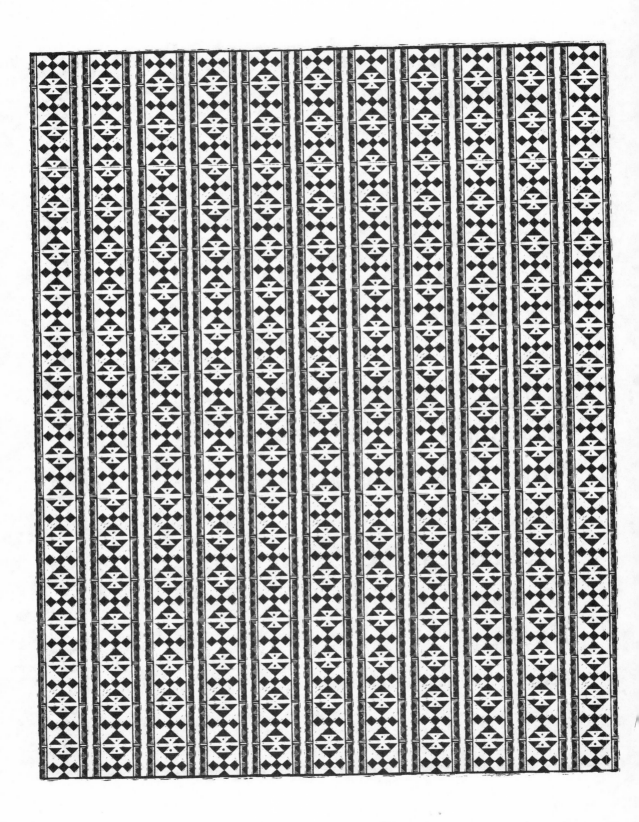

INTRODUCTION

My father was livid. Even that's a mild description. Actually I'd never seen him angrier. But fortunately, he couldn't see me.

I was hiding in one of my grandmother's large kitchen cabinets, and as I was only a shade over four feet tall at the time, it was easy to do. I crouched under the lowest shelf, looking out into the kitchen through a small hole in the door. There was my father, stomping around the large kitchen table, knocking over a chair, shouting, "Felipe! Felipe! Where are you? Come here this instant. I know you're somewhere in this damn kitchen. Come out! Now!"

Scared, knowing I was in for it, I meekly opened the cabinet door and crawled out. My father glared at me. "How many times do I have to tell you to stay out of this kitchen? This is not a place for little boys. You should be out playing soccer with your cousins and brothers. Now go out there!"

I didn't want to go out and play. I never wanted to go out and play. I loved my grandmother's kitchen—its smells, its tastes; for me this was an enchanted place. My grandmother, and even my mother, could take food of one kind or another and magically make it into something delicious and wondrous. Outside all you could do was kick around a dirty leather ball!

My father was a very stern, very proper South American businessman, and he expected that I, his oldest son, would grow up to be a carbon copy of himself, although he wanted me to be a lawyer. So I was to play sports with the other boys and leave things that were done in the kitchen to the women—my mother, my grandmother, and my sister. I was to look at life as he looked at life. And that was that.

Only that wasn't that. I can't remember a time when food wasn't the most important thing in my life. And I can't remember a time when the kitchen wasn't my favorite place in the house. Especially in my grandmother's house, where I had been sent to live at a very early age. My father's mother was a proud woman who had come from Chile to Peru, met and married my grandfather, and raised a large family. She was the dominant figure in our family circle. My father wanted me to live in his mother's large house in Lima because he wanted me, as his oldest child, to learn all of his family's traditions. To an extent I did: I learned all of his family's *food* traditions!

Grandmother's house was the gathering place for our very large extended family. All great family holidays, events, and birthdays took place in her home, and her kitchen was kept busy day and night, most of the year, with the preparation of wonderful dishes to please the multitudes.

My grandmother was master, and very much the lady of her kitchen. Though not an absolute monarch, she came as close as possible, or as close as my mother would allow. For all great family feasts, my mother and her mother-in-law shared the responsibility of creating the meal. If Catherine the Great had been asked to share the duties of the kitchen with Queen Victoria—well, you have some idea of what it was like in the kitchen Rojas-Lombardi!

Each woman carved out a personal domain in that (fortunately) large room. Each had her own helpers. Few words passed between them as they went about their chores, even on those occasions when several days of preparation were required for a single meal. I loved it! Mother and Grandmother vied with each other to see how much they could teach me, and I was the very willing student of two great chefs. A child in love with food could have asked no more.

The cuisine of my childhood was very eclectic. My grandmother's influences were those of her native Chile—heavily Spanish—with touches of her German background. Of course, she loved seafood, the predominant food in Chile, a long, coastal country. My mother's parents were Italian, so the Italian influence was there, though it was not as strong as that of their adopted country, Peru. Peruvian cuisine reflects the country's mixture of cultures: those of the Spanish, the native Quechua Indians, and the black Africans, who were brought over as slaves by the Spanish colonials. The kitchen in my grandmother's house was an even greater cultural melting pot as a result of the kitchen helpers who worked for my mother and grandmother. Around great feast days extra help was needed, and women from all over South America—including Bolivia and Brazil—would be brought in, as well as Peruvian Indian women. My kitchen education was a United Nations of cultural influences.

The influence of the Quechuas is the dominant factor in the food culture of Peru. Unlike Chile, which is primarily desert and produces few agricultural products, Peru is a highly developed agricultural country. Peru, too, is desert along the coast, but the Andes mountain ranges that occupy most of Peru are very wide, unlike the Chilean Andes. And the Quechuas, who live in the Andes, hundreds of years ago learned how to terrace the mountains and turn them into some of the finest farming land in the world.

The Quechuas, often referred to by the title of their leader, the Inca, developed a very sophisticated agricultural science. They are credited with discovering, developing, and breeding hundreds of varieties of such staple items as corn, potatoes, and hot peppers. Even today Peru can boast some thirty or more varieties of potatoes, some of them very exotic and colored purple or yellow, and one that is as white and soft as cotton. There's even a potato that appears transparent when sliced, the *olluco*. The several dozen different types of hot peppers grown in Peru vary in hotness depending on how high up in the Andes they are cultivated. And the corn! You've never seen anything like the corn in Peru, with kernels that are as large as cherry tomatoes. Once, when my mother came to visit me in the United States, she decided to prepare one of my favorite corn dishes as a special treat. She went to the supermarket and found to her dismay the normal North American corn. She couldn't believe the kernels were so small, but since she was determined to make this dish, which consists of corn kernels threaded on toothpicks, dipped in batter, and sautéed, she spent the whole day painfully threading the minuscule kernels onto toothpicks. In the end all she was left with were toothpicks with the flavor of corn! She was so disappointed. In Peru you actually peel the kernels before using them for cooking. Try doing that with the corn you're familiar with!

It's impossible to talk about the foods of South America without stating at the very beginning the fact that Peru was and is the epicenter of that continent's food culture. Peru, to a large extent, is what South American cooking is all about.

If you were to narrow it down to two words that could be called the keys to Peruvian cuisine, and thus to South American cooking, they would have to be *water* and *llama*.

Water, and the incredible way the Quechuas controlled and used water, made it possible to irrigate whole mountain ranges and to turn otherwise inhospitable soil into fertile, creative laboratories where the Quechua agricultural "scientists" could experiment and work their wonders.

Picture, if you can, the very high mountain ranges called the Andes, which virtually divide the South American continent in two. The Andes start almost at the very top of South America and continue down to the very tip. Looking at the map, to the west of the Andes we have Colombia, Ecuador, Peru, and Chile. Smack in the middle of the Andes is Bolivia, once part of Peru and now separated from it by that large mountain lake, Lake Titicaca.

To the east of the Andes are Venezuela, Guiana, Surinam, Inini, Paraguay, Uruguay, and Argentina. The differences in foods in South America, from country to country, are greatly influenced by which side of the Andes the country is on and how, in fact, those mountains are actually *arranged* within those countries. For example, the Peruvian Andes consist of wide ranges with some valleys. They are relatively easily terraced, or cultivated, and Peru was thus able to create a very advanced agricultural base. Chile, Peru's neighbor to the south, is home to a much narrower strip of the Andes that seems to rise straight up from the edge of the seacoast, not really allowing for an agricultural economy. Therefore, Chile's food mainstay is from the sea rather than from the land or the mountains.

The Incas built sophisticated aqueducts, the equal of any built by the Romans. The Peruvian aqueducts not only carried water great distances over land horizontally, they actually carried the water high up into the Andes by an ingenious method.

First the water was carried downhill for a distance, building up speed as it traveled. The water trough would then turn sharply, forcing the water to bounce off the curve, thus giving it a degree of force so that it could "climb" up to the next level, the next lengths of trough rising slightly. It would continue its journey a bit, then the trough would go slightly downhill again to build up speed, then bounce, then climb up, and so on, until it reached, ultimately, great heights. The water actually bounced *up* the mountains, level by level, providing irrigation for large terraced farmlands, called *andenas,* that to this very day cover the Peruvian Andes, a veritable Garden of Eden. The altitude at the various terraced levels produces some strikingly different effects on the same plants.

I mentioned how the heat of hot peppers varies with the altitude; the size and type of potato or corn are similarly affected. At one level, for example, kernels of hominy are as big as strawberries; in fact, these kernels have a name of their own, *mote,* and they're called the "snack of the Andes"; the Indians carry them around in small sacks and nibble on them all day long.

Altitude also plays a role in some of the unique contributions the Incas made in the field of food preservation. They used the universal techniques of air-drying and salting to preserve perishable foods. They also discovered dehydration and freeze-drying.

Dehydration was used by the Incas to preserve potatoes. The resulting product was and is called *chuño* by the Quechuas. Potatoes are put out in the sun at a high altitude, covered in the evening so they do not absorb any night moisture, then exposed to the sun again the next day. This goes on for a few weeks, until all of the water has evaporated from the potatoes and they have shriveled. At this point they are soft and light and as white as cotton on the inside. From these processed potatoes is made some of the finest starch, which is used not only for cooking but also as a baby powder.

The Quechuas also freeze-dried potatoes, also at high altitudes. The resulting product is called *papa seca*. In this method, the potatoes are cooked first, then dried in the cold air and sun until they are hard as rocks. The potatoes are then broken up into small pieces, which makes them easier to pack in bundles to be carried down from the mountains by llamas. By freeze-drying the potatoes and then breaking them into small pieces, the Quechuas could load much more onto the llamas, their prime means of transportation. (Llamas can only carry loads of about thirty-five pounds at a time—if the load gets any heavier, the llama simply sits down!) The *papa seca* is restored to an edible condition by roasting, then soaking in water.

The Quechuas had means of preserving all of the food they grew or raised, and they would store it in silos for winter or periods of drought or other natural calamities that could cause temporary food shortages. At its peak, the Inca Empire numbered some twelve million people, living over a vast area. By means of the above-mentioned food preservation techniques and the silos that were situated throughout the country, the leaders were able to make certain that a crop failure in one part of the empire wouldn't have a great effect on the people of that region. Everyone in the empire was assured of a full stomach.

The other key word pertaining to Peruvian food is *llama*. The llama is the miracle animal of the Andes. I remember a famous comic strip that was very popular when I first arrived in the United States, *Li'l Abner,* by Al Capp. Mr. Capp created the world's greatest animal, truly man's best friend, and he called it the *schmoo*. The schmoo looked like a simple, formless creature, with big eyes and a great smile. The schmoo adored people. It would do anything for mankind. If you wanted a steak, or merely looked hungry, the schmoo became a steak. If you wanted eggs or milk, the schmoo produced eggs in cartons and milk in bottles. If you wanted a fur coat, the schmoo obliged by becoming a mink coat. And so on. Well, the llama is the closest living thing we've found in this world to the schmoo. I've mentioned that the llama was and is the main transportation system in Peru, up and down the Andes. But it is much more than that. Wool from the llama makes wonderful material for clothing (as does that from the alpaca and the vicuña, much smaller llamalike animals with far fewer virtues then the llama). Llama dung is used for fuel, as fertilizer, and even for building construction. And yes, like the schmoo, the llama also provides meat. Air-dried strips of llama meat, called *charquí,* are a staple of the Quechuas. For all of this, and perhaps because of it, they love and cherish their llamas and live day and night in close proximity to the herds. They play with their llamas as one would with pets, and serenade them with mountain flutes or whistles. They even get drunk with their llamas! The favorite drink of the Andeans, a corn-based beer called *chicha,* is a favorite with the llamas, too.

Other animals and birds were domesticated and cultivated by the Indians, long before Spanish colonial times: wild pigeon or squab, duck, and rabbit. Rabbit is still one of the major meats of South America. In Argentina, for example, there is a very large rabbit or hare, called *viscacha,* which lives on the pampas. Deer and wild boar can also be found. One of the most popular animals raised for food is a large South American guinea pig, called the *cuy,* and it is very much a staple.

One more factor that has greatly influenced Peruvian cuisine, both in terms of the foods grown and produced and to some extent in terms of the way they are prepared, is the climate. Peru has three distinct climatic zones. Along the coast, and in cities such as Lima, the climate is that of a desert, which is what the coast, in fact, is. There is virtually no rainfall along the coast. Any growing done there is accomplished by bringing water from the mountains by way of the famous aqueducts. The second climatic zone is that of the mountains. In total contrast with the coastal areas, the mountains actually have seasons. And finally, in the inland valleys of the Andes, there is a tropical region, very hot and very humid. With these three climates, almost any product known to man can be developed and grown. And it is because of this variety of climates that Peruvian cuisine became so varied and so interesting; became, in fact, the bellwether cuisine for all of South America.

Cuisines throughout the world are the result of the mix of peoples that come and control regions for long or sometimes short periods of time. With each wave of migration, or conquest, the cuisine of a country changes—takes on new colors, flavors, and styles, and sometimes even new products. This has certainly been the case for all of the countries of South America.

The influence of the Quechuas was felt throughout the entire western coast of South America and even extended to some degree to the eastern parts of the continent, to Brazil and Argentina. There was some influence by other Indian tribes in other parts of South America, but none so great as that of the Inca, certainly the dominant peoples of South America prior to the Spanish and Portuguese conquests.

When the Spanish conquistador, Francisco Pizarro, destroyed the Inca Empire, he brought with him Spanish cuisine, which mixed with that of the Quechuas. It's a familiar story by now—how Pizarro tricked the Inca ruler Atahualpa into allowing him to enter the Inca capital, Cuzco, with a small group of thirty men, then murdered the emperor and his entire court, destroyed the city, and literally captured a country of millions who wouldn't fight back. But because the Indians wouldn't fight didn't mean they gave in easily to the Spanish.

The Incas lived by only three laws: no killing, no lying, no stealing. That was all. When the Incas conquered they did so mainly by building roads and tunneling through the Andes from village to village. As a result of these roads, the residents of each town would become a part of the whole empire. The roads, plus a record-keeping system that used not written words but rather knotted ropes called *quipus*, kept the empire together. Just to give you an idea of the Incas' road-building prowess, they built two main highways, one along the coast and one inland through the Andes, which ran the length of the empire, each close to 2,500 miles long.

So the Incas had no need of war or of killing. They did demand service from their "conquered" peoples; everyone in the empire had to perform some kind of public service for a period of time, whether building roads or growing food for common use and storage in the silos.

The Incas, like the Aztecs farther north in Mexico, were ill-equipped to deal with the amoral, murderous Spanish outcasts who had come to plunder gold from the New World in the name of their king. They didn't fight; but they didn't give in either.

The Spanish had fully expected to enslave the Quechuas, but they were unslavable. They wouldn't work. They wouldn't obey. They wouldn't even acknowledge the presence of these strange conquerors on their frightening horses, animals that the Indians had never before seen.

The Spanish had their own way of dealing with the recalcitrant Quechuas. They shot them. By the millions. Those the Spanish didn't finish off with bullets they almost did in with disease brought from Europe. The Quechuas survive to this day, but the sixteenth century in Peru was a bloody place to be.

Unsuccessful at getting the Incas to work for them, the Spanish decided to bring in their own black African slaves, and thus the third major influence in Peruvian, and South American, cuisine came to be.

While I've only pointed out the Peruvian story, it's roughly the same throughout South America: Indian influence in those countries that had a significant Indian population; then the invasion of the Spanish (Portuguese in Brazil); and finally the Africans.

Some countries simply had no real food culture prior to the Spanish. Colombia had a few Indian tribes, as did Venezuela, but we know little about them, and their influence is nil. Over the years there has been a great deal of cross-cultural exchange from country to country, just as there has been throughout Europe and North America.

In the nineteenth and twentieth centuries, there have been some additional influences, primarily the Italians in Argentina and the Germans in Chile. If you go to Buenos Aires, for example, it's almost impossible to find a restaurant that's not Italian.

Chile, like Colombia and some other countries, really had little or no serious culinary culture prior to the Spanish. The northern part of Chile was influenced by the Incas and was a part of the Inca Empire. As is true with all countries, Chile's cuisine is determined by its geography. It relies a great deal on food from the sea. The ocean off Chile provides abundant anchovies, giant clams, mussels, and other seafood, due primarily to the Humboldt Current, which brings cold water filled with oxygen and rich plankton.

While Chile is weak as an agricultural country, it does have perfect soil—rich and sandy—for growing grapes, and Chilean wine is valued throughout the world. Other foods that grow well in the Chilean climate are fruit, the *topinambur,* known outside Chile as the sunchoke or Jerusalem artichoke, and beans—kidney, red, black, white, and yellow beans. The Chileans love their beans, or *porotos,* and they include them in absolutely everything, including desserts.

Right next door to Chile, but separated by the Andes to such a degree that they might be on different continents, is Argentina. Argentina, like Paraguay and Uruguay, which don't really have distinct cuisines of their own, is a country where meat is king. Paraguay was populated by the Guarani Indians, and today the Guarani language officially coexists with Spanish in Paraguay. The famed *mate* tea originated in Paraguay. What seafood is to Chile, beef is to Argentina. No meal is served in Argentina that does not include meat of some kind, and it doesn't have to be beef. Rabbit, popular throughout South America, is very popular in Argentina.

It's a country in which a good deal of food is grilled. Argentina also produces some really lovely wines.

Bolivia's cuisine is almost identical to that of Peru; it was, after all, once part of Peru. In some ways it's an unfortunate country, landlocked and located almost entirely up in the Andes. It shares Lake Titicaca with Peru, the dividing line being exactly in the middle. One thing Bolivia is famous for comes from the lake: giant frogs' legs from the giant frogs that inhabit that great inland sea.

Brazil is the largest country in South America, and one of the largest in the world, stretching from the tropics in the north to the more temperate zone of the south, and it has a long coastline. Most of the territory is covered by the thick Amazon jungle, populated by small local Indian tribes—basically large family groups gathering food, hunting, and living together.

Brazil, by its sheer size and ethnic mix, gave rise to the development of interesting, authentic, regional cooking. As with most of its neighbors —Argentina, Uruguay, and Venezuela—Brazil did not have a great Indian civilization to speak of, and thus the Brazilian cuisine did not begin to take shape until the arrival of the Portuguese. It continued to evolve with the arrival of the African slaves who were brought in to work in the sugar-cane fields. This ethnic mixture, along with the later arrival of other Europeans, who brought their native foods and cooking techniques with them, is what now makes Brazilian cooking so colorful and varied.

The Portuguese influence in Brazilian cooking is very much alive, in the heavy use of egg yolks and sugar in the preparation of rich desserts, for example, and in the fondness for frying. The African contribution includes *dendê* (palm) oil, which is used for cooking and gives food its characteristic nutty flavor and color, and the extensive use of coconuts, fresh and dried shrimp, beans, yuca or manioc, cashews, almonds, peanuts, and, of course, hot peppers. The African influence gives this cuisine much of its distinguishing personality.

Like the Argentineans, Uruguayans, and Paraguayans, the Brazilians also love to grill their meats. As a matter of fact, many restaurants— *churrasquerías*—specialize in serving a variety of grilled meats. The exuberant cuisine of Brazil contributes greatly to the variety and excitement of South American cooking.

While new cooking techniques were introduced with the colonization of the South American continent, the ancient ways of cooking are still often used, especially for celebrations. In the Andes of Peru, for example, the Quechuas simply dig a deep hole, fill it with extremely hot stones, layer the foods to be cooked in between the stones, cover the hole with dirt, and then let the heat from the stones do the cooking over a period of time. They call this a *pachamanca,* or earth oven (literally "earth" and "pot" in Quechuan). In Chile, they cook shellfish between layers of seaweed in a *curanto,* which is similar to a North American clambake.

The foods of South America are rich and lively, fun to make, and delicious to eat. It is very much a creole cuisine: a mixture of Europe and Africa, but with a distinctive twist—the significant contributions of the indigenous Indians, who are still there. There is creole cuisine in some of the Caribbean and in parts of the United States, of course, but none that involves the original inhabitants of those places, peoples who are still alive today.

I hope you have as much fun cooking these recipes as I did finding them and preparing them myself. *Provecho!*

THE ART OF
SOUTH
AMERICAN
COOKING

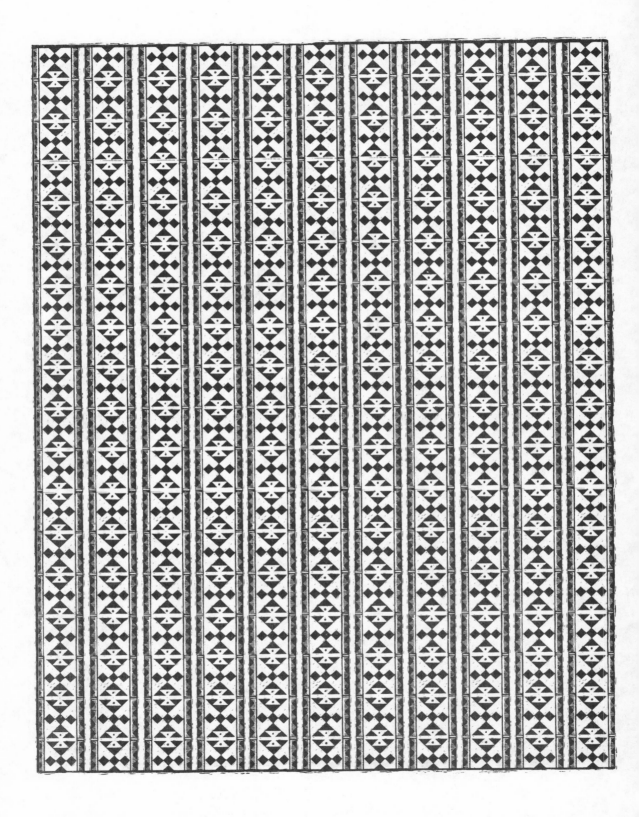

CEVICHES

Cebiche de Atún
Tuna Ceviche
—

Cebiche de Lenguado
Flounder Ceviche
—

Cebiche de Pez Espada
Swordfish Ceviche
—

Cebiche de Choros
Mussel Ceviche
—

Cebiche de Camarones
Shrimp Ceviche
—

Cebiche de Almejas
Clam Ceviche
—

Cebiche de Conchitas
Bay Scallop Ceviche
—

Cebiche de Calamares
Squid Ceviche
—

Cebiche Mixto
Seafood Ceviche
—

Cebiche de Pulpo
Octopus Ceviche
—

Cebiche de Hongos
Mushroom Ceviche
—

Cebiche de Pato
Duck Ceviche

W hen lemons were first paired with South America's wonderful seafood, one of the world's greatest culinary techniques was born. Using such citrus fruits as lemon and lime to flavor and to "cook" fish and shellfish is at the heart of that unforgettable gastronomic experience known variously as *seviche, ceviche,* or *cebiche,* as it is written and pronounced in its land of origin, Peru. Peru, Ecuador, and Chile are acknowledged as having the best ceviches, followed by the rest of the Spanish-colonized countries of South America. Zesty with minced hot peppers, red onions, and fresh cilantro, ceviche is a memorable dish.

When I was growing up in Lima, my friends and I would often end up just before dawn in the *cebicherias* that lined the shore. Who could resist the remarkably fresh ceviche, maybe eight or twelve different kinds, its fiery peppers so invigorating after a long night of partying? Then there was the ice-cold beer, the perfect accompaniment to ceviche —or to a *cebichada,* that is, a dinner or feast in which ceviche is the principal, or sometimes the only, dish.

Actually, with the exception of a normal breakfast, I cannot think of a time of the night or day when it would not be appropriate to serve ceviche. It makes a fine appetizer for lunch or dinner and a good snack throughout the day. Ceviche can be a light meal in itself, especially if it is served as part of a salad with interesting garnishes.

Ceviche takes no time at all to prepare: it is just a matter of squeezing some lemons, chopping some fresh herbs and peppers, and cutting up the fish. It is unthinkable, however, to use anything but utterly fresh seafood. Frozen fish simply will not do, as the taste and texture are destroyed by the freezing process, and nothing in the preparation of ceviche will disguise this.

The only way you can be certain your fish is absolutely fresh is to have some eye contact with the whole fish itself. Only when you have

seen for yourself that the eyes are plump and clear without any cloudy trace can you know for sure that it is fresh. If you are uncertain about the eyes, then lift up the gills and sniff underneath. The fish should give off a clean sea smell, and there should be no visible mucus under the light pinkish gills. If you still don't trust your judgment, lift the fish up in the middle. If the tail flops down, then you know that the fish has been in the company of the fishmonger too long. Fresh fish will not flop, since its muscles are still firm.

A word about lemons. In South America, the big, fleshy yellow lemon that is common in North America is quite a novelty and is thought of as a "sweet" lemon. What we call *limón* is more like the North American lime, although much juicier by far. For the preparation of ceviche, either lemon or lime, or a combination of the two, will do. To my palate, lime has a stronger, more perfumed flavor. Because of its more intense acidity, it also "cooks" the fish faster. So I often combine the two to bring together the mild bouquet of the lemon and the strong character of the lime.

In South America we make ceviche to flavor food as well as to "cook" it. Certain shellfish, such as shrimp and other crustaceans, in fact, are not palatable when "cooked" in lemon juice, for the process makes the flesh disintegrate. Shellfish must be blanched first and then tossed in lemon or lime juice just long enough to flavor them. Crab, crayfish, prawns, and lobster must also be blanched and just briefly tossed in juice. The same is true for octopus, squid, and mussels.

To limit the amount of acid that comes into contact with these types of seafood, they are coated with oil first. The oil prevents acid burn and discoloration. This kind of ceviche should never marinate in lemon juice for more than five or ten minutes.

The other ingredients that go into ceviche can vary tremendously. They may include hot peppers, red onions, scallions, garlic, julienned raw vegetables, cilantro and other herbs, and even chunks of avocado, tomato, or boiled potato. The garnishes also vary a great deal, but I think the best are a lettuce-leaf cup, preferably of Boston lettuce, a few tasty black olives, some slices of hard-boiled egg, chunks of fresh hard goat cheese or feta, or a slice or two of corn on the cob. A garnish of sliced sweet potato makes a ceviche characteristically Peruvian.

You need not get carried away with the garnishes, though, because any ceviche made of impeccably fresh fish or shellfish, no matter how simple, will be a superb experience—so superb that virtually every country in South America claims ceviche as its own invention.

Cebiche de Atún
Tuna Ceviche

—

Serves 6 to 8

Anyone who has lived on the Pacific coast of South America knows and appreciates the flavorful fish known as *bonito*, which resembles a small tuna. Both tuna and bonito work well in a ceviche. Be sure to use a very sharp knife with a smooth blade to cut the fish; otherwise the edges of the fish cubes will shred when they are marinated.

2½ pounds fresh tuna
1 cup lemon juice (about 6 lemons)
1 cup lime juice (about 6 limes)
1½-inch piece fresh ginger, grated (2 tablespoons)
2 jalapeño or serrano peppers, seeded and chopped
6 scallions, thinly sliced (½ cup)
2 tablespoons coarse salt
1 red bell pepper, very finely diced
3 tablespoons olive oil
¼ cup finely chopped fresh cilantro leaves

1. Wipe the fish with a damp cloth. Remove any skin and bones and cut into ¼-inch cubes. Set aside.

2. In a large stainless-steel, porcelain, or glass bowl, combine the lemon and lime juices, ginger, peppers, scallions, salt, and the tuna cubes. Marinate, covered, in the refrigerator for 2 hours.

3. Toss the diced red pepper with the olive oil and add to the marinated tuna cubes. Just before serving, correct the seasoning with salt to taste and gently toss in the cilantro.

Cebiche de Lenguado
Flounder Ceviche

Serves 6 to 8

Among the most popular fish for ceviche is *lenguado,* or flatfish. This kind of lean, delicate, and sweet fish marries well with lemon and lime juice. For this recipe I chose flounder, but sole, turbot, and halibut would be just as delicious.

2½ pounds skinless flounder fillets
2 cloves garlic, peeled
2 tablespoons coarse salt
¼ teaspoon ground white pepper
2 cups lime juice (12 to 14 limes)
2 or 3 fresh jalapeño or serrano peppers or dried mirasol peppers
    (see Note)
1 small red onion, peeled and thinly sliced
¼ cup olive oil

GARNISH
6 to 8 Boston lettuce leaves, washed and dried
1 ear corn, cooked and cut into 6 to 8 slices
1 cooked sweet potato, cut into 6 to 8 slices
12 to 24 alfonso or Kalamata olives
3 tablespoons chopped fresh cilantro leaves

  1. Wipe the flounder fillets with a damp cloth and cut on the diagonal into ¼-inch x 4-inch strips. Set aside.

  2. In a mortar with a pestle, pound the garlic, salt, and white pepper to a smooth paste. Add the paste to the lime juice and mix thoroughly. Pour over the strips of flounder. Let marinate for 1 hour, covered, in the refrigerator. Remove from the refrigerator, add the peppers, onion, and olive oil, and mix well. Let rest 5 to 10 minutes before serving.

3. To serve, place a lettuce leaf on 6 to 8 small plates. With a slotted spoon, scoop a helping of ceviche onto the leaf. Garnish each plate with 1 slice of corn, 1 slice of sweet potato, and 2 or 3 olives. Sprinkle with chopped cilantro. To serve in a serving bowl, cover the bottom of the bowl with lettuce leaves and arrange the ceviche on top. Surround with slices of corn and sweet potatoes and the olives and sprinkle with chopped cilantro.

NOTE   If using dried peppers, remove the seeds, crumble the peppers, and pound them together with the garlic and salt.

Cebiche de Pez Espada
Swordfish Ceviche

—

Serves 6 to 8

Swordfish is so luxurious that I prefer to cook it as simply as possible. One of the simplest ways I know is in a ceviche. The combination of red and green peppers, scallions, and cilantro in this ceviche makes it very colorful and adds extra richness to the fish.

3 pounds skinless and boneless swordfish
1½ cups lemon juice (8 to 10 lemons)
1½ cups lime juice (8 to 10 limes)
1 tablespoon coarse salt
½ teaspoon ground white pepper
10 scallions, thinly sliced (1 cup)
1 small red bell pepper, very finely diced
1 small green bell pepper, very finely diced
¼ cup tightly packed fresh cilantro leaves, chopped
2 tablespoons olive oil

1. Wipe the swordfish with a damp cloth and cut into ½-inch cubes. Set aside.

2. In a large stainless-steel, porcelain, or glass bowl, combine the lemon and lime juices, salt, pepper, and swordfish cubes. Mix well and let marinate, covered, in the refrigerator for 3 to 4 hours.

3. Add the scallions, red and green pepper, cilantro, and olive oil and toss gently. Correct the seasoning with salt to taste and serve.

Cebiche de Choros
Mussel Ceviche

Serves 6 to 8

It is important to select the freshest live mussels. Whether black or green, the shells should be tightly closed. Any mussels that are open must be discarded.

5 pounds mussels
½ cup plus 2 tablespoons olive oil
½ cup dry white wine
4 sprigs fresh thyme or 1 teaspoon dried thyme
3 large new potatoes, washed, cooked, and cut into ½-inch cubes
1½ pounds tomatoes, cut into ½-inch cubes
½ small Bermuda onion, peeled and thinly sliced
4 tablespoons fresh or frozen green peas
⅓ cup fresh lemon juice
1 teaspoon coarse salt
⅓ cup chopped fresh Italian parsley

1. Clean the mussels as described on page 486.

2. In a 12-inch sauté pan with a tight-fitting lid, combine 2 table-spoons of the oil, 2 tablespoons of the wine, the thyme, and mussels. Cover the saucepan and steam the mussels over high heat until they are barely open, 5 to 8 minutes. Discard any that have not opened.

3. Let the juices in the saucepan stand for a few minutes so that any sediment settles to the bottom. Carefully strain these juices into a bowl through a sieve lined with a double layer of cheesecloth, making sure to leave any sediment in the sauté pan.

4. Using a paring knife, detach the mussels from their shells, being careful not to tear them. Remove and discard any beards that might still remain attached to the mussels. Place the mussels in the bowl containing the mussel juices. Add the potatoes, tomatoes, onion, peas, lemon juice, salt, parsley, and the remaining oil and wine. Toss gently, being careful not to damage the mussels. Transfer to a serving dish and serve at room temperature.

Cebiche de Camarones
Shrimp Ceviche

Serves 8 to 10

In this ceviche, lemon juice is used to flavor, rather than "cook," the ingredients. The shrimp are cooked in rapidly boiling water. The cleaned shrimp are dumped into the water and taken out of it *before* it returns to a boil. This should not take more than a minute. As my mother used to say, "Just say two 'Our Fathers' and they will be done."

3 pounds medium shrimp (16 to 20 per pound)
8 stalks celery, strings removed and julienned
12 scallions, julienned
1 carrot, peeled and julienned
1 red bell pepper, seeded and julienned
1 cup lemon juice (about 6 lemons)
2 large cloves garlic, peeled and crushed
2 tablespoons coarse salt
½ teaspoon ground fennel
2 jalapeño or serrano peppers, seeded and thinly sliced,
    or ½ teaspoon ground white pepper
¼ cup olive oil
2 tablespoons chopped fresh cilantro leaves or dill

1. Peel the shrimp, leaving the last segment of tail shell attached. Devein and rinse them. Drop the shrimp in boiling water and blanch for no longer than 1 minute. Drain and set aside to cool.

2. Place the julienned celery, scallions, carrot, and bell pepper in a small bowl with ice water until crisp, about 30 minutes to 1 hour.

3. In a stainless-steel, porcelain, or glass bowl, combine the lemon juice, garlic, salt, fennel, and hot peppers. Add the olive oil and mix well. Drain the julienned vegetables thoroughly. Add the shrimp and drained vegetables, toss, and marinate for 10 to 15 minutes before serving. Sprinkle with the chopped cilantro or dill and serve.

Cebiche de Almejas
Clam Ceviche

Serves 8 to 10

I love clams, especially in ceviches. Cherrystone clams remind me of those wonderful Pacific *almejas*. But wherever your clams come from, and regardless of whether you shuck them yourself or buy them already shucked, always make sure they are free of sand, which ruins the dish.

1 quart plus ½ pint shucked clams, drained
¾ cup lemon juice (4 or 5 lemons)
2 jalapeño peppers, seeded and minced
1 teaspoon coarse salt
3 large new potatoes, washed, cooked, and cut into ½-inch cubes
2 large tomatoes, cut into ½-inch cubes
1 small Bermuda onion, peeled and thinly sliced
¼ cup olive oil
3 tablespoons chopped fresh cilantro leaves or dill
8 to 16 Boston lettuce leaves

1. In a stainless-steel or glass bowl, combine the clams, lemon juice, peppers, and salt. Mix, cover, and place in the refrigerator to marinate for about 2 hours.

2. Remove the bowl from the refrigerator and add the potatoes, tomatoes, and onion. Toss and let stand for 5 minutes at room temperature. Add the olive oil, toss well, correct the seasoning with salt to taste, and sprinkle with the cilantro or dill. Serve on Boston lettuce leaves.

NOTE   Cherrystone clams in the shell may be used instead of already shucked clams. Clean them as directed on page 486 and shuck them. You will need about 100 clams (25 pounds).

Cebiche de Conchitas
Bay Scallop Ceviche

Serves 6 to 8

Tiny bay scallops are the perfect size for a delicious mouthful of ceviche. Sea scallops are also good for this dish, but they do have to be cut in half.

2¼ pounds bay scallops (see Note)
1¼ cups lemon juice (about 9 lemons)
1½ teaspoons minced fresh ginger
1 jalapeño or serrano pepper, seeded and finely chopped
1 teaspoon coarse salt
1 red bell pepper, very finely diced
8 scallions, white parts only, thinly sliced
¼ cup olive oil
4 tablespoons chopped fresh dill

1. Place the scallops in a strainer and dip in a bowl containing cold water. Shake the strainer to loosen any sand and particles of shell. Remove the strainer from the bowl and set aside to drain.

2. In a stainless-steel, porcelain, or glass bowl, combine the lemon juice, ginger, hot pepper, and salt. Mix in the scallops and marinate, covered, in the refrigerator, for about 3½ hours.

3. When ready to serve, combine the red pepper, scallions, and olive oil in a separate bowl. Add this mixture to the marinated scallops; add the dill and toss gently. Correct the seasoning with salt to taste and serve.

NOTE   An equal amount of sea scallops may be substituted for the bay scallops. Using a very sharp knife, cut the sea scallops in half against the grain horizontally into disks or vertically into half-moons.

Cebiche de Calamares
Squid Ceviche

Serves 6 to 8

When I get my hands on baby squid—maybe three or four inches long—I cannot help but see it as a candidate for ceviche. The squid must be cut in circles at an angle, no more than a quarter of an inch thick. Larger squid should be cut even thinner, about an eighth of an inch, for best taste and texture.

Blanching is key: it should be done in a flash. Overcooked squid becomes yellowish and tough. Properly cooked squid is white and tender, a real treat.

2 to 2½ pounds squid
8 scallions, white parts only, julienned
1 red bell pepper, seeded and julienned
2 or 3 jalapeño or serrano peppers, seeded and julienned
1 large clove garlic, peeled and crushed
1 tablespoon coarse salt
1 cup lime juice (about 6 limes)
¼ cup olive oil

1. Clean the squid as described on page 487. Slice the squid on the diagonal about ¼ inch thick. If the tentacles are small, leave them whole; if they are large, cut them in half or quarters. Blanch all the pieces for less than 1 minute in 8 cups of boiling water. Drain and drop the pieces in a bowl containing ice water, and let them cool. Drain thoroughly and set aside.

2. Place the julienned scallions, bell pepper, and hot peppers in ice water for 10 minutes. Drain well and set aside.

3. In a small bowl, combine the garlic, salt, and lime juice and let sit, undisturbed, at room temperature for 10 minutes. Discard the garlic and save the flavored lime juice.

4. In a ceramic, porcelain, or glass bowl, combine the squid, scallions, bell pepper, and hot peppers. Add the flavored lime juice and oil, toss, correct the seasoning with salt to taste, and serve.

Cebiche Mixto
Seafood Ceviche

Serves 8 to 10

The success of a *cebiche mixto* depends on the right contrast of color, shape, taste, and texture created by the different varieties of fish and shellfish.

When I plan to make *cebiche mixto,* I go to the market with an open mind—and open eyes—and look for what is freshest. For good contrast you need three to four different kinds of seafood.

½ pound medium shrimp (16 to 20 per pound)
1½ pounds blanched octopus (page 487)
1 pound small squid, cleaned (page 487)
2 pounds bay scallops
2 cups lemon juice (about 12 lemons)
2 cloves garlic, peeled and crushed
2 to 3 jalapeño or serrano peppers, seeded and finely chopped
2 teaspoons coarse salt
½ teaspoon ground white pepper
8 scallions, julienned
5 stalks celery, strings removed and julienned
1 large carrot, peeled and julienned
1 red bell pepper, seeded and julienned
¼ cup olive oil
2 tablespoons chopped Italian parsley

1. Peel the shrimp, leaving the tails attached. Devein and rinse them under running water and blanch them for about 1 to 2 minutes in boiling water. Remove from water and set aside.

2. Slice the octopus body, head, and tentacles on the diagonal about 1 inch thick, and set aside.

3. Slice the squid bodies on the diagonal about ⅛ inch thick. If the heads and tentacles are small enough, leave them whole; if they are large, cut them in half or quarters. Blanch all the squid pieces for less than 1 minute in 8 cups of boiling water. Drain and drop them in a bowl of ice water and let them cool. Drain thoroughly and set aside.

4. In a stainless-steel, glass, or porcelain dish, marinate the scallops in the lemon juice together with the garlic, hot peppers, salt, and white pepper for about 2 hours, covered, in the refrigerator.

5. While the scallops are marinating, place the julienned scallions, celery, carrot, and bell pepper in ice water until ready for use.

6. Remove the vegetables from the ice water, drain well, and place in a large serving bowl. Add the olive oil and toss lightly. Remove the garlic from the scallops and discard it. Add the scallops, shrimp, octopus, and squid to the vegetables and toss again. Correct the seasoning with salt to taste, sprinkle with parsley, and serve.

Cebiche de Pulpo
Octopus Ceviche

Serves 6 to 8

The way they caught *pulpo*, or octopus, next to the jagged cliffs along the coast of Peru fascinated me as a young man. The fisherman would throw himself down on his belly right at the edge of the mussel-black-ened rocks and stretch his arm as far as it would go into the water. As the sea came up, his arm was submerged to the shoulder. The fisherman jumped up quickly and wrapped around his arm was an octopus. With one stroke of his free hand he flipped the tiny head inside out, and the octopus immediately let go. He would casually drop it into the fishing basket along with the rest of his catch.

I have always had a tremendous love for *pulpo*, but it has to be cooked just right. If overcooked it is mushy; undercooked, it is just too much exercise for the jaw.

1½ to 2 pounds blanched octopus (page 487)
1 small red onion, washed, peeled, and thinly sliced
1 pound red potatoes, washed, cooked, and quartered
1½ cups frozen peas, thawed, rinsed, and drained
  (1 10-ounce package)
1 jalapeño or serrano pepper, seeded and julienned
½ cup lemon juice (about 3 lemons)
½ cup lime juice (about 3 limes)
¼ cup tightly packed fresh cilantro leaves, washed and drained
2 teaspoons coarse salt
¼ teaspoon ground white pepper
¼ cup olive oil
1 avocado, peeled and sliced

1. Slice the octopus body, head, and tentacles on the diagonal, about 1 inch thick.

2. In a porcelain or glass bowl, combine the octopus, onion, potatoes, peas, and hot pepper. Add the lemon and lime juices, cilantro, salt, and pepper and toss gently. Add the olive oil, toss again, and serve at once, garnished with avocado slices.

Cebiche de Hongos
Mushroom Ceviche

Serves 6 to 8

From the vegetable kingdom, I find domestic mushrooms best suited to the ceviche treatment. The lemon juice enhances the rather bland flavor of the mushrooms and also bleaches them beautifully white. Because the flavor of mushrooms is so mild, it is especially important to use a fine-quality olive oil for this ceviche.

Little mushroom caps are charming in ceviche, but any size mushroom will do. Larger ones should be quartered or cut in half. It is not a good idea to slice the mushrooms for ceviche. In general, wild mushrooms (with a few exceptions) are not suitable for this treatment. Best are those firm domestic mushrooms you might use raw in a salad.

1 pound white button mushrooms
¼ cup olive oil
1½ cups lemon juice (about 10 lemons)
2 cloves garlic, peeled and crushed
½-inch piece fresh ginger, peeled and minced
1 jalapeño pepper, seeded and finely chopped,
*   or ⅛ teaspoon cayenne*
½ teaspoon coarse salt
6 to 8 scallions, white parts only, thinly sliced (about ¼ cup)
2 tablespoons chopped fresh dill
1 small red bell pepper, seeded and very finely diced (⅛ inch)

1. Cut the stems of the mushrooms flush with the caps and wipe the caps clean with a damp cloth. Save the stems for another purpose. Place the caps in a stainless-steel bowl, toss with the olive oil, and set aside.

2. In a stainless-steel, porcelain, or glass bowl, combine the lemon juice, garlic, ginger, hot pepper, and salt. Mix well with a wire whisk, add the mushroom caps, and let marinate for 30 minutes at room temperature. Add the scallions and dill. Toss well and let marinate again for another 30 minutes. Correct the seasoning with salt to taste. Sprinkle with the diced red bell pepper and serve.

Cebiche de Pato
Duck Ceviche
—
Serves 6 to 8

This unusual ceviche is found in the ancient city of Huacho on the Pacific coast north of Lima. It seems to break every rule of ceviche making. The duck is not only "cooked," or marinated, in lime juice softened with orange juice, it is actually braised in it.

In Peru, duck ceviche is often served as an appetizer or as a snack. I like it as a main course for lunch or as a refreshing dinner on a hot summer night. If you plan to do this, use two ducks instead of one; the rest of the ingredients and the cooking time remain the same.

1 duck (about 5½ pounds)
2 dried mirasol peppers, seeded and crumbled, or 2 or 3 dried
   red chili peppers
½ cup lime juice (about 3 limes)
1 teaspoon coarse salt
1 large clove garlic, peeled and crushed
1¾ cups fresh orange juice (about 4 oranges)
2 medium red onions, peeled and thinly sliced
1 large clove garlic, peeled and minced
1 teaspoon ground cumin
¼ teaspoon ground white pepper
2 sprigs fresh cilantro
2 sprigs Italian parsley
1 pound yuca, peeled, cored, and cooked (page 394), cut into
   6 to 8 serving pieces

1. Wipe the duck inside and out with a damp cloth. Cut the duck into 6 serving pieces; cut away the wings and cut the breast in half. Cut away the thighs and separate them from the drumsticks. Remove and reserve the skin from the breast pieces and thighs. Place the duck pieces in a stainless-steel bowl and set aside.

2. Cut the reserved duck skin into thin strips. In a small saucepan, cook the duck skin over low heat with ½ cup cold water, stirring now and then, until the water has evaporated and the skin is golden and has released all its fat, about 8 minutes. Reserve the golden skin or cracklings, and ¼ cup of the fat.

3. In a cup, mix the crumbled hot peppers with the lime juice, salt, and crushed garlic and let soak for 15 minutes, or until the pepper is soft. Place the pepper with the lime juice and crushed garlic in the jar of a blender or work bowl of a food processor and blend or process until smooth. Pour this mixture over the duck pieces. Add the orange juice and onions, mix well, and let marinate for 2 hours at room temperature. Transfer the duck pieces from the marinade to a plate and set aside. Strain the onion and reserve both the onion and the marinating juices.

4. In a sauté pan, heat the ¼ cup reserved duck fat. Add the duck pieces and over medium heat sear them all over, without browning them, for about 5 minutes. Push the duck pieces to the sides of the pan, making a well in the center. Add the minced garlic, half of the strained marinated onion, the cumin, and white pepper. Sauté, stirring, until the onion is barely translucent, about 2 minutes.

5. Add all the marinating juices, stir, and bring to a boil. Lower the heat, add the cilantro and parsley, cover, and cook for 30 minutes, or until the duck is tender. Add the remaining marinated onion, stir, and cook for 1 minute longer.

6. Remove from the heat and let cool. Transfer the ceviche to a serving dish, sprinkle with the reserved cracklings, garnish with cooked yuca, and serve at room temperature.

VARIATION

To make this ceviche with wild duck, substitute 2 wild ducks for the domestic duck. Cut each one into 4 pieces, leaving the legs and thighs together. Do not remove the skin. Where the recipe calls for duck fat, use olive oil. There will be no cracklings.

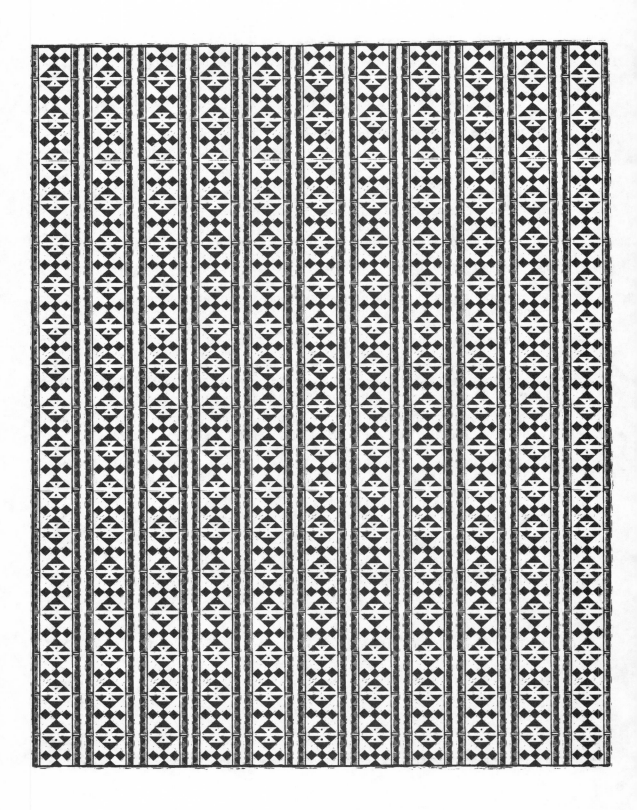

ESCABECHES

Escabeche de Pescado
Fish Escabeche

—

Escabeche de Trucha
Trout Escabeche

—

Escabeche de Camarones
Shrimp Escabeche

—

Escabeche de Pollo
Chicken Escabeche

—

Escabeche de Pato
Duck Escabeche

—

Escabeche de Pavo con Higos
Wild Turkey Escabeche with Figs

—

Escabeche de Alcachofas
Artichoke Escabeche

—

Escabeche de Huevo
Egg Escabeche

T he original purpose of escabeche as a method of cooking was to preserve food with vinegar. Arab in origin, the principle has remained unchanged for many centuries. This way of cooking has been totally absorbed into the food culture of South America, where a wide array of colorful dishes with interesting flavorings and textures has evolved.

No longer viewed as simply a way to preserve food, escabeches are now considered everyday dishes. Hot peppers or a combination of sweet and hot peppers, along with fresh herbs and spices, give the dish its piquancy. The vinegar is mellowed by aromatic vegetables, sweet spices, and, on occasion, dried fruits like figs, dates, prunes, or raisins, which give the escabeche a subtle sweet-and-sour flavor. It is not uncommon to find whole or chopped nuts—peanuts, cashews, hazelnuts, almonds, or walnuts—added to an escabeche for extra texture, especially one made with meat. To give escabeche an appetizing color, aromatic spices, such as achiote, turmeric, *palillo,* or paprika, are added. Besides color, they contribute a range of tones and flavors.

Making an escabeche is quick and uncomplicated. All that is required is to cook some fresh fish, poultry, game, or vegetables, pour over just enough hot vinegar to cover the ingredients, then let the dish cool so the flavors have a chance to mingle. The acidity of the dish is usually tempered by simmering the vinegar with water, wine, stock, coconut milk, or almond milk.

For a fine escabeche, it is essential to start with a good vinegar, one that was allowed to mature without pasteurization or the addition of chemicals. The flavor of the vinegar is very important, as it will determine the flavor of the dish. It should be clean with a pleasant bite, and the aroma should have a good suggestion of the wine or other liquid from which the vinegar was made.

A wide variety of high-quality vinegars is available nowadays. The best are the true vinegars, which are pure and made from fruit or grain.

Vinagre, the Spanish word for "vinegar," means sour wine, and that is what vinegar, red or white, is: an acid fermentation of fresh wine. Wine vinegar is easy to make. Back home, any leftover wine went automatically into the big vinegar jug, to give the already-existing vinegar a boost and to keep an endless supply of good vinegar going. It was always used for making escabeches.

Besides simple red- and white-wine vinegars, there are others made by the same process but with distinctive flavors and different degrees of acidity. Among them are slightly sweet champagne vinegar, rich and smooth sherry vinegar, and long-aged sweet Italian balsamic vinegar.

Malt vinegar, made from grain, and cider vinegar, made from apples, are both tart. Chinese and Japanese rice vinegars are smooth and almost sweet.

There are also many flavored vinegars, made by letting garlic, chili peppers, cinnamon, achiote, cloves, fennel, lemon or orange peel, flower petals, and other flavorings steep in a good-quality white-wine vinegar for about two weeks. Herb vinegars are created by letting herbs (thyme, tarragon, coriander, sage, rosemary, and mint) steep in white- or red-wine vinegar for one week. Flavored or herb vinegars should be decanted into a clean jar after steeping. Fruit vinegars are made by infusing soft fruits, such as currants, raspberries, or blueberries, in red- or white-wine vinegar. Larger fruits, such as pears, can also be used. (See page 488 for directions.)

If, when the vinegar is opened, it smells too strongly acidic, decant it carefully into a clean bottle and let it stand, open, for a month, to mature and mellow before using. If the vinegar is cloudy, it is evidence of the fermentation process. Cloudiness can be eliminated by straining the vinegar or heating it without boiling, then rebottling it.

Escabeche is usually served at room temperature, but it is also good served hot or warm. There are many ways to present or garnish an escabeche. The most common is to serve it with thin slices of cooked corn, juicy black olives, wedges of hard-boiled egg, cubes of feta cheese, and potatoes. Escabeche in all its incarnations is always suitable as an appetizer or snack and fabulous as a main course on a hot day.

Escabeche de Pescado
Fish Escabeche

—

Serves 6 to 8

Cod, bass, snapper, halibut, hake, or any other firm-fleshed white fish, with or without skin and bones, is ideal for escabeche. In this recipe I suggest using a skinless and boneless fillet of cod, but you can also use a whole fish. It is customary throughout South America to prepare escabeche with a whole fish, and with good reason: the skin and bones keep the fish in one piece, and they add extra richness to the sauce.

1 skinless cod fillet (about 3½ pounds)
¾ cup all-purpose flour
3 tablespoons coarse salt
2 tablespoons Spanish paprika
½ teaspoon cayenne
2 quarts vegetable oil for frying (see Note)
12 cloves garlic, peeled
8 to 10 jalapeño peppers
4 bay leaves
2 cups red-wine vinegar
2 cups red wine
2 cups Fish Stock (page 466) or Chicken Stock (page 461)
1 large bunch fresh thyme sprigs (1 ounce) or 6 sprigs fresh cilantro

1. Cut the cod fillet into 6 to 8 even pieces. In a bowl, combine the flour, 1 tablespoon salt, 1 tablespoon paprika, and the cayenne. Coat the fish with the flour mixture, shaking off any excess.

2. In a large sauté pan, heat the vegetable oil to about 365 degrees. Quickly add the fish and fry until barely golden all over, about 5 minutes. Remove from the oil with a slotted spatula, drain on paper towels, and place in an earthenware, glass, or porcelain casserole just large enough to hold all the liquid and the fish comfortably in a single layer; set aside. When the oil is cool enough to handle, strain it through a sieve lined with cheesecloth. Reserve ½ cup and discard or save the rest.

(Continued)

3. In a large sauté pan, heat the reserved ½ cup oil. Add the garlic and sauté until slightly golden. Add the jalapeño peppers, bay leaves, and the remaining tablespoon of paprika and cook for about 1 minute. Add the vinegar, bring to a boil, lower the heat, and simmer for about 5 minutes. Add the wine, bring back to a boil, and continue to simmer for 5 minutes. Add the stock, thyme, and the remaining 2 tablespoons of salt, bring to a boil, lower the heat, and gently simmer for 10 to 15 minutes. Pour this hot mixture over the fried fish in the casserole, let cool to room temperature, and serve.

NOTE   A large quantity of oil is needed to fry the fish properly; after frying, a small amount is used to finish the dish. The remaining oil can be saved. Filter it through several layers of cheesecloth or a paper coffee filter and pour it into a jar with a tight-fitting lid. Store it in the refrigerator. Keep in mind that oil that was used to fry fish will retain some of its bouquet, so it is best to reuse it only for frying fish.

STORAGE NOTE   Fish escabeche keeps well, covered tightly, for about 5 days in the refrigerator.

VARIATION

To use fish with skin and bones, scale and clean the fish, if necessary, then cut it crosswise through the backbone into steaks about 1½ inches thick. Proceed as with filleted fish.

Escabeche de Trucha
Trout Escabeche

—

Serves 6 to 8

4 trout (about ½ pound each), scaled, or 8 large sardines
    or 3 pounds small sardines
3 cups red-wine vinegar (see Note)
2 cups dry white wine
4 bay leaves
½ cup olive oil
10 large cloves garlic, peeled

16 pearl onions, blanched and peeled (page 484)
¼ teaspoon cayenne
4 tablespoons Spanish paprika
15 sprigs fresh thyme
2 tablespoons coarse salt

1. With a paring knife or scissors, slit open the underside of each fish and remove the entrails and gills with your fingers. Gently rinse the fish in cold water and wipe dry with towels or paper towels.

2. In an enameled or stainless-steel saucepan, combine the vinegar, wine, 1 cup of water, and bay leaves. Bring to a boil, lower the heat, and simmer until the liquid has reduced to 3 cups, about 20 minutes.

3. In an earthenware casserole or a skillet, heat the oil. Add the trout or sardines and sauté them until they are golden brown on both sides, turning them once. With a slotted spatula, transfer the fish to a plate and set aside.

4. Add the garlic and pearl onions to the remaining hot oil in the casserole and sauté until the onions are lightly browned. Quickly add the cayenne, paprika, and thyme, then add the reduced vinegar mixture. Stir, cook for a few minutes longer, and add the salt.

5. Remove the casserole or skillet from the heat and add the trout or sardines. Return it to the heat and cook for 1 minute longer. Serve warm or at room temperature, right from the casserole.

NOTE Any good wine vinegar, including vinegar flavored with herbs and spices, can be substituted for red-wine vinegar. A well-aged sherry vinegar will make the trout irresistible.

STORAGE NOTE This escabeche keeps well, covered tightly, for up to 5 days in the refrigerator.

VARIATION

Sauté about ½ cup whole nuts, such as almonds, hazelnuts, or even peanuts, with the pearl onions in Step 4 and proceed with the recipe.

Escabeche de Camarones
Shrimp Escabeche

Serves 6 to 8

This recipe calls for shelled shrimp, which are always available, but it is far more colorful to use whole shrimp, complete with heads and tails, and cook them in the shell. It's great fun to eat whole shrimp, using your fingers to peel the shells away and pop the succulent little tidbits into your mouth.

Since shrimp escabeche is such an orgy of flavor and color, garnishes are not really necessary, but a few black olives and slices of corn on the cob will provide nice accents of color. I like to serve the shrimp on a bed of cold, finely shredded lettuce. The best variety for this purpose is iceberg, which has no real flavor but does have a refreshing crunchiness.

2½ pounds jumbo shrimp or prawns
⅔ cup olive or peanut oil
6 cloves garlic, peeled
2 or 3 dried red chili peppers (optional)
2 bay leaves
1 teaspoon Spanish paprika
3 cups red- or white-wine vinegar
3 small sprigs fresh rosemary or 6 to 8 sprigs fresh thyme
1 teaspoon coarse salt

GARNISHES
3 tablespoons coarsely chopped Italian parsley or cilantro leaves
2 ears corn, cooked and sliced
¼ pound feta, cut into 6 to 8 cubes
12 alfonso or Kalamata olives

1. Peel the shrimp, leaving the last part of the tail attached, and devein them. Rinse and pat dry. In an 8-inch skillet, heat the oil. Add the shrimp, a few at a time so as not to crowd the skillet, and quickly toss them over high heat to sear them, about 1 to 2 minutes. As the shrimp are cooked, transfer them with a slotted spoon to a deep serving dish. Set aside.

2. To the same skillet, add the garlic, optional hot peppers, and bay leaves. Sauté over medium heat until the garlic is barely golden (be careful not to let it burn); quickly add the paprika and vinegar. Stir and bring to a boil over medium-high heat. Lower the heat, add the rosemary and salt, and simmer gently for 5 to 10 minutes, stirring now and then.

3. Let the flavored liquid cool for about 20 minutes, undisturbed, and pour, while still warm, over the shrimp. Let cool to room temperature. Toss in the parsley, garnish with the rounds of corn, feta, and olives, and serve.

STORAGE NOTE   This escabeche will keep in the refrigerator, well covered, for 2 to 3 days.

Escabeche de Pollo
Chicken Escabeche

Serves 6 to 8

Achiote gives a rich, reddish color to this dish and an interesting aromatic flavor as well. I have also made it with curry oil, which gives it a different but still dramatic personality and an appetizing golden color. (See Variation at end of recipe.)

Bell peppers, fresh herbs, onions, and carrots make the escabeche very colorful, so there is no need for additional garnishes. For luncheons or special occasions, however, you might want to use some of the customary garnishes, such as sprigs of fresh herbs, wedges of hard-boiled egg, slices or chunks of cooked corn on the cob, juicy black olives, and a few boiled potatoes or pieces of boiled yuca. Serve the escabeche on a bed of watercress, mâche, shredded lettuce, or lettuce leaves to add a summery feeling to the dish.

1 chicken, cut into 8 to 10 serving pieces (about 3½ pounds)
2½ tablespoons coarse salt
¾ cup Achiote Oil (page 472)
12 large cloves garlic, peeled
12 small onions, about 1½ inches in diameter, peeled, and a small
*   X cut into the root ends*
3 serrano or jalapeño peppers, seeded and julienned
4 bay leaves
½ teaspoon cayenne
8 to 12 sprigs fresh thyme, tarragon, or sage or 1 tablespoon dried
2 carrots, peeled and cut into sticks, about 2½ × ¼ inch
4 cups red-wine vinegar
2 cups red wine
4 stalks celery, washed, strings removed, and sliced ½ inch thick
*   on the diagonal*
2 red bell peppers, seeded, stems and ribs removed,
*   and cut into 1½-inch triangles*
2 green bell peppers, seeded, stems and ribs removed,
*   and cut into 1½-inch triangles*

1. Wipe the chicken parts with a damp cloth and sprinkle them with ½ tablespoon of the salt.

2. In an earthenware casserole or a large skillet, heat the oil. Add the chicken parts and sauté over medium heat until golden on all sides. With a slotted spoon or tongs, transfer the chicken to a plate and set aside.

3. To the remaining oil in the skillet, add the garlic and onions and cook over low heat for about 5 minutes, or until the onions are slightly golden all around. Add the hot peppers, bay leaves, cayenne, the remaining salt, and the sprigs of thyme. Add the carrot sticks, vinegar, and red wine. Bring to a boil, lower the heat, and simmer for 15 minutes. Add the celery and continue cooking for 10 minutes longer.

4. Add the red and green bell pepper triangles; cook for 3 minutes. Add the chicken pieces and let cool to room temperature. Serve right from the casserole.

STORAGE NOTE This escabeche keeps well, tightly covered, for up to 10 days in the refrigerator.

VARIATIONS

A 5-pound stewing hen, cut into serving-size pieces, or 3 or 4 1-pound Cornish hens, split, can be substituted for the chicken.

If a hen is used, add the sautéed pieces with the celery in Step 3. Let cook for about 2 minutes in the sauce, add the bell pepper triangles, and proceed with the recipe.

Curry Oil (page 473) may be substituted for the Achiote Oil. Use a plain or flavored white-wine vinegar instead of the red, and white wine instead of red wine.

Escabeche de Pato
Duck Escabeche

—

Serves 6 to 8

Duck, domestic or wild, is stupendous when prepared as an escabeche. The excellent flavor of the rich meat is intensified by that great pepper from Cuzco known as *mirasol* and further enhanced by sweet spices and vegetables. For this escabeche, I have suggested using a red-wine vinegar, but you could replace all or some of it with a flavored variety such as raspberry or pear wine vinegar, which will add its perfume to the dish.

This recipe calls for two ducks, which might appear to be quite generous, but the fact is that two will give you just six to eight comfortable servings. When using mallards or other wild ducks, drop in an extra one for the same number of servings. Geese are larger than ducks, so a single one should be sufficient. Another red-meat bird, squab, though not a water bird, is great for this escabeche. (See Variation at end of recipe.)

2 ducks (5 to 6 pounds each)
2½ tablespoons coarse salt
1 teaspoon Spanish paprika
⅓ cup Achiote Oil (page 472)
12 small red onions about 1½ inches in diameter, peeled, and a small
*   X cut into the root ends*
2 3-inch cinnamon sticks
4 bay leaves
2 dried or fresh mirasol or ancho peppers, seeded and chopped
*   or quartered lengthwise*
1 or 2 sprigs fresh rosemary or sage or ½ teaspoon dried
*   rosemary or sage*
3 carrots, peeled and cut into sticks, 2½ × ¼ inch
4 cups red-wine vinegar
2 cups red wine
2 red bell peppers, seeded, stems and ribs removed, and cut into
*   1½-inch triangles*
2 green bell peppers, seeded, stems and ribs removed,
*   and cut into 1½-inch triangles*
Sprigs of fresh rosemary or sage

1. Wipe the ducks inside and out with a damp cloth. Cut each duck into 8 serving pieces.

2. In a small cup, mix the salt and paprika. Coat the duck pieces with this mixture.

3. In an earthenware casserole or a skillet, heat the achiote oil over medium heat. Add the duck pieces, skin side down, and sauté until slightly brown. Remove the pieces with a slotted spoon or tongs to a plate; set aside.

4. Discard all but about 1 cup of the oil and fat in the skillet. Add the onions and sauté them until they are slightly golden all around. Add the cinnamon, bay leaves, hot peppers, rosemary, and carrot sticks. Add the vinegar and wine. Bring to a boil, lower the heat, and simmer for 15 minutes.

5. Add the red and green bell pepper triangles and continue cooking for 3 minutes longer. Add the duck pieces and any accumulated juices from the plate, and serve right from the casserole, either warm or at room temperature, garnished with the sprigs of fresh rosemary.

STORAGE NOTE   This escabeche keeps well, tightly covered, for about 2 weeks in the refrigerator.

VARIATION

For squab escabeche, substitute at least 4 squab for the ducks. To cook the squab, add ½ cup olive, peanut, or vegetable oil to the achiote oil to compensate for the birds' lack of fat. All other ingredients and procedures remain the same.

Escabeche de Pavo con Higos
Wild Turkey Escabeche with Figs

Serves 6 to 8

The sweet-and-sour taste produced by combining dried fruits with good vinegar is a perfect foil for wild turkey. This is a superb escabeche, one that leaves your palate with a tantalizing memory.

Feel free to omit the dates and prunes or add other dried fruits, but under no circumstances change the figs, for they provide a special texture and go beautifully with game. Select dried figs that are large and plump and feel moist and soft to the touch. If the figs are of excellent quality, drop a few extra into the pot—because turkeys really *love* good figs!

You could use pheasant, wild or farmed, a stewing hen, rabbit, or domestic turkey instead of wild in this escabeche. (See Variation at end of recipe.)

1 wild turkey (about 7 pounds)

TURKEY STOCK
1 large onion, unpeeled, roots trimmed, and chopped
1 large carrot, washed and chopped
3 stalks celery, with leafy tops, washed and chopped
2-inch piece fresh ginger, sliced
2 dried mirasol peppers or dried hot red chili peppers
3 or 4 sprigs fresh mint
2 teaspoons cumin seed
½ teaspoon turmeric
12 whole cloves
12 to 15 allspice berries
3 cups white wine
2 tablespoons coarse salt
2 or 3 leafy celery tops (optional)
1 or 2 sprigs fresh mint or parsley (optional)

½ cup olive oil
¼ cup plus 1 tablespoon Curry Oil (page 473)

1 cup whole blanched almonds or Brazil, cashew,
 or macadamia nuts (4 ounces)
4 large onions, peeled and sliced into ⅛- to ¼-inch rings
 (about 2½ pounds)
1 cup port or Madeira or marsala or Pernod
3 cups sherry vinegar or white-wine vinegar, plain or flavored
8 large dried figs (about ½ pound)
20 dried pitted dates (about ¼ pound)
12 to 15 pitted prunes (about ¼ pound)

1. With a damp cloth, wipe the turkey inside and out and cut it into 8 pieces: 2 thighs, 2 drumsticks, 2 wings (cut off tips sticking out at the first joint), and the breast cut in half lengthwise. Spread a piece of cheesecloth, about 30 to 34 inches square, on your work surface. Arrange the turkey pieces as close together as possible in the middle, gather the cheesecloth, twist to close tightly, and tie with kitchen twine to make a compact bag. Set aside.

2. With a cleaver, chop all the bones, including the neck, head, feet (if any), wing tips, and the heart and gizzard (no liver), and place in a stockpot or a large saucepan. Add the onion, carrot, celery, ginger, hot peppers, mint, cumin, turmeric, cloves, allspice, wine, 12 cups of water, and salt, and bring to a boil. Lower the heat and simmer, covered, for about 45 minutes, stirring now and then.

3. Submerge the cheesecloth bag containing the turkey pieces in the hot stock and poach, covered, for 1½ to 2 hours, turning once during cooking. Remove the bag from the stock, let it drain over the pot, then place it on a tray. Cut the strings, open the bag, and transfer the turkey pieces to a plate to cool; discard the cheesecloth.

4. Strain the stock through a fine sieve, let sit for about 5 minutes, undisturbed, then remove and discard all the fat that has risen to the surface. Strain the degreased stock through a strainer lined with several layers of cheesecloth; you should have 4 to 5 cups. If you have more than 5 cups, place the clean stock in a large sauté pan or skillet, add the optional celery tops and mint or parsley sprigs, and cook over medium heat until reduced to 4 to 5 cups. Discard the celery tops and mint or parsley sprigs.

5. In a large sauté pan, heat the olive oil and ¼ cup of the curry oil. Add the turkey pieces and sauté over medium heat until light brown on all sides, about 8 minutes.

(Continued)

6. Remove the turkey pieces to a plate and strain the oil through a fine sieve into a large earthenware casserole or enameled or stainless-steel sauté pan. Heat the strained oil over medium heat, add the tablespoon of curry oil, stir in the nuts, and cook for a few seconds. Add the onions and sauté, while stirring, until the onions are barely translucent, about 3 minutes.

7. Push the mixture to the sides of the casserole, pour the wine or Pernod into the center, and bring to a full boil. Stir, including the onions and nuts, and continue to cook until almost all of the liquid has evaporated, about 5 minutes.

8. Add the vinegar and stock and bring to a boil. Lower the heat and gently simmer for 10 minutes. Add the figs and cook for 15 minutes. Add the dates and continue cooking for 5 minutes, then add the prunes and cook for 10 minutes more. Arrange the turkey pieces in the vinegar sauce and let simmer for 1 or 2 minutes. Remove from heat, let cool to room temperature, and serve.

NOTE   For this recipe, the turkey breast has been left in two pieces to cook properly. They can be cut into smaller serving pieces, either before the turkey is added to the finished vinegar sauce or just before serving. If you like, you can thinly slice the turkey breast against the grain before serving and serve it with the sauce, garnished with the fruits.

STORAGE NOTE   This dish keeps well, tightly covered, for up to 10 days in the refrigerator.

VARIATION

Substitute 3 wild pheasants for the wild turkey; proceed as for the turkey. You may also substitute farmed pheasants, a domestic turkey, stewing hen, or 2 rabbits for the wild turkey. Poach these meats in the stock for only about 1 hour in Step 3. Proceed with the recipe.

Escabeche de Alcachofas
Artichoke Escabeche

—

Serves 8

Certain vegetables are fabulous when prepared in an escabeche, especially those rich in natural sweetness, such as artichokes. The sweetness contrasts with the tartness of the vinegar, creating a well-balanced and aromatic dish.

Many vegetables can be substituted in this escabeche—cauliflower, broccoli, okra, and fennel are all good choices. (See Variations at end of recipe.) All of these vegetables prepared in escabeche make a good garnish or side dish, as well as a colorful appetizer.

8 medium artichokes (about 8 ounces each) or 16 baby artichokes (about 2 ounces each)
1 lemon
2 tablespoons coarse salt
1 cup olive oil
4 cloves garlic, peeled
2 medium onions, peeled and sliced into ¼-inch rings
2 large carrots, peeled and cut into sticks, 3 × ⅛ inch
1 serrano or jalapeño pepper, seeded and julienned
1 bay leaf
12 black peppercorns
6 to 8 sprigs fresh oregano, chopped, or ½ teaspoon dried oregano
⅛ teaspoon ground nutmeg
½ cup red-wine vinegar
1½ cups white wine
Sprigs of fresh oregano

1. Wash the artichokes in cold water. Fill a bowl large enough to hold all of the artichokes with about 2 quarts of cold water, and squeeze and mix in the juice of ½ lemon. With a large knife, cut off the stem flush with the base of each artichoke. Pull off and discard any small or discolored leaves around the base. Remove one or two rows by bending each leaf outward and down so that the top part snaps off the leaf's fleshy base. Place the artichoke on its side on a cutting board, and with a sharp

(Continued)

knife, cut off about 1 to 1½ inches of the top. With kitchen scissors, trim off the thorny tips of the remaining leaves. When each artichoke has been trimmed, drop it immediately into the water with the lemon juice to prevent discoloration, and keep the artichokes there until ready to cook.

2. In a large enameled or stainless-steel pot, bring 4 quarts of water, 1 tablespoon of the salt, and the juice of the remaining ½ lemon to a boil. Drop the artichokes into the boiling water and cook them for about 15 to 20 minutes, or until they are barely tender. Remove the artichokes from the water; turn them upside down in a colander or on a rack to drain.

3. In an earthenware casserole, heat the olive oil. Add the garlic and sauté over medium heat for just 1 or 2 seconds. Do not let the garlic brown or burn. Add the onions, carrots, pepper, bay leaf, peppercorns, oregano, nutmeg, and the remaining 1 tablespoon salt. Sauté for 2 minutes, stirring. Add the artichokes, cook for 1 minute, and pour in the vinegar and white wine. Stir and bring to a boil. Lower the heat and simmer for 5 minutes. Remove from the heat and set aside to cool to room temperature. Serve right from the casserole, garnished with the oregano sprigs.

NOTE   In this recipe the artichokes are left whole, but they can be cut lengthwise into halves or quarters, especially if they are very large. Do this after trimming them. Then, using a paring knife or teaspoon, cut off or scoop out the fuzzy chokes, discard them, and proceed with the recipe.

STORAGE NOTE   Escabeches made with artichokes, broccoli, cauliflower, fennel, or okra, alone or in combination, all keep well, tightly covered, for up to 10 days in the refrigerator.

VARIATIONS

Substitute 2 or 3 heads of broccoli or cauliflower for the artichokes. Separate the heads into florets, blanch, and drain. Proceed with the recipe from Step 3 on.

Substitute about 5 pounds okra for the artichokes. Trim the stems without cutting into the pods, then blanch in salted water and drain. Proceed with the recipe from Step 3 on.

Substitute 4 to 8 fennel bulbs, depending on the size, for the artichokes. Trim the bulbs and cut in half if large, then blanch and drain. Proceed with the recipe from Step 3 on.

Substitute a combination of vegetables, trimmed, blanched, and drained, for the artichokes. You will need 8 to 12 cups, depending on how small or large the vegetables are cut.

Escabeche de Huevo
Egg Escabeche

Makes 18 to 24 eggs

The flavoring in this escabeche is quite special: fresh coconut milk with its rich oils is used instead of wine, stock, or water to mellow the vinegar. The sweetness of this escabeche is brought out by the addition of onions and raisins and further enhanced by saffron.

Any type of eggs can be used in this escabeche, but some, like duck or goose eggs, are richer in taste than others. They are also larger than chicken eggs, so you would use fewer of them. Ten to twelve dozen tiny quail eggs may also be substituted for the chicken eggs in this recipe.

18 to 24 large chicken or duck eggs (see Note)
2 fresh coconuts (about 2 pounds each)
3 or 4 dried mirasol peppers or dried red chili peppers, crumbled
1-inch piece fresh ginger, chopped
2 or 3 cinnamon sticks (2 inches each)
18 to 20 allspice berries
1 teaspoon sugar
2 tablespoons coarse salt
2 tablespoons olive oil
1 cup blanched whole almonds, macadamia nuts, hazelnuts, or peanuts (4 ounces) (optional)
4 medium onions, peeled and thinly sliced (2½ pounds)
1 teaspoon Spanish saffron threads (1 vial)
1 cup light sherry vinegar or dry sherry wine
2 cups sherry vinegar, red-wine vinegar, or rice vinegar
1 to 1¼ cups golden raisins

(Continued)

1. Place the eggs in a pot deep enough to hold them without crowding and add cold water to cover by at least 2 to 3 inches (about 3 quarts). Bring to a full boil, cover, remove from heat, and let sit, undisturbed, 10 minutes for chicken eggs, 15 minutes for duck eggs. Transfer the eggs to a bowl of cold water and let them cool. Gently crack the shell of each egg all around, then, starting at the large end, peel under a thin stream of cold water; set aside.

2. With a pointed instrument, such as an ice pick, pierce two of the three soft "eyes" of the coconuts. Shake the whitish opaque liquid into a measuring cup and add enough warm water to make 5 cups. Crack open the coconut shells, remove the meat, and discard the shells.

3. Chop the coconut meat; place half into the jar of a blender or the work bowl of a food processor, together with half the coconut liquid, and blend thoroughly. Repeat this operation with the remaining coconut meat and liquid.

4. Pour all the blended coconut into an enameled saucepan. Add the hot peppers, ginger, cinnamon, allspice, sugar, and salt, and bring to a boil. Lower the heat, cover the pot, and simmer for 45 minutes, stirring now and then.

5. Remove from the heat, and when cool enough to handle, take out and reserve the cinnamon sticks. Pour the rest through a large fine sieve or in several batches through a strainer lined with a double layer of cheesecloth. Twist the cheesecloth to extract all the juices, discarding the dry pulp. You should have about 4 cups of coconut milk. Set aside.

6. In a medium saucepan, heat the olive oil. Add the nuts, if using, and sauté while stirring for 1 minute. Stir in the sliced onion and sprinkle in the saffron; sauté over high heat until the onion is soft, about 3 to 5 minutes. Add the sherry or sherry vinegar, the rice or wine vinegar, and the reserved cinnamon sticks, and bring to a boil. Lower the heat and simmer for about 10 minutes.

7. Add the coconut milk and bring to a boil again. Lower the heat and continue to simmer for 10 to 15 minutes. Add the raisins and cook for 5 minutes longer. Place the hard-boiled eggs in a deep porcelain, glass, or earthenware serving dish and pour the hot sauce over the eggs. Let the escabeche cool to room temperature and serve.

NOTE   If using goose eggs, proceed as with chicken or duck eggs, but in Step 1, let them sit in the hot water, covered and undisturbed, for 17 to 20 minutes. If using quail eggs, proceed with Step 1 but let them sit in the hot water for only 1 minute, covered. Rinse them under cool water, then place them in a bowl with white vinegar to cover. Let them stand for 4 to 5 hours. Rinse in cold water and then peel.

STORAGE NOTE   This escabeche keeps well, tightly covered, in the refrigerator for up to 10 days.

VARIATION

Almond milk may be used in place of coconut milk. Substitute 1 pound of shelled, blanched almonds for the 2 coconuts, and use 8 cups of water instead of 5. Finely grind the almonds in a food processor. Cook the almonds (instead of the coconut) with the hot peppers and spices in Step 4, then strain through cheesecloth in several batches, twisting to extract all the milk. You should have about 4 cups. If not, put the squeezed-out pulp back in the saucepan and add 4 cups of water. Bring to a boil, let simmer for 15 minutes, then strain and squeeze out again. Add as much of the liquid as needed to make 4 cups of almond milk. Proceed with the recipe, starting with Step 6.

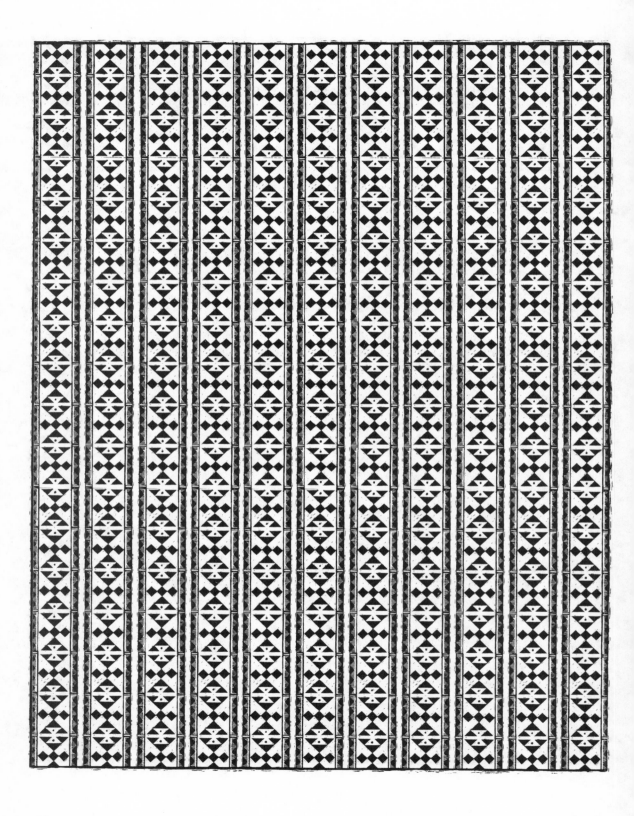

EMPANADAS

Caldudas
Chilean Empanadas

—

Empadas de Carne
Beef Empadas

—

Empanadas de Cerdo
Pork Empanadas

—

Empanadas de Pollo
Chicken Empanadas

—

Empanadas de Cordero
Lamb Empanadas

—

Empanadas de Pato
Duck Empanadas

—

Empanadas de Bacalao
Cod Empanadas

—

Empanadas de Atún
Tuna Empanadas

—

Empadinhas de Camarão
Shrimp Empadinhas

Pastel de Pescado
Fish and Swiss Chard Pie

—

Pastel de Choclo
Meat and Corn Pie

—

Empanadas Vegeterianas
Vegetable Empanadas

—

Empanadas de Espinaca
Spinach Empanadas

—

Empanaditas de Maíz
Corn Empanadas

—

Salteñas de Queso
Cheese Empanadas

SWEET EMPANADAS

Empanadas Dulces de Queso
Sweet Cheese Empanadas

—

Empanadas de Manzana
Apple Empanadas

One of the great food passions all South Americans share is for those tasty savory pastries called *empanadas, empadas, pasteles,* or, in Bolivia, *salteñas.* The word *empanada* is Spanish for "breaded," and it has come to mean a filled pastry turnover, patty, or pie. The average-size empanada yields about three handsome bites. Those consisting of just one bite are usually referred to as *empanaditas, empanadillas, pastelitos,* or *empadinhas,* though the diminutive is sometimes used more as a term of affection than description.

I will always remember my grandmother's empanadas. The pastry was impeccable and the fillings were fabulous. Her empanadas made with leftover squab were unforgettable. Most of her empanadas, in fact, were made from leftovers. Now as then, makng empanadas should be as casual as looking into the refrigerator or pantry and using your imagination, guided by your palate, to transform ingredients into food that is sensible and delicious to eat.

For a tasty empanada, you need both a dough with personality and a well-seasoned filling, which can be made from meat, poultry, seafood, cheese, vegetables, or even fruit. Generally, two kinds of dough are used for empanadas and *pasteles:* the more common one is pastry dough, somewhat dry and delicate (at times puff pastry is used); the other is a breadlike dough, leavened with yeast or baking powder. White flour is almost always used for both.

The other basic dough ingredients are water, eggs, and lard or shortening. Flour and vegetable starch are sometimes combined to produce unusual textures and flavors. Mashed potatoes, for example, make the dough very robust; yuca (see page 394) lends it great elasticity. The dough is often enriched with spices or cheese.

Flavorful fats, such as butter, lard, or rendered duck or goose fat, make the dough richer than plain vegetable shortening. I like to incorporate a strong oil, such as olive, sesame, or *dendê* (palm) oil, or an oil imbued with achiote, paprika, or curry powder. These flavors capture the spirit of South American cooking and give the pastry an irresistible bouquet and appealing color.

Of the many kinds of empanada fillings, I confess to a special weakness for lamb, goat, and rabbit; I am also very fond of game: *jabalí,* or boar, venison, pheasant, quail, partridge, and especially duck. But I definitely would not turn down an empanada with a more common (yet no less delectable) pork, beef, chicken, turkey, or veal stuffing.

Seafood empanadas are made with almost any kind of fish or shellfish. *Bacalao,* or salt cod, is very popular as a filling, as is river shrimp, which is always served on special occasions.

No matter what the filling, it had better be extremely flavorful! Since there is so little of it in an empanada, you want the flavor to be overwhelmingly satisfying, to give the sensation that there is much more. To achieve that explosion of flavors, I sometimes cook the ingredients slowly in a rich stock, reducing it to a mere glaze. I use plenty of spices and hot peppers. Sometimes I put in nuts for crunch and texture or raisins and spices to bring out the sweetness of the meat.

Empanadas can be either baked or fried. Baked empanadas are best served warm, not hot; they need to rest for a few minutes after being removed from the oven so the flavors can settle. Fried empanadas, on the other hand, should be served immediately, without allowing them to cool—not even slightly. That way the pastry will retain all its wonderful crispiness.

Empanadas are appropriate on any occasion. Bite-size empanadas are perfect with cocktails or for snacks; larger ones are just right for an appetizer or first course, or even as a light lunch dish, with a crisp salad on the side and a cold glass of beer.

The doughs and fillings that follow are interchangeable. Sizes and shapes—triangles, half-moons, or patties—can be tailored to suit the occasion. You can follow my suggestions or, better still, apply your own personal style and flair.

Caldudas
Chilean Empanadas

Makes about 16 empanadas

While many kinds of empanadas are found in Chile, *calduda* is considered *the* Chilean empanada. The meat is slowly cooked in a *caldo,* or stock, and as the stock evaporates to almost nothing, the meat becomes soft as butter and very moist.

The filling, or *pino,* is sweetened with raisins, which also contrast with the tart taste of olives.

DOUGH
3 cups all-purpose flour
1 teaspoon coarse salt
8 tablespoons (1 stick) unsalted butter, at room temperature,
*   cut in bits*
2 egg yolks
2 tablespoons tarragon vinegar or white-wine vinegar
9 tablespoons cold water

FILLING
1 tablespoon Paprika Oil (page 474) or olive oil mixed with
*   1 teaspoon Spanish paprika and ⅛ teaspoon cayenne*
2 tablespoons unsalted butter
2 medium onions, peeled and finely chopped (2 cups)
½ pound ground lean beef
1 teaspoon finely chopped fresh oregano or ¼ teaspoon dried oregano
2 teaspoons coarse salt
1 bay leaf
½ cup Beef Stock (page 462)
3 tablespoons seedless raisins
8 Kalamata olives, pitted and chopped
1 hard-boiled egg, chopped

GLAZE
1 egg yolk
1 whole egg
1 tablespoon cold water

(Continued)

1. Sift the flour and salt into a bowl. Add the butter, egg yolks, and vinegar and mix quickly and thoroughly with your fingertips until all ingredients are well incorporated. Add 5 tablespoons of the water and continue mixing, adding just enough of the remaining water, a little at a time, to make a firm dough. Refrigerate until ready to use.

2. For the filling, heat the oil and butter in a sauté pan. Add the onions and sauté over medium heat until light brown around the edges, about 5 minutes. Add the beef, oregano, salt, and bay leaf and cook until all the liquid has evaporated. Add the stock and continue cooking until the stock has almost—but not quite—evaporated. Mix in the raisins and olives. Remove from heat and let cool. Stir in the chopped hard-boiled egg. Correct the seasoning with salt to taste; set aside.

3. Preheat the oven to 375 degrees.

4. On a floured board, roll out the dough about ⅛ inch thick, shaping it into a 16-inch square. Cut out circles about 5 inches in diameter. Knead and re-roll the scraps and cut into additional circles. Place a heaping tablespoon of the meat filling about ½ inch from the edge of each circle. Brush the border of the circle with juices from the filling or with water. Fold the dough over to form a half-moon, pressing the edges together with your fingertips or the tines of a fork to seal. Prick the top of each empanada once or twice with the tines of the fork. Repeat this process until all the empanadas are assembled.

5. Make the glaze by beating the egg yolk and egg with the water.

6. Spread parchment paper on a baking sheet. Arrange the empanadas on top and brush with glaze. Bake for 30 minutes, or until golden. Remove the baking tray from the oven, transfer the empanadas to a serving platter or individual plates, and serve hot.

Empadas de Carne
Beef Empadas

—

Makes about 16 empadas

The Brazilians call their empanadas *empadas* or, when they are little, *empadinhas*. Many kinds of fillings, including beef, shrimp, and, on occasion, chicken, are used, and sizes range from generous (enough for a meal) to tiny. The *empadas* in this recipe are intended to be served as appetizers or snacks, but you can easily make them larger by simply doubling the size of the squares to eight inches and adjusting the amount of the filling accordingly. For bite-size *empadinhas*, which are lovely with drinks, cut the dough into two-inch squares.

DOUGH
3 cups all-purpose flour
3 tablespoons lard or vegetable shortening, chilled
1 egg
1 egg white
½ cup cold water

FILLING
2 tablespoons olive oil
½ pound ground lean beef (see Note)
½ teaspoon ground cardamom
1 bay leaf
1 jalapeño or serrano pepper, seeded and chopped,
    or ⅛ teaspoon cayenne
2 teaspoons coarse salt
1 medium potato, peeled and cut into ¼-inch dice (1 cup)
1 cup water
8 scallions, white parts only, chopped (½ cup)
1 tablespoon chopped Italian parsley

SEALER and GLAZE
1 egg yolk
1 tablespoon cold water

   1. Sift the flour into a bowl, add the chilled lard, and mix quickly and thoroughly with your fingertips until the mixture resembles coarse meal.

(Continued)

Add the egg, egg white, and ¼ cup of the cold water. Continue mixing, adding the rest of the cold water, a little at a time, just until you have a firm dough. Knead the dough for a few seconds until smooth, then wrap it and chill for 15 to 30 minutes. (It can be used immediately or kept refrigerated, well wrapped, for up to 1 week.)

2. In a small frying pan, heat the olive oil. Add the meat, cardamom, bay leaf, pepper, and salt and sauté over medium heat, stirring, until the liquid has evaporated. Add the potatoes and the water and simmer over very low heat, stirring now and then, until the potatoes are tender and all the liquid has evaporated. Add the scallions and cook for 2 to 3 minutes longer. Remove from the heat, stir in the parsley, and correct the seasoning with salt to taste. Set the filling aside and let cool thoroughly or refrigerate overnight, well covered.

3. Make the sealer and glaze by beating the egg yolk and the cold water together. Set aside.

4. Preheat the oven to 375 degrees.

5. On a floured board, roll out the dough ⅛ inch thick. Cut the dough into 4-inch squares. Knead the scraps and re-roll them, and cut into additional squares. Put 1 full tablespoon of the filling into the center of each square. Moisten the edges of the dough lightly with the sealer. Fold the dough over the filling to form a triangle; press the edges together with your fingertips or the tines of a fork to seal. Repeat until all the *empadas* are assembled.

6. Place the *empadas* on a baking sheet lined with parchment paper. Brush them with the remaining glaze and bake for about 25 minutes, or until golden. Remove from the oven; transfer the *empadas* to a rack to cool slightly. Serve warm.

NOTE   Ground pork or chicken, or a combination of both, may be substituted.

VARIATION

Pasteles de Carne
Fried Empadas
—

Complete the recipe through Step 5. Heat 6 cups of oil to between 365 and 375 degrees. Gently drop the *empadas* into the hot oil and fry until golden. Serve immediately.

Empanadas de Cerdo
Pork Empanadas

Makes about 16 empanadas

Pork is the most extensively used of all meats in South America. Since it is so rich in flavor, pork makes excellent fillings, just right for savory pastries. In this recipe, it is combined with onions, spices (cumin, cloves, and allspice), and raisins.

This filling can also be made with pork's wild cousin, boar (or *jabalí*, as that beast is called in Spanish), or venison.

Achiote Dough (page 52)

FILLING
3 tablespoons Achiote Oil (page 472) or Paprika Oil (page 474)
   or 3 tablespoons olive oil mixed with ½ teaspoon paprika
1 large clove garlic, peeled and finely chopped
1 large onion, peeled and minced (1½ cups)
1 jalapeño or serrano pepper, seeded and finely chopped,
   or ⅛ teaspoon cayenne
¼ teaspoon ground cloves
1 teaspoon ground cumin
¼ teaspoon ground allspice
2 teaspoons coarse salt
½ pound lean pork, coarsely chopped
¼ cup raisins soaked in ⅓ cup light rum
8 alfonso or Kalamata olives, pitted and coarsely chopped
¼ cup chopped fresh cilantro or Italian parsley

SEALER and GLAZE
1 whole egg or 2 egg yolks
2 tablespoons cold water or milk or heavy cream

1. Prepare the achiote dough.

2. In a small frying pan, heat the oil. Add the garlic, onion, pepper, cloves, cumin, allspice, and salt and sauté until the onion is totally translucent, about 4 or 5 minutes. Add the pork and cook for 5 to 8 minutes, stirring now and then. Add the raisins with the rum and con-

(Continued)

tinue cooking until all the liquid has evaporated. Stir in the olives. Remove from heat to cool thoroughly or refrigerate overnight, well covered. Just before using, correct seasoning with salt to taste and mix in the cilantro.

3. Make the sealer and glaze by mixing the egg with the water.

4. Preheat the oven to 375 degrees.

5. On a lightly floured pastry board, roll out the dough about ⅛ inch thick, shaping it into a 16-inch square. Cut the dough into 4½-inch squares. Knead and re-roll the scraps to cut into additional squares. Place a full tablespoon of filling in the center of each square. Moisten the edges of the dough lightly with the egg sealer. Fold the dough over the filling to form a triangle, and press the edges together with your fingertips or the tines of a fork to seal. Prick the empanada once or twice with the tines of the fork. Repeat until all the empanadas are assembled.

6. Line a baking sheet with parchment paper and arrange the empanadas on top. Brush the surface of the empanadas with the remaining egg glaze and bake for 25 to 30 minutes, or until golden brown. Remove the baking sheet from the oven, transfer the empanadas to a rack to cool slightly, and serve warm.

STORAGE NOTE   These empanadas freeze extremely well. To freeze, assemble the empanadas but do not glaze them. Wrap or cover them tightly and put them in the freezer; they will keep in good condition for up to three months. When they are ready to be used, either let them thaw in the refrigerator, glaze, and bake, or bake, glazed, directly from the freezer.

Masa de Achiote
Achiote Dough

—

Makes enough for 2 9-inch shells, 16 to 18 individual pastries,
or 32 bite-size pastries

The fiery hue and woody aroma of achiote, or annatto, imbue this pastry dough with an appetizing color and flavor, which come from an essence of annatto seeds and oil. This oil can be replaced with Paprika Oil or paprika, which will give the pastry a somewhat similar flavor and good color. (See Variations at end of recipe.)

3 cups all-purpose flour
2 teaspoons coarse salt
1 teaspoon sugar
9 tablespoons lard, chilled (see last Variation, at end of recipe)
3 tablespoons Achiote Oil (page 472)
½ cup cold water

Sift the flour, salt, and sugar into a bowl. Add the lard and oil and mix quickly with your fingertips until the mixture resembles coarse meal. Add ¼ cup of the water. Continue mixing, adding the rest of the water a little at a time, just until you have a firm dough. Knead the dough for a few seconds until smooth, wrap well, and let rest in the refrigerator for about 10 minutes, or until ready to use.

STORAGE NOTE   Achiote dough stores well for up to 10 days in the refrigerator, tightly wrapped. For longer storage, freeze the dough, tightly wrapped. It will keep for at least 6 months. When the frozen dough is ready to be used, defrost it, preferably in the refrigerator overnight, until malleable enough to roll out.

VARIATIONS

For a milder, lighter flavor, use only 2 tablespoons of achiote oil. Do not change anything else in the recipe.

Paprika Oil (page 474) may be substituted for achiote oil. Use the same amount.

To substitute ground paprika for the achiote oil, sift 1 teaspoon of paprika together with the flour, salt, and sugar. Use 11 tablespoons of lard instead of 9.

Vegetable shortening may be substituted for the lard; it will make a lighter pastry. For better flavor, use half vegetable shortening and half butter.

Empanadas de Pollo
Chicken Empanadas

Makes about 16 empanadas

With few exceptions, empanada dough consists of flour, lard, eggs, and water. This one, however, stands apart. It has a special zest that comes from a splash of flavorful vinegar. This crisp, slightly tart pastry is the ideal envelope for white meats—chicken, turkey, and rabbit—though game birds, such as pheasant, partridge, and quail, should definitely not be overlooked.

DOUGH
3 cups all-purpose flour
1 teaspoon coarse salt
6 tablespoons unsalted butter, chilled and chopped
2 tablespoons lard or vegetable shortening
1 egg yolk
1 egg
3 tablespoons sherry vinegar or cider vinegar or white-wine vinegar
7 tablespoons cold water

FILLING
2 tablespoons unsalted butter
1 large onion, peeled and finely chopped (1½ cups)
⅛ teaspoon ground allspice
2 teaspoons coarse salt
¾ pound boneless and skinless chicken or turkey meat,
  coarsely chopped (see Note)
1 or 2 teaspoons chopped fresh oregano or
  ¼ teaspoon dried oregano
3 tablespoons chopped walnuts or black walnuts or hazelnuts
  (optional)

SEALER and GLAZE
1 egg white
1 tablespoon cold water

1. Sift the flour and salt into a bowl. Add the chilled butter and lard and mix quickly and thoroughly with your fingertips until the mixture resembles coarse meal. Add the egg yolk, egg, vinegar, and half of the cold water and mix, adding the remaining water, a tablespoon at a time, just until you have a firm dough. Knead the dough until smooth. This dough can be used immediately, kept wrapped in the refrigerator until ready to use, or stored, well covered, in the refrigerator for up to 1 week.

2. In a small sauté pan, heat the butter. Add the onion, allspice, and salt and cook over medium heat until the onion is golden around the edges, about 5 minutes. Add the chicken and oregano and cook until all the liquid has evaporated. Mix in the nuts, if using; remove from heat and set aside to cool thoroughly, or refrigerate overnight, tightly covered. Just before using, correct seasoning with salt to taste.

3. Make the sealer or glaze by beating the egg with the cold water; set aside.

4. Preheat the oven to 375 degrees.

5. On a floured board, roll out the dough ⅛ inch thick, shaping it into a 16-inch square. Cut the dough into 5-inch squares. Knead and re-roll the scraps to make additional squares. Place 1 heaping tablespoon of the filling ¼ inch from the edge of the square. Moisten the border of the square with the sealer and fold the dough over the filling to form a triangle, pressing the edges together with your fingertips or the tines of a fork to seal. Prick the top of the empanada once or twice with the tines of the fork. Repeat until all the empanadas are assembled.

6. Line a baking sheet with parchment paper and arrange the empanadas on top. Brush the empanadas with the glaze and bake for 25 to 30 minutes, or until golden. Remove the baking sheet from the oven and transfer the empanadas to a rack to cool slightly. Serve warm.

NOTE   Rabbit, pheasant, partridge, or quail may be substituted, but grind the meat instead of chopping it.

STORAGE NOTE   These empanadas may be frozen once they are assembled but not yet glazed. When ready to use, remove from the freezer and place directly on a baking sheet lined with parchment paper. Brush with egg glaze and bake in a preheated 375-degree oven until golden.

VARIATION

Olive oil or, for more dramatic flavoring, Curry Oil (page 473), Achiote Oil (page 472), or Paprika Oil (page 474) may be substituted for the butter.

Empanadas de Cordero
Lamb Empanadas

—

Makes about 16 empanadas

Curry Dough (page 58)

FILLING
2 tablespoons raisins
3 tablespoons rum
2 tablespoons olive oil
3 large cloves garlic, peeled and minced
1 or 2 jalapeño or serrano peppers, seeded and minced,
    or ⅛ teaspoon cayenne
2-inch piece fresh ginger, peeled and minced
1 large onion, peeled and finely chopped (1½ cups)
¼ teaspoon ground cloves
1 to 1½ tablespoons finely chopped fresh mint or 2 teaspoons
    dried mint, crumbled
2 teaspoons ground cumin
1 teaspoon coarse salt
¼ teaspoon ground white pepper
½ pound lean lamb, coarsely ground
3 tablespoons roasted pignolis (page 485) (see Note)
3 tablespoons chopped fresh cilantro leaves or Italian parsley

SEALER and GLAZE
1 egg white (see Variation)
2 tablespoons water or milk or heavy cream

1. Prepare the curry dough.

2. Place the raisins and rum in a cup and let soak for 15 to 20 minutes.

3. To prepare the filling, heat the olive oil in a sauté pan. Add the garlic, hot pepper, ginger, onion, cloves, mint, cumin, salt, and white pepper; sauté over medium heat until the onion is totally translucent, about 4 or 5 minutes. Add the lamb and cook for 10 minutes, stirring, until the lamb is thoroughly cooked. Add the raisins with the rum and stir constantly until all the liquid has evaporated. Mix in the pignolis and remove from the heat. Cool thoroughly or store, well covered, overnight in the refrigerator. Just before using, add the cilantro and mix; correct the seasoning with salt to taste.

4. To prepare the sealer and glaze, mix the egg white with the water.

5. Preheat the oven to 375 degrees.

6. On a lightly floured board, roll out the dough about ⅛ inch thick, shaping it into a 16-inch square. Cut the dough into 4-inch squares. Knead and re-roll the scraps and cut into additional squares. Place 1 full tablespoon of filling in the center of each square. Moisten the edges of the dough lightly with egg sealer. Fold the dough over the filling to form a triangle, and press the edges together with your fingertips or the tines of a fork to seal. Prick the surface of the empanada once or twice with the tines of the fork. Repeat this process until all the empanadas are assembled.

7. Spread parchment paper on a baking sheet. Arrange the empanadas on the parchment paper and brush with the remaining egg glaze. Bake for about 25 minutes, or until golden brown. Remove from oven; place the empanadas on a rack and let them cool slightly. Serve warm.

NOTE   Walnuts, almonds, or hazelnuts may be substituted for the pignolis. They should be toasted, then coarsely chopped.

STORAGE NOTE   These empanadas can be frozen after they have been assembled but not yet glazed. Wrap them tightly and place them in the freezer. They will keep for about 3 months. When ready to use, place frozen empanadas on a baking sheet lined with parchment paper, brush with egg glaze, and bake until golden in a preheated 375-degree oven.

VARIATION

To give the pastry extra sheen, substitute 1 whole egg or 1 egg yolk for the egg white in the sealer and glaze. Plain water may also be used for the sealer.

Masa de Curry
Curry Dough

—

Makes enough for 2 9-inch shells, 16 to 18 individual pastries,
or 32 bite-size pastries

3 cups all-purpose flour
2 teaspoons coarse salt
1 teaspoon sugar
8 tablespoons lard, chilled (see last Variation, at end of recipe)
3 tablespoons Curry Oil (page 473)
1 egg yolk
½ cup cold water

Sift the flour, salt, and sugar into a bowl. Add the lard and oil and mix quickly with your fingertips until the mixture resembles coarse meal. Add the egg yolk and ¼ cup of the water. Continue mixing, adding the rest of the water, a little at a time, just until you have a firm dough. Knead the dough for a few seconds until smooth. Wrap the dough and let it rest in the refrigerator for about 10 minutes, or until ready to use.

STORAGE NOTE   Curry dough stores well for 1 week in the refrigerator, tightly wrapped or covered. It will keep for about 6 months in the freezer. When ready to use, defrost it, preferably in the refrigerator overnight, until malleable enough to roll out.

VARIATIONS

For a milder, somewhat subdued, curry flavor, add only 1 or 2 tablespoons of curry oil. Do not change anything else in the recipe.

To substitute curry powder for the curry oil, sift 1 teaspoon curry powder together with the flour, salt, and sugar. Use 10 tablespoons of lard instead of 8.

For a very strong, robust dough, use 2 or 3 egg yolks or 1 egg in addition to the egg yolk in the recipe. You may also substitute 1 whole egg for the egg yolk.

Vegetable shortening may be substituted for the lard; it will make a lighter pastry. For more flavor, use half vegetable shortening and half butter in place of the lard.

Empanadas de Pato
Duck Empanadas
—

Makes about 16 empanadas

Duck, domestic or wild, is a superb bird, and its succulent red meat makes an excellent empanada. Other red-meat birds, such as goose, squab, woodcock, and snipe, are also good in this filling.

While wild ducks are relatively lean, the domestic ones are enveloped in fat. This fat is excellent for cooking; you will find many uses for it in your kitchen. (See page 475 for directions for rendering duck fat.) So, even though this recipe calls for meat without skin, bones, or fat, do not discard those parts. Save the bones for stock and the skin and fat for rendering. If you like, you can use rendered duck fat instead of lard in the pastry dough and instead of olive oil in the filling.

Curry Dough (page 58)

FILLING
2 tablespoons olive oil
1 large clove garlic, peeled and minced
1 medium onion, peeled and finely minced (about 1 cup)
¼ teaspoon ground juniper berries or ground allspice
¼ teaspoon ground white pepper
¾ pound boneless and skinless duck meat, finely chopped
    (about 1 breast)
1 to 2 teaspoons finely chopped fresh cilantro leaves or 1 teaspoon
    finely chopped fresh tarragon or ¼ teaspoon dried tarragon,
    crumbled
½ cup white wine or Quick Duck Stock (page 60) or Beef Stock (page
    462) or Chicken Stock (page 461)
1 teaspoon coarse salt
1 teaspoon fresh thyme, chopped
¼ cup chopped Italian parsley

SEALER and GLAZE
1 egg white
2 tablespoons water or milk or heavy cream

(Continued)

1. Prepare the curry dough.

2. In a sauté pan or small frying pan, heat the olive oil. Add the garlic, onion, ground juniper berries, and white pepper and sauté over medium heat until the onion is totally translucent, about 2 to 3 minutes. Add the duck and cilantro and cook, stirring, for 2 more minutes. Add the wine, salt, and thyme and continue to cook for about 15 minutes longer, or until all the liquid has evaporated. Remove from heat and set aside to cool thoroughly, or refrigerate overnight, well covered. Just before using, mix in the chopped parsley and correct seasoning with salt to taste.

3. Prepare the sealer and glaze by mixing the egg white with the water.

4. Preheat the oven to 375 degrees.

5. On a lightly floured board, roll out the dough about ⅛ inch thick, shaping it into a 16-inch square. Cut the dough into 4- or 5-inch squares. Knead and re-roll the scraps into additional squares. Place 1 to 1½ tablespoons of the filling in the center of each square and moisten the edges lightly with the sealer. Fold one corner of the square over the filling to form a triangle, pressing the edges together with your fingertips or with the tines of a fork. Prick the top of the empanada once or twice with the tines of the fork. Repeat until all the empanadas are assembled.

6. Line a baking sheet with parchment paper and arrange the empanadas on top. Brush the empanadas with the remaining glaze and bake for about 25 to 30 minutes, or until they are golden. Remove the baking sheet from the oven, transfer the empanadas to a rack to cool slightly, and serve warm.

Caldo de Pato
Quick Duck Stock

—

Makes 1 to 1½ quarts

2 or 3 stalks celery, with leafy tops, washed and chopped
1 parsnip or carrot, washed and sliced
1 leek, washed and chopped
1 medium onion, peeled and sliced

½ orange, sliced
Duck bones, neck, and giblets (not the liver) from 1 or more ducks
6 cloves
½-inch piece fresh ginger
2 or 3 cloves garlic, unpeeled and crushed
6 sprigs fresh dill or thyme or oregano

1. Preheat the oven to 400 degrees.

2. Spread the celery, parsnip, leek, onion, and orange slices on the bottom of a roasting pan and put the duck bones, neck, and giblets on top. Place in the oven and roast for about 25 minutes, or until the bones are slightly browned.

3. Transfer the bones, vegetables, and orange to a stockpot. Deglaze the roasting pan with about 1 cup water and add this to the pot, together with the cloves, ginger, garlic, and dill. Pour in enough water to cover all the ingredients. Bring to a boil, lower the heat, and simmer gently until the liquid has reduced by half, stirring now and then.

4. Remove from heat and strain through a fine sieve or strainer lined with several layers of cheesecloth, pressing to extract all the juices from the bones and vegetables. Let the strained stock sit for a few minutes to allow the fat to rise to the surface, then remove and discard it.

5. Use the stock immediately or store in the refrigerator, well covered, for up to 5 days. (The stock may also be frozen.) For a finer, more concentrated stock, place the stock in a saucepan over very low heat and let simmer to reduce to the amount needed.

Empanadas de Bacalao
Cod Empanadas

Makes about 16 empanadas

The Spanish and Portuguese brought salt cod to South America, and South Americans have become addicted to it. There are two types of salt cod (*bacalao* in Spanish, *bacalhau* in Portuguese): one is partially dried

(Continued)

after salting; the other is totally dried. When selecting salt cod for this recipe, look for the moist variety. Gaspé-cured salt cod is readily available; it is a fleshy, opal-colored chunk of clean fillet, often marketed as Canadian salt cod. Like all salt cod, it will need to be presoaked, both to remove excess salt and to reconstitute the fish.

For this dish, I prefer to use *aceittunas de botijas* from Peru, known in the United States as alfonso olives. They are big, juicy, and purplish-black in color. (If they are not available, you can substitute Greek Kalamata olives.) The very thought of this combination of olives with cod, sweet bell peppers, and a touch of cardamom, encased in a crunchy pastry, makes my mouth water.

Achiote Dough (page 52)

FILLING
½ pound skinless and boneless fresh cod or 1 cup tightly packed
    presoaked Canadian salt cod (see Note)
1 tablespoon Achiote Oil (page 472) or Paprika Oil (page 474)
    or 1 tablespoon olive oil mixed with ½ teaspoon Spanish paprika
2 cloves garlic, peeled and minced
1 large onion, peeled and finely chopped (1½ cups)
1 or 2 jalapeño or serrano peppers, seeded and finely chopped,
    or ⅛ teaspoon cayenne
1 teaspoon ground cardamom
1 large tomato, peeled, seeded, and chopped
½ large green bell pepper, seeded and finely diced (¼ cup)
½ large red bell pepper, seeded and finely diced (¼ cup)
1 teaspoon lemon juice
6 to 8 alfonso or Kalamata olives, pitted and coarsely chopped
2 tablespoons finely chopped Italian parsley
2 teaspoons coarse salt (if fresh cod is used)
Ground white pepper

SEALER and GLAZE
1 egg or 2 egg yolks
2 tablespoons cold water or milk or heavy cream

1. Prepare the achiote dough.

2. Shred the fresh cod or the soaked salt cod, discarding the skin and bones, if any. Set aside.

3. In a small frying pan, heat the oil and add the garlic, onion, hot pepper, and cardamom. Cook over medium heat until the onion is translucent, about 5 minutes. Add the tomato, bell peppers, lemon juice, and cod, stir, and cook for 8 to 10 minutes, until the fish is cooked and the mixture is quite dry. (If salt cod is being used, add ½ cup of water and cook until all the liquid has evaporated and the mixture is dry. This will take about 10 to 15 minutes.) Mix in the olives and parsley. Correct seasoning with salt, if using fresh cod, and white pepper to taste. Cool thoroughly or refrigerate overnight, well covered.

4. Prepare the sealer and glaze by mixing together the egg and water.

5. Preheat the oven to 375 degrees.

6. On a lightly floured pastry board, roll out the dough about ⅛ inch thick, shaping it into a 16-inch square. Cut the dough into 4-inch squares. Knead and re-roll the scraps into additional squares. Place 1 full tablespoon of filling in the center of each square. Moisten the edges of the dough lightly with the sealer. Fold a corner of the square over the filling to form a triangle, and press the edges together with your fingertips or the tines of a fork to seal. Prick the top of the empanada once or twice with the tines of the fork. Repeat until all the empanadas are assembled.

7. Spread parchment paper on a baking sheet. Arrange the empanadas on the parchment paper, brush with the remaining glaze, and bake for 25 to 30 minutes, or until golden brown. Remove the baking sheet from the oven and transfer the empanadas to a rack to cool slightly. Serve warm.

NOTE   If using dried cod, soak it in cold water for 24 hours, changing the water several times.

STORAGE NOTE   The empanadas may be frozen once they have been assembled but not glazed. When ready to use, remove from the freezer and place directly on a baking sheet lined with parchment paper. Brush with egg glaze, and bake in a 375-degree oven until golden.

Empanadas de Atún
Tuna Empanadas

Makes about 16 empanadas

Tuna is quite common along the Pacific coast. Bonito *(Sarda orientalis)*, a type of tuna quite similar in taste and appearance to the Atlantic bonito *(Sarda sarda)*, but much smaller, is found everywhere. Bonito and tuna are interchangeable in this recipe.

Other firm-fleshed fish, such as swordfish, yellowtail, salmon, or even bluefish, can be substituted for the tuna. Even canned tuna can be used. (See Variation at end of recipe.)

DOUGH
2½ cups all-purpose flour
1 teaspoon coarse salt
1 large potato, cooked, peeled, and mashed
8 tablespoons lard, butter, or solid vegetable shortening, chilled
2 egg yolks
1 egg
¼ cup cold water

FILLING
2 tablespoons olive oil
1 medium onion, peeled and finely chopped (1 cup)
½ teaspoon Spanish paprika
⅛ teaspoon ground white pepper
1 teaspoon coarse salt
½ pound boneless and skinless fresh tuna, coarsely chopped
2 tablespoons chopped fresh dill or Italian parsley

SEALER and GLAZE
2 egg whites
2 tablespoons milk

1. Sift the flour and salt into a bowl. Add the mashed potato and mix into the flour thoroughly. Add the lard and quickly mix with your fingertips until the mixture resembles coarse meal. Blend in the egg yolks, egg, and half of the water and mix, adding the remaining water, a bit at a time, if necessary, to form a firm dough. Knead the dough for a few minutes until smooth and let rest, covered with a moist cloth, for about 10 minutes. Use the dough immediately or store it for up to 5 days, well wrapped, in the refrigerator.

2. In a small frying pan, heat the olive oil. Add the onion, paprika, pepper, and salt and sauté over medium heat until the onion is totally translucent, about 2 minutes. Add the tuna and cook, stirring frequently, for 1 to 2 minutes. Remove from heat and set aside to cool, or refrigerate overnight, well covered. Just before using, mix in the dill and correct the seasoning with salt and white pepper to taste.

3. Make the sealer and glaze by beating the egg whites with the milk.

4. Preheat the oven to 375 degrees.

5. On a lightly floured board, roll out the dough about ¼ inch thick, shaping it into a 16-inch square. Cut into circles about 4½ inches in diameter. Knead and re-roll the scraps and cut into additional circles. Place a generous tablespoon of the filling on one side of the circle, leaving about a ¼-inch border of dough. Brush all around with the sealer and fold half of the circle over the filling, forming a half-moon. With the tines of a fork or with your fingertips, press the edges together to seal. Prick the top of the empanada once or twice with the tines of the fork. Repeat until all the empanadas are assembled.

6. Line a baking sheet with parchment paper and arrange the empanadas on top. Brush the empanadas with the remaining egg glaze and bake for 25 to 30 minutes, or until golden. Remove the baking sheet from the oven, transfer the empanadas to a rack to cool for a few minutes, and serve warm.

VARIATION

Substitute ¾ cup well-drained canned white-meat tuna (1 6½-ounce can) for the fresh tuna. Off the heat, mix the tuna with the cooked onion in Step 2; correct the seasoning and proceed with the recipe.

Empadinhas de Camarão
Shrimp Empadinhas

—

Makes about 16 empadinhas

If I had to say what kind of seafood Brazilians enjoy most, it certainly would be *camarão,* or shrimp; they are passionate about it. The wonderful flavor and aroma of Brazilian shrimp, whether large or small, from sea or stream, are often captured in *empadas* or, as they are called familiarly, *empadinhas.*

You could fill these crusty pastry cases with lobster or crab, instead of shrimp. A filling of all three—shrimp, lobster, and crab—enhanced by a hint of cardamom and cloves and enlivened by some nutty hearts of palm, makes one of the finest of all *empadinhas.*

To give a truly Brazilian character to your *empadinhas,* use some *dendê* (palm) oil in the dough.

DOUGH
3 cups all-purpose flour
1 teaspoon coarse salt
½ teaspoon ground turmeric
¼ teaspoon ground white pepper
10 tablespoons unsalted butter, chilled and chopped
6 tablespoons lard or solid vegetable shortening, chilled
1 egg
1 egg yolk
½ cup light beer or water

FILLING
2 tablespoons unsalted butter
1 large onion, peeled and finely chopped (1½ cups)
2 cloves garlic, peeled and chopped
3 to 4 medium tomatoes, peeled, seeded, and chopped
½ teaspoon ground cardamom
⅛ teaspoon ground cloves
¼ teaspoon ground white pepper
1 teaspoon coarse salt
*1½ cups hearts of palm, drained and coarsely chopped
    (1 14-ounce can)*
3 tablespoons chopped Italian parsley

SEALER and GLAZE
1 egg white
2 tablespoons cold water or milk or heavy cream

1 pound medium shrimp (16 to 20 per pound), shelled, deveined,
   rinsed, and patted dry

1. Sift the flour, salt, turmeric, and white pepper into a bowl. Add the butter and the lard and mix quickly and thoroughly with your fingertips until the mixture resembles coarse meal. Add the egg and egg yolk and half of the beer and continue mixing, adding just enough of the remaining liquid, a tablespoon at a time, until you have a firm dough. Knead the dough until smooth, cover with a moist towel, and let rest in a cool spot for about 15 minutes, or until ready to use. (This dough keeps well, tightly wrapped, in the refrigerator for up to 1 week.)

2. In a small frying pan, heat the 2 tablespoons butter. Add the onion and garlic and cook over medium heat until the onion is translucent, about 5 minutes. Add the chopped tomatoes, cardamom, cloves, white pepper, and salt and cook for about 8 minutes, stirring now and then. Add the hearts of palm and continue cooking for about 5 minutes longer, or until all the liquid has evaporated. Remove from heat and set aside to cool thoroughly, or store overnight in the refrigerator, tightly covered. Just before using, correct the seasoning with salt to taste and mix in the parsley.

3. Make the sealer and glaze by mixing the egg white with the water. Set aside.

4. Preheat the oven to 400 degrees.

5. On a lightly floured pastry board, roll out the dough ¼ to ⅛ inch thick and shape into a 16-inch square. Cut the dough into 4-inch circles, then knead and re-roll the scraps and cut more circles. Place 1½ to 2 tablespoons of filling into the center of each circle, and arrange 1 shrimp on top. Brush the edges of the dough lightly with the egg sealer. Fold the dough over the filling to form a half-moon, and press the edges together with your fingertips or the tines of a fork to seal. Prick the top of the *empadinhas* once or twice with the tine of the fork. Repeat until all of the *empadinhas* are assembled.

6. Preheat the oven to 400 degrees.

7. Line a baking sheet with parchment paper and arrange the *empadinhas* on top. Brush the surface of the *empadinhas* with the remain-

(Continued)

ing egg glaze and bake for 25 minutes, or until golden. Remove the baking sheet from the oven, transfer the *empadinhas* to a rack to cool slightly, and serve warm.

NOTE   You may substitute 1 or 2 tablespoons of *dendê* (palm) oil for 1 or 2 tablespoons of the lard. *Dendê* oil is available in specialty food shops.

Pastel de Pescado
Fish and Swiss Chard Pie

Serves 6 to 8

A *pastel* is a type of pie, and it comes in different shapes, usually round or rectangular; some are closed, some are left open. The filling can be made with vegetables, meat, fish, or cheese, or combinations of ingredients.

Like the filling, the pastry of a *pastel* can vary, though basically there are only two types: yeast dough, as in this recipe, or something more akin to pastry dough. For this recipe I suggest a mild-flavored yeast dough, but if you prefer a gutsier one, you could replace some or all of the butter with lard or rendered duck or goose fat.

DOUGH
*2 packages active dry yeast (2 scant tablespoons) or 1 ounce
    compressed yeast, crumbled*
1 teaspoon sugar
¾ cup warm milk or water (100 to 115 degrees)
3½ cups all-purpose flour
1 teaspoon coarse salt
6 tablespoons unsalted butter, softened, or lard
2 tablespoons olive oil

FILLING
*2 pounds skinless and boneless fresh cod or other firm
    white-fleshed fish fillets*
Grated rind of 1 lemon
3 to 4 pounds Swiss chard, washed, drained, and coarsely chopped
2 tablespoons unsalted butter

2 tablespoons olive oil
3 cloves garlic, peeled and finely chopped
2 jalapeño peppers, seeded and finely chopped
1 large onion, peeled and chopped (1½ cups)
1-inch piece fresh ginger, peeled and grated
⅛ teaspoon grated nutmeg or ground mace
2 teaspoons coarse salt
1 tablespoon chopped fresh oregano or dill or thyme
Juice of ½ lemon
1 egg yolk mixed with 1 teaspoon cold water or cream
1 to 2 teaspoons black mustard or sesame or poppy seeds (optional)

1. In a small bowl, combine the yeast, sugar, and milk or water and stir until the yeast is dissolved. Let the mixture sit in a warm, draft-free spot (such as a turned-off oven), undisturbed, for about 10 minutes.

2. In a mixing bowl, combine 3 cups of the flour with the salt. Add the butter or lard and the olive oil and mix with your fingertips until the butter is thoroughly absorbed and the mixture resembles coarse meal. Mix in the yeast and water, a little bit at a time, to form a compact dough. Knead the dough on a lightly floured board for about 8 to 10 minutes, until smooth and elastic. Place the dough in a lightly buttered or oiled bowl, cover with a moist towel or plastic wrap, and let stand in a warm, draft-free spot for about 2 hours, or until almost doubled in bulk. The dough should spring back slowly when gently poked.

3. Meanwhile, rub the fillets all around with the grated lemon rind, cover with a damp towel, and refrigerate until ready to use.

4. Blanch the Swiss chard for a few seconds in boiling water. Drain thoroughly and squeeze dry. Chop the chard, both leaves and stems, and set aside.

5. In a large skillet over medium heat, heat the 2 tablespoons butter and the 2 tablespoons olive oil. Add the garlic and hot peppers and stir; add the onion, ginger, nutmeg, and salt and cook, stirring, until the onion is translucent, about 6 minutes. Add the Swiss chard and cook, stirring, until completely dry. Remove from heat, mix in the chopped oregano, and season with a few drops of lemon juice and salt to taste; set aside.

6. Punch down the dough. Transfer it to a lightly floured board and knead for a few minutes. Roll out the dough, dusting it with flour to

(Continued)

prevent sticking, into a circle 18 to 19 inches in diameter and about ¼ inch thick. Gently fold the dough in half and in half again without pressing. Carefully lift the wedge and place the point in the center of a lightly buttered springform or layer-cake pan, about 9½ inches round and 2 or 3 inches deep. Unfold the dough loosely into the pan, and with the help of your knuckles, gently press the dough into the bottom and against the sides of the pan. Let the dough drape over the edge, with a generous overhang. Brush the bottom and sides of the dough with some of the egg/water mixture, and let it dry for a few minutes.

7. Spread the bottom evenly with half of the Swiss chard, and arrange the fish fillets on top. Then spread the remaining chard over the fish.

8. Preheat the oven to 375 degrees.

9. Begin to fold in the dough hanging over the edges of the pan. To do this, draw the sides of the dough up over the filling toward the center, evenly pleating the dough into loose folds. Rotate the pan as you continue to pleat the dough. Gather together the ends of the dough that meet in the center, and twist them into a small knob.

10. Brush the dough with the remaining egg wash and sprinkle with the seeds, if using. Place the pan on a baking sheet and bake for 1 to 1¼ hours, or until golden. Remove from the oven, place on a rack, and let cool slightly. Unmold and serve warm.

NOTE   Curry Oil (page 473) or Achiote Oil (page 472) may be substituted for some or all of the olive oil.

VARIATION

Pastel de Jamón con Queso y Acelgas
Ham, Cheese, and Swiss Chard Pie

—

Make the dough, as described in Steps 1 and 2, and prepare the Swiss chard or spinach as described in Steps 4 and 5. Line the pan with dough and brush the bottom with Dijon mustard instead of the egg wash. Use ½ pound thinly sliced ham and ½ pound thinly sliced Emmenthal, Gruyère, or Jarlsberg. Line the pastry shell with half the ham and half the cheese. Spread with the Swiss chard or spinach, then cover with the remaining ham and cheese, 1 roasted bell pepper, cut in strips, and a few pitted black olives, if desired. Close the pastel, brush with egg wash, and bake as directed in Step 10.

Pastel de Choclo
Meat and Corn Pie

Serves 6 to 8

I love *pasteles* made with corn. Sweet corn has a wonderful flavor, but it is a bit too juicy when ground. To compensate, I add some yellow or white hominy to the grated sweet corn, which gives the dough the right consistency and flavor.

Beef is the usual filling for a *pastel de choclo,* but chicken, rabbit, or lean pork are also good. No matter what kind of meat you use, be sure to season it well to bring out the rich taste of the corn.

FILLING
1½ *pounds lean beef, chicken, rabbit, or pork*
3 *tablespoons olive oil*
2 *medium onions, peeled and finely chopped (2 cups)*
½ *teaspoon dried oregano*
1 *teaspoon ground cumin*
1 *tablespoon coarse salt*
1 *tablespoon Spanish paprika*
½ *teaspoon white pepper*

DOUGH
5 *tablespoons plus 1 teaspoon unsalted butter*
12 *ears fresh corn, husked and silk removed, grated*
1 *tablespoon coarse salt*
1 *tablespoon plus 1 teaspoon sugar*
5 *cups drained and ground canned yellow or white hominy*
   (3 16-ounce cans)
3 *hard-boiled eggs, sliced*
12 *black alfonso or Kalamata olives, pitted and chopped*

1. Grind the meat in a meat grinder and set aside.

2. In a skillet, heat the olive oil. Add the onion, oregano, cumin, and salt and sauté over medium heat until the onion is slightly brown around the edges, about 6 to 8 minutes. Add the meat, paprika, and pepper. Mix well and cook, stirring occasionally, until all the liquid has evapo-

(Continued)

rated. Remove from heat. (If the meat has released too much fat, drain it.) Correct seasoning with salt to taste and set aside.

3. In a separate skillet, heat 4 tablespoons of the butter. Add the grated corn, salt, and 1 tablespoon sugar; cook over low heat for about 10 minutes, or until the mixture has thickened, stirring and scraping the bottom to prevent the corn from sticking to the pan. Add the ground hominy and cook for a few minutes longer, until the mixture becomes a thick paste. Remove from heat and set aside.

4. Preheat the oven to 375 degrees.

5. Butter a shallow 2- to 2½-quart baking dish (about 2½ inches deep) with 1 teaspoon of the butter and fill the baking dish with half of the corn mixture. Add all the beef filling, arrange the slices of hard-boiled eggs and the chopped olives on top, and cover the filling with the rest of the corn, smoothing out the surface. Melt the remaining table-spoon of butter and brush the top of the *pastel*. Sprinkle with the re-maining teaspoon of sugar and bake for 1 hour and 15 minutes, or until the top of the *pastel* is light golden in color. Remove from the oven and let rest in a warm spot for 5 to 10 minutes. Serve hot or at room temper-ature.

STORAGE NOTE   Well covered, this *pastel* will keep in the refrigerator for up to 5 days. It can be warmed to room temperature or reheated and served hot.

Empanadas Vegetarianas
Vegetable Empanadas

Makes about 16 empanadas

Vegetable empanadas are quite common and are just as suitable as meat or fish empanadas for practically any occasion. Some vegetables, such as spinach, Swiss chard, or broccoli, are traditionally used alone, while others are combined. The combination of spices and hot peppers with sweet bell peppers, peas, tomatoes, and potatoes almost fools you into thinking some meat was slipped into the filling when no one was watching!

Curry Dough (page 58)

FILLING
*2 tablespoons Curry Oil (page 473) or 2 tablespoons olive oil mixed
    with ½ teaspoon curry powder*
1 large clove garlic, peeled and minced
2-inch piece fresh ginger, peeled and minced
1 medium onion, peeled and chopped (1 cup)
*1 jalapeño or serrano pepper, seeded and finely chopped, or
    ⅛ teaspoon cayenne*
1½ teaspoons ground cumin
⅛ teaspoon ground cloves
2 teaspoons coarse salt
¼ teaspoon ground white pepper
1 large tomato, peeled, seeded, and chopped
¾ pound potatoes, cooked, peeled, and cut into ⅛-inch dice (1 cup)
1 cup peas, fresh or frozen (see Note)
½ cup seeded and finely diced red bell pepper
3 tablespoons chopped Italian parsley

SEALER and GLAZE
1 egg white
2 tablespoons water or milk or heavy cream

1. Prepare the curry dough.

2. In a small sauté pan, heat the oil and add the garlic, ginger, onion, hot pepper, cumin, cloves, salt, and white pepper. Sauté over medium heat until the onion is totally translucent, about 2 to 3 minutes. Add the chopped tomato pulp and cook, stirring, for 5 minutes. Add the potatoes and ¾ cup of water and simmer for 10 minutes longer. Add the peas and red pepper and continue cooking for 2 to 3 minutes longer, or until all the liquid has evaporated. Remove from heat and set aside to cool thoroughly, or refrigerate overnight, well covered. Just before using, mix in the chopped parsley and correct seasoning with salt to taste.

3. Make the sealer and glaze by mixing the egg white with the water. Set aside.

4. Preheat the oven to 375 degrees.

5. On a lightly floured board, roll out the dough about ⅛ inch thick, shaping it into a 16-inch square. Cut the dough into circles 4½ inches in diameter. Knead and re-roll the scraps for additional circles. Place 1

(Continued)

full tablespoon of the filling to one side of the circle, leaving a ½-inch border. Brush the border of the circle with the egg sealer, and fold half the circle over the filling, forming a half-moon. Press the edges together with your fingertips or with the tines of a fork to seal. Prick the top of the empanada once or twice with the tines of the fork. Repeat until all the empanadas are assembled.

6. Line a baking sheet with parchment paper and arrange the empanadas on top. Brush them with the glaze, and bake for about 25 to 30 minutes, or until golden. Remove the baking sheet from the oven and transfer the empanadas to a rack to cool slightly. Serve warm.

NOTE   If you are using frozen peas, just rinse and drain them well and add them with the parsley in Step 2. (Do not cook.)

STORAGE NOTE   You can freeze the empanadas unglazed and bake them while they are still frozen. Simply arrange them on a baking sheet covered with parchment paper, brush with the egg glaze, and bake until golden.

Empanadas de Espinaca
Spinach Empanadas

Makes about 16 empanadas

In Paraguay yuca, also called manioc, is much appreciated, not only as a root vegetable but as a base for empanada dough. Although there are no eggs in this dough, it has incredible elasticity, which comes from the yuca.

This recipe calls for a spinach filling, but other vegetables, such as Swiss chard or broccoli, also work quite well. (See Variations at end of recipe.)

DOUGH
12 ounces yuca, boiled (page 394)
4 tablespoons unsalted butter
2 teaspoons coarse salt
2½ cups all-purpose flour

FILLING

2½ pounds fresh spinach, stems removed, washed, and drained, or 2
    10-ounce packages frozen spinach, defrosted and drained
1 tablespoon olive oil
4 slices bacon, minced
2 large cloves garlic, peeled and minced
1 jalapeño pepper, seeded and finely chopped
2 medium onions, peeled and finely chopped (2 cups)
⅛ teaspoon grated nutmeg
1 teaspoon ground fennel
⅛ teaspoon ground cloves
⅛ teaspoon ground mace
1 teaspoon coarse salt
3 sprigs fresh tarragon or basil or oregano, finely chopped
¼ pound fresh mozzarella or Fontina or Jarlsberg, coarsely grated or
    finely chopped

2 quarts vegetable oil for frying
Lemon wedges

1. After the yuca has been cooked and cored, and while it is still hot, place it in the bowl of a food processor. Add the butter and salt and blend until smooth. Add 1 cup of the flour and blend for a few seconds longer to make a dough. Add the remaining flour, ½ cup at a time, blending after each addition until all of the flour has been thoroughly absorbed. Transfer the dough to a bowl, dredge it with additional flour all around, and set aside in a cool place, undisturbed, for about 20 minutes, or until the dough has cooled to room temperature.

2. In a pot containing boiling water, blanch the fresh spinach for 1 second. Remove the spinach from the water to a colander and let drain. When cool enough to handle, squeeze out the water from the leaves, chop them, place them in a clean cloth, and squeeze, extracting and discarding any remaining water. Set aside. If using defrosted frozen spinach, remove and discard the stems, chop the leaves, place them in a clean cloth, and squeeze out all the water. Set aside.

3. In a frying pan, heat the olive oil. Add the bacon and sauté over medium heat until the bacon has released most of its fat, about 5 minutes. Add the garlic and hot pepper and stir. Add the onions, nutmeg, fennel, cloves, mace, and salt and cook until the onions start to get golden around the edges, about 8 minutes. Add ½ cup of water and the

(Continued)

tarragon, lower the heat, and continue cooking until the water has evaporated, about 5 minutes. Add the spinach and cook, stirring, for a few minutes longer. Remove from heat and set aside to cool. Just before assembling the empanadas, mix in the cheese and correct seasoning with salt to taste.

4. On a floured pastry board, knead the dough, dredging with flour as needed, for a minute or so, or until it is smooth, soft, and not sticky. Roll out the dough about ⅛ inch thick, shaping it into a 16-inch square. Cut into 4-inch squares; knead and re-roll the scraps to make additional squares. Place 1 full tablespoon of filling in the center of the square. Brush the edges with water and fold a corner of the dough over the filling to make a triangle. Press the edges together with your fingertips or the tines of a fork to seal. Repeat until all the empanadas are assembled.

5. In a fryer, heat the vegetable oil to between 365 and 375 degrees. Gently drop the empanadas into the hot oil and fry them until they are golden brown, about 6 minutes. Remove them from the oil, drain them on towels or paper towels, and serve immediately, accompanied by lemon wedges.

VARIATIONS

For Swiss chard empanadas, substitute the same amount of Swiss chard for the spinach and follow the recipe exactly.

For broccoli empanadas, substitute 1 to 1½ pounds of broccoli for the spinach. Wash and chop the broccoli but do not blanch it. Add it instead of the spinach in Step 3.

Empanaditas de Maíz
Corn Empanadas

Makes about 32 empanadas

In Venezuela and Colombia one finds two distinctly different kinds of empanadas. The same fillings are used in both, but the dough varies dramatically. One is a traditional dough made with flour, lard, and eggs; the other is prepared by cooking finely milled white or yellow cornmeal in water with butter or lard. This cornmeal dough can be further enriched with grated cheese, or achiote or paprika, which also give the dough a deeper color. (See Variations at end of recipe.)

Empanadas made with cornmeal dough are shaped by hand into half-moons or patties; they can be made large or small. The ones in this recipe are a good size for hors d'oeuvres, appetizers, or snacks. You can make them larger if you want.

DOUGH
2 tablespoons unsalted butter
2 teaspoons coarse salt
4 cups finely ground white or yellow cornmeal

FILLING
3 tablespoons olive oil
1 medium onion, peeled and finely chopped (1 cup)
¼ teaspoon ground cinnamon
½ teaspoon sugar
⅛ teaspoon ground cloves
1 teaspoon coarse salt
⅛ teaspoon ground white pepper
½ pound ground lean pork
2 medium tomatoes, peeled, seeded, and chopped
1 tablespoon capers, well drained

2 quarts vegetable oil for frying
Onion Relish (page 481)

1. In a saucepan, heat 6 cups of water with the butter and salt. Add the cornmeal while stirring and bring to a boil. Continue cooking until

(Continued)

the mixture has become thick, about 5 minutes. Remove from heat and set aside to cool.

2. In a frying pan, heat the olive oil. Add the onion, cinnamon, sugar, cloves, salt, and pepper and cook over medium heat until the onion is slightly golden around the edges, about 8 minutes.

3. Add the pork and continue cooking, stirring now and then, for 10 to 15 minutes, or until the pork is thoroughly cooked. Add the tomatoes and capers and continue cooking until all liquid has evaporated. Remove from heat and set aside to cool; correct the seasoning with salt to taste.

4. Moisten your hands with cold water and roll a lime-size ball of the cooled cornmeal dough into a smooth ball (continue moistening your hands if the mixture sticks to your hands). Make an indentation in the ball. Place about 1 heaping teaspoon of the pork mixture into the indentation and close by pressing the edges together with your fingers; shape the ball into a half-moon. To shape into patties, place the filling into the dough as described and close to form a ball. Roll the ball between the palms of your hands to smooth out the entire surface evenly, and then gently flatten it into a circle about 3 inches in diameter. Repeat until all the patties or half-moons are assembled.

5. Heat the vegetable oil to 375 degrees. Gently drop in the empanadas and fry them until they are golden all around. Remove to towels or paper towels and let drain. Serve hot, accompanied by Onion Relish.

STORAGE NOTE   These empanadas can be prepared up to 3 days in advance and kept, well covered, in the refrigerator. They can also be frozen. They do not need to be defrosted before frying; just drop them right into the hot oil.

VARIATIONS

Stir ½ to 1 cup grated parmesan into the dough right after removing it from the heat in Step 1.

Substitute 1 tablespoon Achiote Oil (page 472) or 1 tablespoon Paprika Oil (page 474) for 1 tablespoon of the butter. Add it to the water with the remaining tablespoon of butter in Step 1.

Salteñas de Queso
Cheese Empanadas

—

Makes about 16 salteñas

*S*alteña is what they call an empanada in Bolivia. Many kinds of filling are used for *salteñas;* cheese is one of the most interesting. This recipe calls for a blend of sharp cheddar and Emmenthal, but other cheeses or combinations may be used. Select cheeses that have good bouquet and that melt well.

The dough for these Bolivian empanadas has a biscuitlike texture and is made rich with egg yolks and butter. For a lighter but still flavorful pastry, you could use half butter and half vegetable shortening. If you can find it, try goat butter instead of cow butter.

DOUGH
2½ cups all-purpose flour
1 teaspoon sugar
½ teaspoon coarse salt
⅛ teaspoon ground mace
1 teaspoon baking powder
8 tablespoons (1 stick) unsalted butter, chilled and chopped
4 egg yolks
½ cup milk

FILLING
½ pound sharp Cheddar, grated
¼ pound Emmenthal or mozzarella, grated
½ teaspoon Spanish paprika
½ teaspoon coarse salt (see Note)
4 egg whites

SEALER and GLAZE
1 egg
1 tablespoon milk or water

1. Sift the flour, sugar, salt, mace, and baking powder into a bowl. Add the butter and mix quickly and thoroughly with your fingertips or with the help of a fork until the mixture resembles coarse meal. Add the

(Continued)

egg yolks and half of the milk and mix, adding the remaining milk, 1 tablespoon at a time, to form a soft dough. In a floured bowl, knead the dough for a minute or so until smooth, then set aside in a cool spot, wrapped in a moist towel, for about 10 to 15 minutes, or until ready to use.

2. In a bowl, mix the cheeses with the paprika and salt. In a separate bowl, preferably copper, beat the egg whites to soft, dry peaks. Fold well into the cheese mixture and set aside.

3. Make the sealer and glaze by beating the egg with the milk. Set aside.

4. Preheat the oven to 375 degrees.

5. On a lightly floured board, roll out the dough about ⅛ inch thick, shaping it into a 16-inch square. Cut into 4½-inch circles. Knead and re-roll the scraps and cut more circles. Place a generous tablespoon of the cheese filling to one side of the circle, leaving a ½-inch border of dough. Brush all around with the sealer and fold half the circle over the filling, forming a half-moon. Press the edges together with the tines of a fork or your fingertips to seal thoroughly. Prick the surface of the empanada several times with a toothpick or with the tines of the fork. Repeat until all the empanadas are assembled.

6. Line a baking sheet with parchment paper and arrange the empanadas on top. Brush the empanadas with the remaining glaze and bake for about 30 minutes, or until light golden. Remove the baking sheet from the oven and transfer the empanadas to a rack to cool for a few minutes. Serve warm.

NOTE   If using mozzarella, add an extra ½ teaspoon coarse salt to the filling.

SWEET EMPANADAS

Empanadas Dulces de Queso
Sweet Cheese Empanadas

—

Makes about 8 empanadas

Although the most popular empanadas are savory, there are some spectacular sweet empanadas, like this one from Ecuador. The cheese-and-raisin filling, flavored with a strong dose of rum, has a creamy, luscious texture.

Many kinds of cheese can be used in this filling. Choose a cheese similar in consistency to cream cheese but not necessarily totally smooth. A moist, fresh goat cheese resembling *queso fresco,* the common South American fresh cheese, is a fine choice. A combination of cream cheese and unsalted fresh goat cheese makes an exceptional sweet empanada. Traditionally, these empanadas are fried, but they can also be baked. (See Variation at end of recipe.)

FILLING
¼ *cup dark rum*
⅛ *teaspoon cayenne*
¼ *cup seedless raisins or currants*
½ *pound cream cheese, at room temperature*
Yolk of 1 hard-boiled egg
1 egg yolk
1 tablespoon sugar
⅛ *teaspoon coarse salt*

DOUGH
2 cups all-purpose flour
⅛ *teaspoon coarse salt*
1 teaspoon sugar
3 tablespoons unsalted butter, chilled and chopped
1 egg
¼ *cup cold water*

2 quarts vegetable oil for frying
½ *cup confectioners' sugar*

(Continued)

1. In a cup, mix the rum with the cayenne. Add the raisins and let them soak in this mixture at room temperature for 2 hours, or until ready to use.

2. Place the cream cheese in a bowl. Force the hard-boiled egg yolk through a strainer over the cream cheese and beat until creamy. Add the egg yolk, sugar, and salt and beat until all the ingredients have been well absorbed and turned into a smooth, rich paste. Drain the soaked raisins and mix them into the cheese mixture. Set aside, covered, in the refrigerator for about 10 minutes, or until ready to use.

3. Sift the flour, salt, and sugar into a bowl. Add the butter, egg, and 2 tablespoons of the cold water and mix to obtain a soft dough, adding the remaining water, if necessary, to make a smooth, malleable dough. Set aside in a cool spot, wrapped in a moist towel, until ready to use.

4. On a floured pastry board, roll out the dough ⅛ to ¼ inch thick, shaping it into a 14-inch square. Cut into squares, about 4½ inches each; knead and re-roll the scraps into more squares. Place about 1½ tablespoons of the cheese mixture in a corner of each square, leaving about a ½-inch border. Brush the border with water and fold one corner of the square over the filling to form a triangle. Press the edges together with your fingertips or the tines of a fork to seal. Repeat until all the empanadas are assembled.

5. In a fryer, heat the oil to between 365 and 375 degrees. Drop the empanadas into the hot oil and fry them until golden, about 5 minutes. With a slotted spoon, remove the empanadas from the oil and drain them on towels or paper towels. Place the confectioners' sugar in a fine sieve and shake over the empanadas to dust them evenly. Serve hot.

STORAGE NOTE After the empanadas have been assembled, they can be frozen. Wrap them tightly and place them in the freezer where they will keep in perfect condition for up to 3 months. When needed, drop them, still frozen, directly into the hot oil. Continue as in Step 5.

VARIATION

To bake the empanadas, preheat the oven to 375 degrees. Arrange the empanadas on a baking sheet lined with parchment paper and bake for 20 minutes, or until golden. Dust with confectioners' sugar and serve warm.

Empanadas de Manzana
Apple Empanadas

Makes about 16 empanadas

The dough of this empanada is made with plantains, a versatile fruit that looks something like bananas. Plantains contain enough starch to produce a dough that is easy to handle, and their natural richness works well with all sorts of sweet fillings, especially fruit. You can substitute ripe quince or unripe pears for the filling, if you like. (See Variations at end of recipe.)

DOUGH
3 large green plantains (about 2½ pounds)
4 tablespoons unsalted butter
1 tablespoon sugar
⅛ teaspoon ground mace
1 teaspoon grated lemon rind
3 egg yolks

FILLING
5 large tart apples, such as Granny Smith
Juice of 1 lemon
1 tablespoon unsalted butter
1 cup light brown sugar
1-inch piece fresh ginger, peeled and grated
Grated rind and juice of 1 orange
⅛ teaspoon ground cloves
¼ teaspoon ground cinnamon
½ cup dark rum or calvados
½ cup walnuts, coarsely chopped

2 quarts vegetable oil for frying
¼ cup confectioners' sugar

1. Peel the plantains and cook them in 6 cups of water for about 40 to 45 minutes, or until they are quite soft. Remove from the water, let drain thoroughly, and place them, while they are still hot, in the work bowl of a food processor. Add the butter, sugar, mace, and lemon rind

(Continued)

and blend for 1 minute, or until smooth. Add the egg yolks and blend a few seconds longer, or until the egg yolks have been thoroughly absorbed into the dough. Transfer the dough to a bowl, dredge lightly with flour, and set aside for 25 minutes, undisturbed, at room temperature, or until thoroughly cooled.

2. Peel, core, and finely chop 3 of the apples. Peel and core the remaining 2 apples and cut each into 8 wedges. Drop the wedges immediately into a bowl of cold water with lemon juice to cover.

3. In a small enameled saucepan, heat the butter. Add the brown sugar and cook over medium heat, stirring, until the sugar has melted (do not let it burn). Add the chopped apples, ginger, orange rind, cloves, and cinnamon; stir. Add 1 cup water and continue cooking for about 15 minutes, or until most of the water has evaporated, stirring now and then. Add the orange juice and rum. Cook until all the liquid has evaporated and the spoon leaves a track at the bottom of the pan, about 5 minutes. Drain, and add the apple wedges; cook over low heat, covered, until wedges are barely soft, about 8 minutes. Mix in the walnuts and remove the saucepan from the heat. Set aside to cool.

4. On a floured board, roll out the dough ¼ inch thick, shaping it into a 16-inch square. Cut into 4½-inch squares; knead and re-roll the scraps to make more squares. Place 1 apple wedge in the center of each square and top it with some of the sauce. Leave about a ½-inch edge on all sides of the square. Brush with water and fold a corner of the square over to make a triangle. Press the edges together with your fingertips or the tines of a fork to seal. Repeat until all the empanadas are assembled.

5. In a fryer, heat the vegetable oil to between 365 and 375 degrees. Gently drop the empanadas into the hot oil and fry until golden, about 6 minutes. With a slotted spoon, remove from oil and drain on towels or paper towels. Place the confectioners' sugar in a sieve and shake it over the empanadas to dust them evenly. Serve hot.

STORAGE NOTE   Once assembled, the empanadas can be frozen, well wrapped, for up to 3 months. When ready to use, drop the frozen empanadas into the hot oil and cook until golden. Dust with confectioners' sugar and serve piping hot.

Empanadas de Membrillo
Quince Empanadas

—

Substitute an equal number of ripe quince for the apples and proceed with the recipe.

Empanadas de Peras
Pear Empanadas

—

Substitute an equal number of hard, unripe Bartlett or Bosc pears for the apples. Use a pear eau-de-vie or liqueur instead of rum or calvados.

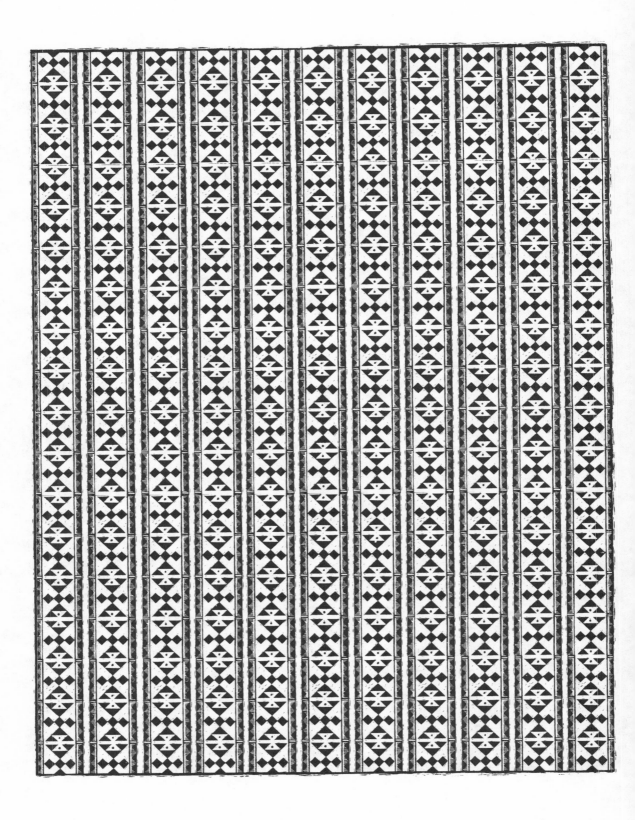

TAMALES

Tamal Cuzqueño
Cuzqueño Tamale
—

Tamal de Pollo
Chicken Tamale
—

Tamal de Pato
Duck Tamale
—

Tamales Navideños
Christmas Tamale
—

Tamal de Vegetales
Vegetable Tamale
—

Tamal de Mariscos
Seafood Tamale
—

Tamal de Quinua
Quinoa Tamale
—

Tamal de Fuente
Pan-Baked Tamale
—

Juanes
—

Hallacas de Cumaná
Cumaná Hallacas
—

Bollos
Plantain Bollos
—

Bollos de Ternera
Veal Bollos
—

Humitas
Savory Corn Humitas

SWEET TAMALES

Humitas de Manjar Blanco
Sweet Corn Humitas
—

Pamonhas do Norte
Brazilian Sweet Pamonhas
—

Chapanas de Cañete
Chapanas with Golden Raisins

Whenever I get a longing for the foods of my childhood, visions of tamales fill my mind.

Before any big family celebration, I would find my grandmother sitting at the kitchen table, only the silver-gray bun on the top of her head visible above a mountain of hominy. As she and her helpers performed the monotonous task of picking off the tips and hulling the immaculate white corn kernels, the warm, earthy aroma of simmering hominy would begin to waft through the house. It was only a matter of time before my grandmother started to pass the banana leaves over an open flame to bring out their flavor. She did this with a certain elegance and precision as she swept her outstretched arms across the fire.

My mother and grandmother could never agree on kitchen matters, especially when it came to what made a proper *tamal*. For my grandmother there was only one correct filling, and that was pork. For my mother pork was not the only answer: she loved chicken. Once my mother brought a huge casserole to the table; the top was entirely covered with steaming banana leaves. Rather than wrapping the filling in separate little packets, she had lined a *fuente,* or a large baking dish, with banana leaves, buried her chicken mixture in the masa, or dough, and covered it with more banana leaves. She called this giant tamale a *tamal de fuente*. To this day I like to prepare my mother's *tamal de fuente* for large parties and buffets. But for my grandmother, a tamale made in the *fuente* was a disgrace, a violation of all the rules of tamale-making. "Well, what do Italians know about making tamales anyway?" the German lady concluded.

The arguments about tamales went back and forth at home over the years. No one could win these arguments because in South America there are as many ways to make tamales as there are cooks. The dough can be based on corn (hominy, corn flour, or grated fresh corn), other grains, or starchy vegetables. They can be savory or sweet; filled with meat, seafood, or vegetables; wrapped in corn husks, banana leaves, or other leaves; tied with banana or corn-husk "strings" or kitchen twine; steamed or simmered. But however they are prepared, tamales are quintessentially South American.

Tamales go by different names in different places, though if you use the word *tamal,* everyone will know what you mean. This is because the Spanish colonists, as they traveled southward, introduced the word, which was derived from *tamalli* in Nahuatl, the language of the Aztecs.

The word *tamal* is used all over Central America and throughout Peru, Ecuador, and Colombia. But in Venezuela they call it *hallaca,* after the native Indian name, and *bollo,* a term also used in parts of Colombia and along the coast of Ecuador. In other parts of Ecuador and in Bolivia, the term *humita* is used. In towns along the Amazon, they call their tamales *juanes,* while in other parts of Brazil they call them *pamonhas.* It becomes complicated to summarize the similarities and differences between all these kinds of tamales—after all, South America is a large continent—so I have described them instead in the introductions to the recipes in this chapter.

A Few Hints on Preparing Tamales

Most tamales have three parts: the dough, the filling, and the wrapping. Here are some suggestions for preparing each of these and for assembling, cooking, and storing tamales.

THE DOUGH

The masa, or dough, which surrounds the filling, is traditionally made from a fine corn flour or finely ground cornmeal called *harina de masa.* This flour is also used for making tortillas and is often called *tortilla flour.* It comes in white and yellow varieties; the latter is preferred for the preparation of tamales and Venezuelan bollos and hallacas. The masa may also be made from *mote,* the Quechuan name for hominy. Although these two traditional masas differ somewhat in taste and texture, in the recipes in this chapter, one may be substituted for the other. Grated fresh corn and other grains and starches or starchy vegetables are also used, including rice, quinoa, potatoes, yuca, and plantains.

The dough for tamales should always be moist; this is achieved by adding a flavorful fat or oil and/or well-seasoned stock. The dough is colored with annatto, paprika, curry, or even saffron, which also lend it their characteristic flavors.

The texture of the masa is the most important aspect of tamale-making. It can vary from coarse to smooth. I prefer the texture to be a little coarse.

The finest and smoothest texture is obtained when the masa is made with corn flour. If you use hominy, it must be ground. All you need for grinding hominy is a meat grinder. You can also use a food processor; it may not be as romantic, but it is faster. With the food processor you have to be careful not to overprocess the hominy and end up with a dough that is too pasty. To be sure of a nice texture when making the dough from hominy, you can do one of four things:

Grind the hominy in a meat grinder, passing it through two or three times until you get the desired texture.

—

Grind the hominy in a food processor, using the pulser and keeping a very close watch, until you have achieved the desired texture.

—

Grind three-quarters of the hominy in a food processor until you have a very fine, smooth paste (this does not require careful watching). Transfer the paste to a bowl. Grind the remaining hominy to a coarse texture and mix the two batches together.

—

Grind or process the hominy to a smooth paste; add some cooked rice or other grains and mix well.

THE FILLING

Anything goes when it comes to a tamale filling, as long as it is tasty. I have eaten some delicious vegetarian tamales, filled with well-seasoned assortments of vegetables, peas, beans, nuts, and *alcaperones*, or ca-perberries. I am always experimenting with mushrooms, berries, game, and all kinds of fish and shellfish.

The filling must be well seasoned. Chances are you will be using some chili peppers to give the filling heat, and paprika, curry or annatto oil, or saffron for a fiery color and woodsy taste. If you use meat in the filling, it must be cooked slowly until it is so tender that it practically collapses under the touch of a fork.

THE WRAPPING

The wrapping is an important element of the tamale: it holds it together and protects it during the cooking process, and adds a subtle and haunting dimension of flavor to the filling. Several kinds of green leaves are used for wrapping. Banana leaves are standard, but you can also use *hojas de achira,* or canna lily leaves, *maxan,* or Palmyra palm leaves, or leaves of *bijao,* a common Amazonian plant.

Fresh and dried corn husks are also used as wrappers. If neither banana leaves nor corn husks are available, you can use aluminum foil or parchment paper cut to size. In fact, parchment paper is the wrapper of choice for many Caribbean tamales; for South Americans it would be totally unacceptable.

Banana Leaves

Fresh banana leaves. Fresh banana leaves are exceptional in taste; they are my first choice. Banana leaves grow up to nine feet long and twenty inches wide. They have a strong fibrous vein or cord running down the middle. The color is shiny green on top and slightly duller green underneath. Leaves used for wrapping tamales should not have any brown spots or tears.

To prepare fresh leaves, use scissors to clip about one or two inches through the middle of the vein, starting at the base. Tear the remaining length of the vein, separating the leaf into two halves, each attached to half the vein. Wipe the leaves with a damp cloth, going with the grain to avoid tearing. For easy handling, cut the leaves to the size indicated in the recipe. Pass each piece through an open flame to bring out the natural oils and flavor, or for a milder flavor blanch them by dipping them in boiling water for a second.

To store the leaves and keep them fresh, sandwich them between moist towels and refrigerate for up to ten days. For longer storage, freeze the leaves. Stack the pieces of banana leaf neatly on top of one another, fold the stack in half, and place it in a plastic bag in the freezer. The leaves will remain in perfect condition for up to three months.

Frozen banana leaves. Frozen banana leaves are available all year round; they are sold in one-pound packages. The leaves have already been cut in half and the central vein removed.

To use frozen banana leaves, remove them from the freezer and let them thaw, undisturbed, at room temperature. Open the package and carefully unfold the leaves. Cut them to size with scissors and wipe them with a damp cloth, going with the grain to avoid tearing. Any leftover pieces of banana leaf can be wrapped in a damp cloth and refrigerated for up to one week. Do not refreeze.

Dried banana leaves. To dry frozen or fresh banana leaves, place them in direct sunlight and let them dry naturally; this will take several days. The sun will not only dry them but will bleach them to a rich, silky brown color. The dried leaves are extremely brittle and delicate. Do not attempt to straighten or unfold them.

There is a quicker way to dry banana leaves, but the taste and color will not be as good as with sun-drying. Preheat the oven to 350 degrees. After the leaves have been cut to size, place them on a rack in the oven and cook until totally dry, about twenty minutes for frozen leaves, a little longer for fresh. Very carefully remove them from the oven and let cool. Dried banana leaves can be stored in a container in a cool, dry, dark place almost indefinitely.

To reconstitute sun-dried or oven-dried banana leaves, use tongs to lower them into boiling water and cook until soft, about one minute. Remove and drain. At this point they will be pliable and strong enough to withstand rougher handling. Wipe dry, always going with the grain.

Wrapping tamales with banana leaves. Once your dough and filling are ready and the banana leaves prepared, place the leaves on the work surface with the grain running from left to right. Place the dough and filling on the leaf as directed in the recipe. Wrap each tamal as you would wrap a package, using the banana leaf as wrapping paper. First, fold the closest edge of the leaf over the dough, covering all of it. Then lift the leaf with the filling, and continue folding until you reach the opposite edge. Fold each of the ends toward the center, overlapping them to form a neat, compact square or rectangular package.

Repeat if necessary with a second leaf, placing the side with the overlapping ends down on it. This double-wrapping is important if you notice a tear or if the tamales are to be simmered. If the leaves are in perfect condition, a single leaf is all you need, but in most of the following recipes, double-wrapping is suggested to securely encase the filling.

To tie, take a length of kitchen string, about thirty inches long. Place the tamale on the center of the string. Bring each end of the string to the middle, twist, and bring the ends of the string over and around to the other side. Tie tightly in the middle, making four sections on each side. This method is fine for steaming.

For simmering, it is preferable to take a longer piece of string and tie the tamale more securely. Place the middle of the string under the top third of the tamale, slightly off center. Bring the ends up and twist. Bring one end of the string over and the other under the tamal lengthwise to the bottom third; twist. Bring the longer end of the string under and around the tamale; twist again. Now take each string around to the back; going lengthwise in opposite directions, turning the tamale over as you do so; twist. Bring the ends of the string to the center of the tamal; twist. Bring both ends of the string around the tamal and knot tightly. You should have twelve sections on each side.

There is a third way to tie tamales. Sweet chapanas, which are wrapped in sun-dried banana leaves, for example, are tightly tied in the center to resemble bow ties.

Corn Husks

Fresh corn husks. When corn is in season, you can use the husks as wrappers. Cut the corn cob with a very sharp knife at the point where the husks are attached. Carefully peel off the husks one at a time, selecting the largest, most perfect ones for wrappers. They can be used as is or dried.

Dried corn husks. Dried corn husks are commercially available in large and small packages. To dry your own, place fresh husks on a piece of paper in a sunny spot and leave them to dry until they become silky brown, stiff, and brittle. Store the dried husks, well wrapped, in a dark, dry place. They will last almost indefinitely.

Dried husks need to be reconstituted. Without unfolding, submerge them in boiling water for about one minute, then carefully remove them with tongs. Drain the husks in a colander and pat them dry with a cloth or paper towel.

Wrapping tamales with corn husks. Once your dough and filling are ready and the corn husks reconstituted (if dried), place two corn husks with the wide ends overlapping on the work surface. Place a third corn husk in the middle. Place the dough and filling on the corn husks as directed in the recipe. Fold the near edge up over the filling, covering it, and fold the opposite edge down. Fold the sides in to make a neat rectangular package. Sometimes the tamale is double- or triple-wrapped. You can also fold the edges over to cover the filling, then bring one tapered end up to meet the other and tie them together.

Corn husk–wrapped tamales can also be tied with a simple four-way package tie or with a tight tie in the middle that makes the tamale look like a bow tie. You can use kitchen string or, preferably, strips of corn husk to tie the tamales. This is the South American way to tie corn-husk tamales, especially humitas and pamonhas. When using fresh husks, pick soft, young husks from close to the cob. Tear the husks, starting at the base, into one-inch-wide strips. Tie a tight knot at the pointed end of the strip, then tear the knotted strip down the middle. This will give you a length of natural "string" with a small knot in the middle. Use the same method with fresh or reconstituted dried corn husks.

COOKING THE TAMALES

There are two traditional ways to cook tamales: steaming and simmering. Before embarking on either, check all of your tamales to be sure there are no slits or cracks in the wrapping. Should you discover any, simply use another leaf or husk, or a piece of aluminum foil or parchment paper, for a second, protective layer.

Steaming Tamales

Steaming is the simplest and most common way to cook tamales. I definitely prefer it. You can use a vegetable steamer or any other steamer, or improvise your own. I find a Chinese steamer with bamboo baskets perfect for steaming tamales. Alternatively, you can line a pot containing one inch of water with leftover banana leaves or corn husks, making a thick bed for the tamales. This gives them additional flavor as they are steamed.

When steaming the tamales, make sure there is always water in the pot, and always use a pot with a tight lid so that none of the steam escapes.

Simmering Tamales

In this technique, the tamales are cooked by submerging them in a large quantity of very hot water. Bring the water to a boil. Lower the heat to a simmer, place the tamales in the water, and simmer them. The water must remain at a gentle simmer; any vigorous movement of the water might force it into the packet.

STORING TAMALES

Tamales store extremely well. Actually, they improve by standing for a day. After they have been simmered or steamed, allow them to cool completely. Tightly wrap them individually in plastic wrap, parchment paper, or aluminum foil, and place them in the refrigerator. (You can also place them in an airtight container and store the container in the refrigerator for up to ten days.)

When ready to serve, remove as many tamales as needed and heat them thoroughly for fifteen to twenty minutes by steaming or simmering. Certain sweet tamales are best served at room temperature. Just remove them from the refrigerator a few hours before serving.

Tamales made with seafood should be eaten right after they have been cooked. They do not store well nor should they be reheated.

Tamal Cuzqueño
Cuzqueño Tamale

—

Makes 8 tamales

In Cuzco, a city in the Peruvian Andes that was once the seat of the Inca Empire, they hold to the tradition of wrapping tamales in corn husks. In this recipe, I use a lot of paprika to permeate the dough as well as the meat. The special flavor of the dough comes from *chicha de jora*, or corn beer, its lightness from a touch of baking powder. Every time I eat one, it reminds me of the air in the Andes, clean and light.

1½ pounds boneless pork loin
1 tablespoon coarse salt
½ cup lard, Rendered Bacon Fat (page 476), or olive oil
2 cloves garlic, peeled and minced
½ cup Spanish paprika
¼ teaspoon ground white pepper
2 teaspoons ground cumin
6 cups canned white hominy, rinsed and well drained
  (4 16-ounce cans)
2 eggs
3 tablespoons Corn Beer (page 470) (see Note)
1 teaspoon baking powder
72 dried corn husks
2 hard-boiled eggs, chopped

1. Cut the pork into 8 equal pieces. In a saucepan, combine 4 cups of water with the salt; add the pork and simmer for about 25 minutes. Remove the pork pieces to a plate and set aside. Reserve the cooking liquid. You should have about 2 cups.

2. In a skillet, heat ½ tablespoon of the lard. Add the cooked pork pieces and sauté them until golden all around. Add the garlic, paprika, pepper, and cumin and continue to sauté for 1 more minute. Add the reserved 2 cups of cooking liquid from the pork and cook over low heat until the pork is tender to the touch of a fork and all but ¾ cup of the liquid has evaporated, about 35 to 40 minutes.

3. In a food processor, process the hominy, alternating with the remaining lard, the 2 eggs, corn beer, baking powder, and the ¾ cup of liquid from the skillet. Transfer to a stainless-steel bowl and knead into a smooth, moist dough or masa. Set aside.

4. Prepare the dried corn husks as described on page 94. Place 2 corn husks on your work surface, overlapping the wide ends. Place a third one in the middle. Spoon 3 tablespoons of the dough in the center, place 1 piece of the pork and 1 heaping teaspoon of the chopped hard-boiled eggs on top, and cover with another 3 tablespoons of dough, making sure that the filling is totally sealed between the 2 layers of dough. Wrap the tamale as described on page 94. Repeat twice to triple-wrap the tamale. Tie securely as described. Repeat this process until all the husks, dough, and filling are used up to make 8 tamales.

5. Arrange all the tamales in a pot just large enough to hold them upright, tightly packed, and pour just enough boiling water into the pot to cover the tamales. Cover the pot with a tight-fitting lid and simmer (do not allow to boil) for 1 to 1¼ hours. Maintain the water level at all times by adding boiling water as necessary. Remove the tamales from the water and drain them on a rack for a few minutes, keeping them covered to stay hot. Cut and discard the strings, open the husks, and serve at once.

NOTE Pisco, a brandy from the coast of Peru, or light rum can be substituted for corn beer. The dough will not have quite the same flavor, but it will be fantastic just the same.

Tamal de Pollo
Chicken Tamale

—

Makes 6 tamales

½ pound skinless and boneless chicken breast, legs, or thighs
1 pound new potatoes
4 cups white hominy, rinsed and well drained (3 16-ounce cans)
1 tablespoon coarse salt
½ teaspoon ground white pepper
½ cup Rendered Bacon Fat (see page 476) or solid
    vegetable shortening
12 banana leaf pieces, 15 × 14 inches (2 1-pound packages)
¼ pound bacon, blanched, divided into 12 pieces
½ cup cooked or canned chick-peas or blanched and toasted
    hazelnuts (see Note)
6 Kalamata olives, pitted and cut in half

1. Cut the chicken into 1-inch cubes and set aside.

2. Boil the potatoes in water to cover until done. Peel and set aside to cool.

3. Process the hominy in a food processor for about 1 minute, or grind in a meat grinder two or three times. Transfer the hominy to a stainless-steel bowl. Mash the potatoes and add to the hominy, along with the salt and the pepper. Blend well. Add the bacon fat or shortening and knead to a smooth dough.

4. Prepare the banana leaves as described on page 92. Place one on the work surface with the grain running from left to right.

5. Divide the dough into 6 equal portions. Take 1 of the portions and divide it in half. Place this half 3 inches from the lower edge of the banana leaf and flatten it into a 4 × 3-inch rectangle. Arrange on top: 2 pieces of chicken; 2 pieces of bacon; a few chick-peas; and 2 olive halves. Cover with the other half of the dough, shaping with your hands to cover completely, and seal the filling. Repeat until all the leaves, dough, and filling are used. Double-wrap and securely tie each tamale as described on pages 93–94.

6. Place the tamales in a pot large enough to hold all of them in one layer, upright. Add just enough boiling water to cover, so that the tops of the tamales break the surface of the water. Cover the pan and simmer over low heat for 1½ hours, maintaining the water level with additional boiling water. Remove the tamales from the water and drain them on a rack for a few minutes, keeping them covered so they stay hot. Cut and remove the strings, open the leaves, and serve them at once.

NOTE   If canned chick-peas are used, pour them into a strainer, rinse under cold running water, and drain thoroughly.

Tamal de Pato
Duck Tamale

Makes 8 to 10 tamales

In South America *pato criollo,* or Muscovy duck, is *the* domestic duck; it is leaner and larger than the Peking duck raised in the United States. Usually marketed as Long Island duckling, this duck works very well in this recipe; its fat adds flavor and moisture to the tamales. You may substitute the same amount of goose for the duck in this recipe.

The dough for these tamales is made with potatoes; it has a rich, velvety texture that complements the duck perfectly. Chocolate is sometimes added to the dough for a *tamal negro,* or black tamale. (See Variation at end of recipe.)

3½ pounds large boiling potatoes, washed
1 duck (5 to 6 pounds), with neck and giblets but without the liver
6 cloves garlic, crushed
1 carrot, washed and sliced
2 dried mirasol peppers
1 large bunch fresh thyme (1 ounce)
3 sprigs fresh sage
6 whole cloves
2 tablespoons coarse salt
1 medium onion, peeled and finely minced (1 cup)
¼ cup dry sherry (optional)
8 or 10 banana leaf pieces, 15 × 14 inches (1 16-ounce package)
8 or 10 Kalamata olives, pitted

(Continued)

1. Place the potatoes and about 12 cups of cold water in a large pot. Bring to a boil, lower the heat, and cook for about 45 minutes, or until the potatoes are done. When cool enough to handle, peel them and mash them by forcing them through a strainer with the back of a large spoon. Set aside.

2. Wipe the duck inside and out with a damp cloth and cut up: remove the thighs with the legs and the 2 breast pieces. Save the carcass, neck, and giblets. Remove the bones from the thighs and legs, leaving the meat in one piece. Score the skin of the breast pieces at an angle three or four times with a sharp knife (do not pierce the meat). Place the breast pieces and thigh-leg pieces, skin side down, in a skillet and cook over low heat to release all the fat, shaking the skillet now and then to prevent the duck pieces from sticking to the bottom, about 30 minutes. Turn the pieces and continue to cook for another 20 to 25 minutes, shaking the skillet from time to time. Remove the pieces to a plate and set aside, reserving the rendered fat.

3. Trim off and discard any excess fat from the reserved duck carcass and chop it. Place the chopped carcass, neck, giblets, and gizzard (but not the liver) in a small stockpot or saucepan. Add the garlic, carrot, mirasol peppers, thyme, sage, cloves, 1 tablespoon of salt, and 5 cups of water, and bring to a boil. Lower the heat and simmer for about 45 minutes. Remove from heat and strain through a fine sieve or through a strainer lined with 2 layers of cheesecloth. Discard the contents of the sieve or strainer. Let the duck stock sit for about 10 minutes, undisturbed, and then degrease thoroughly. Set aside.

4. In a saucepan, heat 1 tablespoon of the reserved duck fat. Add the onion and sauté over medium heat for about 2 minutes. Add the sherry, if using, and continue to sauté until all the liquid has evaporated, about 1 minute. Add the cooked duck pieces and 2 cups of the degreased duck stock, and cook over low heat until most of the liquid has evaporated and the duck pieces are tender, about 25 minutes. Remove the duck pieces to a plate. Continue cooking the sauce until all of the liquid has evaporated, leaving just the onion mixture in the saucepan. Remove from heat and set aside. Cut the duck pieces to obtain 8 to 10 smaller pieces.

5. Add the remaining 1 tablespoon salt and 3 tablespoons reserved duck fat to the mashed potatoes and mix until the fat is totally absorbed. Mix in ⅓ cup duck stock. Knead the potatoes to a smooth dough.

6. Prepare the banana leaf pieces as described on page 92. Place one on the work surface with the grain running from left to right.

7. Divide the dough into 8 to 10 equal portions. Place half of one portion on a banana leaf, about 3 inches from the near edge, and flatten it into a 4 × 2-inch rectangle. Arrange on top: 1 piece of duck breast and 1 piece of thigh-leg; 1 pitted olive; and about 1 tablespoon of the reserved onion sauce. Cover with the remaining half of the dough, shaping with your hands to seal the filling completely. Wrap and securely tie the tamale as described on pages 93–94. Repeat this process until all the tamales are assembled.

8. Steam the tamales over boiling water, tightly covered, for about 45 minutes to 1 hour. Maintain the water level at all times by adding boiling water as necessary. Remove the tamales from the steamer, cut and discard the strings, open the steaming leaves, and serve at once.

STORAGE NOTE   The steamed tamales can be stored, well covered, in the refrigerator for up to 5 days. Reheat them in a steamer for 15 to 20 minutes and serve hot.

VARIATION

Tamales Negros
Black Tamales
—

Chop 1½ to 2 ounces unsweetened chocolate, place in a small saucepan with ¼ cup duck stock, and heat just long enough for the chocolate to melt. Add the chocolate-stock mixture instead of the ⅓ cup stock to the mashed potatoes (along with duck fat and salt) in Step 5. Proceed with the recipe.

Tamales Navideños
Christmas Tamales

Makes 8 tamales

Potatoes and other starchy vegetables are often used in tamales for texture. In this tamale they are part of the filling, which is incorporated right into the dough.

It is a good idea to prepare these tamales the day before cooking them as they taste best when the flavors have had a chance to mingle.

4 cups canned white hominy, rinsed and well drained
(3 16-ounce cans)
½ pound pork loin, chopped
¼ pound salt pork, blanched with rind removed, finely chopped
1 large potato, peeled, cooked, and finely chopped
2 cups canned chick-peas, rinsed and well drained (1 19-ounce can)
1 small onion, peeled and chopped (½ cup)
1 large clove garlic, peeled and minced
2 tablespoons lard, Rendered Bacon Fat (page 476), or olive oil
2 tablespoons Spanish paprika
2 teaspoons coarse salt
1 teaspoon ground black pepper
2 hard-boiled eggs, chopped
16 banana leaf pieces, 15 × 14 inches (2 1-pound packages)
8 green olives, pitted

1. Place the hominy in a food processor and process for about 1 minute. Transfer to a stainless-steel bowl and set aside.

2. In another bowl, combine the pork, salt pork, potato, chick-peas, onion, and garlic.

3. In a small saucepan, heat the lard or oil and quickly add the paprika; stir vigorously for about 60 seconds. Remove the saucepan from the heat and add the contents to the bowl containing the meat mixture. Add the ground hominy, salt, and pepper and mix well. Gently fold in the chopped eggs. Correct seasoning with salt to taste.

4. Prepare the banana leaf pieces as described on page 92. Place one on the work surface with the grain running from left to right. Place 6 to 7 tablespoons of the tamale mixture about 3 inches from the lower edge of the leaf and shape it into a 4 × 3-inch rectangle. Set 1 olive on top. Double-wrap the tamales and use a simple tie as described on pages 93–94. Repeat until all the tamales are assembled.

5. Store the tamales in the refrigerator overnight so the mixture absorbs all of the seasonings. Then steam them, tightly covered, for 2 hours over medium heat. Maintain the water level at all times by adding boiling water as necessary. Remove the tamales from the steamer and let rest, covered, for 5 to 10 minutes. Cut the strings and discard, open the leaves, and serve at once.

VARIATION

The dough or masa for these tamales may also be made with corn flour. Mix 2 cups of corn flour with 6 cups of cold water, 1 tablespoon coarse salt, and ⅓ cup Rendered Bacon Fat (page 476) or olive oil in a saucepan. Cook over medium heat for 20 to 25 minutes, stirring constantly and scraping the bottom of the pan to prevent sticking. Remove from the heat and let cool. If the dough has lumps, force it through a strainer with the back of a spoon. Substitute this dough for the ground hominy in Step 3 and proceed with the recipe.

Tamal de Vegetales
Vegetable Tamale

—

Makes 8 to 10 tamales

This tamale from Colombia is made with vegetables only. In this recipe, I have suggested carrots, fennel, and mushrooms, with roasted red bell peppers and asparagus tips or peas for extra color and flavor. You can substitute any vegetable you want; just keep the quantities about the same.

Since these tamales are simmered rather than steamed, they must be double-wrapped.

3 dried mirasol peppers
3 cups Chicken Stock (page 461) or water
3 cups corn flour (1 pound)
3 tablespoons coarse salt
¾ cup Rendered Bacon Fat (page 476) or Rendered Duck Fat
*   (page 475) or Clarified Butter (page 476)*
4 cloves garlic, peeled
2 bay leaves
1 small fennel bulb, cut into 8 or 10 wedges
3 tablespoons Achiote Oil (page 472)
1 large onion, peeled and minced (1½ cups)
1 carrot, peeled and cut into 8 or 10 sticks
16 or 20 banana leaf pieces, 15 × 14 inches (2 1-pound packages)
1 roasted red bell pepper (page 484), cut into 8 to 10 strips
8 to 10 small mushroom caps
8 to 10 asparagus tips or ¼ cup fresh or frozen peas

1. Seed and crumble the peppers and soak in 1 cup warm stock or water with 1 tablespoon coarse salt for 15 minutes, or until ready to use.

2. In a 3-quart saucepan, combine the corn flour, 8 cups water, and 2 tablespoons salt. Mix well and let the mixture stand for about 5 to 10 minutes. Mix again and cook over low heat, constantly stirring and scraping the bottom of the pan to prevent sticking, until the dough is very thick, about 25 minutes. Remove from heat and set aside. If lumps form, force the dough through a strainer.

3. Place the fat or butter in a skillet. Add the garlic and bay leaves and sauté over low heat until the garlic is light golden all around, about 3 to 4 minutes. Do not let the garlic get too dark or burn. Remove from heat and let cool. Add ½ cup of fat to the dough and mix and knead until the fat is totally absorbed and the dough is smooth. Set aside.

4. Meanwhile, in a clean saucepan, heat the remaining 2 cups of stock or water. Add the fennel wedges and blanch them for a few minutes, just until barely tender. Remove them from the stock to a plate, and set both stock and fennel aside.

5. In the jar of an electric blender or work bowl of a food processor, combine the soaked mirasol peppers and stock with the sautéed garlic and blend or process until smooth.

6. In the skillet containing the remaining fat and bay leaves, heat the achiote oil and the minced onion. Sauté over medium heat until the onion is translucent, about 5 minutes. Add the blended hot pepper-garlic mixture and continue cooking for 2 minutes. Add the set-aside stock and the carrot sticks and cook until the carrots are tender and all of the liquid has evaporated. Remove from heat and transfer the carrots to a plate. Place a strainer over the dough and with a rubber spatula scrape in the contents of the skillet. Let drain for a few minutes; discard the bay leaves and save the onion sauce in the strainer. Knead the dough until all the fat has been absorbed and it is smooth.

7. Prepare the banana leaf pieces as described on page 92. Place one leaf on the work surface with the grain running from left to right.

8. Divide the dough into 8 or 10 equal portions. Place half of one portion on a banana leaf, about 3 inches from the near edge, and flatten it into a 4 × 2-inch rectangle. Arrange on top: 1 fennel wedge; 1 strip of roasted bell pepper; 1 carrot stick; 1 mushroom cap filled with a bit of the onion sauce; 1 asparagus tip or a few peas. Top the vegetables with a bit more of the onion sauce. Cover this with the other half portion of the dough, shaping it with your hand to seal the filling completely. Double-wrap the tamale and tie it securely as described on pages 93–94. Repeat until all tamales are assembled.

9. Steam the tamales over boiling water, tightly covered, for 45 minutes to 1 hour. Maintain the water level at all times by adding boiling water as necessary. Remove the tamales from the steamer, cut and discard the strings, open the steaming leaves, and serve.

Tamal de Mariscos
Seafood Tamale

—

Makes 8 tamales

You can capture the beautiful smell of the sea in a seafood tamale as in nothing else. The fish cooks as the tamales are steamed, releasing a wonderful bouquet and rich juices that are absorbed by the dough. Timing and temperature are critical in this recipe.

I use at least three, sometimes four kinds of fish in seafood tamales. For this recipe, I combined shrimp, scallops, and mussels with a piece of fish. The recipe calls for jumbo shrimp, one per tamale, but you can use large shrimp (16 to the pound) and put two in each tamale.

Seafood tamales must be eaten as soon as they are made. They should not be stored or reheated.

8 large mussels

8 jumbo shrimp

8 sea scallops

*½ pound skinless and boneless cod or swordfish, cut into
    8 1-inch pieces*

2 thin slices bacon, minced

¼ cup Achiote Oil (page 472)

3 tablespoons olive oil

3 large cloves garlic, peeled and finely minced

2-inch piece fresh ginger, peeled and finely minced

*1 to 2 dried mirasol peppers, seeded, crumbled, and finely minced,
    or 2 to 3 dried red chili peppers*

2 medium onions, peeled and minced (2 cups)

1 tablespoon plus 1 teaspoon coarse salt

½ teaspoon ground cumin

3 tablespoons dry vermouth

2 tablespoons sweet sherry

*10 cups canned white hominy, rinsed and well drained
    (7 16-ounce cans)*

16 banana leaf pieces 15 × 14 inches (2 1-pound packages)

1. Clean the mussels as described on page 486. Steam them until they are barely open. Remove the meat and set aside; discard the shells.

2. Peel, devein, and rinse the shrimp. Set aside. Coarsely chop the shells; place them in a small saucepan with 1 cup of water and cook over low heat for about 10 minutes. Strain through a fine sieve, pressing out all the juices from the shells. Discard the shells and set the liquid aside.

3. Place the scallops in a strainer; dip into a bowl containing cold water and shake to release any leftover particles of shell or sand. Quickly remove the strainer from the water and set aside to drain.

4. Wipe the swordfish cubes with a damp cloth and set aside.

5. In a skillet, heat the bacon and achiote and olive oils. Sauté until the bacon has rendered most of its fat and is slightly golden. Add the garlic, ginger, and peppers and sauté for just a second or two. Do not allow the mixture to burn. Add the onions, 1 tablespoon salt, cumin, vermouth, and sherry. Mix well and cook over medium-high heat for about 6 minutes. Add the reserved shrimp broth and continue cooking for about another 20 minutes, or until all the liquid has evaporated and only sauce and oil remain in the skillet. Scrape this mixture into a glass measuring cup and let it sit long enough for the oil to rise to the top. Skim the oil and reserve; you should have at least ½ cup. Set aside.

6. In a food processor, process half of the hominy to a very smooth paste. Transfer to a stainless-steel bowl. Process the remaining hominy to a more granular texture and add this to the hominy paste in the bowl. Add the remaining 1 teaspoon salt and the reserved ½ cup of the flavored oil. Mix well and knead to a smooth dough.

7. Prepare the banana leaf pieces as described on page 92. Place one on the work surface with the grain running left to right.

8. Divide the dough into 8 equal portions. Shape half of 1 portion into a 6 × 4-inch rectangle and place in the center of a leaf. Arrange on top: 1 shrimp; 1 scallop; 1 mussel; and 1 piece of fish. Spoon about 1 tablespoon of the reserved sauce over the seafood and cover with the remaining portion of dough, shaping with your hands to cover completely, and seal the filling. Double-wrap and tie the tamale, using a simple tie, as described on pages 93–94. Repeat this process until all the tamales are assembled.

9. Steam the tamales over boiling water, tightly covered, for 20 to 30 minutes. Maintain the water level at all times by adding boiling water as necessary. Remove from steamer, cut and discard the strings, open the leaves, and serve at once.

Tamal de Quinua
Quinoa Tamale

Makes 7 or 8 tamales

One of the grains I like best for tamales is quinoa, because of its wonderful nuttiness and its ability to absorb flavor. If you like, you can substitute rice in this recipe. (See Variation at end of recipe.)

2⅓ cups quinoa (1 pound)
2 dried red chili peppers, seeded
½ cup lard, solid vegetable shortening, or Rendered Bacon Fat
   (page 476)
¼ teaspoon annatto seeds
1 medium onion, peeled and finely chopped (1 cup)
1 clove garlic, peeled and crushed
¼ teaspoon ground cumin
⅛ teaspoon ground white pepper
3 teaspoons coarse salt
10 ounces lean, boneless pork loin, cut into ½-inch cubes
14 to 16 banana leaf pieces, 15 × 14 inches (2 1-pound packages)
14 to 16 peanuts, roasted (page 485)
7 or 8 Kalamata olives, pitted

1. Place the quinoa in a bowl; wash under running water, rubbing the quinoa between the palms of your hands. Drain.

2. In a 2½- to 3-quart saucepan, combine the quinoa and 8 cups of water. Bring to a boil, stirring now and then; lower the heat and simmer, uncovered, for about 10 minutes, or until the quinoa is barely done. Do not overcook. Pour through a strainer and drain well. In a food processor, process the quinoa with 3 quick on-off pulses; place in a bowl and set aside.

3. In a small bowl, soak the chili peppers in 1 cup hot water until soft. Drain and finely chop them, reserving both the peppers and the water.

4. In a saucepan, melt the lard with the annatto seeds over low heat until the seeds turn the melted lard bright red-orange. Remove the seeds with a slotted spoon and discard. Add the onion, garlic, cumin, pepper, salt, and pork pieces. Add the chili peppers and sauté for 1 minute more. Add the reserved water from the peppers and continue cooking for about 10 to 15 minutes, or until the pork is nearly tender and all the liquid has evaporated. Transfer the pork from the saucepan to a plate and set aside. Add the cooked quinoa and 2 cups of water. Cook over low heat, stirring constantly and scraping the bottom of the pan, until all the liquid has been absorbed by the quinoa.

5. Prepare the banana leaf pieces as described on page 92. Place one on the work surface with the grain running from left to right.

6. Preheat the oven to 400 degrees.

7. Place about 3 tablespoons of the quinoa mixture on the leaf, about 3 inches from the near edge. Flatten it into a 4 × 3-inch rectangle. Place a piece of meat, 2 peanuts, and 1 olive in the middle of the rectangle. Cover the filling with about 3 more tablespoons of the quinoa mixture, shaping it to cover completely, and seal the filling. Repeat until all of the leaves, grain, and filling are used. Double-wrap and securely tie the tamales, as described on pages 93–94.

8. Place the tamales in a baking dish large enough to hold them all in one layer. Pour just enough boiling water into the dish to cover the surface of the tamales. Cover the baking dish tightly with aluminum foil and bake for 1 hour. Keep adding enough boiling water to maintain its level. Remove the tamales from the water and drain them on a rack for a few minutes, keeping them covered so they stay hot. Cut and remove the strings, open the leaves, and serve.

VARIATION

Substitute 2 cups rice for the quinoa and cook it until barely done. Proceed with the recipe, starting with Step 3.

Tamal de Fuente
Pan-Baked Tamale

Serves 6 to 8

This nontraditional, king-size tamale is a clever invention of my mother's. By lining the baking dish with banana leaves and placing the filling on top of them, you enjoy all the flavor and scent of the leaves without having to wrap the tamales individually. Just be sure you have enough leaves to cover the bottom of the pan, leaving a generous overhang to pull up over the top. This dish is an easy way to put tamales on the buffet table.

6 cups canned white hominy, rinsed and well drained
(4 16-ounce cans)
½ cup Achiote Oil (page 472)
1 pound skinless and boneless chicken breast, cut into 1-inch pieces
2 dried red chili peppers, seeded and chopped
1 clove garlic, peeled and crushed
2 teaspoons coarse salt
1¼ cups Chicken Stock (page 461)
4 to 6 banana leaf pieces, 15 × 14 inches (1 16-ounce package)
8 Kalamata olives, pitted and sliced
2 jalapeño or serrano peppers, seeded and cut lengthwise into
5 strips each
20 peanuts, roasted (page 485)

1. Place the hominy in a food processor and process for about 1 minute. Transfer to a stainless-steel bowl and set aside.

2. In a skillet, heat the oil. Add the chicken pieces, hot peppers, garlic, and salt and sauté until the chicken is slightly brown on all sides. Add 1 cup of the stock and cook over medium heat until the liquid has evaporated and only the oil and flavorings remain. Transfer the chicken pieces to a plate and set aside.

3. Add the oil and flavorings left in the skillet to the bowl containing the hominy and mix well. Add the remaining ¼ cup of stock and knead the mixture to a smooth dough.

4. Preheat the oven to 400 degrees.

5. Prepare the banana leaf pieces as described on page 92. Line a 10-inch square baking dish or a 9-inch pie plate with the leaves. Arrange them by overlapping them in the center to cover the bottom and sides, with almost half the leaves draping over the edge of the baking dish or pie plate. Spread half the hominy mixture on top of the leaves in the pan. Evenly distribute the chicken pieces, olives, pepper strips, and peanuts. Cover the filling with the remainder of the hominy mixture. Fold the overhanging leaves over the filling toward the center, so that the mixture is completely covered by the leaves.

6. Place a sheet of wax paper or parchment paper over the dish and cover tightly with aluminum foil. Set the dish inside a larger baking dish or pan. Pour enough boiling water into the bottom of the larger dish to reach a third of the way up the sides of the smaller one. Place on the middle rack of the oven and bake for 1 hour. Keep adding enough boiling water to maintain the water level.

7. Remove from the oven and discard the foil and paper. Open the leaves and cut the tamale into wedges. Serve hot.

Juanes

Makes 8 juanes

These tamales from the Amazon are traditionally wrapped in delicate *bijao* leaves, which have long, thin stems. The stem is not detached, so a juane looks a little like a hobo's bundle on the end of a stick. If *bijao* leaves are unavailable, I wrap these in banana leaves.

The dough for these tamales is made with rice, which is flavored and colored with *palillo,* also known as *guisador,* a spice native to the Amazon. It is similar in color to turmeric, which is a good substitute. Saffron, though not normally used, would give the rice a rich color and flavor. You could also use curry. (See Variation at end of recipe.)

1 bay leaf
4 cloves garlic
8 to 10 black peppercorns
4 stalks celery, cut into quarters
1½ tablespoons coarse salt
3 chicken legs with thighs (about 2 pounds)
¼ pound slab bacon, blanched with rind removed, or 1 chorizo
    (about ¼ pound)
1 large carrot, peeled
1 teaspoon palillo or turmeric, or ¼ teaspoon saffron threads
¼ cup dry sherry (optional)
3 tablespoons olive oil
2 cloves garlic, peeled and finely chopped
2 medium leeks, white parts only, finely chopped
⅛ teaspoon cayenne
2 medium tomatoes, peeled, seeded, and chopped
1¾ cups rice, cooked until barely tender
16 banana leaf pieces, 15 × 14 inches (2 1-pound packages)
8 alfonso or Kalamata olives, pitted and cut in half
4 prunes, pitted and cut in half
¼ cup canned chick-peas, rinsed and drained

1. In a stockpot, combine the bay leaf, garlic, peppercorns, celery, salt, and 8 cups of water. Bring to a boil, lower the heat, and simmer, uncovered, for 10 to 15 minutes. Add the chicken, bacon, and carrot and cook until the chicken and carrot are tender, about 20 minutes. Remove the chicken, bacon, and carrot. Skin and debone the chicken, putting the skin and bones back in the stockpot. Reduce the stock to about 2 cups; strain through a fine sieve or cheesecloth and degrease; set aside. Cut the chicken, bacon, and carrot into 8 pieces each.

2. If using saffron, finely crumble the threads and soak them in the sherry for 10 minutes.

3. In a large skillet, heat the olive oil. Add the chopped garlic, leeks, and cayenne and sauté, stirring now and then, for 4 minutes, or until the leeks are totally translucent. Add the *palillo* and the tomatoes and continue cooking over medium heat for 5 minutes, or until the tomatoes have softened and all the liquid has evaporated. Add the reserved 2 cups of chicken stock and continue cooking over low heat for 20 to 25 minutes, stirring now and then. Add the cooked rice and continue to cook, stirring constantly, until the rice has absorbed all the juices. Correct the seasoning with salt to taste and set aside.

4. Prepare the banana leaves as described on page 92. Place one on the work surface with the grain running from left to right.

5. Divide the flavored rice into 8 portions. Break 1 portion in half and place the half in the center of the leaf, flattening it into a 6 × 5-inch rectangle. Arrange on top: 2 olive halves; 1 prune half; 1 piece of chicken; a few chick-peas; 1 piece of bacon; and 1 slice of carrot. Place the other half portion of rice over the filling and flatten it down to cover it completely. Double-wrap the tamale and tie it, as you would a package, as described on pages 93–94. Repeat until all the tamales are assembled.

6. Steam over boiling water, tightly covered, for 1 hour. Maintain the water level at all times by adding more boiling water as necessary. Remove the tamales from the steamer, cut and discard the strings, open the leaves, and serve at once.

VARIATION

For a curry-flavored dough, substitute 3 tablespoons of Curry Oil (page 473) for the olive oil in Step 3 and omit the *palillo* or turmeric.

Hallacas de Cumaná
Cumaná Hallacas

—

Makes 8 hallacas

A specialty of Cumaná, a Venezuelan port on the Caribbean, these hallacas are a riot of color and flavor. The dough gets its color from annatto and tomatoes, which also give it a refreshing taste. Potatoes and peas add a final note of emphasis. Hallacas can be made in advance and reheated.

1 carrot, washed and sliced
2 stalks celery, washed and sliced
1 large onion, quartered
1 bay leaf
1 or 2 fresh jalapeño peppers or dried red chili peppers
2 tablespoons coarse salt
1 whole chicken breast with skin and bones (1¼ pounds)
5 tablespoons olive oil
1 pound boneless pork loin, cut into 8 equal cubes
3 cloves garlic, peeled and minced
4 medium-large tomatoes, peeled, seeded, and finely chopped
3 cups corn flour (1 pound)
3 tablespoons Achiote Oil (page 472)
16 banana leaf pieces, 15 × 14 inches (2 1-pound packages)
1 medium potato, cooked, peeled, and cut into 8 cubes
½ cup fresh or frozen peas

1. In a stockpot, combine the carrot, celery, onion, bay leaf, hot peppers, 1 tablespoon of salt, and 6 cups of water; bring to a boil. Lower the heat and simmer, uncovered, for about 10 minutes. Add the chicken breast and cook until the meat is tender to the touch of a fork, about 20 minutes. Remove the chicken from the liquid; remove the skin and bones and put them back into the stock. Reduce the stock to 3 cups. Strain through a fine sieve or a strainer lined with cheesecloth and degrease the stock; set aside. Cut the chicken into 8 equal pieces and set aside.

2. Heat the olive oil in a skillet. Add the pork cubes and sauté until all the pieces are light brown on all sides. Add the garlic, tomatoes, and the reserved 3 cups of stock. Cook over medium heat for 45 minutes, or until the pork is tender and most of the liquid has evaporated. Transfer the pork pieces to a plate and set aside. Let the reduced tomato mixture cool slightly.

3. In a 3-quart saucepan, combine the corn flour, 8 cups of cold water, the remaining 1 tablespoon of salt, and the achiote oil. Mix well and let stand for 5 to 10 minutes. Mix again and cook, over low heat, constantly stirring and scraping the bottom of the pan to prevent sticking, until the dough is very thick, about 25 minutes. Remove from heat, and when cool enough to handle, force the mixture through a strainer to remove any lumps. Scrape the reduced tomato mixture from the skillet into the dough; mix and knead the dough until smooth.

4. Prepare the banana leaves as described on page 92. Place one on the work surface with the grain running from left to right.

5. Divide the dough into 8 equal portions. Take one of the portions and divide it in half. Place one half in the center of the banana leaf; flatten it into a 4 × 3-inch rectangle. Arrange on top: 1 piece of chicken and 1 potato cube, then in a second row, 1 cube of pork and a few peas. Slightly flatten the remaining half of the dough and cover the filling, shaping with your hands to seal the edges completely. Double-wrap the hallaca and tie as you would a package, as described on pages 93–94. Repeat until all the hallacas are assembled.

6. Steam the hallacas over boiling water, tightly covered, for 1 to 1½ hours. Maintain the water level at all times by adding more boiling water as necessary. Remove the hallacas from the steamer, cut and discard the strings, open the leaves, and serve at once.

Bollos
Plantain Bollos

Makes 6 bollos

These bollos are typical of Ecuador. The dough is made with plantains, which look like unripe bananas. I like to use them when they have just begun to ripen, and the skin is pale yellow. This gives the bollo a pleasant, sweet undertone. Chicken is used in this recipe; I generally reserve other poultry, such as turkey, duck, or pigeon, for special occasions.

1 carrot, washed and sliced
2 stalks celery, washed and sliced
1 large onion, unpeeled and quartered
1 bay leaf
1 or 2 dried chili peppers
3½ tablespoons coarse salt
1 chicken breast with skin and bones (1¼ pounds)
6 tablespoons lard or Rendered Bacon Fat (page 476) or olive oil
1 medium onion, peeled and minced (about 1 cup)
2 tablespoons Spanish paprika
10 plantains, peeled (8 to 10 pounds)
1 egg white
12 banana leaf pieces, 15 × 14 inches (2 1-pound packages)
¼ cup raisins
¼ cup fresh or frozen peas
1 baking potato, peeled, cooked, and cut into 30 cubes
3 tablespoons butter, cut into small pieces

1. In a small stockpot, combine the carrot, celery, onion, bay leaf, chili peppers, and ½ tablespoon of salt with 3 cups of water. Bring to a boil, lower the heat, and let simmer, uncovered, for about 10 minutes. Add the chicken breast and cook until the meat is tender, about 20 minutes. Transfer the chicken to a plate. Remove the skin and bones and put them back in the stock. Continue to simmer the stock until it has reduced to about 1¾ cups. Strain through a fine sieve or several layers of cheesecloth, degrease, and set aside. Cut the chicken into 18 pieces and set aside.

2. In a skillet, heat the lard and add the minced onion; sauté until translucent, about 2 to 3 minutes. Add the paprika, the chicken pieces, and 1½ cups of the stock. Stir and bring to a boil; lower the heat and simmer, uncovered, for about 25 minutes, or until all the liquid has evaporated and only the fat, onion, and chicken pieces remain in the skillet. Pour the contents of the skillet through a fine sieve and reserve both the oil and the chicken pieces with the onion.

3. Meanwhile, in a large pot, bring 16 cups of water with the remaining 3 tablespoons salt to a boil. Add the peeled plantains, bring to a boil again, lower the heat, and simmer for 25 to 30 minutes, or until the plantains are soft to the touch of a fork. With tongs or a fork, remove 1 or 2 plantains at a time and mash them immediately with a potato ricer or masher, directly into a stainless-steel bowl, or in the work bowl of a food processor. Repeat until all the plantains are mashed. While they are still warm, add the egg white and mix. Then add the reserved fat and 3 tablespoons of the remaining stock. Knead this mixture into a smooth dough. Correct the seasoning with salt to taste and set aside.

4. Prepare the banana leaves as described on page 92. Place one lengthwise on the work surface.

5. Divide the dough into 6 portions. Divide one portion in half and place the half in the middle of the leaf, forming a 4 × 3-inch rectangle. Arrange on top: 3 pieces of chicken in the first row; followed by a few raisins and a few peas; then in the last row, 5 potato cubes. Spoon a bit of the reserved onion mixture over the filling and cover with the other half of the dough portion, making sure that the edges are well sealed. Just before wrapping the filling with the banana leaf, take several pieces of the butter and put them around the filling as if to frame it. Double-wrap the bollo and tie it like a package, as described on pages 93–94. Repeat until all the bollos are assembled.

6. Steam the bollos over boiling water, tightly covered, for 45 minutes to 1 hour. Remove them from the steamer, cut and discard the strings, open the leaves, and serve hot.

Bollos de Ternera
Veal Bollos

Makes 10 to 12 bollos

The dough for these bollos is made with yellow corn flour or tortilla flour, which is preferred in Venezuela. This dough is like a batter, and the filling is folded right into it. Meat does not have to be cooked especially for this recipe; leftover chicken, turkey, pork, ham, beef, or lamb would all work well. A combination of meats could also be used.

1 veal shank or piece of veal breast (5 pounds)
2 cloves garlic, peeled
2 tablespoons coarse salt
1 teaspoon ground cumin
1 teaspoon red-wine vinegar
2 teaspoons olive oil
2 cups yellow corn flour
1¾ cups warm Chicken Stock (page 461) or water
*6 tablespoons Rendered Bacon Fat (page 476), Rendered Duck Fat
    (page 475), or solid vegetable shortening*
3 scallions, including some green parts, thinly sliced
2 jalapeño peppers, seeded and finely chopped
½ cup roasted peanuts, pignolis, or hazelnuts (page 485)
¼ cup fresh peas
10 to 12 banana leaf pieces, 15 × 14 inches (2 1-pound packages)

1. Preheat the oven to 475 degrees.

2. Trim off any excess fat and wipe the veal on all sides with a damp cloth. In a mortar with a pestle, pound the garlic, 1 tablespoon salt, and cumin to a paste. Add the vinegar and mix thoroughly. Blend in the oil and rub this mixture generously all over the veal. Place on a rack in a roasting pan and roast for 45 minutes to 1 hour. Remove from oven, and when cool enough to handle, slice all the meat off the bone and cut into ¼-inch cubes. If using veal breast, remove and discard any excess fat. You should have 2½ to 3 cups of meat cubes.

3. In a bowl, combine the corn flour with the warm stock. Add the fat and 1 tablespoon salt and mix thoroughly. Let sit, undisturbed, for 30 minutes to 1 hour. Mix well again. Mix in the veal cubes, scallions, peppers, peanuts, and peas.

4. Prepare the banana leaf pieces as described on page 92. Place a leaf on the work surface with the grain running from left to right. Place ⅓ cup of the corn mixture on the leaf, about 3 inches from the near edge. Wrap the hallaca and tie as you would a package, as described on pages 93–94. Repeat until all the hallacas are assembled.

5. Steam the hallacas over boiling water, tightly covered, for 45 minutes to 1 hour. Maintain the water level at all times by adding more boiling water as necessary. Remove from steamer, cut and discard the strings, open the leaves, and serve at once.

Humitas
Savory Corn Humitas

Makes 18 humitas

Humitas are what tamales are called in Argentina, Chile, and Bolivia. Most are savory, though there are some fantastic sweet ones. (In Peru, the term *humitas* is used only for sweet corn tamales.) But no matter where they come from, whether they are savory or sweet, humitas are always made with grated fresh corn and wrapped in fresh husks, which contribute to the humitas' sweet bouquet.

I like to serve these savory humitas, which are typical of Argentina and Chile, at the beginning of a meal. For even more fragrant humitas, add some cheese, as is done in Bolivia. (See Variation at end of recipe.)

When selecting corn, always check for fresh, healthy-looking husks. To examine the cob without tearing the husks, move your fingers over the entire surface, pressing hard, and feel for any soft spots or gaps. A good ear will feel firm all over. Each ear should have about twelve usable husks.

24 to 30 ears corn
¼ cup Rendered Bacon Fat (page 476) or butter
1 medium onion, peeled and finely chopped (1 cup)
1 large tomato, peeled, seeded, and finely chopped
1 tablespoon coarse salt
1 cup corn flour

1. Carefully remove the husks from the corn. Cut the corn with a very sharp knife at the point where the husks are attached. Gently peel off the husks one at a time, saving the young husks without tears and setting them aside. Remove and discard the silk. Grate the kernels off the cobs. You should have about 7 cups of grated corn. Set aside.

2. In a skillet, heat the fat or butter. Add the onion and sauté over medium heat until the onion is translucent, about 3 minutes. Do not brown the onion. Add the chopped tomato and continue cooking for about 4 minutes, stirring. Remove from heat and add the grated corn and salt. Sprinkle with corn flour and thoroughly mix it in. Let the mixture sit for about 30 minutes, stirring now and then.

3. Place 2 fresh corn husks on the work surface, overlapping, with the pointed ends of the husks facing away from each other, as described on page 94. Place a third husk in the middle. Place 1 heaping tablespoon of the corn mixture in the center. Wrap the humita as you would a package: fold one side of the husks up over the filling to cover it completely. Then fold down the opposite side of the husks. Fold each of the ends toward the middle, overlapping, to form a neat rectangular package. Tie the humita in the middle with strips of corn husk or kitchen string. Continue until all the humitas are assembled.

4. Place the humitas in a steamer, cover tightly, and steam for 45 minutes, maintaining the water level with more boiling water. Remove from steamer; let cool slightly, cut and discard the strings, open the husks, and serve warm.

STORAGE NOTE These humitas keep well under refrigeration. After they have cooled thoroughly, cover them tightly and refrigerate. They should keep well for up to 1 week. Before serving, place them in the steamer and heat for about 10 minutes.

VARIATION

Humitas de Queso
Cheese Humitas

—

Add ⅓ cup grated cheese, such as Parmesan, Emmenthal, or Jarlsberg, to the finished corn mixture at the end of Step 2 (immediately after mixing in the corn flour).

SWEET TAMALES

Humitas de Manjar Blanco
Sweet Corn Humitas

—

Makes 36 humitas

Dulce de leche, known in sophisticated culinary circles as *manjar blanco,* contributes to the wonderful flavor of these humitas. This thick milk pudding, made by cooking down fresh or condensed milk to a soft ball, is very sensitive to heat; it tends to stick to the pan and burns easily. Keep the flame low and use a flame tamer under the pan. As the pudding gets thicker and thicker, it needs to be stirred more and more.

20 to 24 ears corn
½ cup corn flour
¼ cup cornmeal
⅛ teaspoon ground mace
2 tablespoons sugar
1 teaspoon coarse salt
11 tablespoons (1 stick plus 3 tablespoons) unsalted butter
1¾ cups sweetened condensed milk (1 14-ounce can)
1 1½-inch cinnamon stick
¼ cup dark rum
1 teaspoon vanilla extract
⅛ teaspoon cayenne
Grated zest of 1 lemon

1. Carefully remove the husks from the corn. Cut the corn with a very sharp knife at the point where the husks are attached. Gently peel off the husks one at a time, saving the young leaves without tears and setting them aside. Remove and discard the silk and grate the kernels off the cobs. You should have about 4½ cups.

2. In an enameled saucepan, combine the grated corn, corn flour, cornmeal, mace, sugar, salt, and 8 tablespoons of the butter, chopped. Mix well and let sit, undisturbed, for 15 to 20 minutes.

3. In another small, enameled saucepan, combine the sweetened condensed milk, cinnamon stick, rum, vanilla, and cayenne. Place the saucepan over very low heat and cook, stirring from time to time, for 40 to 45 minutes, until a spoon leaves a track on the bottom of the pan when drawn through the mixture. Remove from heat and scrape the pudding off the cinnamon stick; discard the stick. Stir in 1 tablespoon butter and the grated lemon rind and beat vigorously until the milk pudding is cool to the touch. Divide it into 36 equal portions. Set aside.

4. Place the saucepan containing the grated corn mixture over medium heat, mix well, and cook, stirring constantly and scraping the bottom of the pan, for 20 minutes. The corn mixture will leave a film on the bottom of the pan. Remove from the heat and beat in the remaining 2 tablespoons butter. When cool enough to handle, divide the dough into 36 portions.

5. Place 1 corn husk horizontally on the work surface. In the palm of your hand, slightly flatten 1 portion of the corn mixture and place 1 portion of the milk pudding in the middle. Fold over so that the pudding is enclosed in the corn mixture. Place the filling in the middle of the husk. Fold one side of the husk up to cover the filling completely. Then fold the opposite side of the husk down over it. Place this filled husk into another one, but with the pointed end of the husk facing in the opposite direction. Fold one side and then the other over the first husk. Repeat with a third husk. Fold each end toward the middle, overlapping, to form a neat rectangular package. Tie the humita tightly in the middle, so it resembles a bow tie, with a strip of corn husk or kitchen twine. Repeat until all the humitas are assembled.

6. Place the humitas in a steamer, cover tightly, and steam for 1 hour. Remove from steamer; let cool slightly, cut and discard the strings, open the husks, and serve warm or at room temperature. (The humitas can also be gently simmered for 45 minutes to 1 hour.)

STORAGE NOTE These humitas store well, both before and after cooking. They can be assembled, placed in a container with a tight lid or individually wrapped in plastic wrap or aluminum foil, and stored in the refrigerator for several days. When ready to serve, unwrap them and steam or simmer them. To store already cooked humitas, let them cool to room temperature before wrapping or placing them in a container. Warm them by steaming or simmering for about 15 minutes, or until heated through.

Pamonhas do Norte
Brazilian Sweet Pamonhas

—

Makes 22 pamonhas

These coconut and corn pamonhas steamed in fresh corn husks will transport you straight to the northern regions of Brazil—Bahia, Paraíba, Recife, Ceará—where they are considered a great treat. It's not just the tropical twist of combining coconut with corn, but also the way the pamonhas are folded into purses that makes them so charming.

5 to 8 ears corn
⅓ cup sugar
⅛ teaspoon ground cloves
⅛ teaspoon ground cardamom
1 cup freshly grated coconut
9 ounces yuca, peeled, cored, and grated (about 1 cup)
*   (see Variations)*
2 tablespoons unsalted butter, melted

1. Carefully remove the husks from the corn. Cut the corn with a very sharp knife at the point where the husks are attached. Gently peel off the husks one at a time, saving the young husks without tears, and set aside. Remove and discard the silk. Grate the kernels off the cobs. You should have about 2½ cups.

2. In a bowl, combine the grated corn, sugar, cloves, cardamom, coconut, yuca, and melted butter. Mix well.

3. Take 3 large fresh corn husks for each pamonha. Place 2 husks on the work surface, overlapping (except for 2 inches at each end), with the ends pointing in opposite directions. Place a third husk in the middle. Place 1½ tablespoons of the coconut mixture in the middle but closer to one of the ends. Fold both sides of the husks over the filling, overlapping them in the center. Fold the husks in half, so that the pointed ends come together as one. Tie securely about 1 inch below the points with kitchen string or a strip of husk. Repeat until all the pamonhas are assembled.

4. Cook the pamonhas in a steamer, tightly covered, for 35 to 40 minutes, maintaining the water level with additional boiling water. Remove the pamonhas from the steamer, place them on a rack to cool thoroughly, and serve.

STORAGE NOTE   Pamonhas can be stored, well wrapped or well covered, in the refrigerator for up to 1 week.

VARIATIONS

Rinse and drain a 16-ounce can of white or yellow hominy; you should have about 1½ cups. Grind it in a food processor for 1 minute. Add this instead of grated yuca to the corn-and-coconut mixture in Step 2. Mix thoroughly and proceed with the recipe.

Add ¼ cup corn flour instead of yuca to the grated corn-and-coconut mixture in Step 2.

Chapanas de Cañete
Chapanas with Golden Raisins

Makes 12 chapanas

I remember as a child running around the corner from home and finding the woman who sold chapanas crouched on the edge of the sidewalk, her brightly patterned wool *polleras* billowing out like an umbrella tied to her waist. Set before her was a board covered with old burlap and semidried banana leaves. Resting on it was a gigantic pile of chapanas, neatly stacked one on top of the other. I was drawn to them like a fly to honey.

Chapanas are a specialty of southern Peru, and these are the pride of Cañete, a little town south of Lima. They are always better served the next day.

2 tablespoons annatto seeds
½ cup pisco, aguardiente, or light rum
2½ pounds yuca, peeled and finely grated (3½ cups)
¼ teaspoon ground cloves
1 cup sugar
⅛ teaspoon cayenne
¼ cup golden raisins
24 dried banana leaf pieces, 12 × 10 inches (2 1-pound packages)
  (see Variation)
Extra banana leaves (optional)

1. In a small saucepan, combine the annatto seeds, pisco, and ½ cup water and allow to soak for at least 15 to 20 minutes, or until ready to use. Place over medium heat and bring to a boil. Lower the heat and simmer, stirring now and then, until the liquid has reduced to ¾ cup. Pour through a strainer, reserve the liquid, and discard the seeds.

2. In a stainless-steel bowl, combine the yuca, cloves, sugar, cayenne, raisins, and the reserved liquid. Mix well and set aside.

3. Dip the dried banana leaf pieces into boiling water to soften them, about 1 minute. Wipe the leaves along the grain with a cloth. With a pair of scissors cut the cords from the leaves and set them aside. These will be used later to tie the chapanas.

4. Place a leaf on the table with the grain running vertically. Place 3 tablespoons of the filling about 2 inches from the near edge. Fold the edge of the leaf over the filling to cover. Fold both sides of the leaf toward the center and roll until you reach the opposite end of the leaf. Double-wrap with a second leaf with the grain running horizontally. Repeat until all the chapanas are assembled.

5. Place the chapanas in a steamer, cover with the extra banana leaves, if desired, and a tight-fitting lid. Steam for 2 hours 40 minutes. Maintain the water level at all times by adding more boiling water as needed. Remove the chapanas from the steamer and let them cool thoroughly on a rack, preferably overnight. Remove the cords, unfold the leaves, and serve.

STORAGE NOTE   These chapanas will keep well for several days in the refrigerator. A little while before serving, remove them from the refrigerator and let them come to room temperature.

VARIATION

Reconstitute 72 dried corn husks and double-wrap the chapanas as described on page 94, using 3 tablespoons of filling. Tightly tie the package in the middle with a strip of husk to look like a bow tie. Steam the chapanas as described in Step 5.

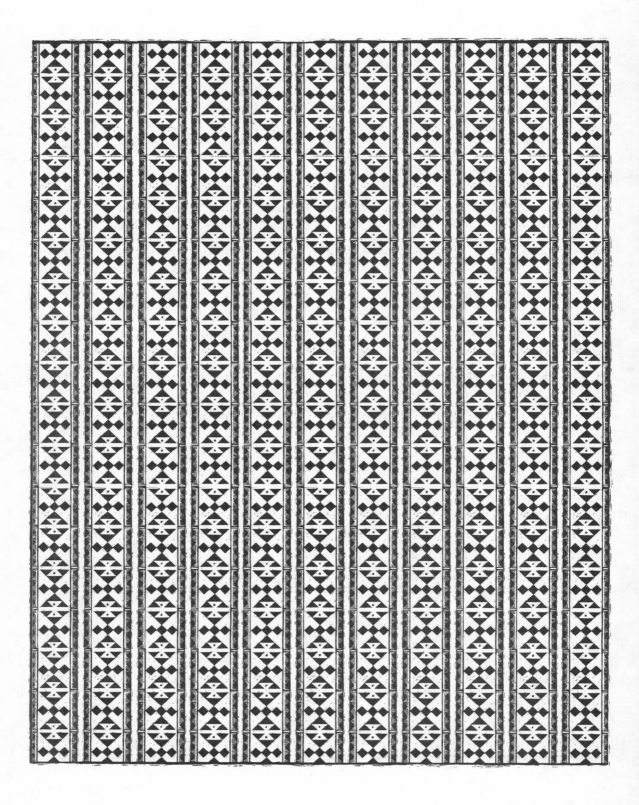

Soups

MEAT SOUPS

Sancocho
—

Sancochado
—

Puchero
—

Olla Podrida
Puchero with Morcilla Sausages
—

Cozido
—

Cruzado
—

Chairo
Beef and Vegetable Soup
—

Carbonada Criolla
Carbonade of Beef, Squash, and Peaches
—

Caldo de Patita
Calves' Feet and Peanut Soup
—

Cazuela de Pollo con Hinojo
Cazuela with Chicken and Fennel
—

Canja
Brazilian Chicken Soup with Rice
—

Bori-Bori
Paraguayan Dumpling Soup
—

Caldo de Bolas
Ecuadorian Dumpling Soup
—

SEAFOOD SOUPS

Chupe de Camarones
Shrimp Chowder
—

Chupe de Cangrejo
Crabmeat Chowder
—

Chupe de Loco
Chilean Clam Chowder
—

Mariscada de Mejillones y Almejas
Mariscada of Mussels and Clams
—

Caldito de Pescado
Chilean Fish Soup

Caldo de Bagre
Catfish Soup
—

Caldo de Peixe
Brazilian Coconut Soup with Fish

VEGETABLE SOUPS

Sopa de Yuyo
Sea Greens Soup
—

Crema de Apio
Venezuelan Cream of Celeriac Soup
—

Sopa de Chuchu
Brazilian Chayote Soup
—

Caldo Verde
Brazilian Kale and Potato Soup
—

Sopa de Zapallo
Winter Squash Soup
—

Chupe de Choclo
Corn Chowder
—

Sopa de Feijão Preto
Brazilian Black Bean Soup
—

Chupe de Porotos
Chilean Bean Chowder
—

Sopa de Habas
Fava Bean Soup
—

Chupe de Quinua
Quinoa Chowder
—

FRUIT SOUPS

Champus
Chirimoya Soup
—

Sopa de Tomatitos Verdes
Tomatillo Soup
—

Sopa de Palta
Avocado Soup

In South America no proper meal starts without soup. And it is served piping hot no matter what the season.

When I was growing up, my grandmother's soups were wonderful and portions were generous. It seemed to take forever to get to the bottom of the soup plate, and in her house the soup had to be finished to the last drop before we were allowed to continue with the rest of the meal. I knew I was licked even before I began when one of her *chupes,* or chowders, appeared on the table.

Today I appreciate those hearty chowders with their fabulous combinations of ingredients. I have a particular weakness for *chupes* made with shrimp, crab, and corn. I like to make them the focus of a meal. I am perfectly content to have a bowl of *chupe* for lunch or dinner with some crusty bread and a salad. When I eat *chupe,* I am transported back home to Peru. Among my most vivid food memories are those Peruvian *chupes de cangrejo* (with crab) and *chupes de camarones* (with shrimp). I can almost see the soup plate in front of me, filled to the brim with a thick, milky broth chockful of whole sweet Pacific shrimp still in the shell. What a *chupe* that was!

Chupes also make me think of the magnificent chowders you get along the Chilean coast. An authentic Chilean *chupe* must also have some *porotos,* as they call beans. *Chupe de loco* is filled with the abalone that grows so large and tender in that part of the world. *Caldito de Pescado,* another great seafood soup from Chile, is a combination of fish and shellfish in a flavorful clear broth.

Chupes are found in an almost unlimited variety all the way up the Pacific coast as far north as Ecuador. There, *chupes* are prepared not only with fish and shellfish but with meat, poultry, beans, grains, potatoes, and corn.

Soup is not indigenous to South America. Although our forefathers had the vessels, understood the concept of boiling, and used it to tenderize and cook foods—and to make *chicha,* or corn beer—they cooked mainly over an open flame or on flat hot stones or in primitive ovens. But once the Spanish colonists introduced the idea of soup making, soups started taking form throughout the continent. New ingredients were combined with local products, and the extraordinary soups of South America were born.

Squash, the most ancient of Indian crops, and beans in every size, shape, and color are transformed everywhere into soup. Whether it's in a Brazilian *sopa de feijão preto,* rich and inky black, or a Chilean *chupe de porotos,* made with three kinds of beans, the unassuming dried bean is a star in the South American kitchen.

Pureed soups are found everywhere in South America as well. We call them cream soups, even though no cream ever comes near the soup pot. Rather, they are thickened with starchy vegetables, beans, or grains. I have even used stems of cauliflower or broccoli to get the satiny effect I look for in a pureed soup.

Cold soups are not popular in South America, but they certainly are in my kitchen. *Sopa de tomatitos verdes* (with tomatillos) and *sopa de palta* (with avocados) can be served hot or cold. Actually, almost all pureed soups are candidates for chilling. They are simple enough to make with a food processor or blender, though any vegetable or fruit with seeds (including tomatillos) should be passed through a food mill first. Just be sure to taste the soup once it has been chilled, and adjust the seasoning, especially salt.

One type of soup found in every South American country, though the name and traditional ingredients vary from place to place, is what in North America is called a boiled dinner. Meat, poultry, fish, and/or sausages are cooked in water or stock with vegetables. In Peru this is called *sancochado;* in Ecuador and Colombia, *sancocho;* in Venezuela, *hervido;* in Chile, *cazuela,* after the earthenware pot in which it is cooked; in Brazil, *cozido;* and in Argentina, Uruguay, Paraguay, and Bolivia, *puchero.* When the *puchero* is made with sausages in Uruguay, it is called *olla podrida,* literally "rotten pot," and it is delicious despite its name.

To make a good soup, all you really need is water and flavorings. Sometimes a water-based soup is enriched with an *aderezo,* which is made by sautéing garlic, onion, and hot peppers along with seasonings, aromatic vegetables, herbs, and, in some cases, tomatoes. How many times have I seen my mother make a quick garlic soup! She would take a good quantity of chopped garlic and sauté it in olive oil in her favorite little black pot. Then she would add as many cups of water as there were guests. Just before serving the soup, she quickly stirred in a well-beaten egg to give it body. Then she adjusted the seasoning with salt and freshly cracked pepper and sprinkled the soup with chopped fresh herbs.

A rich, well-seasoned broth is a heavenly beginning for a meal. It can be garnished with a few plain croutons and chopped herbs. Other interesting additions include a raw egg with chopped herbs, julienned vegetables, julienned or diced meat, pieces of fish or shellfish, and pasta and grains of all kinds. Throughout Chile and Peru, *yuyo*, an edible seaweed that ranges in color from translucent green to purple, is added to the broth.

Whether simple or complex, light or robust, a true South American soup must have exciting flavor, strong body, appetizing color, and, of course, a touch of heat. Oh yes! One more thing—a group of hungry people sitting around the table.

MEAT SOUPS

Sancocho

—

Serves 8 to 10

*S*ancocho, as this dish is called in Ecuador and Colombia (they call it *hervido* in Venezuela), is one of the many South American soups that resemble a North American boiled dinner. This *sancocho* is made with a brisket of beef, but other cuts, such as shank, rump, eye of round, short ribs, or flank steak, can be substituted. A good *sancocho* can also be made with chicken, pork, or veal. Seafood, too, is often used.

I find it a good idea to roll and tie the brisket. This keeps it in a compact shape and also makes it easier to remove it from the broth after cooking. When you add the vegetables, make sure there is enough broth to cover them. If not, add just enough additional stock or water to keep them barely covered. There is nothing wrong with adding the vegetables just as they are, without wrapping them in cheesecloth, but I find it much easier to wrap them at the beginning than to fish them out one by one at the end.

1 whole brisket of beef, rolled and tied (5 to 6 pounds)

BOUQUET GARNI
6 sprigs Italian parsley
2 or 3 sprigs fresh mint
1 small sprig fresh rosemary
8 sprigs fresh thyme
1 or 2 jalapeño peppers, cut in half and seeded

6 quarts Beef Stock (page 462) or water
2 tablespoons coarse salt

VEGETABLES
6 small carrots, peeled
6 medium potatoes, peeled (2 pounds)
6 small onions, peeled (1½ pounds)

3 plantains (green), peeled and cut in half (10 to 12 ounces each)

1 small Savoy cabbage, outer leaves removed (about 2 pounds)

6 small leeks, white and some part of green only, roots trimmed and thoroughly washed (about 2 pounds)

4 ears corn, husked, silk removed, and cut across in half

2 tablespoons chopped fresh cilantro leaves or Italian parsley or dill

1. Wipe the brisket on both sides with a damp cloth. Trim off all excess fat. Roll and tie the meat securely with kitchen string. Set aside. Wrap the parsley, mint, rosemary, thyme, and peppers in a 10-inch-square piece of cheesecloth and tie securely. Set aside.

2. Place the beef in a large stockpot. Add stock or water, bouquet garni, and salt and bring to a boil, skimming the foam as it rises to the surface. Lower the heat, cover, and gently simmer for 3 hours, or until the meat is tender.

3. While the meat is cooking, wrap and tie each of the vegetables in an 18-inch-square piece of cheesecloth. Immerse the packages in a bowl of cold water. Set aside until ready to use.

4. With a spoon or ladle, skim off and discard the fat on the surface of the broth. Add the packages containing the carrots, potatoes, onions, plantains, and cabbage. Cook for 25 to 30 minutes. Add the leeks and corn and cook for 5 to 10 minutes longer, or until the corn is done.

5. Remove the packages containing the vegetables from the broth and drain the liquid back into the pot. Place the meat on a large serving platter and cut and discard the strings. Unwrap the vegetables, arrange them around the meat, and sprinkle with chopped cilantro leaves. Remove and discard the bouquet garni from the broth and correct the seasoning with salt to taste. Pour the broth into a soup tureen and serve along with the meat and vegetables. Or, serve individually in large soup plates or bowls with a slice of meat, an assortment of vegetables around the meat, and hot broth sprinkled with chopped cilantro leaves.

Sancochado

Serves 8 to 10

At its simplest, Peruvian *sancochado* is just a matter of placing a piece of beef in a pot, filling it up with water, adding some vegetables, and cooking until the meat is tender and the vegetables are done. For a more flavorful *sancochado,* the water is replaced with stock. For a magnificent one, the meat is marinated first and browned, as in this recipe; this gives the broth a wonderfully rich flavor and an amber color.

There are many marinades for *sancochado.* One of the most unusual comes from Cuzco, a city in the Andes, where they use *chicha de jora,* or Corn Beer (page 470) (see Variation at end of recipe).

When Peruvians serve a *sancochado,* they offer up to three different sauces: hot-pepper; aioli; and one made with fresh herbs (pages 477–479).

> To make a simple hot-pepper sauce, take some fresh hot peppers, remove and discard the seeds, and grind or finely mince the peppers. Add a few drops of vinegar and oil, season with salt, mix well and serve.

1 brisket of beef, rolled and tied, or short ribs in 1 piece
   (6 to 7 pounds)

SPICE RUB
4 cloves garlic, peeled
3 tablespoons coarse salt
1 or 2 dried mirasol or red chili peppers, seeded and crumbled
1 teaspoon ground cumin
1-inch piece fresh ginger, peeled and grated
4 tablespoons olive oil

BOUQUET GARNI
6 to 8 cloves
4 sprigs fresh oregano
10 sprigs fresh thyme
1 bay leaf
½ teaspoon black peppercorns
2 tablespoons coarse salt

VEGETABLES

3 small yuca, peeled and cut into 2-inch pieces (about 2½ pounds)
6 small carrots, peeled (about 1½ pounds)
6 small turnips, peeled (about 1½ pounds)
3 chayotes, peeled, cut lengthwise into quarters, and seeded
3 small bunches celery, leafy tops cut off, leaving 6 inches of stalk
6 small onions, peeled (1 to 1½ pounds)
6 small leeks, tops and roots trimmed, washed thoroughly
   (about 2 pounds)
2 tablespoons chopped fresh cilantro leaves or Italian parsley or dill

1. With a damp cloth, wipe the brisket or short ribs on both sides and trim and remove all excess fat. Roll and tie the meat. Set aside.

2. In a mortar with a pestle, pound the garlic, salt, peppers, and cumin to a smooth paste. Add the grated ginger and continue pounding until thoroughly blended. Rub the meat all over with this mixture and let it sit at room temperature for several hours, or refrigerate overnight, tightly covered.

3. In a large stockpot, heat the olive oil over medium heat. Add the marinated meat and brown on both sides, about 8 minutes per side, or until the meat has a thick brown crust. Add 6 quarts of water, the bouquet garni, and salt. Bring it to the boil, skimming the foam as it rises to the surface. Lower the heat and let simmer, covered, for 3 hours, or until the meat is tender.

4. While the meat is cooking, wrap and tie each of the vegetables into an 18-inch-square piece of cheesecloth. Immerse the packages in a large bowl of cold water. Set aside until ready to use.

5. With a spoon or ladle, skim off and discard the fat from the surface of the broth and add the package of yuca. Cook for 15 minutes. Add the carrots and cook for 5 minutes more. Add the turnips, chayotes, celery, and onions and cook for 8 minutes more. Finally, add the leeks and continue to simmer until all the vegetables are tender, about 5 to 10 minutes more.

6. Remove the packages and drain back into the broth. Take out the meat and place it on a serving platter. Unwrap the vegetables, arrange them around the meat, and sprinkle with the chopped cilantro leaves.

(Continued)

Remove and discard the bouquet garni from the broth and correct the seasoning with salt to taste. Pour the broth into a tureen and serve along with the meat and vegetables. Or, serve in individual soup plates or bowls with a slice of meat, an assortment of vegetables, and hot broth sprinkled with chopped cilantro.

VARIATION

Sancochado Cuzqueño

Cuzqueño Sancochado

—

Add 1 cup Corn Beer (page 470) to the marinade in Step 2. Pour and rub this mixture all over the meat and let marinate in the refrigerator for 24 hours. Proceed with the recipe.

Puchero

—

Serves 8 to 10

Chorizo gives this particular dish, which is from Argentina, its distinctive flavor. A fresh chorizo is moist and soft to the touch, with a smooth, tight skin and a fiery reddish color. Although fresh chorizo can be tossed right into the *puchero* pot along with the rest of the ingredients, I prefer to blanch it first. Dried chorizo *must* be blanched long enough to soften it before adding it to the pot.

1 stewing hen, with giblets and neck (about 6 pounds)
1 brisket of beef or rump roast or eye of round, or 2 flank steaks
    (about 3 pounds)
3 chorizos (about 1 pound, total)
2 tablespoons olive oil
1 bay leaf
2 or 3 dried red chili peppers, seeded
2 tablespoons coarse salt

VEGETABLES
1 small whole green cabbage (about 2½ pounds)
6 small carrots, peeled (about 1½ pounds)

6 small red potatoes, scrubbed (1 pound)

6 small onions, peeled and roots trimmed (1½ pounds)

*6 medium leeks, white parts and about 1 inch of green parts,
  roots trimmed and thoroughly washed (3 pounds)*

2 tablespoons chopped Italian parsley

1. Rinse and wipe the hen inside and out and truss it as described on page 257. Set aside. Wipe the meat with a damp cloth, trim off any excess fat, and secure tightly with kitchen string. Set aside. Bring about 8 cups of water to a boil in a saucepan. Add the chorizos and blanch for 5 to 8 minutes. Remove the sausages from the water and set them aside. Discard the water.

2. In a large stockpot, heat the olive oil. Add the brisket and the neck, gizzard, and heart but not the liver from the chicken and quickly brown the meat over high heat, about 10 minutes. Add 6 quarts of water, the bay leaf, hot peppers, and salt. Bring to a boil, skimming the foam as it rises to the surface. Stir from time to time. Lower the heat, cover, and simmer for 1 hour 30 minutes, or until tender. Add the chicken and continue simmering for about 15 minutes, constantly skimming.

3. While the meat and chicken are cooking, wrap and tie each vegetable in an 18-inch-square piece of cheesecloth. Immerse the packages in a bowl of cold water. Set aside until ready to use.

4. Add the chorizos and the cabbage to the stockpot, cover, and cook for 30 minutes. Add the carrots and potatoes and cook for 10 minutes. Add the onions and cook for 5 minutes. Add the leeks and cook for 10 minutes more.

5. Take out the packages and drain the liquid back into the broth. Remove the brisket, chicken, and chorizos and place them in the center of a large serving platter. Remove and discard the strings from the chicken and meat. Unwrap the vegetables, arrange them around the meats and sausages, and sprinkle with chopped parsley. Degrease the broth, correct the seasoning with salt to taste, and pour into a soup tureen and serve along with the meats, sausages, and vegetables. Or, serve individually in large soup plates or bowls: place a slice of each of the meats and a piece of sausage in the plate or bowl. Surround it with vegetables, and fill the plate with broth. Serve sprinkled with chopped parsley.

Olla Podrida
Puchero with Morcilla Sausages
—

Serves 8 to 10

When they add sausage to *puchero* in Uruguay, they call it *olla podrida,* literally "rotten pot"—not a very appetizing name for a truly delicious dish. Morcilla sausage, a blood sausage that is quite popular throughout South America (it's called *morcilha* in Portuguese), is generally used, but other blood sausages, such as the French *boudin noir,* will work. Other kinds of sausage, especially well-seasoned and garlicky ones like kielbasa or cotecchino, can also be substituted. When using these sausages, blanch them for ten minutes before adding them to the pot.

4 pounds beef shank or oxtails or short ribs, cut into 2-inch pieces

MARINADE
4 large cloves garlic, peeled
2 tablespoons coarse salt
2 teaspoons ground cumin
*3 tablespoons sherry vinegar or 2 tablespoons sweet sherry
    mixed with 1 tablespoon vinegar*

1 stewing hen (about 6 pounds)
3 morcilla sausages
⅓ cup vegetable oil
24 juniper berries
12 allspice berries
6 to 8 cloves
1 tablespoon coarse salt

VEGETABLES
6 medium carrots, peeled (about 1½ pounds)
6 small turnips, peeled (about 1 pound)
6 small red potatoes (about 1 pound)
4 medium onions, peeled and roots trimmed (about 2 pounds)
*1 large butternut squash, cut in half lengthwise and seeded, each half
    sliced to yield 1½-inch pieces (about 2½ pounds)*
4 ears corn, husked, silk removed, and cut across in half

BOUQUET GARNI
1 or 2 jalapeño or serrano or arbol peppers, sliced,
  or dried red chili peppers
2 or 3 leafy celery tops, washed
6 to 8 sprigs fresh oregano
12 to 15 sprigs fresh thyme
3 sprigs fresh mint

2 tablespoons chopped fresh cilantro leaves or Italian parsley

1. Wipe the meat with a damp cloth. Set aside.

2. In a mortar with a pestle, pound the garlic, 2 tablespoons salt, and cumin to a smooth paste. Add the vinegar and mix thoroughly. Rub the meat with this mixture and let it marinate for about 2 hours at room temperature or, preferably, overnight, tightly covered, in the refrigerator.

3. Rinse the hen and wipe dry, reserving the neck and giblets; discard the liver. Truss the hen as described on page 257. Set aside.

4. In a saucepan, bring 6 to 8 cups of water to a boil. Add the morcillas and blanch them for 2 to 3 minutes. Remove the sausages from the water, set aside, and discard the blanching liquid.

5. In a large stockpot, heat the oil over high heat. Add the chicken neck, gizzard, and the meat and quickly sear them over high heat on all sides for about 8 minutes. Add 6 quarts of water, the juniper berries, allspice, cloves, and 1 tablespoon salt. Bring to a boil over high heat and skim the foam as it rises to the surface. Lower the heat, cover the pot, and simmer gently for 1½ to 2 hours.

6. Meanwhile, wrap and tie each of the vegetables in an 18-inch-square piece of cheesecloth. Immerse the packages in a bowl of cold water until ready to use. Wrap and tie the peppers, celery, oregano, thyme, and mint in a 10-inch-square piece of cheesecloth.

7. Transfer the meat to a clean but larger stockpot. Degrease the stock thoroughly and strain through a fine sieve lined with a double layer of cheesecloth. Add the cleaned stock to the stockpot containing the meat. Add the chicken and the bouquet garni. Bring to boil, skimming the foam as it rises to the surface. Lower the heat and simmer, covered, for 20 minutes. Add the carrots, turnips, and potatoes and cook for 15 minutes. Add the onions and cook for 5 minutes more. Add

(Continued)

the blanched morcillas and butternut squash and cook for 10 minutes more. Add the corn and cook for 10 minutes more.

8. Remove the vegetables from the broth and let the liquid drain back into the broth. Remove the sausages, chicken, and meat and place them on a large serving platter. Cut and remove the trussing strings. Unwrap the vegetables, arrange them around the chicken, meat, and sausages, and sprinkle with the chopped cilantro leaves. Remove and discard the bouquet garni from the broth. Correct the seasoning with salt to taste. Pour the broth into a soup tureen and serve along with the rest. Or serve individually in large soup plates or bowls.

Cozido
—
Serves 8 to 10

This Brazilian dish, with its various meats and vegetables, is ideal for entertaining. It creates a mood of festivity because the very nature of *cozido* is abundance. A proper *cozido* must have two different meats, usually pork and beef, plus sausage. Sometimes a piece of *carne seca* or *carne de sol,* Portuguese for sun-dried beef, is also added. At least one and sometimes two kinds of sausage are found in a *cozido.* Most typical is *paio,* a well-seasoned and lightly smoked pork sausage. Other Portuguese sausages, such as salpicão, chouriço, or lingüiça, can also be used.

Vegetables should also be plentiful. Yuca, cabbage, corn, and green plantains are always found in a *cozido.* (Plantains are what distinguish the Brazilian *cozido* from the Portuguese one.)

1 brisket of beef (about 5 pounds)
6 fresh ham hocks (about 6 pounds)
3 or 4 sprigs fresh cilantro leaves or Italian parsley
4 tablespoons coarse salt
1½ pounds paio, lingüiça, kielbasa, or any other garlic sausage

AROMATICS
2 large heads garlic, unpeeled and cut in half horizontally
2 large onions, unpeeled, roots trimmed, and cut into quarters
    (about 1½ pounds)

1 large leek, white and green parts, washed and chopped

1 large carrot, washed and chopped

6 stalks celery with leafy tops, washed and chopped

1-inch piece fresh ginger, sliced

6 to 8 sprigs fresh oregano

6 sprigs fresh mint

20 sprigs fresh thyme

1 or 2 dried red chili peppers, seeded

1 bay leaf

2 teaspoons cumin seeds

12 cloves

24 black peppercorns

VEGETABLES

1 Savoy or green cabbage, outer leaves removed (about 3 pounds)

*3 small yuca, peeled, washed, and cut crosswise into 3-inch pieces,
   each piece quartered lengthwise, central fibrous cord
   removed and discarded (about 2 pounds)*

3 green plantains, peeled and cut in half crosswise (about 3 pounds)

3 large carrots, peeled and cut in half crosswise (about 1½ pounds)

3 ears corn, husked, silk removed, and cut in half crosswise

4 tablespoons chopped fresh cilantro leaves or Italian parsley

1. Wipe the brisket with a damp cloth and trim and discard most of the fat. Roll and tie the brisket securely with kitchen string and set aside. Wipe the ham hocks with a damp cloth. In a saucepan, combine 4 quarts of water, the cilantro sprigs, and 1 tablespoon of the salt. Bring to a boil and add the ham hocks. Bring back to a boil, lower the heat, and simmer for 25 minutes. Remove the ham hocks from the water, drain, and set aside. Strain the blanching liquid through a strainer lined with several layers of cheesecloth and set aside. Cut the sausage into 6 to 8 serving pieces and wrap and tie them in an 18-inch-square piece of cheesecloth. Set aside.

2. In a large stockpot, combine 8 quarts of water, the garlic, onions, leek, carrot, celery, ginger, oregano, mint, thyme, hot peppers, bay leaf, cumin, cloves, peppercorns, and the remaining 3 tablespoons of salt. Bring to a boil, lower the heat, and simmer for 30 minutes. Add the brisket and bring to a boil again, skimming the foam as it rises to the surface. Lower the heat and continue to simmer for 2 hours. Transfer the brisket from the broth to a tray and set aside.

(Continued)

3. While the meat is cooking, wrap each vegetable in an 18-inch-square piece of cheesecloth and tie securely. Immerse in cold water until ready to use.

4. Strain the stock through a strainer lined with several layers of cheesecloth, pressing out all of the juices from the vegetables. Discard the cheesecloth and its contents. Let the stock sit, undisturbed, for about 10 minutes, to allow the fat to rise to the surface. Remove and discard all the fat. Measure the stock and add enough of the strained ham-hock blanching liquid to make 8 quarts. Pour the stock into a pot large enough to hold all the meats and the vegetable packages.

5. Add the brisket and ham hocks. Bring to a boil, lower the heat, and simmer for 15 minutes. Add the packages with the cabbage and yuca and continue to simmer, covered, for 45 minutes. Add the plantain and carrot packages and the *paio* or sausage, and cook for 20 minutes more. Add the corn and cook for 5 to 10 minutes more, or until tender.

6. Remove the ham hocks and the brisket, cut and discard the strings, and place the meats on a large serving platter or earthenware dish with 4- to 6-inch-high sides. Take out the packages containing the sausage and the vegetables and let the liquid drain back into the pot. Unwrap the sausage and vegetables and arrange them around the brisket and ham hocks. Correct the seasoning of the broth with salt to taste and pour enough hot broth over the meats and vegetables to barely cover them. Sprinkle with chopped cilantro and serve.

Cruzado

—

Serves 6 to 8

In a *cruzado*, beef, chicken, and fish or shellfish are combined with vegetables and served in broth. This Venezuelan soup is a very versatile dish; with just a few simple adjustments you can create several different *cruzados*. (See Variations at end of recipe.)

1 piece brisket of beef or beef shank or chuck (3½ pounds)
1 large frying chicken, with neck, gizzards, and head and feet if
*   available (3½ pounds)*
24 cherrystone or littleneck clams (about 3 pounds)

AROMATICS

2 large onions, unpeeled and cut into quarters (1 pound)
1 large carrot, washed and cut into 3 pieces
4 stalks celery with leafy tops, washed and chopped
12 cloves garlic, crushed
1 jalapeño pepper or 1 dried red chili pepper
18 sprigs fresh thyme
1 bay leaf
12 cloves
2 tablespoons coarse salt

VEGETABLES

1 small Savoy cabbage (about 1½ pounds)
8 small white or red new potatoes (about 1 pound)
3 large ears corn, husked, silk removed, and cut into 6 or more pieces

2 tablespoons chopped fresh cilantro leaves or Italian parsley

1. Wipe the beef with a damp cloth and trim off any excess fat. Roll and tie the meat tightly. Wipe the chicken inside and out with a damp cloth; truss as described on page 257. Using a vegetable brush, scrape the sand off the clamshells. Rinse several times, and keep the clams submerged in plenty of cold water until ready to use.

2. In a stockpot, combine the brisket and the neck, giblets (not the liver), and head and feet, if available, of the chicken with the onions, carrot, celery, garlic, hot pepper, thyme, bay leaf, cloves, salt, and 4 quarts of water. Bring to a boil, skimming the foam as it rises to the surface. Lower the heat, cover, and simmer for about 2 hours, stirring now and then. Remove the brisket and set aside. Strain the broth through a fine sieve, pressing to extract all the juices from the vegetables. Let the broth sit for about 5 minutes, undisturbed, so that all the fat can rise to the surface; then degrease it thoroughly. Measure the broth: you should have about 13 cups. If not, add enough water to make 13 cups. Correct the seasoning with salt to taste.

3. In a large, clean stockpot, combine the brisket, chicken, cabbage, and the 13 cups of clean broth. Slowly bring to a boil, lower the heat, and simmer, covered, for 45 minutes to 1 hour. Skim the excess fat from the surface of the broth, add the potatoes, and continue cooking until the potatoes are tender, about 30 minutes.

(Continued)

4. Add the corn and clams, making sure that the hinges of the clams are submerged in the hot broth. Cover the pot tightly and continue cooking until the clams start to open, about 8 to 10 minutes.

5. Remove from the heat and transfer the meat and chicken to a large serving platter or earthenware casserole. Cut off and discard the trussing strings. Arrange the clams, cabbage, potatoes, and corn around the meats. Correct the seasoning of the broth with salt to taste. Pour the hot broth through a strainer lined with several layers of cheesecloth right over the meats, vegetables, and clams. Sprinkle with the chopped cilantro and serve at once.

VARIATIONS

Omit the chicken and increase the amount of beef to 5 pounds.

Omit the beef and use a 5-pound (instead of a 3½-pound) chicken.

Substitute about 4 pounds of cod, bass, snapper, or other firm-fleshed fish, with skin and bones, for the clams. Cut into serving pieces and add to the broth in place of the clams in Step 4. Cook for about 8 minutes, or until the fish is done.

Chairo
Beef and Vegetable Soup
—
Serves 6 to 8

This Bolivian soup has *chuño,* a dehydrated potato unique to the Andes (see page 366), in it. *Chuño* is available in food specialty stores, both loose in the dry form or canned in brine; the latter is called *chuño-tunta.* Beef is used in this recipe, but *charqui,* or dried llama meat, is more authentic. If you ever find a piece of *charqui,* try it (see Variation at end of recipe).

3½ to 4 pounds chuck
½ teaspoon freshly cracked black pepper
3 stalks celery with leafy tops, washed and cut into pieces
2 medium onions, unpeeled and cut into quarters

1 small head garlic, unpeeled and cut in half horizontally
2 dried mirasol peppers or red chili peppers
1 tablespoon cumin seeds
4 sprigs fresh Italian parsley
1 tablespoon coarse salt
3 quarts Beef Stock (page 462)

VEGETABLES
½ cup barley, rinsed and drained
½ pounds chuño, reconstituted and broken into small pieces
   (optional) (see Note)
1 large onion, peeled and cut into ¼-inch dice
1 carrot, peeled and cut into ¼-inch dice
2 large potatoes, peeled and cut into ¼-inch dice
1 cup canned white hominy, rinsed and drained

2 tablespoons chopped Italian parsley

1. Wipe the meat with a damp cloth and cut into 1½-inch cubes. Place the meat on a baking tray, sprinkle with pepper, and broil it as close to source of heat as possible, turning to brown all sides, for about 10 minutes.

2. In a stockpot, combine the browned chuck, celery, onions, garlic, hot peppers, cumin, parsley, salt, and stock and bring to a boil. Lower the heat and let simmer for about 1½ hours, or until the meat is tender. Remove from the heat, remove the meat, and set aside. Strain the broth through a strainer lined with a double layer of cheesecloth, squeezing and pressing to extract all the juices. Let the broth sit for a few minutes until all of the fat rises to the surface. Degrease thoroughly, discarding the fat. You should have about 9 cups of broth. Correct the seasoning with salt to taste.

3. In a large saucepan or casserole, combine the broth, meat, barley, *chuño*, if using, diced onion, carrot, and potatoes and bring to a boil. Lower the heat and simmer for 10 minutes. Add the hominy and continue cooking for 15 minutes more, or until the vegetables and the barley are tender. Sprinkle with chopped parsley and serve at once.

NOTE Soak the *chuño* in warm water for 2 to 4 hours. Drain well and squeeze gently between towels to extract the excess water. Peel away the outer skin. If using *chuño-tunta*, drain and rinse well, then pat dry.

(Continued)

Soak a piece of *charqui* in cold water for about 4 hours, changing the water several times. When soft, add it to the pot in Step 2. (Omit the cracked pepper and browning in Step 1.) Cook for 1½ hours, then remove from the broth. When the meat is cool enough to handle, shred it with the grain and set aside. Return it to the broth with the hominy in Step 3.

Carbonada Criolla
Carbonade of Beef, Squash, and Peaches

—

Serves 6 to 8

Yellow-fleshed winter squash is used extensively in the cuisine of Argentina, as a vegetable, in desserts, and as a thickener in soups, stews, and other dishes. In this unique dish it is combined with meat, corn, and peaches. *Carbonada criolla* is usually cooked on top of the stove in a casserole, but for a more festive look, it can be baked in a hard-shelled squash or pumpkin, which then serves as a terrine at the table.

4 pounds short ribs or chuck, cut into 2- to 3-inch pieces
½ teaspoon coarsely cracked black pepper
¼ cup plus 1 tablespoon olive oil
¼ cup all-purpose flour
2 tablespoons red-wine vinegar or balsamic vinegar
1 large bunch fresh thyme, coarsely chopped (1 ounce)
8 sprigs fresh oregano, coarsely chopped
4 sprigs Italian parsley, coarsely chopped
1 dried red chili pepper, crumbled
2 carrots, washed and peeled (peels saved), sliced ¼ inch thick on the diagonal
1 large onion, peeled (skins saved) and cut into ¼-inch dice
4 stalks celery, with leafy tops, washed, strings removed, and tops saved, sliced ¼ inch thick on the diagonal
1½ tablespoons cumin seed

4 cloves garlic, crushed
1 bay leaf
2 tablespoons coarse salt
½ cup sherry (optional)
1 large butternut squash, peeled, seeded, and cut into 1½-inch cubes
1 ear corn, husked, silk removed, and cut crosswise into
  8 equal slices
3 large firm peaches, pits removed and cut into quarters
  (about 1 pound)
2 tablespoons chopped fresh cilantro leaves

1. Wipe the meat with a damp cloth and trim off and discard any excess fat. Sprinkle with cracked pepper and set aside.

2. In a large saucepan, heat ¼ cup of the olive oil over high heat and brown the meat on all sides, about 12 minutes. Remove from the pan and set aside. Add the flour to the same pan and cook for 1 minute over medium heat, stirring; do not brown.

3. With a wire whisk, stir in 8 cups of water and the vinegar, while scraping the bottom of the pan. Add the thyme, oregano, parsley, hot pepper, carrot peels, onion skins, celery tops, cumin, and garlic and bring to a boil, stirring. Lower the heat and let simmer for 30 minutes, stirring from time to time.

4. Remove from the heat and strain through a strainer lined with several layers of cheesecloth, squeezing the cheesecloth to extract all the juices; discard the cheesecloth. Measure the stock and add enough water to make 10 cups.

5. Place the browned meat in a stockpot and add the 10 cups of stock. Add the bay leaf and salt and bring to a boil over high heat, skimming the foam as it rises to the surface. Lower the heat, cover the pot, and simmer for 1 hour 15 minutes.

6. Remove from the heat; take out the meat and set it aside. Strain the stock through a strainer lined with a double layer of cheesecloth; discard the cheesecloth. Let the stock sit for a few minutes until all the fat rises to the surface. Degrease thoroughly and discard the fat. Measure the stock: you should have at least 8 cups. If not, add enough water to make 8 cups. Correct the seasoning with salt to taste. Set aside.

(Continued)

7. In a casserole over high heat, heat the remaining tablespoon of olive oil. Add the onion and sauté until the pieces start to get golden around the edges, about 3 minutes. Add the sherry, if using, and continue cooking until all the liquor has evaporated, about 2 minutes. Add the meat, carrot slices, celery slices, and reserved stock and bring to a boil, skimming the foam as it rises to the surface. Lower the heat and simmer for 10 minutes. Add the squash pieces, cover the casserole, and cook for 15 minutes. Add the corn and peaches and cook for 10 to 15 minutes longer, or until all the vegetables and fruit are tender. Sprinkle with chopped cilantro leaves and serve at once.

VARIATION

This dish may be baked in a large pumpkin. Omit the butternut squash called for in the recipe. While the meat is cooking (Step 5), preheat the oven to 375 degrees. Wash a 10- to 12-pound pumpkin under cold running water. With a sharp knife, cut out a lid about 6 to 8 inches in diameter, leaving the stem intact to use as a handle. Lift off the lid. With a large spoon, scrape out and discard the seeds and the long, stringy fibers from the lid and the inside of the pumpkin. Brush the underside of the lid and the inside of the pumpkin generously with oil or butter. Place them on a baking sheet and bake for about 45 minutes, or until the flesh is barely tender. Fill the shell with the finished soup, the corn, and the peaches, cover with the lid, and continue baking for 20 minutes longer. Remove the pumpkin from the oven, transfer to a serving platter, and serve from the pumpkin.

Caldo de Patita
Calves' Feet and Peanut Soup

Serves 6 to 8

Calves' feet are enjoyed throughout South America. This soup, in which they are combined with peanuts, is unique to Ecuador, though.

The appeal of calves' feet is their wonderful gelatinous quality. In this recipe, it is made even more pronounced by putting the bones back into the stock after the meat is tender and has been removed from the bones. This second, slow cooking melts the remaining gelatin into the broth, making it very thick and sleek.

5 calves' feet (about 8½ pounds)
4 stalks celery, washed and cut into large pieces
1 carrot, washed and cut into 3 pieces
1 large leek, with green parts, washed and cut into large pieces
2 medium onions, cut into quarters
1 jalapeño pepper
8 cloves
2 teaspoons coriander seed
1 bay leaf
2 heads garlic, unpeeled and cut in half, horizontally
4 sprigs fresh mint
4 sprigs Italian parsley
2 tablespoons coarse salt
4 quarts Veal Stock (page 464) or Chicken Stock (page 461)
   or a combination of both
1 yuca, peeled, washed, cored, and cut into 1½-inch cubes (1 pound)

BOUQUET GARNI
1 medium bunch fresh thyme (½ ounce)
6 sprigs fresh dill
1 dried mirasol or red chili pepper, crumbled
3 to 4 celery tops

⅓ cup unsalted peanuts, roasted (page 485)
1 cup canned white hominy, rinsed and drained
2 tablespoons heavy cream
2 tablespoons chopped fresh cilantro leaves

1. Wipe the calves' feet with a damp cloth.

2. In a stockpot, combine the calves' feet, celery, carrot, leek, onions, hot pepper, cloves, coriander seeds, bay leaf, garlic, mint, parsley, salt, stock, and 2 cups of water. Bring to a boil, skimming the foam as it rises to the surface. Lower the heat and let simmer, covered, stirring now and then, for 1½ hours. Remove from the heat, take out the calves' feet, and while they are still hot, cut and scrape off all the meat from the bones. Slice the meat into bite-size pieces, set aside, and place the bones back into the stock.

3. Continue to simmer the stock with the bones, covered, for another 1½ to 2 hours. Remove from the heat and strain the stock through a strainer, pressing to extract all the juices from the vegetables, herbs,

(Continued)

and spices; discard them along with the bones. Let the stock sit for a few minutes until all the fat rises to the surface; then degrease it. While the stock is still hot, strain through a strainer lined with a double layer of cheesecloth and discard. Measure the broth: you should have 8 cups. If not, add enough extra stock or water to make 8 cups. Set aside.

4. Blend 3 pieces of cubed yuca and 1 cup of broth in the jar of an electric blender until smooth. Wrap and tie the thyme, dill, hot pepper, and celery tops in a 10-inch-square piece of cheesecloth.

5. In a stockpot, combine the remaining 7 cups of veal broth and the yuca mixture, well mixed, and bring to a boil, while stirring. Lower the heat, add the bouquet garni and the remaining yuca pieces, and simmer for 30 minutes.

6. Add the peanuts and hominy and continue cooking for 10 minutes more. Remove the bouquet garni, squeezing out the juices, and discard. Add the meat and heat through thoroughly. Correct the seasoning with salt to taste. Just before serving, mix in the heavy cream and sprinkle with chopped cilantro. Serve hot.

NOTE   A 16-ounce can of hominy yields 2 to 2½ cups. Save the leftover hominy for another purpose, or if you are fond of hominy, add the entire amount to the soup.

VARIATION

Substitute the same number of pigs' feet or ham hocks for the calves' feet without changing anything else in the recipe.

Cazuela de Pollo con Hinojo
Cazuela with Chicken and Fennel
—
Serves 6 to 8

A *cazuela* is an earthenware casserole; in Chile it is also the name of the soup that is cooked in it. For this dish, the best chicken to use is a hen, either whole or cut up. You could also use game birds, such as pheasant, wild turkey, partridge, grouse, or quail; just allow them more time to cook.

Fennel, with its light and delicate licorice flavor, is perfect in this dish, but you could replace it or add to it with celery, leeks, chayotes, corn, or even cabbage. Whole hot peppers are used in this recipe, not only to give heat to the soup but to serve as a condiment with the dish. If your hot peppers have little or no bite, increase the amount and serve one per person with the other vegetables.

1 stewing hen (about 5½ pounds)

BOUQUET GARNI
1-inch piece fresh ginger, thinly sliced
16 sprigs fresh thyme
8 sprigs fresh dill

1 piece yuca (about 10 ounces)
4 large fennel bulbs (about 3 pounds)
6 to 8 small red or white new potatoes (about 1¼ pounds)
3 tablespoons olive oil
1 large clove garlic, peeled and minced
5 large tomatoes, peeled, seeded, and minced, juices saved
 (about 2½ pounds)
1 teaspoon ground fennel
1 cup dry sherry
2 tablespoons coarse salt
1 or 2 jalapeño peppers
2 tablespoons chopped fresh dill or feathery green fennel tops

1. Rinse the hen inside and out and wipe dry. Wrap and tie the ginger, thyme, and dill in a 10-inch-square piece of cheesecloth. Place the bouquet garni into the cavity and truss as directed on page 257. Set aside.

2. Peel the yuca and cut into quarters lengthwise. Remove and discard the fibrous cord with a sharp paring knife. Chop the yuca. Pour 2 cups of water into the jar of an electric blender, add the yuca pieces, and blend thoroughly at top speed for a minute or so. Strain the liquidized yuca through a fine sieve or a strainer lined with a double layer of cheesecloth. Add 2 more cups of water to the yuca pulp in the sieve or cheesecloth and strain again. Press against the sieve or gather the cheesecloth and squeeze to extract all the extra juices from the pulp. Save the yuca liquid and set aside. Discard the cheesecloth and the pulp.

(Continued)

3. Trim off the feathery green tops and wash the fennel. Save some of the young feathery tops, if they are to be used as garnish; discard the rest. Cut the fennel in half lengthwise and place in a bowl of cold water. Set aside. Scrub and wash the potatoes. Add them to the cold water with the fennel, and let them sit until ready to use.

4. In a stockpot, heat the olive oil. Add the garlic (do not brown), the tomatoes with their juices, and the fennel and stir. Cook over medium heat for about 10 minutes, stirring constantly. Add the sherry and continue cooking, stirring, until all the liquid has evaporated, about 4 minutes. Thoroughly mix the yuca liquid and add, along with 8 cups of water, salt, and hot peppers. Bring to a boil, stirring constantly. Lower the heat, cover, and simmer for 15 minutes, skimming the foam as it rises to the surface.

5. Immerse the hen in the broth, bring back to a boil, lower the heat, and simmer gently, covered, for about 1 hour. Add the potatoes. Cook for 10 minutes. Add the fennel halves. Cook for 15 minutes, or until all the vegetables are tender.

6. Transfer the hen to a large serving bowl, tureen, or casserole. Cut and discard the trussing strings. Remove and discard the bouquet garni from the cavity of the chicken. With a slotted spoon, remove the vegetables from the broth and arrange them around the hen. Correct the seasoning of the broth with salt to taste and pour over the hen and the vegetables. Sprinkle with chopped dill and serve. Or serve individually: place a piece of chicken in a large soup plate or soup bowl, arrange 1 piece of fennel and 1 potato around it, fill the plate or bowl with hot broth, sprinkle with the chopped dill, and serve.

VARIATIONS

Substitute a 3½-pound chicken for the hen. Simmer for only 25 minutes before adding the potatoes in Step 5.

Add 2 cups of cooked or canned beans to the soup 10 minutes before it is ready. White, canary, lima, or fava beans and chick-peas are all suitable. If using canned beans, rinse them under cold running water and drain first.

Canja
Brazilian Chicken Soup with Rice

Serves 6 to 8

One of the most popular soups in Brazil is *canja,* or chicken soup with rice. Chicken soup, in fact, is overwhelmingly popular all over the continent. Every home has its version, from the simplest—chicken cooked in water with aromatic vegetables and herbs—to very complex dishes made with stock, carefully selected vegetables, and beans, grain, or pasta.

Northern Brazilian cooking is characterized by the use of the malagueta pepper and, most important, *dendê,* or palm, oil. It is a dense and yellowish oil. You can use the more readily available jalapeño pepper and olive oil, but do try to get the others. They will give an authentic Bahian flavor to the soup.

4 whole chicken breasts (about 4½ pounds)
6 tablespoons olive oil
1 large onion, unpeeled and coarsely chopped
1 large carrot, washed and coarsely chopped
2 stalks celery, with leafy tops, washed and coarsely chopped
1-inch piece fresh ginger, chopped
1 bay leaf
1 malagueta or jalapeño pepper, chopped
2 cloves garlic, unpeeled and crushed
1 small ear corn, husked, silks removed, and cut into 8 equal slices
  (save and chop 5 of the most tender husks)
1 small sprig fresh rosemary (optional)
2 tablespoons coarse salt
1 tablespoon dendê or olive oil
1 clove garlic, peeled and minced
1⅓ cups rice, rinsed and drained (do not use instant rice)
2 tablespoons chopped fresh cilantro leaves

1. Wipe the chicken breasts with a damp cloth. Remove the skins, debone the breasts, and cut them in half lengthwise. Set aside chicken breasts, skins, and bones.

(Continued)

2. In a saucepan, heat the olive oil over medium heat. Add the chicken breasts, skin side down first, and brown until golden on all sides, about 12 to 14 minutes. Remove them from the pan and set aside.

3. Place the skins and bones in the same saucepan and brown over medium heat until totally golden, about 8 minutes. Push the skins and bones to one side and add the onion, carrot, celery, ginger, bay leaf, hot pepper, and crushed garlic. Stir and sauté for about 5 minutes.

4. Add the chopped corn husks, rosemary sprig, if using, 1 tablespoon of the salt, and 3 quarts of water and bring to a boil, while stirring and scraping the bottom of the pan. Lower the heat, cover, and let simmer for 45 minutes.

5. Remove from the heat and strain through a fine sieve. Discard the contents of the sieve and let the strained stock sit for a few minutes so that all the fat rises to the surface. Degrease the stock and discard the fat. Strain the stock again through a strainer lined with several layers of cheesecloth; discard the cheesecloth. Measure the stock; you should have about 8 cups. If not, add enough water to make 8 cups. Set aside.

6. In a saucepan, heat the *dendê* oil and the minced garlic over medium heat. Do not brown the garlic. Add the rice and sauté, stirring, for about 2 to 3 minutes. Add the remaining tablespoon of salt and reserved 8 cups of stock and bring to a boil. Lower the heat, cover, and cook for 35 minutes.

7. Add the browned chicken breasts with the accumulated juices and the corn slices and continue cooking for another 5 minutes, or until the corn is tender and chicken has heated through thoroughly. Correct the seasoning with salt to taste. Sprinkle with chopped cilantro and serve.

VARIATION

Cut a 3½-pound chicken into serving pieces. Use all the parts except the liver but including the head and feet, if available. The skin of the feet should be peeled. If they are not, pass the feet over an open flame to char them. Then rub off the skin with a clean cloth.

Bori-Bori
Paraguayan Dumpling Soup
—
Serves 6 to 8

Bori-bori, a specialty of Paraguay, is, at its simplest, broth with dumplings. Sometimes, as in this recipe, chunks of meat are added as well. The dumplings are made with cornmeal and cheese. Although I have suggested parmesan in this recipe, any good hard cheese will do.

2 pounds chuck or beef shank or brisket of beef
1 teaspoon coarsely ground black pepper
2 tablespoons olive oil
4 ounces bacon, chopped
1 large onion, unpeeled, cut into quarters
1 head garlic, unpeeled, cut in half horizontally
3 stalks celery, with leafy tops, washed and cut in half
1 medium carrot, washed and cut in half
1 bay leaf
6 to 8 cloves
1 tablespoon coarse salt

DUMPLINGS
1 cup white or yellow cornmeal
1 cup grated Parmesan
2 teaspoons coarse salt
1 small onion, peeled and minced (about ½ cup)
¼ cup Clarified Butter (page 476)
1 egg
1 egg yolk

⅛ teaspoon saffron (optional)
2 tablespoons chopped Italian parsley
Grated Parmesan

1. Wipe the meat with a damp cloth and cut into 2-inch cubes. Sprinkle with black pepper.

2. In a large saucepan or sauté pan, heat the olive oil and bacon over medium heat. Sauté until the bacon has released most of its fat, about

(Continued)

1 minute. Add the meat cubes and brown on all sides, about 8 to 10 minutes. Add the onion, garlic, celery, carrot, bay leaf, cloves, 1 tablespoon of salt, and 3½ quarts of water and bring to a boil. Lower the heat, cover, and let simmer for 1½ hours, or until the meat is tender.

3. Remove the pot from the heat; remove the meat and set aside. Strain the stock through a fine sieve, pressing to extract all the juices from the vegetables; discard the vegetables. Let the stock sit for a few minutes. Degrease thoroughly, then pour the stock through a strainer lined with several layers of cheesecloth. Discard the cheesecloth and measure the stock; you should have 10 cups. If not, add enough water to make 10 cups. Set aside.

4. Meanwhile, in a bowl, combine the cornmeal, Parmesan, and 2 teaspoons of salt and mix well. Add the minced onion and butter and, with your fingers or a fork, incorporate all the ingredients well. Make a well in the center and place the egg and egg yolk in it. Mix with a fork until the eggs have been thoroughly absorbed. With your hands, knead all the ingredients right in the bowl for a minute or so, until you have a smooth and compact dough. Tightly cover the dough with a piece of plastic wrap and let it rest at room temperature, undisturbed, for about 30 minutes or more.

5. Divide the dough into 30 equal portions (each 1 scant tablespoonful), and with the palms of your hands, gently roll each portion into a small dumpling.

6. In a large saucepan, bring 3 quarts of water to a boil. Lower the heat to a gentle simmer, drop the dumplings into the water, and let cook for 15 minutes. Remove them from the water with a slotted spoon and set aside.

7. In a large pot or sauté pan, bring the reserved 10 cups of broth to a boil, adding saffron, if using. Lower the heat and add the meat; cook for 15 minutes and correct the seasoning with salt to taste. Gently place the dumplings into the broth and continue simmering 15 minutes more. Serve the soup at once sprinkled with chopped parsley. Pass Parmesan at the table.

Caldo de Bolas
Ecuadorian Dumpling Soup

Serves 6 to 8

*B*olas are small filled dumplings. In this soup they are made with plantains, which produce a smooth, rich dough that is neutral enough to set off various fillings. This recipe calls for a meat filling, but vegetables and seafood are often used. (See Variation at end of recipe.) You can add extra flavors and colors to the filling once it is cooked with such extras as hard-boiled eggs, slivered black olives, peanuts or walnuts, and chopped fresh herbs.

4 green plantains (about 2½ pounds)
1 tablespoon seedless raisins
¼ cup Amontillado sherry or rum
1 dried red chili pepper, seeded
1 large clove garlic, peeled
3 tablespoons olive oil or Achiote Oil (page 472)
4 ounces bacon, minced
1 large onion, peeled and finely chopped (1½ cups)
1 small carrot, peeled and grated (⅓ cup)
2 teaspoons Spanish paprika (see Note)
2 small tomatoes, peeled, seeded (juices saved), and finely chopped
3 tablespoons coarse salt
¼ pound ground veal or chicken or lean beef or pork
4 quarts Chicken Stock (page 461) or Veal Stock (page 464)
1 small sprig fresh rosemary or 10 sprigs fresh thyme or oregano
3 leafy celery tops
1¼-inch slice fresh ginger, cut on the diagonal (optional)
¼ cup freshly grated parmesan
1 whole egg plus 1 egg yolk
2 tablespoons unsalted butter, softened
1 bay leaf
2 tablespoons chopped Italian parsley

(Continued)

1. Peel the plantains and put them in a bowl of cold water. Set aside.

2. In a cup, place the raisins with the sherry or rum to soak. Set aside.

3. Mince the hot pepper and garlic together. Set aside.

4. In a skillet, heat the olive oil over low heat. Add the bacon and sauté, stirring, until the bacon has released most of its fat and starts to get golden around the edges, about 3 minutes. Stir in the hot pepper-garlic mixture; add the onion, carrot, and paprika, if using, and sauté, stirring now and then, for about 10 minutes, or until the onion is translucent.

5. Add the raisins, together with the sherry or rum, and continue cooking until all the liquor has evaporated. Add the tomatoes, with their juices, and 1 tablespoon of the salt. Cook, while stirring, until the liquid had evaporated, about 10 minutes.

6. Mix in the ground meat and cook for 10 minutes more, stirring now and then. Remove from the heat; strain the contents of the skillet through a fine sieve or strainer into a bowl and let drain, pressing gently to extract most of the oil and juices. Reserve both the oil and the meat. Set aside.

7. Meanwhile, in a large enameled sauté pan, bring 8 cups of the stock to a boil together with the rosemary, celery tops, ginger, if using, and 1 tablespoon of the salt. Remove the peeled plantains from the water and add them to the boiling stock. Lower the heat and let simmer, covered, for about 40 to 45 minutes, or until the plantains are soft. Remove from the heat; remove the plantains, saving the stock.

8. Place the piping-hot plantains in the work bowl of a food processor together with the reserved oil, the cheese, and the remaining 1 tablespoon of salt. Process for about 1 minute, or until you have a totally smooth dough. Transfer the dough to a stainless-steel bowl and let cool. When cool, incorporate the egg and the egg yolk with a rubber spatula until they are totally absorbed. Knead in the butter.

9. Divide the dough into 16 equal portions. Place 1 portion in the palm of your hand, and with your hand slightly cupped, flatten the dough into a circle 3 to 3½ inches in diameter; form a well in the center. Place 1 tablespoonful of filling in the middle and close the dough over the filling by pinching the edges together. Gently roll between your palms to shape into a perfectly smooth ball. Repeat this process until all the dumplings are assembled.

10. Strain the reserved stock in which the plantains were cooked through a strainer lined with several layers of cheesecloth. Add enough of the remaining chicken stock to make about 13 cups.

11. In a pan just large enough to hold the 16 dumplings comfortably, bring the stock with the bay leaf to a boil. Correct the seasoning with salt to taste. Lower the heat, carefully drop all the *bolas* into the stock, and simmer gently, without boiling, for 10 minutes. Remove from the heat. Serve the *bolas* in the broth. Sprinkle with chopped parsley.

NOTE   Omit the paprika if achiote oil is used.

VARIATION

Substitute ½ pound of peeled, cleaned, and chopped shrimp for the ground meat. Add to the onion mixture in Step 6 but cook for only 1 minute, not 10 as for meat. Remove from heat and proceed with the recipe.

SEAFOOD SOUPS

Chupe de Camarones
Shrimp Chowder

Serves 6 to 8

This invigorating soup is one of the most vibrant of the *chupes,* or chowders. All parts of the shrimp are used to create an incredible bouquet and bring out the flavor of the shrimp to its fullest.

2 pounds jumbo shrimp, peeled and deveined, shells saved
    (8 to 10 shrimp per pound)
1 yuca or 2 potatoes (1 pound)
3 tablespoons olive oil
3 large cloves garlic, peeled and finely chopped
4 leeks, white parts only, washed and chopped
5 or 6 celery tops, washed and chopped
2 teaspoons annatto seed
2 teaspoons fennel
1/8 teaspoon cayenne
1 tablespoon coarse salt
4 tablespoons all-purpose flour
8 cups whole milk
6 sprigs fresh thyme
4 tablespoons Clarified Butter (page 476)
18 pearl onions, peeled (page 484), or 1 pound frozen pearl onions,
    thawed and drained
1/4 cup heavy cream, at room temperature
1/4 cup chopped fresh dill or Italian parsley or cilantro leaves

1. Rinse the shrimp and drain well. Crush or chop the shells and heads, if any, and set aside. Slice each shrimp on the diagonal into 3 pieces.

2. Peel and wash the yuca and cut into quarters lengthwise. With a sharp paring knife, remove and discard the fibrous cord and cut the yuca into ½-inch cubes. Place them in a bowl of cold water and set aside until ready to use. If using potatoes, peel them and dice into ½-inch cubes. Keep the cubes in cold water until ready to use.

3. In an enameled or stainless-steel saucepan, heat the olive oil. Add the garlic, leeks, and celery tops; stir and sauté for a few seconds. Add the annatto and fennel, cayenne, and salt. Sauté, stirring, until the leeks are totally wilted. Do not brown.

4. Sprinkle in the flour and cook, stirring, for a few seconds. Add the chopped shrimp shells and heads. Stir in the milk, scraping the bottom of the pan. Add the thyme sprigs and bring to a boil, stirring. Lower the heat and simmer for about 10 minutes, stirring now and then.

5. Remove the pan from the heat. Strain the contents through a fine sieve or a strainer lined with a double layer of cheesecloth, pressing the shells and vegetables against the sides of the sieve or strainer to extract all the juices; discard.

6. Pour the strained flavored milk into a clean enameled saucepan. Add the yuca or potatoes, bring to a boil, and cook for another 15 minutes for yuca, 10 minutes for potatoes, over low heat, or until tender. Remove from the heat and keep hot.

7. In an enameled or stainless-steel sauté pan or earthenware casserole, heat the butter and quickly sauté the pearl onions until they are soft and lightly golden all around. Push the onions to the sides of the pan. Add the shrimp to the center and quickly sauté them over high heat for 1 minute, stirring. Pour in the hot soup; let heat through, while stirring, and mix in the heavy cream. Correct the seasoning with salt to taste, sprinkle with the chopped dill, and serve at once.

VARIATION

Chupe de Langosta
Lobster Chowder

—

Substitute 3 live lobsters, about 1½ pounds each, for the shrimp. Cut them up with a knife, separating the bodies from the tails. Cut the tails, shells and all, in half; remove and crack the claws and set aside with the tails. Crush and chop the bodies and legs to use in place of the shrimp shells for the broth in Step 4. Add the tails and claws with the sautéed pearl onions in Step 7. Cook, stirring, for a few minutes, just long enough to heat and firm up the lobster meat. Proceed with the recipe.

Chupe de Cangrejo
Crabmeat Chowder

—

Serves 6 to 8

For this recipe, I suggest using lump crabmeat, which is readily available, but you can make the chowder with soft-shell crabs when in season. They are at their very best when you clean them yourself just minutes before dropping them into the soup.

1 pound fresh lump crabmeat
1 piece yuca (about ½ pound)
6 cups Fish Stock (page 466) or Chicken Stock (page 461)
2 tablespoons olive oil
1 large clove garlic, peeled and minced
1 large onion, peeled and finely chopped (1½ cups)
½ teaspoon ground cumin
⅛ teaspoon ground mace
½ cup light beer
1 dried red chili pepper, seeded
1 large potato, peeled and cut into ¼-inch cubes
2 leeks, white parts only, thinly sliced (about 1 cup)
1 cup cooked or canned chick-peas or hominy or white beans
*   or lima beans (see Note)*
½ cup heavy cream or half-and-half
1 tablespoon fresh thyme leaves

1. Handling the crabmeat gently and as little as possible to prevent the lumps from falling apart, check for and discard any bits of cartilage or shell. Set aside.

2. Peel the yuca and cut into quarters lengthwise. Remove and discard the fibrous cord with a sharp paring knife. Chop the yuca. Add 2 cups of the stock to the jar of an electric blender, add the chopped yuca, and blend at top speed for a minute or so. Pour the liquidized yuca through a fine sieve or a strainer lined with two layers of cheesecloth, pressing out all the juices from the pulp. Discard the pulp and set the yuca liquid aside until ready to use.

3. In a saucepan, heat the olive oil over medium heat. Add the garlic, onion, cumin, and mace and sauté until the onion is translucent, about 2 to 3 minutes. Add the beer and cook until all of the beer has evaporated, about 3 minutes. Stir the yuca liquid thoroughly and add, together with the remaining 4 cups of stock. Add the hot pepper and, while stirring, bring to a boil. Lower the heat and simmer for 5 minutes.

4. Add the potato and leeks and cook until the potato is tender, about 12 minutes. Add the chick-peas and cook for 2 minutes longer. Stir in the heavy cream and season with salt to taste. Gently fold in the crabmeat, sprinkle with thyme leaves, and serve at once.

NOTE   If canned chick-peas, hominy, or beans are used, place them in a strainer, rinse under cold running water, and let drain thoroughly.

VARIATION

Allow 1 soft-shell crab per person. To clean the crabs, use kitchen shears to cut off the face, including the eyes, and remove the tail. Lift up the apron, and remove the feathery gills. For easier serving, cut each crab in half lengthwise. (Or have the fishmonger clean the crabs for you.) Add the crabs with the chick-peas or beans and cook for a few minutes. Proceed with the recipe.

Chupe de Loco
Chilean Clam Chowder

Serves 6 to 8

This wonderful soup from Chile pairs abalones or clams with beans. In Chile, *chupes* are made with a variety of fish and shellfish. Besides shrimp, clams and abalones (called *locos*) are used. For this recipe, I have used small quahogs, but if abalone comes your way, by all means drop it in the soup pot. Use the same amount of abalone as clams, but cut it into bite-size pieces.

1 pound dried white beans (2½ cups)
1 quart shucked cherrystone clams, with their liquor
1½ to 2 pounds fish heads and bones, from cod, bass, flounder, or any other lean fish, chopped
2 stalks celery with leafy tops, washed and chopped
1 leek, with some green parts, washed and chopped
1 small carrot, washed and chopped
1-inch piece fresh ginger, chopped
3 sprigs fresh mint
8 sprigs fresh oregano
2 teaspoons fennel seed or 8 cloves
2 dried red chili peppers, crumbled
3 large tomatoes, peeled (skins saved), seeded (seeds and juices saved), and minced
2 tablespoons olive oil
2 cloves garlic, peeled and minced
2 tablespoons chopped Italian parsley

1. Place the beans in a colander and rinse them under cold running water. Soak them overnight or for 8 to 10 hours in 8 cups of water.

2. Place the soaked beans in a saucepan with the soaking water and bring to a boil. Lower the heat and let simmer over very low heat for about 35 minutes, or until the beans are tender but still retain their shape. Drain them and save both beans and water. You should have about 3 cups of water. Set aside.

3. Meanwhile, place the clams in a colander or strainer over a bowl to separate the clams and liquor. Set the clams aside. Measure the clam liquor, adding enough bean water and plain water, if necessary, to make a total of 5 cups. Set aside.

4. In a small stockpot or saucepan, combine the fish heads and bones, celery, leek, carrot, ginger, mint, oregano, fennel, hot peppers, and the reserved tomato skins, seeds, and juices. Add the 5 cups of clam and bean liquor and bring to a boil, skimming the foam as it rises to the surface. Lower the heat and let simmer gently for 20 to 25 minutes, stirring now and then.

5. Remove from the heat, let cool slightly, and strain through a strainer lined with a double layer of cheesecloth, pressing or squeezing to extract all the juices. Discard the contents of the strainer and save the fish stock. You should have 4 cups or more.

6. Combine 4 cups of the cooked beans with 4 cups of fish stock in an electric blender and blend in several batches until totally smooth. Strain the blended beans through a fine sieve to remove the skins, pressing to extract all the juices; discard the pulp. In an enameled saucepan, combine the strained blended beans with the remaining whole beans and heat the soup thoroughly over low heat, while stirring, or heat and keep hot in a double boiler until ready to serve.

7. In a saucepan, heat the olive oil over high heat. Add the garlic and stir. Add the minced tomatoes and cook for 10 minutes, stirring, until all the liquid has evaporated. Push the tomato mixture around the edges of the pan; place the clams in the middle and quickly toss just to sear them, then mix with the tomatoes. This should not take more than a few seconds. Mix in the hot bean soup and correct the seasoning with salt to taste. Sprinkle with chopped parsley and serve at once.

Mariscada de Mejillones y Almejas
Mariscada of Mussels and Clams

Serves 6 to 8

There are as many kinds of mariscadas, or shellfish soups, as there are mollusks and crustaceans in the sea. This one has clams and mussels, but you could use shrimp, crayfish, or periwinkles.

What really counts in a mariscada is freshness. Fresh shellfish still has the sweet smell of the sea on it. Both clams and mussels feel heavy when fresh, and their shells should be tightly closed. If not, they should close when tapped; discard any that do not.

All shellfish is extremely perishable and should be used within a day of purchase. If it must be stored, place the pieces between moistened towels in the refrigerator.

24 clams
24 mussels
2 tablespoons olive oil
2 large cloves garlic, peeled and minced
1 large onion, peeled and cut into ¼-inch dice
2 bay leaves
2 large tomatoes, peeled, seeded, and minced
1 teaspoon Spanish paprika
1 tablespoon coarse salt
6 cups Fish Stock (page 466) or Chicken Stock (page 461)
1 or 2 jalapeño peppers, quartered lengthwise and seeded (optional)
4 tablespoons chopped cilantro leaves or Italian parsley

1. Clean the clams as described on page 486. Spread them out on a tray, cover with a damp cloth, and set aside until ready to use.

2. Clean the mussels as described on page 486. Set them aside, covered with a damp cloth, until ready to use.

3. In a large sauté pan or earthenware casserole with a tight-fitting lid, heat the olive oil. Add the garlic, onion, and bay leaves and sauté, stirring, until the onion is barely translucent, about 4 minutes. Add the minced tomatoes, paprika, and salt and cook over medium heat, stirring now and then, for 5 minutes. Add the stock and hot peppers, if using, and bring to a boil. Lower the heat and simmer for 5 minutes. Correct the seasoning with salt to taste.

4. Arrange the clams and mussels in the bottom of the pan, burying their hinges in the liquid. Cover the pan tightly and cook over high heat until both the clams and mussels have barely opened, about 5 to 10 minutes. Do not overcook. Remove from the heat, sprinkle with chopped cilantro, and serve immediately.

Caldito de Pescado
Chilean Fish Soup

—

Serves 6 to 8

*C*aldito de Pescado, a simple fish soup popular along the Chilean coast, is basically no more than fish and/or shellfish stewed in a good fish stock. Corn, potatoes, squash, beans, and grains are often added to the *caldito*. In this recipe, I've added only potatoes, but I've enriched the broth with an *aderezo* of ripe tomatoes and onions and, of course, a jalapeño or two for heat.

1 whole cod, blackfish, snapper, bass, or hake, with head and tail, cleaned (about 6 pounds)
2 large onions, unpeeled and quartered
1 carrot, washed and chopped
4 stalks celery, with leafy tops, washed and chopped
6 cloves garlic, crushed
16 sprigs fresh thyme or 3 sprigs Italian parsley
4 sprigs fresh dill
1 bay leaf
8 cloves
12 black peppercorns
½ teaspoon fennel seed
1 tablespoon coarse salt
2 tablespoons olive oil
1 medium onion, peeled and thinly sliced
4 medium tomatoes, peeled, seeded (juices saved), and minced
1 or 2 jalapeño peppers, seeded and julienned, or ⅛ teaspoon cayenne
8 small white or red potatoes (about 1 pound)
2 tablespoons chopped fresh dill or Italian parsley

1. Remove and discard the gills from the head of the fish and wipe inside and out with a damp cloth. Cut the head, tail, and fins away from the body and cut the fish into 6 to 8 serving pieces. Set aside.

2. Place the head, tail, and fins in a stockpot. Add the onions, carrot, celery, garlic, thyme, dill, bay leaf, cloves, peppercorns, fennel seeds, salt, and 7 cups of water. Bring to a boil; lower the heat and simmer, covered, for 25 minutes.

3. Remove from the heat and let cool slightly. Pour the broth through a fine sieve, pressing out all the juices from the vegetables and fish parts; discard them, saving the fish stock. Set aside.

4. In a large sauté pan or earthenware casserole, or *cazuela*, heat the olive oil over medium heat. Add the thinly sliced onion and sauté, stirring, until the onion has softened, about 1 or 2 minutes. Add the minced tomatoes and juices and the hot peppers, and continue cooking, stirring now and then, for 8 minutes. Add the fish broth and bring to a boil; correct the seasoning with salt to taste.

5. Add the potatoes, lower the heat, and simmer gently for 35 minutes, or until the potatoes are nearly done. Add the fish pieces and continue to simmer (do not let boil), covered, for 8 minutes longer, or until the fish is barely done. Remove from the heat, sprinkle with chopped dill, and serve at once.

Caldo de Bagre
Catfish Soup

—

Serves 6 to 8

*C*aldo de bagre is a favorite soup in Ecuador. It consists of a delicate light broth in which *bagre*, or catfish, is poached, along with one or more vegetables. Catfish is a white, firm-fleshed fish. Any kind—saltwater or freshwater, wild or farmed—can be used for this soup, as can other white, firm-fleshed fish, such as cod, bass, or sea trout. Whatever fish you use, be sure to leave the bones and skin. They will add depth to the broth, and the skin will keep the fish from falling apart as it cooks.

2 small or 1 large catfish (4 to 4½ pounds)
1 large onion, peeled and chopped
1 head garlic, unpeeled and cut in half horizontally
3 stalks celery, with leafy tops, washed and chopped
1 small carrot, peeled and chopped
1 leek, with some green parts, washed and chopped
½-inch piece fresh ginger, sliced
1 or 2 jalapeño peppers, cut in half
1 tablespoon coarse salt
3 sprigs Italian parsley
1 small bunch fresh thyme (½ ounce)
2 large sprigs fresh tarragon or cilantro
5 sprigs fresh oregano or dill
6 cloves
1 yuca, peeled, cored, and cut into 12 2½-inch pieces (1 pound)
8 medium white or red potatoes (2 pounds)
2 chayotes, peeled, cut into 8 equal wedges, and seed removed (1 pound)
1 acorn squash or butternut squash with or without skin, cut into 8 equal wedges and seeded (about 1½ to 2 pounds)
½-inch piece lemon or lime rind
2 tablespoons chopped Italian parsley or fresh cilantro leaves

1. Wipe the fish inside and out with a damp cloth. Cut off and save the fins and tails. Separate the heads from the bodies. Remove and discard the gills; with the help of a cleaver, chop the heads and set aside. Cut the fish bodies crosswise into 6 to 8 equal pieces. Set aside.

2. In a small stockpot, combine the onion, garlic, celery, carrot, leek, ginger, hot peppers, salt, parsley, thyme, tarragon, oregano, cloves, the fish heads, tails, and fins, and 3 quarts water. Bring to a boil, lower the heat, and simmer for about 25 minutes.

3. Remove from the heat and pour through a strainer, pressing to extract all the juices. Discard the contents of the strainer; clean the stock again by pouring it through a strainer lined with a double layer of cheesecloth into an earthenware casserole or a sauté pan.

4. Place the casserole or sauté pan over high heat; add the yuca and potatoes and bring to a boil. Lower the heat, cover the casserole or saucepan, and simmer gently until the yuca and potatoes are almost tender, about 30 to 35 minutes.

5. Add the chayote and squash wedges, cover, and continue cooking for 10 minutes longer, or until all the vegetables are done. Correct the seasoning with salt to taste.

6. Add the fish pieces, placing them among the vegetables. Add the lemon rind. Cover and cook for another 4 minutes, or until the fish is done. Remove from the heat, sprinkle with chopped parsley, and serve.

Caldo de Peixe
Brazilian Coconut Soup with Fish

Serves 6 to 8

No cuisine has mastered the coconut as skillfully and imaginatively as that of Brazil. Their *caldo de peixe*, in which fish or shellfish is poached in coconut milk enhanced with tomatoes and onions, is a good example of this remarkable creativity.

3 pounds whole cleaned whiting or catfish fillets or thick cod steaks,
   with bone and skin
1 fresh coconut
3 inner stalks celery, with leafy tops, chopped
1-inch piece fresh ginger, peeled and chopped
3 sprigs fresh oregano or dill
3 sprigs fresh mint
1 bay leaf
2 tablespoons coarse salt
1 piece yuca (about ½ pound)
1 tablespoon olive oil or dendê (palm) oil
1 large clove garlic, peeled and minced
2 large onions, peeled and cut into ¼-inch squares
½ teaspoon sugar
1 teaspoon ground fennel
2 medium tomatoes, peeled, seeded (juices saved), and chopped
1 or 2 jalapeño peppers, seeded and cut lengthwise into quarters or
   eighths
2 tablespoons chopped Italian parsley, dill, or cilantro

1. Wipe the fish with a damp cloth and set aside.

2. With a pointed instrument, such as an ice pick, pierce two of the three soft "eyes" of the coconut. Drain the juice and set it aside. Crack open the nut, peel and discard the thin brown skin from the meat, and chop the meat. You should have about 3 cups. Place 2 cups of water and half of the chopped coconut in the jar of an electric blender and blend at top speed for 1 minute, until totally liquidized. Pour the liquid into an enameled saucepan and repeat with the remaining chopped coconut and another 2 cups of water.

3. Add the celery, ginger, oregano, mint, bay leaf, and salt. Bring to a boil, stir, lower the heat, and simmer very gently, covered, for 20 to 25 minutes.

4. Remove from heat and let cool slightly. Strain through a strainer lined with a single layer of cheesecloth and squeeze all the juices from the coconut pulp to make about 5 cups of coconut broth. Return the broth to the saucepan and set aside. Discard the pulp.

5. Peel the yuca, cut lengthwise into quarters, remove the fibrous cord, and rinse under cold running water. Drain and chop. Measure the reserved coconut juice (*not* the broth) and add enough water to make 1 cup. Pour into the jar of an electric blender, add the yuca pieces, and blend at top speed for 1 minute. Strain in a strainer lined with a single layer of cheesecloth, squeezing to extract all the liquid. Discard the pulp and save the yuca liquid.

6. Stir the yuca liquid well and add it to the saucepan containing the strained coconut broth. Bring to a boil, constantly whisking with a wire whisk, and let cook for 3 minutes. Remove from the heat and set aside.

7. In an earthenware casserole or large sauté pan, heat the olive oil over medium heat. Add the garlic and the onion and sauté, stirring, until the onion starts to turn golden around the edges, about 4 minutes. Sprinkle in the sugar and the fennel and stir; add the chopped tomatoes with the juices and cook for another 5 minutes, stirring, or until most of the liquid has evaporated. Add the reserved coconut broth and the hot peppers and bring to a boil, stirring. Correct the seasoning with salt to taste.

8. Lower the heat, arrange the fish in the broth, cover, and gently simmer (do not boil) for 8 to 10 minutes, or until the fish is barely cooked. Sprinkle the dish with chopped parsley and serve at once.

VEGETABLE SOUPS

Sopa de Yuyo
Sea Greens Soup

—

Serves 6 to 8

I prefer to call *cochayuyo* (*yuyo* for short) and other edible seaweed *sea greens* rather than *seaweed*. Many kinds of sea greens can be found fresh when in season, but they are more commonly used (and more desirable) dried. The best sea greens for soup look like long, thin ribbons and are dark green in color; also good are those that resemble curly, thin ribbons, and are dark green or purplish-red.

Many Oriental and other specialty markets carry a large selection of sea greens. Although the names differ according to their origin, their characteristics do not. For this recipe, I have used what the Japanese call *wakame*, a ribbonlike sea green that, at its best, is very dark green in color. *Alaria,* which is very similar to *wakame,* can also be used. All dried sea greens become somewhat translucent after soaking. Dried sea greens can be stored for a fairly long period of time, tightly covered or wrapped and kept in a container in a cool, dark, dry place.

1 cup dried chick-peas
1½ ounces dried wakame *or* alaria, *reconstituted (see Note)*
1 tablespoon olive oil
4 ounces bacon, thinly sliced
2 large cloves garlic, peeled and minced
½-inch piece fresh ginger, peeled and minced
1 large onion, peeled and thinly sliced (about 2 cups)
1 jalapeño pepper, seeded and julienned
½ teaspoon ground fennel
1 tablespoon coarse salt
4 medium tomatoes, peeled, seeded (juices saved), and minced
2 potatoes, peeled and cut into ½-inch cubes

1. Rinse and drain the dried chick-peas thoroughly. Place them in a bowl and soak them overnight or for 12 hours in 5 cups of cold water. Strain, reserving both the chick-peas and the water: you should have 4 cups. If not, add enough water to make 4 cups. Set aside.

2. Rinse the sea greens and drain well. Cut into 3-inch pieces and set aside.

3. In a small soup kettle, heat the olive oil and bacon over high heat and sauté until the bacon has released most of its fat and starts to get golden around the edges, about 3 minutes. Stir in the garlic and ginger. Add the onion, hot pepper, and fennel and cook for about 1 minute, stirring. Add the tomatoes with the juices and the salt and continue to cook for 10 minutes.

4. Add the chick-peas, potatoes, sea greens, and the reserved soaking liquid and bring to a boil. Lower the heat and simmer gently, stirring now and then, for 40 minutes, or until the chick-peas and the potatoes are tender. Correct seasoning with salt to taste and serve steaming hot.

NOTE   Without separating the leaves, place the sea greens in water to cover. When soft, separate them; continue soaking for about 30 minutes, changing the water two or three times. This long soaking removes any sand or excess salt used in the drying process.

Crema de Apio
Venezuelan Cream of Celeriac Soup

—

Serves 6 to 8

A*pio* means "celery" in Spanish, and it refers to both celery and celeriac, also known as celery root or celery knob. The root has a distinctive flavor and is eaten both cooked and raw. This soup from Venezuela has both, a combination that I find excites the palate.

The leaves of celeriac are strong and sharp, very good for flavoring stocks, sauces, and soups. If you are making this soup with water rather than stock, simmer some stalks and leaves in the water for a few minutes, then remove them and use the flavored water.

3 medium celeriac or celery roots (about 2 pounds)
½ lemon
2 tablespoons olive oil
1 large clove garlic, peeled and finely chopped
1 large onion, peeled and finely chopped (about 1½ cups)
1 teaspoon ground fennel or ground coriander
½ teaspoon ground cardamom
⅛ teaspoon cayenne
1 medium leek, white part only, washed and finely chopped
    (about 1 cup)
½ cup dry vermouth or white wine
1 teaspoon sugar
1 tablespoon coarse salt
½ teaspoon ground turmeric (optional)
5 cups Chicken Stock (page 461) or water
4 tablespoons crème fraîche or heavy cream (optional)
2 tablespoons chopped fresh dill

1. Trim off and discard any stalks and the rootlets from the celeriac. Peel, wash, and cut each in half. Julienne half of one. Pour 4 cups of cold water in a bowl, squeeze the lemon juice into the water, mix, and add the julienned celeriac. Set aside. Coarsely chop the rest of the celeriac; you should have about 4 cups. Set aside.

2. In a saucepan, heat the olive oil. Add the garlic, onion, fennel, cardamom, and cayenne and sauté, stirring, until the onion is translucent, about 2 to 3 minutes (do not brown). Add the leek, vermouth, sugar, salt, and turmeric, if using, and cook over medium heat, stirring, until all the liquid has evaporated, about 8 minutes.

3. Add the chopped celeriac. Mix well and add the stock. Bring to a boil, skimming the foam as it rises to the surface; lower the heat and simmer for 15 to 20 minutes.

4. Remove from the heat and blend in several batches in the jar of an electric blender. The soup should be slightly thicker than heavy cream. If it is too thick, add extra stock or water to obtain the right consistency.

5. Drain the julienned celeriac. Pour the blended soup into a double boiler, mix in the julienned celeriac, reserving about ¼ cup, and let heat through for about 5 to 10 minutes. Mix in the crème fraîche, if using, and correct the seasoning with salt to taste. Sprinkle with chopped dill, garnish the center of the soup with the remaining julienned celeriac, and serve.

Sopa de Chuchu
Brazilian Chayote Soup

Serves 6 to 8

Chayote, which the Brazilians call *chuchu,* almost an affectionate name, is a pear-shaped squash with a delicate flavor.

6 chayotes (about 4 pounds)

BOUQUET GARNI
1 dried chili pepper
4 or 5 sprigs fresh tarragon or thyme or oregano
3 or 4 sprigs fresh mint
4 sprigs fresh dill or Italian parsley
1 thin slice fresh ginger (optional)

2 tablespoons olive oil
2 medium onions, peeled and finely chopped (2 cups)
1 teaspoon sugar
½ teaspoon ground mace
3 stalks celery, washed and finely chopped (1 cup)
1 large cucumber, peeled and finely chopped (1 cup)
4 cups water
1 tablespoon coarse salt
Fresh mint leaves

1. Peel the chayotes and cut them in half. Remove and discard the large seeds, chop the flesh, and set aside.

2. Wrap and tie the hot pepper, tarragon, mint, dill, and ginger, if using, in a 10-inch-square piece of cheesecloth.

3. In a saucepan, heat the olive oil. Add the onions, sugar, and mace and sauté until the onion is translucent, about 4 minutes. Do not brown. Add the celery and cucumber and continue cooking until the vegetables are soft, about 3 minutes. Add 4 cups of water, the bouquet garni, and the salt. Bring to a boil and simmer for a few minutes. Add the chopped chayote, cover, and continue to simmer, stirring now and then, for 10 to 15 minutes, or until the chayote is barely tender.

4. Remove from the heat, discard bouquet garni, and blend in batches in a blender until smooth. Transfer to an enameled saucepan and heat thoroughly over low heat, stirring; or reheat and keep hot in a double boiler until ready to serve. Correct the seasoning. Serve hot, garnished with mint leaves.

VARIATION

To serve the soup chilled, cool thoroughly over ice for several hours in the refrigerator. Adjust the seasoning with salt and garnish each serving with mint and a dot of crème fraîche or sour cream.

Caldo Verde
Brazilian Kale and Potato Soup

Serves 6 to 8

This classic soup of kale and potato is found wherever the Portuguese settled, and although the Brazilians have made *caldo verde* their own, it if definitely part of their Portuguese heritage.

1 pound kale or mustard greens
3 tablespoons olive oil
3 cloves garlic, peeled and minced
*3 medium leeks, white parts and some green, washed and chopped
    (about 1⅔ cups)*
1 bay leaf
1 teaspoon ground coriander
⅛ teaspoon ground mace
1 baking potato, peeled and chopped (about 1⅔ cups)
6 cups Chicken Stock (page 461) or water
1 tablespoon coarse salt
4 to 6 ounces chouriço or lingüiça, cut into ¼-inch dice
Extra-virgin olive oil

1. Wash the kale very well. Drain and dry thoroughly. Cut off the stems. Chop the stems and set aside; you should have about 3 cups. Chop all the leaves and set aside; you should have 4 cups tightly packed.

(Continued)

2. In a large sauté pan, heat 2 tablespoons of the olive oil and ⅔ of the minced garlic over medium heat. Add the leeks, bay leaf, coriander, and mace and sauté, stirring, until the leeks have wilted, about 2 to 3 minutes. Add the stems from the kale, stir, and cook for a few minutes longer. Add the chopped potato, stock, and salt. Bring to a boil, skimming the foam as it rises. Lower the heat and simmer for 20 minutes.

3. Remove from the heat and blend in several batches at top speed in the jar of an electric blender until smooth; set aside.

4. In a saucepan, heat the remaining tablespoon of the olive oil, the remaining minced garlic, and the diced sausage over high heat. Sauté and stir for a few seconds. Do not brown the garlic. Add the chopped kale leaves and, stirring constantly, cook for another minute, or until the kale has softened. Add the blended soup and simmer, stirring, until thoroughly hot. Correct the seasoning with salt to taste, and serve garnished with a few drops of olive oil, if desired.

Sopa de Zapallo
Winter Squash Soup

—

Serves 6 to 8

*C*alabaza is the general term for "squash" in Spanish. *Zapallo* is a winter or hard squash of considerable size, with bright-orange flesh, pale or speckled. Its flavor is a cross between that of pumpkin and acorn squash. *Zapallo* is not widely available in North America, but butternut squash is quite similar, and I have used it in this recipe.

2 large butternut squash (about 2 pounds each)
1 tablespoon coarse salt
1 bay leaf
2 tablespoons olive oil
1 large clove garlic, peeled and finely chopped
1 large onion, peeled and finely chopped (about 1½ cups)
½ teaspoon sugar
2 medium leeks, white parts only, washed and finely chopped (about 1 cup)
⅛ teaspoon ground cloves

⅛ teaspoon cayenne
¼ teaspoon ground mace or nutmeg
1 cup milk
Ground white pepper

GARNISH
3 tablespoons chopped fresh dill or cilantro leaves or Italian parsley
Crème fraîche or sour cream (optional)

1. Peel and seed the squash. Cut 1 pound into ¼-inch dice; you should have about 2¾ cups. Chop the remaining squash; you should have about 6 heaping cups. Set aside.

2. In a saucepan, combine 6 cups of water, the salt, and the bay leaf and bring to a boil. Lower the heat and simmer for 4 to 5 minutes. Blanch the squash cubes in the simmering water for 3 to 5 minutes, or until they are tender. Do not overcook. With a slotted spoon, remove the cubes and set aside. Remove and discard the bay leaf and measure the cooking water. You should have 5 cups. If not, add enough water to make 5 cups. Set aside.

3. In a saucepan, heat the oil. Add the garlic, onion, and sugar and sauté until the onion is translucent, about 3 to 4 minutes. Add the leeks, cloves, cayenne, and mace and cook, stirring, for about 1 minute longer, or until leeks are soft. Add the raw chopped squash and the reserved cooking water. Stir, bring to a boil, lower the heat, and simmer for 15 minutes, or until the squash is very tender.

4. Remove from the heat and blend in several batches in the jar of an electric blender, adding the milk a little at a time.

5. Heat the blended soup in a double boiler; add the blanched squash cubes, stir, and correct the seasoning with salt and pepper to taste. Serve piping hot, sprinkled with fresh dill. For extra richness, top each bowl with crème fraîche.

VARIATION

Corn can be added to this soup. Husk and remove the silk from 1 ear of corn. Blanch the corn, covered, in the boiling salted water (with the bay leaf) in Step 2 for 5 minutes. Remove the corn and save the water to continue with the recipe. When the cob is cool enough to handle, cut off the kernels. Add them to the soup together with the blanched cubes of squash in Step 5.

Chupe de Choclo
Corn Chowder

—

Serves 6 to 8

Maíz, or corn, is grown in a wide range of colors in South America—white, yellow, red, orange, purple, and even black, as well as bicolored and multicolored Indian varieties. It also varies in texture, from mealy to juicy. Most of the corn commercially available and eaten today in the United States is what is called *sweet corn*.

Corn husks are full of flavor, and when I make this chowder I extract some of it by adding them to the water in which the corn and potato are cooked. This brings out the full intensity of the corn.

20 ears corn
1 tablespoon coarse salt
1 medium potato, peeled
4 tablespoons butter
1 large clove garlic, peeled and finely chopped
1-inch piece fresh ginger, peeled and finely chopped
3 medium leeks, white parts only, washed and finely chopped
    (about 1 cup)
1 medium onion, peeled and finely chopped (1½ cups)
⅛ teaspoon cayenne
⅛ teaspoon ground cloves
½ teaspoon ground mace
½ teaspoon ground turmeric
1 teaspoon sugar
1 tablespoon coarse salt
¼ cup Pernod
4 cups milk
½ cup fresh or frozen peas
2 or 3 tablespoons crème fraîche or sour cream (optional)

1. Husk all the ears of corn, saving some of the young husks. Set aside 2 ears of the husked corn. Finely grate the 18 remaining ears. You should have 3 heaping cups.

2. In a saucepan, combine 2 quarts of water, the salt, and the reserved husks. Bring to a boil; add the potato and the 2 reserved ears of corn. Lower the heat and simmer for about 5 minutes, or until the corn is tender. Remove the corn and set aside. Continue cooking for 15 to 20 minutes, or until the potato is done; remove and set aside. If using fresh peas, place them in a strainer, lower the strainer into the boiling water, and blanch the peas for 2 to 3 minutes. Drain and set aside. Discard the cooking water.

3. In an enameled saucepan or earthenware casserole, heat the butter. Add the garlic and ginger and stir. Add the leeks and cook until soft, about 2 to 3 minutes. Add the onion, cayenne, cloves, mace, turmeric, sugar, salt, and Pernod and continue cooking over medium heat, stirring now and then, until all the liquid has evaporated and the onion is totally translucent. Do not brown. Add the grated corn and stir; add the milk and over medium heat, bring to a boil while constantly stirring. Lower the heat and simmer, stirring, for 8 to 10 minutes.

4. Remove from the heat and place in a food mill with a fine disk. Force the mixture through the mill, leaving only the corn skins. Discard the corn skins.

5. Pour half the chowder in the jar of an electric blender and blend thoroughly. If a smoother texture is desired, blend the entire mixture. Combine the blended and unblended mixtures in a double boiler. If a thinner texture is desired, mix in an extra ½ cup of milk

6. Cut the cooked potato into ¼-inch dice and add to the soup. Cut the kernels off the 2 ears of cooked corn and discard the cobs. Add all but ½ cup of the kernels. Add the peas (if frozen peas are used, rinse and drain them first) and mix. Heat the chowder thoroughly; add the crème fraîche, if desired. Mix well and correct the seasoning with salt to taste. Serve piping hot, garnished with the reserved ½ cup of corn kernels.

Sopa de Feijão Preto

Brazilian Black Bean Soup

—

Serves 6 to 8

They call beans *feijão* in Brazil, *porotos* in Chile, and *frijoles* in the rest of the continent, but whatever they call them, South Americans love their beans! They are used in all courses of the meal and are found in all sizes, shapes, and colors.

12 ounces dried black beans
1 small smoked or fresh ham hock or ham bone
2 tablespoons olive oil
2 cloves garlic, peeled and minced
1 or 2 jalapeño peppers, seeded and minced
1 large leek, white part only, finely chopped (⅔ cup)
2 medium onions, peeled and chopped (about 2½ cups)
3 stalks celery (strings removed), finely chopped (about ⅔ cup)
2 tablespoons Pernod
2 tablespoons sweet vermouth
1 tablespoon dark soy sauce
1 teaspoon ground cumin
⅛ teaspoon ground cloves
8 cups Beef Stock (page 462)

GARNISH
4 thin slices Black Forest ham, julienned
1 hard-boiled egg, finely chopped
Crème fraîche (optional)
Thin slices lemon or lime

1. Wash the beans under cold running water and soak them overnight in 3 cups of water. Drain them and set aside, reserving the soaking water.

2. Place the ham hock and 6 cups of water in a saucepan and bring to a boil. Lower the heat and simmer for about 15 minutes. Remove the ham hock to a plate and set aside. Discard the blanching liquid.

3. In a large sauté pan, heat the olive oil over medium heat. Add the garlic and hot peppers and sauté for a few seconds. Do not burn the garlic. Add the leek and stir; add the onions and celery and sauté, stirring, until the onions are translucent and slightly golden around the edges, about 6 minutes.

4. Mix together the Pernod, vermouth, and soy sauce. Add the cumin, cloves, and the Pernod mixture to the vegetables and cook until all the liquid has evaporated, about 1 or 2 minutes. Add the reserved soaking water from the beans. Bring to a boil, lower the heat, and simmer until most of the liquid has evaporated and leaves a track on the bottom of the pan.

5. Add the beans, stock, and blanched ham hock. Bring to a boil, lower the heat, and simmer, covered, for 1 hour 15 minutes, or until the beans are totally soft. Skim the foam as it rises to the surface and stir from time to time.

6. Remove the ham hock. If you like, it can be boned and cut into bite-size pieces to be added to the finished soup. Or discard it.

7. Blend the soup in several batches in the jar of an electric blender until totally smooth. If the soup seems too thick, add a bit of stock to obtain the desired consistency. Serve the soup hot, garnished with the ham, chopped egg, a dollop of crème fraîche, and/or lemon or lime slices in each bowl.

VARIATION

Substitute an equal amount of pink beans, Borlottis, or white, pinto, or lima beans, or black-eyed peas for the black beans. These beans take longer to cook than black beans, so adjust the cooking time in Step 5 accordingly.

Chupe de Porotos
Chilean Bean Chowder

Serves 6 to 8

——

Bean soups are among the stars of the Chilean kitchen, and the heartiest of them are the *chupes*. Several versions exist, some made with stock, others with milk, still others with water. Besides the beans, *chupes* might include pieces of meat or fish, as well as corn, potatoes, or squash, and even noodles or rice. Although this *chupe de porotos* is water-based, it is thick and robust. It is made with three kinds of beans: white beans for thickness, pinto beans and black-eyed peas for color and texture.

1½ cups dried white beans
1 cup dried pinto beans
1 cup dried black-eyed peas
1 small fennel bulb, trimmed and chopped
2 small leeks, white parts only, washed and chopped
1 small carrot, peeled and chopped
3 stalks celery, washed, strings removed, and chopped
1 bay leaf
2 or 3 dried red chili peppers, seeded
3 tablespoons olive oil
3 cloves garlic, peeled and minced
½-inch piece fresh ginger, peeled and grated
4 tomatoes, peeled, seeded (juices saved), and minced
1 generous pinch saffron threads soaked in ½ cup amontillado sherry
   or Pernod, or 2 teaspoons Spanish paprika
1 tablespoon coarse salt

GARNISH
2 tablespoons chopped Italian parsley
2 slices smoked or cooked ham, julienned (optional)

   1. Place each kind of dried beans in a colander and rinse them under cold running water; soak them separately overnight or for 8 to 10 hours. Soak the white beans in 8 cups of cold water and the black-eyed peas and pinto beans in 4 cups of water each. Reserve the soaking liquid from the white beans only. Measure this soaking liquid and add enough water to make 7 cups. Set aside.

2. Place the soaked white beans and the 7 cups of soaking liquid in a saucepan and bring to a boil. Lower the heat and let simmer for 35 minutes, or until the beans are tender.

3. With a slotted spoon, take out 1 cup of the beans and set aside. To the remaining beans in the saucepan, add the fennel, leeks, carrot, celery, bay leaf, and hot peppers and continue to simmer for another 20 minutes.

4. Remove from the heat; remove and discard the bay leaf and hot peppers and drain, saving the cooking liquid, the beans, and the vegetables. You should have about 5 cups of cooking liquid. If not, add water or chicken stock to make 5 cups. Blend the white beans with the vegetables in several batches in the jar of an electric blender. Strain the pureed soup through a fine sieve and set aside.

5. At the same time, place the soaked pinto beans in a saucepan with 3 cups of water. Bring to a boil. Lower the heat and simmer for about 1 hour 10 minutes, or until the beans are cooked. Drain, discard the cooking liquid, and set the beans aside.

6. At the same time, place the soaked black-eyed peas in a third saucepan with 5 cups of water. Bring to a boil, lower the heat, and simmer for about 45 minutes, or until the beans are tender but still hold their shape. Drain, discard the cooking liquid, and set the beans aside.

7. Heat the olive oil in a saucepan over high heat. Add the garlic and ginger, stir, and add the tomatoes and juices. Cook until all the liquid has evaporated, about 6 to 8 minutes. Add the saffron with the sherry and the salt and continue cooking until the liquor has evaporated, about 2 minutes. Add the reserved 1 cup of white beans, the black-eyed peas, and the pinto beans and mix in the pureed white-bean soup. Heat thoroughly over low heat, stirring. Correct the seasoning with salt to taste and serve garnished with chopped parsley and julienned ham, if desired.

NOTE   If the soup is too thick for your taste, just add a little water, milk, or stock.

Sopa de Habas
Fava Bean Soup

—

Serves 6 to 8

Fresh favas are at their peak in spring and early summer. Look for the smallest, fullest, crispest pods. They should be evenly green, though some discoloration is normal. Sometimes you'll come across very large pods, nearly a foot long, with yellowish beans; these are also good.

10 pounds fresh fava beans (2½ pounds shelled beans)
1 tablespoon olive oil
3 ounces bacon (about 3 thin slices)
2 cloves garlic, peeled and minced
1 jalapeño pepper, seeded and minced
3 medium onions, peeled and minced (about 3 cups)
⅛ teaspoon ground mace
2 tablespoons coarse salt
2 tablespoons chopped fresh cilantro leaves

1. Shell the beans by cutting the tips from the pods and pressing the seams open; or bend the tips, which are partially curved, in the opposite direction, pull along the seams of the beans, and press to open the pods. Remove the beans and discard the pods. Remove and discard the tough rubbery skin by making a tiny slit with the point of a paring knife on the curved side of each bean and peeling off the skin, being careful not to bruise the bean. Set aside.

2. In a soup kettle or small stockpot, heat the olive oil and the bacon over high heat. Sauté until the bacon slices are crisp and have released most of their fat, about 7 minutes. Remove the bacon and set aside. Add the garlic, hot pepper, onions, mace, and salt. Stir and cook over medium heat until the onion is soft, about 10 minutes.

3. Add the beans and continue to cook, stirring, for a few minutes. Add 5 cups of water and bring to a boil. Lower the heat and simmer for 8 minutes. Remove from the heat.

4. Blend about half the soup in several batches in the jar of an electric blender until smooth. Add the pureed soup to the remaining half containing the whole beans and mix gently. Correct the seasoning with salt to taste. Grumble the bacon slices. Serve the soup hot, topped with bacon bits and sprinkled with cilantro.

Chupe de Quinua
Quinoa Chowder

Serves 6 to 8

Quinoa has a good nutritional profile; it is high in protein and other nutrients. It is also exceedingly versatile in the kitchen. It is good by itself and goes well with other foods. A handful of quinoa added to an ordinary vegetable or chicken soup—or any soup for that matter—makes it something special.

8 ounces raw quinoa (1¼ cups)
2 tablespoons olive oil
1 large clove garlic, peeled and minced
1 jalapeño pepper, seeded and minced
¼ teaspoon ground cumin
⅛ teaspoon ground white pepper
1 tablespoon coarse salt
½ pound potatoes, peeled and cut into ¼-inch dice
8 ounces feta, cut into ¼-inch dice
½ pound fresh spinach leaves, shredded about ¼ inch thick
1 or 2 hard-boiled eggs, sliced

1. Rinse the quinoa in a strainer under cold running water. In a saucepan, combine the rinsed quinoa with 6 cups of cold water and bring to a boil over high heat, stirring now and then. Lower the heat and simmer for 10 minutes, or until the quinoa is tender. Remove from the heat, pour through a strainer, and let drain thoroughly. Set aside.

2. In a saucepan, heat the olive oil over low heat. Add the garlic and hot pepper and sauté, stirring, for just a second or two. Do not let the

(Continued)

garlic brown. Add the cumin, pepper, salt, and 5 cups of water and bring to a boil. Add the cooked quinoa and the diced potatoes and cook over medium heat for 10 to 15 minutes, or until the potatoes are done.

3. Stir in the cheese and continue to cook for a few seconds, then fold in the shredded spinach leaves. Correct the seasoning with salt to taste and serve hot, garnished with slices of hard-boiled eggs.

VARIATIONS

Add 1½ pounds of lean meat (lamb, beef, pork, or chicken), cut into 1-inch cubes. Thoroughly brown the meat in the olive oil in Step 2; add the garlic and hot pepper and proceed with the recipe.

Sopa de Beterraga y Quinua
Beet and Quinoa Soup

—

Substitute ½ pound of beets for the potatoes. Peel and cut them into ¼-inch cubes and add them in Step 2. They will take a few minutes longer to cook than potatoes. Already-cooked beets may be added too.

Sopa de Quinua al Estilo Huancayo
Fava Bean and Quinoa Soup

—

Shell and peel 1 to 1½ pounds of fava beans. Substitute them for the potatoes in Step 2.

FRUIT SOUPS

Champus
Chirimoya Soup

Serves 6 to 8

In Colombia and parts of Venezuela, *champus* is a refreshing cold fruit drink. In Peru, it is a hot, creamy soup made with white corn and chirimoya.

Chirimoya, which looks like a large green pinecone, is a fruit native to the Andes. Its name comes from the Quechua (Inca) language and means "gold seeds." The fruit is sweet, with a rich, custardy texture. The flavor is somewhere between that of a banana and a pineapple. Several varieties of chirimoya are marketed in the United States. All are suitable for *champus*.

Chirimoyas, like avocados, are picked green and must be left to ripen at room temperature. Once ripe, they can be stored in the refrigerator for four or five days. Despite its leathery exterior, a ripe chirimoya is a delicate fruit, easily damaged by jostling, pressure, or severe cold.

3 large chirimoyas (about 1 pound each)
3 hard pears (1 pound)
1 lemon or lime
1 small or ½ large ripe pineapple, cut crosswise and chopped,
*   with skin, into 1-inch pieces (about 2 pounds)*
1 large green apple, chopped, with skin and core, into 1-inch pieces
1-inch piece fresh ginger, peeled and thinly sliced
5 sprigs fresh mint
1-inch piece lemon or lime rind
1 dried red chile pepper
2 1½-inch cinnamon sticks
10 cloves
¼ cup sugar
4 tablespoons unsalted butter
2 cups white hominy, rinsed and drained (1 16-ounce can)
Fresh mint leaves (optional)

(Continued)

1. Peel the chirimoyas by piercing the broad part of the fruit with the point of a paring knife and pulling the skin toward the tip. Slice each fruit in half lengthwise and remove and discard the central core. Cut each half into quarters, and with the point of a paring knife, remove the seeds. Then slice each quarter across, exposing the next row of seeds, and remove them. Continue until all the seeds are removed, ending up with as large chunks as possible. Discard the seeds. Place the seedless pulp in a bowl and set aside. (Another way to do this is to cut the fruit into quarters, skin and all, discard the cores, and remove the seeds with the point of a paring knife. Then scrape the soft pulp from the skin or scoop it out with a teaspoon. Either way, the idea is to have as large chunks of fruit as possible without seeds.)

2. Peel the pears, saving the skins. Cut all the pears into quarters; remove and save the cores and place the pears in a bowl containing 2 cups of water mixed with the juice of ½ lemon. Set aside.

3. In a small enameled or stainless-steel stockpot, combine the skins and cores from the pears, the chopped pineapple, chopped apple, ginger, mint, lemon rind, hot pepper, cinnamon, cloves, sugar, and 8 cups of water. Bring to a boil, lower the heat, and simmer, stirring now and then, for 45 minutes to 1 hour.

4. Remove from the heat and let cool slightly. Pour through a fine sieve, pressing against the sides of the sieve to extract all the juices. Discard the contents of the sieve and set the fruit stock aside. You should have about 5 cups.

5. Remove two-thirds of the pears from the lemon water and chop into 1-inch pieces.

6. In a stainless-steel saucepan, melt 2 tablespoons of the butter. Add the chopped pears and sauté, stirring, for 2 minutes. Add 1¼ cups of the hominy, stir, and sauté for about 1 minute longer. Add 4 cups of the reserved fruit stock and bring to a boil, stirring now and then. Lower the heat and simmer for 8 to 10 minutes.

7. Remove from the heat. Blend in several batches in the jar of an electric blender until smooth.

8. Drain the remaining pears and cut into ¼-inch dice.

9. In a stainless-steel or enameled saucepan, melt the remaining 2 tablespoons of butter. Add the diced pears and the rest of the hominy and sauté over medium heat, stirring constantly, for 3 minutes. Do not brown. Add the blended soup and bring to a boil, stirring, over medium heat. Reduce the heat and simmer for about 3 minutes. Mix in the reserved chirimoya pulp and continue to simmer, stirring, for another 5 to 7 minutes. Correct the seasoning with sugar and a few drops of lemon juice to taste and serve hot, garnished with fresh mint leaves, if desired.

NOTE   This soup should be thick. If it seems too thick, however, add a little of the remaining fruit stock.

Sopa de Tomatitos Verdes
Tomatillo Soup

—

Serves 6 to 8

Atomatillo looks like a small green tomato. It is covered with a papery husk, which is easily peeled off. Though tomatillos can be purplish and may ripen to a yellowish color, they are commonly used green.

Tomatillos are available year-round. Pick firm, medium-size ones, with dry, clean, close-fitting husks; there should be no sign of blackness or mold. They can be stored in the refrigerator, in a paper bag, for about three weeks.

2½ to 3 pounds tomatillos

BOUQUET GARNI
4 sprigs fresh tarragon or thyme
2 to 3 sprigs fresh mint
3 sprigs Italian parsley

3 tablespoons olive oil
1 large onion, peeled and finely chopped (about 2 cups)
4 stalks celery, washed, strings removed, and finely chopped
1 to 2 jalapeño peppers, seeded and chopped
1-inch piece fresh ginger, peeled and chopped
¼ teaspoon sugar
3 cucumbers, peeled, seeded, and chopped (about 2 cups)
3 green bell peppers, seeded and chopped
2½ cups cold water or Chicken Stock (page 461)
1 tablespoon coarse salt
3 tablespoons chopped fresh cilantro leaves or Italian parsley

1. Peel off the crackly husks and stems of the tomatillos. Wash the tomatillos well and drain.

2. Wrap and tie the sprigs of tarragon, mint, and parsley in a 6-inch-square piece of cheesecloth. Set aside.

3. In an enameled or stainless-steel saucepan, heat the olive oil over medium heat. Add the husked whole tomatillos and sauté them, stirring now and then, until they are golden all around, about 12 minutes. Stir in the onion, celery, hot peppers, ginger, and sugar and cook until the onion is translucent, about 3 to 4 minutes. Add the cucumbers and bell peppers and continue to cook, stirring, for 5 minutes longer. Add the water or stock, salt, and bouquet garni and bring to a boil. Lower the heat and simmer, stirring from time to time, for 15 to 20 minutes, or until the tomatillos have totally collapsed. Remove from the heat and discard the bouquet garni.

4. Force the soup through a food mill, leaving the skins and seeds behind. Place the soup in a double boiler and heat through. Correct the seasoning with salt to taste, sprinkle with chopped cilantro, and serve hot.

NOTE   For a smoother texture, blend half or more of the soup in the jar of an electric blender and mix it with the remaining soup, or blend all of it to the desired consistency. Do this only after passing the soup through the food mill to remove the seeds and skins.

VARIATION

This soup may be served chilled. Pass the soup through a food mill and puree it in a blender. Cool thoroughly over ice or in the refrigerator for several hours. Correct the seasoning with salt, sprinkle with fresh herbs, and serve.

Sopa de Palta
Avocado Soup

—

Serves 6 to 8

This quick, delicious soup can be made in fifteen minutes from start to finish. It is velvety and thick, with an appetizing pale green color.

Sopa de palta is usually served chilled. It can also be served warm, but never hot.

3 avocados (about 2 pounds, total)
Juice of 1 lemon or lime
2 tablespoons olive oil
2 cloves garlic, peeled and finely chopped
1-inch piece fresh ginger, peeled and finely chopped
1 or 2 jalapeño peppers, seeded and finely chopped
2 medium onions, peeled and finely chopped (2 cups)
3 stalks celery, leafy tops removed, washed, strings removed, and finely chopped
1 teaspoon ground coriander
1 tablespoon coarse salt
4 cups Chicken Stock (page 461) or Vegetable Stock (page 469)
3 or 4 sprigs fresh tarragon or cilantro or basil or 1 or 2 sprigs fresh rosemary

GARNISH
Crème fraîche
2 tablespoons chopped fresh cilantro leaves or Italian parsley
Diced canned potatoes (optional)
Diced cucumbers (optional)
Diced bell peppers (optional)

1. Carefully peel the avocados, cut them in half, and discard the pits. Chop 2 of the avocados, place them in a small bowl, and add the juice of ½ lemon. Toss and set aside. Cut the remaining avocado into ¼-inch dice and place in another small bowl. Add the juice of the other ½ lemon, toss gently, and set aside.

2. In a saucepan, heat the olive oil. Add the garlic, ginger, and hot peppers and stir. Add the onions, celery, coriander, and salt and sauté, stirring, until the vegetables are totally wilted, about 4 minutes. Do not brown the vegetables. Add the stock and the tarragon sprigs. Bring to a boil over high heat, lower the heat, and simmer for 8 minutes, skimming once. Remove and discard the tarragon sprigs.

3. Fill about half of the jar of an electric blender with some stock and vegetables and blend until the vegetables are liquidized. With the machine and blend until the vegetables are liquidized. With the machine running, add some of the chopped avocados and continue blending until smooth. Repeat until all the stock, vegetables, and chopped avocados are used.

4. Thoroughly chill the soup over ice or in the refrigerator for several hours. Correct the seasoning with salt and/or lemon juice to taste and serve. Garnish the cold soup with crème fraîche, chopped cilantro leaves, and/or the optional chopped vegetables.

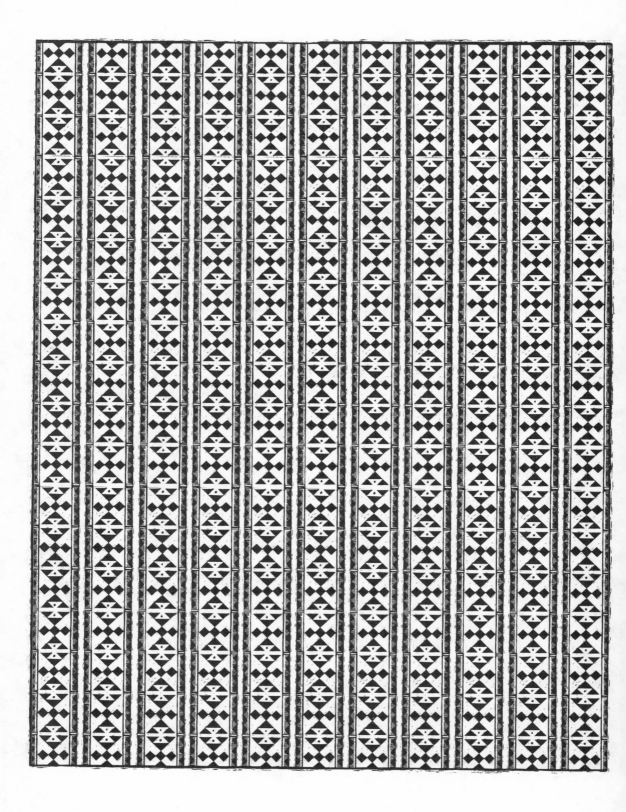

SEAFOOD

FISH

Sudado de Salmón
Steamed Salmon with Vegetables
—

Truchas con Anchoas
Trout with Anchovies
—

Abadejo con Alazán
Cod and Sorrel in Banana Leaves
—

Cría de Bacalao en Tomatitos Verdes
Scrod Braised with Tomatillos
—

Merluza en Salsa de Avellanas
Hake in Hazelnut Sauce
—

Budín de Pescado
Fish Terrine
—

Puré de Bacalao
Salt-Cod Mousse
—

Pescado con Acelgas
Bluefish with Swiss Chard
—

Pargo con Mejillones
Braised Snapper and Mussels
—

Corvina con Frijoles Blancos
Bass and White Beans
—

Fiambre de Bonito
Bonito Fiambre
—

Atún a la Chorrillana
Tuna Steak Chorrillas Style
—

Guiso de Atún
Ragu of Tuna and Thyme
—

Sardinas con Tomillo
Braised Sardines with Thyme

Pejerreyes Arrebosados
Crispy Fried Smelts
—

Cazuela de Pejerreyes
Smelt Casserole
—

SHELLFISH

Parihuela Salvaje
—

Mariscada
—

Migas de Camarones
Shrimp Migas
—

Picante de Camarones
Shrimp in a Picante Sauce
—

Camarão con Coco
Shrimp in Coconut Sauce
—

Salpicón de Cangrejo
Crabmeat Salpicón
—

Tortillas de Cangrejo
Crab Cakes
—

Almejas con Quinua
Clams with Quinoa
—

Mejillones con Hinojo
Mussel Salad with Fresh Fennel
—

Seco de Choros
Mussel Seco
—

Choros a La Perricholi
Mussels à La Perricholi
—

Picante de Calamares
Squid in a Picante Sauce

South American cooks are passionate about seafood and have always given it a great deal of attention. It appears on the table in many guises, from a simple ceviche to a complex mariscada, the South American version of bouillabaisse. Fish and shellfish are treated with an ingenuity that combines an appetite for assertive flavors with an understanding of the inherent character of the ingredients.

South America is rich in fish, both saltwater and freshwater. From a culinary point of view, the most popular fish are the large meaty ones: the *bocachico,* the larger *dorado* and *paiche* (an Amazon fish with delicious fine meat that is eaten fresh as well as dried), the *pavon,* the *sungaro,* and the *paco* or *pacú,* as this fish is called in Brazil.

Chile and Peru have some of the most magnificent seafood in the world as a result of the cold Humboldt Current, which runs along the coast, carrying vast quantities of plankton. Plankton is the main food of anchovies and small shellfish, and they, in turn, provide the diet of many larger fish and shellfish. The waters off Chile and Peru are a vast breeding ground for seafood, the source of an unrivaled gastronomic experience.

As a child, I loved to go fishing. I'd plunk my net down in those clean, clear waters right into the middle of a shimmering silver school of anchovies and scoop them up by the dozens. For every anchovy that got hooked on the fishing line as bait, two or three were popped into my mouth. They were so tiny that the bones didn't even get in the way. I'll never forget how delicious those anchovies tasted—so full of flavor and seasoned with the briny sea water.

Whatever bait was left, I brought home. My mother would quickly clean the fish, gently wiping each one as if it were a jewel, and lay them on a thick bed of coarse salt in a deep earthenware casserole. She would alternate layers of anchovies and salt and then cover the casserole with a heavy wooden lid with a stone on top, to weigh everything down. After a few days the salted anchovies were ready to eat. Or we would brush off the salt and steep them in virgin olive oil, together with a few bay leaves and peppercorns. These marinated anchovies were used for cooking, as garnishes, and as snacks for the family.

The use of all parts of the shrimp also illustrates the economical and practical side of South American cooking. My mother used to buy about a pound of shrimp to serve our large family. She would use the shrimp heads and shells to make a densely flavored sauce and then serve sliced boiled potatoes, beautifully arranged, with a shrimp or two per person as a garnish. The rich sauce gave the dish an intense shrimp taste, and we felt as if we were sitting in the lap of luxury.

As for mussels—which I regard as among the tastiest of shellfish—my mother would steam them open and save the broth, which she considered one of the most precious ingredients in her kitchen. She would use it in soups and sauces and to make rice. The mussels would be used in the preparation of other dishes or simply presented in their shells as an appetizer, topped with a spoonful of *picadillo*—finely minced tomatoes, cucumbers, hot peppers, and fresh herbs with oil and lemon juice or vinegar.

When I was growing up, frozen fish was unheard of, and I took it for granted that any seafood that landed in the cooking pot was spanking fresh. One of the most vivid memories of my youth is of watching a Peruvian Indian woman in her colorful native dress, called a *polleras*, crouched on the bank of a high Andes stream. She yanked squirming trout out of the cold water to cook for her waiting customers. With the fish still on the line, she slit open the belly and threw the guts back into the water. She smacked the fish, still flapping, onto a hot, flat stone that rested on two piles of smaller stones. There was a lively fire going under this crude but effective grill. Within minutes she was serving the fish, along with a scoop of fresh local cheese garnished with a hot pepper. Nothing could be simpler, nothing better. It was incredible!

FISH

Sudado de Salmón
Steamed Salmon with Vegetables

Serves 6 to 8

One of the purest and quickest ways to cook seafood is by steaming it, which is called *sudado* in Spanish. All you need is water and a steamer. For this recipe, I used a tiered steamer with three deep steaming baskets that can be stacked one on top of the other.

1 salmon fillet, cut into 6 to 8 pieces (about 3½ pounds)
1 tablespoon olive oil
1 head garlic, unpeeled and cut in half horizontally
3 jalapeño peppers, with seeds, cut in half
Peel of 1 lemon
6 cloves
1 tablespoon black peppercorns
¼ cup coarse salt
2 sprigs fresh rosemary or 1 tablespoon dried rosemary
16 baby carrots, peeled, with ¼ inch of the tops left on
    (about 6 ounces)
16 Brussels sprouts, outside leaves removed and roots trimmed
    (about ¾ pound)
8 Jerusalem artichokes, peeled, or small new potatoes
    (about 1¼ pounds)
2 large fennel bulbs, cut into 6 to 8 wedges

GARNISH
Melted butter or olive oil
Fresh Cilantro Sauce (page 477) and/or Parsley Sauce (page 479)

1. Rub the salmon with the olive oil and set aside.

2. Place 5 cups of water in the bottom of a steamer and add the garlic, hot peppers, lemon peel, cloves, peppercorns, salt, and rosemary. Bring to a boil, lower the heat slightly, and simmer for a few minutes. Place the carrots, Brussels sprouts, and Jerusalem artichokes

(Continued)

in the first steamer basket. Cover and steam for about 5 minutes. Add the fennel, cover, and steam for 4 more minutes.

3. Arrange the fish in one or two other steamer baskets. Place on top of the vegetables, cover, and steam for 6 minutes, or until all the vegetables and fish are done.

4. Place the salmon on a serving platter or on individual dinner plates, surrounded by the vegetables. Brush with a little melted butter or olive oil and serve with one or both of the sauces.

Truchas con Anchoas
Trout with Anchovies

Serves 6 to 8

The best trout come from cold rivers and lakes. I have used rainbow trout, which I prefer above all, for this recipe. One fish makes an individual serving.

6 to 8 small trout, dressed
1 cup all-purpose flour
½ cup olive oil
1 clove garlic, peeled and finely chopped
1 medium onion, peeled and finely chopped (1 cup)
1 or 2 jalapeño or serrano peppers, seeded and finely chopped
6 to 8 anchovy fillets, drained, wiped dry on paper towels, and finely chopped
2 tablespoons chopped fresh mint
3 tablespoons chopped fresh basil
1 cup light beer
Juice of 1 large lemon

GARNISH
6 to 8 anchovy fillets, drained and wiped dry
3 tablespoons chopped Italian parsley or fresh cilantro leaves

1. Remove the fins and gills from the trout with kitchen shears and discard. Wipe the fish inside and out with a damp cloth. Dredge the trout with flour, shake off the excess, and set aside.

2. In a cast-iron skillet or earthenware casserole large enough to hold all of the fish in one layer, heat the oil over high heat and brown the fish quickly on both sides, a few at a time. Do not cook the fish through. With a spatula, transfer the fish to a plate or tray. Set aside.

3. Discard all but 3 tablespoons of the oil in the skillet. Add the garlic and onion and sauté over medium heat until the onion is translucent but not browned, about 5 minutes. Add the hot pepper and chopped anchovies. Continue to sauté, stirring, for 2 minutes. Add the mint and basil and sauté for 1 minute. Add the beer and lemon juice. Bring to a boil over high heat, lower the heat, and simmer for a couple of minutes.

4. Gently arrange the trout in one layer in the skillet or casserole, cover tightly, and simmer for 5 to 8 minutes or until the trout are done.

5. Serve the trout directly from the skillet or casserole. Garnish each trout with an anchovy fillet and sprinkle with Italian parsley.

Abadejo con Alazán
Cod and Sorrel in Banana Leaves

—

Serves 8 to 10

2 cod fillets, with skin (3 pounds each)
2 cloves garlic, peeled
1 teaspoon coarse salt
5 tablespoons olive oil
2½ pounds sorrel, washed and spun dry
3 cloves garlic, peeled and finely chopped
1 dried mirasol pepper, seeded and finely chopped, or 1 or 2 dried red peppers
1 medium onion, peeled and finely chopped (1½ cups)
½ teaspoon sugar
1 pound fresh or frozen and thawed banana leaves, cut into 30-inch-long pieces
1 cup alfonso or Kalamata olives, pitted

(Continued)

1. Place the cod fillets, skin side down, on a large plate and check for bones; remove and discard any you see. Set aside.

2. In a mortar with a pestle, pound the 2 garlic cloves and the salt to a smooth paste. Add 2 tablespoons of the olive oil and mix thoroughly. Rub most of this mixture over the fillets and set aside.

3. Trim off and discard the stems of the sorrel and coarsely chop the leaves. Set aside.

4. Heat the remaining 3 tablespoons of olive oil in a large sauté pan. Add the chopped garlic and pepper and sauté for a few seconds. Add the onion and continue sautéing for about 2 minutes, or until the onion is totally translucent. Add ½ cup water and the sugar. Mix well and cook over high heat until all the liquid has evaporated and the sauté pan has a slightly brown film on the bottom. Add the sorrel, a bit at a time, and cook until all of it has totally wilted, about 6 minutes. Correct the seasoning with salt to taste.

5. Prepare the banana leaves by very gently wiping them along the grain with a damp cloth. Pass each piece rapidly over an open flame to soften. Do not burn. Line an earthenware, porcelain, or glass baking dish with the leaves: cover the entire bottom, with the leaves overlapping in the center and draping over the sides of the dish.

6. Preheat the oven to 400 degrees.

7. Place one of the cod fillets, skin side down, on the banana leaves. Spread the sorrel mixture evenly over the fish. Add half of the olives and place the second fillet piece, skin side up, on top. Rub the top of the fish with the remaining garlic-and-oil mixture. Spread the remaining olives over and around the fish. Fold the overhanging banana leaves up over the fish and bake for about 45 to 50 minutes. Remove the dish from the oven, open the leaves, and serve.

Cría de Bacalao en Tomatitos Verdes
Scrod Braised with Tomatillos

Serves 6 to 8

The tomatillo has a wonderful lemony-herbal taste that goes exceptionally well with fish. Its gelatinous juice enriches and thickens the fish juices as they cook together, making an excellent sauce.

1 scrod fillet, with or without skin (4 pounds)
2 pounds tomatillos
6 tablespoons olive oil
4 large cloves garlic, peeled and finely chopped
1 or 2 jalapeño or arbol peppers
4 stalks celery, washed, strings removed, and finely chopped
¼ teaspoon ground allspice
1 teaspoon ground cumin
1 tablespoon plus 1 teaspoon coarse salt
1 cup tightly packed chopped fresh cilantro leaves
3 large onions, peeled and thinly sliced

1. Remove and discard any bones left in the fillet. Wipe the fish with a damp cloth, cover with a moist towel, and set aside.

2. Remove and discard all the papery husks and wash the tomatillos. Select 1 pound of the smallest ones and set aside. Coarsely chop the remaining tomatillos and set aside.

3. Heat 4 tablespoons of the olive oil in an earthenware casserole with a cover over medium heat. Add the reserved whole tomatillos and sauté them, shaking the casserole, until they are slightly golden all around. Do not overcook them, or they will collapse very easily. With a slotted spoon, remove the tomatillos to a plate and set aside.

4. Add the garlic and hot peppers to the remaining olive oil in the casserole, stir, and sauté for a second or two. Do not burn the garlic. Add the celery, allspice, cumin, and 1 tablespoon of salt and cook,

(Continued)

stirring, until the celery is translucent. This should not take more than a few minutes. Add the chopped tomatillos and ¼ cup of water. Continue cooking over medium heat for 10 minutes, stirring now and then, until most of the liquid has evaporated and a wooden spoon leaves a track on the bottom of the casserole. Stir in ¾ cup of the chopped cilantro leaves and the sliced onions.

5. Rub the scrod with the remaining oil and sprinkle with 1 teaspoon of salt. Place the fish on top of the onion-celery mixture. Arrange the small sautéed tomatillos and their accumulated juices around the fish, cover the casserole tightly, and braise over medium heat for about 20 to 25 minutes, or until done. Remove from the heat, sprinkle with the remaining ¼ cup chopped cilantro leaves, and serve right from the casserole.

VARIATION

Preheat the oven to 475 degrees. Place the casserole, tightly covered, in the oven and bake for 25 minutes, or until done. Remove from the oven, garnish with chopped cilantro, and serve.

Merluza en Salsa de Avellanas
Hake in Hazelnut Sauce

—

Serves 6 to 8

Cod, pollack, and monkfish can be substituted for hake in this recipe.

1 hake, with tail but no head, dressed (6 to 7 pounds)
1 tablespoon grated lime or lemon rind
4 stalks celery, washed, strings removed, and chopped
7 tablespoons butter
3 tablespoons olive oil
24 cloves garlic, peeled (2 heads)
1 bay leaf
2 dried red chili peppers, seeded

¼ cup all-purpose flour
3 cups milk
1 tablespoon coarse salt
1 cup shelled and blanched hazelnuts (5 ounces)
6 to 8 leeks, white parts only, washed, and cut in half lengthwise
3 tablespoons chopped fresh cilantro leaves or Italian parsley

1. Wipe the fish inside and out with a damp cloth. Rub the inside with the grated lime or lemon peel and fill the cavity with the chopped celery. Set aside.

2. Heat 4 tablespoons of the butter and 2 tablespoons of the olive oil in a saucepan. Add the garlic, bay leaf, and hot peppers; cover the pan and cook over low heat, stirring from time to time, for about 15 minutes, or until the garlic is totally soft to the touch of a fork. Remove and discard the peppers; remove and set aside the bay leaf.

3. Mix in the flour and continue cooking for 2 minutes longer. Do not let the flour brown. With a wire whisk, beat in the milk and salt. Increase the heat to medium and bring to a boil, stirring and scraping the bottom of the saucepan. Lower the heat and cook, stirring, until the sauce has thickened, about 3 to 4 minutes. Add the hazelnuts, stir, and remove from heat. Correct the seasoning with salt to taste.

4. Preheat the oven to 400 degrees.

5. Place the hake in a baking dish large enough to hold the fish and the leeks and rub the surface of the fish with 1 tablespoon of olive oil. Pour the hazelnut sauce around the fish, arrange the leeks, cut side down, on top of the sauce, and place the reserved bay leaf on top of the fish.

6. Melt the remaining butter. Brush the surface of the leeks with 1 tablespoon of melted butter and use the remaining tablespoon to butter a piece of wax paper large enough to cover the top of the baking dish. Place the wax paper, butter side down, over the dish, then cover tightly with foil. Place the baking dish in the oven, lower the temperature to 375 degrees, and bake for 45 minutes to 1 hour.

7. Remove the dish from the oven and let sit for about 5 minutes. Remove and discard the wax paper and foil, sprinkle with chopped cilantro, and serve.

Budín de Pescado
Fish Terrine

—

Serves 12 as an appetizer or 8 as a main dish

To give this terrine a festive look, I suggest a grape-leaf wrapping; another of my favorites is fish skins. (See Variation at end of recipe.)

Any firm, white-fleshed fish can be substituted for cod or halibut, as well as *congrio,* or conger eel, which is common and very much appreciated throughout Chile.

2½ pounds cod or halibut fillets
1 pound bay or sea scallops
2 cups milk or 1 cup milk mixed with 1 cup heavy cream
1 egg white
⅛ teaspoon ground mace
⅛ teaspoon cayenne
1 tablespoon coarse salt
Grated peel of 1 lemon
6 ounces salt pork or slab bacon, blanched with rind removed,
*   cut into chunks*
½ cup fresh bread crumbs
¼ cup pistachios or pignolis
1 tablespoon chopped fresh dill
1 tablespoon olive oil
20 to 25 stemless blanched California or Greek grape leaves, packed
*   in brine, drained, rinsed, and patted dry (preferably Orlando*
*   California Grape Leaves)*

GARNISH
Capers or pickled okra or small gherkins or cornichons
Alfonso or Kalamata olives
Corn on the cob, thinly sliced
Onion Relish (page 481)
Mayonnaise or an herb sauce (pages 477–479)
Salsa Cruda (page 480)

1. Remove and discard any bones left in the fish; cut into small pieces and set aside. Place the scallops in a strainer and dip into a bowl of cold water. Shake the strainer to loosen any particles of sand or shell and immediately remove. Set aside to drain.

2. In a small bowl, combine the milk, egg white, mace, cayenne, salt, and grated lemon peel. Mix and let sit, undisturbed, for 5 to 10 minutes.

3. Place the chunks of salt pork in the work bowl of a food processor and process thoroughly to a paste. Add the bread crumbs and continue processing until they are totally absorbed. With the motor still running, add half of the fish and half of the milk mixture and blend until the fish is finely ground and has absorbed all of the liquid. Transfer this mixture to a mixing bowl.

4. Place about ¾ pound of the scallops in the work bowl of the food processor and process them. Add the remaining fish and milk and continue processing until all the liquid is absorbed and the fish is ground. Add this to the mixing bowl containing the already-ground salt pork and fish and mix thoroughly. Fold in the remaining ¼ pound of scallops, the nuts, and the dill.

5. Preheat the oven to 375 degrees.

6. Brush the bottom and sides of a 10-cup rectangular porcelain, enameled cast-iron, or glass terrine (11¾ × 4½ × 3¾ inches) with some of the olive oil. Line the terrine with parchment paper or wax paper, covering the bottom and sides. Brush the paper lightly but evenly with the remaining oil. Then cover the entire bottom and sides of the terrine with grape leaves, overlapping them. With a rubber spatula, spread the fish mixture into the dish, pressing down slightly to make sure that all sides and corners are well covered. Cover the surface of the fish mixture with grape leaves. Place a piece of oiled parchment paper or wax paper over the top and cover tightly with aluminum foil.

7. Stand the terrine in a larger pan and pour in enough boiling water to reach three-quarters of the way up the sides of the terrine. Bake for 1 hour, or until set. Remove from the oven and let rest for about 15 minutes, with the terrine still in the pan. Remove the terrine from the water and let cool thoroughly. Store in the refrigerator overnight.

8. Remove and discard the aluminum foil and parchment paper or wax paper from the top and place the terrine upside down on a serving platter. Gently shake the terrine to loosen the *budín*, and remove the

(Continued)

mold. Carefully peel off and discard the parchment paper or wax paper Garnish with capers, pickled okra, or gherkins, olives, slices of corn on the cob, and onion relish. Serve with mayonnaise, an herb sauce, or salsa cruda.

STORAGE NOTE   This keeps well in the refrigerator, covered, for up to 5 days.

VARIATION

To wrap the fish loaf in scaled fish skin, take several small pieces or one large piece of skin and use it instead of the grape leaves to line the terrine. After the terrine has been unmolded, brush the top and sides with dissolved gelatin. Put the terrine in the refrigerator for a few minutes to set the gelatin, then serve.

Puré de Bacalao
Salt-Cod Mousse

Serves 8 as an appetizer or 6 as a main dish

Two kinds of salt cod are available. One, Norwegian salt cod, is dry and heavily salted and comes with skin and bones. The other, from Canada, is lightly salted and soft, without skin and bones. Either is suitable for this preparation, though the Canadian is preferable by far.

2 pounds skinless and boneless salt cod
1-inch piece fresh ginger, sliced
3 cups milk
3 cups heavy cream
2 bay leaves
3 or 4 dried red chili peppers, crumbled
2 tablespoons ground fennel
12 to 15 allspice berries
3½ pounds all-purpose potatoes
6 tablespoons olive oil
4 cloves garlic, peeled and slightly crushed
1 clove garlic, cut in half crosswise

4 tablespoons butter, melted
*Slivers of alfonso or Kalamata olives and/or whole caperberries
marinated in a bit of olive oil*

1. Soak the fish for 10 to 12 hours or overnight in generous amounts of cold water, changing the water a few times. Rinse thoroughly and drain the fish.

2. In a large pot, combine 8 cups of cold water and the ginger and bring to a boil. Add the fish and bring back to a rapid boil. Remove from the heat and with a slotted spoon, carefully transfer the fish to a colander; set aside to drain. Discard the water and ginger.

3. In an enameled saucepan, combine the milk and cream with the bay leaves, hot peppers, fennel, and allspice berries and bring to a boil. Lower the heat and simmer over very low heat until the liquid has reduced to 3½ to 4 cups, about 1½ hours. Let cool, then strain through a fine sieve, pressing against the sides of the strainer to extract the flavors from the spices. Discard the contents of the sieve and set aside the reduced cream and milk.

4. Meanwhile, peel the potatoes, place them in a pot with 8 cups of boiling water, and simmer for about 20 minutes, or until they are done. Drain them well. While the potatoes are still hot, mash them in a potato ricer or, for a finer texture, force them through a strainer, one or two at a time, using your hands or a wooden mallet. Set aside.

5. Remove and discard the bones and skin, if any, from the fish and with the back of a fork, shred or flake the fish until very fine or pound it to a paste in a mortar with a pestle.

6. In a large saucepan, heat the olive oil with the crushed garlic over medium heat, and sauté until the garlic is brown on all sides, about 4 minutes. Do not burn the garlic. With a slotted spoon, remove and discard the garlic and add the fish; sauté, stirring constantly, for a few minutes, or until the fish has absorbed all of the oil. Let cool for a few minutes and then scrape into a bowl.

7. Add the mashed potatoes and mix thoroughly until the mixture is smooth. Knead in the reduced flavored cream, a little at a time, making sure that the cream is absorbed each time. Correct the seasoning with salt to taste.

8. Preheat the oven to 400 degrees.

(Continued)

9. Rub the bottom of a baking dish with the cut side of the garlic, pressing to get all the garlic juices into the dish, and discard. Spoon and evenly spread the codfish mixture into the dish and smooth the surface with a wet rubber spatula. With a brush, dot the entire surface with melted butter. Bake for 35 minutes, or until golden. Serve piping hot, garnished with olives and/or caperberries.

VARIATIONS

Soak 1 pound of navy or Great Northern beans or chick-peas overnight. Cook them in plain water for 45 minutes to 1 hour, or until tender. Drain them and pass them through a food mill, or force them through a strainer to remove the skins. Substitute for the mashed potatoes in Step 7.

For individual appetizer portions, preheat the oven to 475 to 500 degrees. Divide the mousse among 8 ovenproof plates or gratin dishes. Smooth the top of the mousse with a wet rubber spatula. Place the dishes in the oven and bake until golden brown, about 8 minutes. The dishes may also be placed under the broiler, as far away from the heat source as possible, and broiled until golden brown, about 8 minutes. Remove from the oven or broiler and garnish each dish with olives or caperberries and serve with triangles of toasted or fried bread.

Pescado con Acelgas
Bluefish with Swiss Chard
—
Serves 6 to 8

Salmon, bass, or grouper can be used instead of bluefish.

1 bluefish, with head and tail, dressed (6 to 8 pounds)
6 pounds Swiss chard
5 tablespoons olive oil
3 cloves garlic, peeled and minced
1 or 2 jalapeño peppers, seeded and finely chopped
1 pound scallions, white parts only, cleaned and chopped (1 generous cup)
¼ cup chopped pitted alfonso or Kalamata olives

1 tablespoon plus 1 teaspoon coarse salt
3 cloves garlic, peeled and chopped
12 whole alfonso or Kalamata olives, pitted

1. With kitchen shears, remove and discard the fins and gills from the bluefish. With a damp cloth, wipe the fish inside and out. Remove and discard the backbone. To do this, place the fish horizontally on the work surface with the cavity facing you. Insert a sharp knife at the tail end, right on top of the backbone, and slide it, cutting to separate the bone from the flesh. Continue cutting until you reach the head. Repeat on the other side of the fish. With your hands, break and detach the loosened backbone at the head and tail end, then pull it out. Check for any leftover bones; remove and discard them. Set the fish aside.

2. Wash the Swiss chard well and drain thoroughly. Cut off the leaves from the stems and set the stems aside. Coarsely chop the leaves and set aside.

3. Preheat the oven to 400 degrees.

4. In a large saucepan, heat 3 tablespoons of the olive oil. Add the minced garlic and hot pepper and sauté over medium heat for a second or two, stirring. Do not let the garlic burn. Add the scallions and chopped olives, stir, and continue to sauté for a few minutes longer until the scallions are soft. Fold in the chopped Swiss chard leaves and 1 tablespoon of salt and cook over high heat until all the liquid has evaporated, about 12 minutes, tossing frequently. Remove from the heat and let cool. Stuff the cavity of the fish with this mixture.

5. In a roasting pan large enough to hold the fish, make a bed with the reserved Swiss chard stems; sprinkle with chopped garlic, whole olives, and the remaining salt. Place the bluefish on top. Rub the surface of the fish with 1 tablespoon of olive oil, cover the head and tail with oiled pieces of foil to protect them from burning, and bake for 45 minutes, or until the fish is done. Transfer to a serving platter with the Swiss chard stems, garnish with olives, and serve.

VARIATION

This dish may also be prepared with 2 fillets, each weighing 3 to 4 pounds. Place one fillet, skin side down, horizontally in front of you on the work surface. Cover with the Swiss chard mixture and fit the other

(Continued)

fillet on top. Tie together with kitchen string, starting at the middle. Tie again 2 inches from the middle on one side and then the other; continue tying on alternate sides at 2-inch intervals to make a compact package. Proceed with the recipe. Remove and discard the strings before serving.

Pargo con Mejillones
Braised Snapper and Mussels

—

Serves 6 to 8

*P*argo, or snapper, is found in abundance in the waters off Venezuela and Colombia. Its simple bone structure—just a spine and a few small bones around the cavity—makes it easy to cut handsome fillets.

Among the many varieties of snapper, red snapper is probably the best known. Other varieties include the yellowtail snapper, which has a milder and somewhat sweeter taste, and, from the same tropical waters, the mutton snapper, vermilion snapper, mangrove or gray snapper, silk snapper, and lane snapper, the smallest of all and abundant from south Florida to Brazil. Any kind of snapper can be used in this recipe.

2 snapper fillets with skin (about 3 pounds each)
1 dozen mussels (about 1½ pounds)
2 tablespoons olive oil
2 tablespoons Achiote Oil (page 472)
3 large cloves garlic, peeled and chopped
1 or 2 jalapeño peppers, seeded and chopped
½ teaspoon ground fennel
2 bay leaves
½ cup chopped Italian parsley
2 teaspoons coarse salt

1. Wipe the snapper fillets with a damp cloth. Remove and discard any bones, cover the fish with a moist cloth, and place in the refrigerator until ready to use.

2. Clean the mussels as described on page 486. Rinse them well, drain, cover with a damp cloth, and set aside until ready to use.

3. In a large oval earthenware or terra-cotta casserole or *cazuela,* heat the olive and achiote oils over medium heat. Add the garlic, hot pepper, fennel, and bay leaves. Sauté for just a second or two. Do not burn the garlic. Stir in ¼ cup of the parsley and place the fillets in the center of the casserole. Cover with a lid or a piece of aluminum foil and gently simmer the fillets for 10 to 15 minutes.

4. Arrange the mussels over and around the snapper. Sprinkle with salt and the remaining chopped parsley. Cover the casserole tightly and continue cooking for another 3 minutes, or until the mussels have opened. Remove from the heat and serve from the casserole.

Corvina con Frijoles Blancos
Bass and White Beans

Serves 6 to 8

Iam always generous with beans, so if when you prepare this dish, all the beans do not fit into the cavity of the fish, surround the fish with the extra beans, sprinkling them with chopped parsley.

1 striped bass, with head and tail, dressed (about 8 pounds)
3 tablespoons Achiote Oil (page 472)
6 thick strips bacon, coarsely chopped (about ½ pound)
6 cloves garlic, peeled and chopped
8 to 10 fresh sage leaves, chopped, or 1 teaspoon dried sage
⅛ teaspoon cayenne
6 cups cooked dried white beans (1 pound)
1 tablespoon plus 1 teaspoon coarse salt
½ cup cooking liquid from the beans or water
¼ cup chopped Italian parsley

1. Wipe the fish inside and out with a damp cloth and place in a roasting pan. Rub the fish inside and out with 1 tablespoon of achiote oil. Set aside.

2. Preheat the oven to 400 degrees.

(Continued)

3. In a large skillet, heat the remaining oil and the bacon and sauté until the bacon has rendered most of its fat, about 2 minutes. Add the garlic, sage, and cayenne; stir and sauté for a few seconds. Do not burn the garlic. Add the beans, salt, and cooking liquid from the beans and cook over medium heat, stirring, until all of the liquid has evaporated, about 8 minutes.

4. Remove from the heat, correct the seasoning with salt to taste, and let the mixture cool slightly. Mix in the chopped parsley and fill the cavity of the fish with the beans. Sew up the cavity with a trussing needle and fine string.

5. Bake the fish for about 45 minutes, or until done. To test, press the fish: it should feel firm but spring back. Transfer the fish to a serving platter, remove and discard the strings, and serve.

Fiambre de Bonito
Bonito Fiambre

—

Serves 8 as an appetizer or 6 as a main course

*F*iambre is a culinary term used throughout South America to denote cold food. Fiambres are served as appetizers or snacks; they also make a good lunch or a light dinner.

2½ pounds skinless bonito or tuna, cut into 2-inch cubes
½ cup all-purpose flour
½ cup olive oil
2 cloves garlic, peeled and crushed
2 large onions, peeled and thinly sliced
6 to 8 black peppercorns
½ cup red-wine vinegar
1 teaspoon sugar
4 sprigs fresh mint or thyme
1 cup Fish Stock (page 466) or Chicken Stock (page 461)
3 red bell peppers, seeded and thinly sliced
1 ear cooked corn, sliced into ¼- to ½-inch rounds

1. Lightly dredge the fish cubes in the flour. Shake off the excess and set aside.

2. In a sauté pan or earthenware casserole large enough to hold the fish in one layer, heat the olive oil over medium heat. Add the fish and brown it on all sides. With a slotted spatula or tongs, remove the fish to a plate and set aside.

3. Sauté the garlic in the remaining oil until golden but not browned. Add the onions and peppercorns and continue cooking until the onions are translucent. Add the vinegar, sugar, and mint. Stir, bring to a boil, and add the stock. Bring back to a boil, stirring frequently. Lower the heat, add the bell peppers, and cook for 1 minute longer. Add the fish with the accumulated juices, cover the sauté pan, and remove from the heat.

4. Let the dish sit, undisturbed, until cool. Serve at room temperature, garnished with rounds of corn.

STORAGE NOTE   This dish will keep well, refrigerated, for up to 2 days.

Atún a la Chorrillana
Tuna Steak Chorrillos Style

—

Serves 6 to 8

A *la chorrillana* is a style of cooking that originated in Chorrillos. Now a neighborhood of Lima, Chorrillos used to be a fishing village that supplied the capital with fish. Everyone understands *a la chorrillana* to mean smothered in onions and fresh hot peppers. This method is now used with both fish and steak. In Peru, bonito, which resembles a small tuna, and *corvina,* a type of bass, are commonly prepared in this style. Although I have used tuna here, swordfish would also be good.

For the dish to be a success, the tuna steaks must be cut thick, no less than 1¼ inches. If the fish is not thick enough, it will be overcooked and dry by the time the surface is golden.

6 to 8 tuna steaks, 1¼ to 1½ inches thick (about 8 ounces each)
2 cloves garlic, peeled
1 tablespoon coarse salt
1½-inch piece fresh ginger, peeled and grated
½ teaspoon ground cardamom
1 tablespoon dry vermouth
1 tablespoon lime juice
½ teaspoon sesame oil
3 tablespoons olive or vegetable oil
3 slices bacon, julienned (3 ounces)
2 cloves garlic, peeled and thinly sliced
3 pounds red onions, peeled and cut into ¼-inch slices
4 jalapeño peppers, seeded and julienned
2 pounds tomatoes, cut into wedges
2 tablespoons fresh thyme leaves
2 tablespoons fresh oregano leaves, coarsely chopped, or dill
3 tablespoons coarsely chopped fresh oregano or Italian parsley

1. Remove and discard the skin from the tuna and trim off any dark sections. Set aside.

2. In a mortar with a pestle, pound the 2 whole cloves of garlic and the salt to a smooth paste. Add the ginger and cardamom and continue pounding. Add the vermouth and lime juice and stir. Let sit for a few minutes and add the sesame oil and 1 tablespoon of the olive oil. Mix thoroughly. Rub the tuna steaks with this mixture and let marinate for 10 to 15 minutes.

3. Preheat the broiler. Broil the steaks in a pan at the middle level, or about 4 inches away from the heat source, for 10 to 15 minutes, or until the fish is golden.

4. Meanwhile, in a large skillet, heat the remaining 2 tablespoons of olive oil over high heat. Add the bacon and sauté until it is golden. Stir in the sliced garlic and onions and continue to sauté, stirring now and then, until all the liquid has evaporated and the onions are golden around the edges. Add the hot peppers, tomato wedges, thyme, and oregano and continue cooking until the tomatoes are heated through.

5. Cover the bottom of a serving platter with the braised onion. Arrange the tuna steaks on top, surrounded by the tomato wedges. Serve immediately, sprinkled with chopped oregano.

Guiso de Atún
Ragu of Tuna and Thyme

Serves 6 to 8

Guisos are stewlike dishes that are usually made with meat and vegetables, but some of the most interesting ones are made with fish. For this guiso, I have selected tuna, a firm-fleshed fish; it holds together well during cooking. Swordfish, bonito, or Pacific yellowtail can be substituted for tuna in this recipe.

2 pounds fresh tuna
¼ cup all-purpose flour
4 tablespoons olive oil
2 cloves garlic, peeled and minced
2 jalapeño peppers, seeded and minced, or ⅛ teaspoon cayenne
2 medium onions, peeled and finely chopped (about 2 cups)
1 tablespoon coarse salt
6 sprigs fresh thyme, tied together with kitchen string
6 medium potatoes, peeled and cut into 4 × 3-inch pieces (about 2 pounds)
4 large green bell peppers, roasted and sliced
1 tablespoon fresh thyme leaves

1. Remove and discard the skin from the tuna and cut the meat into 16 chunks, about 4 × 3 inches. Dredge the chunks in the flour, shaking off the excess.

2. In an earthenware casserole or a saucepan, heat the olive oil. Quickly brown the fish all around. With a slotted spoon, remove the chunks to a plate and set aside.

3. Add the garlic, hot peppers, onions, salt, and thyme to the oil remaining in the casserole and cook, stirring frequently, until the onions are lightly golden. Add 1 quart of water, bring to a boil, and add the potato pieces. Lower the heat and simmer for 20 minutes, or until the potatoes are barely tender.

4. Add the roasted peppers and the tuna and cook for 10 minutes more. Remove from the heat, discard the thyme sprigs, and correct the seasoning. Garnish with thyme leaves and serve right from the casserole.

Sardinas con Tomillo
Braised Sardines with Thyme

—

Serves 6 to 8

Fresh sardines are delightful, but they must be *very* fresh. They are too delicate to hang around the fish market for long. These tasty, tiny fish don't need much fussing. Just gut and grill or broil them for a few minutes, and one of the greatest meals will appear as if by magic. Sardines are also good when cooked with fresh herbs, particularly thyme, as in this recipe.

It is important that the pan in which the sardines are cooked conduct heat as evenly as possible so the fish doesn't stick to the bottom. Copper is good, and a heavy nonstick aluminum pan is fine, but the best is a well-seasoned black cast-iron pan. It heats evenly, retains heat well, and brings out the best in food. And it looks great on the dinner table.

3 pounds fresh sardines (3 to 4 ounces each)
4 tablespoons olive oil
4 cloves garlic, peeled and slivered
2 dried red chili peppers, seeded and crumbled
3 tablespoons fresh thyme leaves
1 teaspoon coarse salt

1. Gut the sardines, leaving the heads and tails attached. Rinse and drain them. Gently pat dry inside and out with paper towels and set aside.

2. In a cast-iron frying pan about 15 inches in diameter, heat the oil over high heat. Add the garlic and hot peppers and sauté for a second. Do not burn the garlic. Remove the pan from the heat and mix in 1 tablespoon of the thyme leaves.

3. Quickly arrange all of the sardines in the pan. Sprinkle with the salt and 1 tablespoon of the thyme leaves. Tightly cover the pan and cook over medium-low heat for 4 minutes, gently shaking the pan from time to time.

(Continued)

4. Remove the lid and cook for another 4 minutes, or until the sardines are done, shaking the pan to prevent the sardines from sticking to the bottom. Remove from the heat; sprinkle with the remaining thyme leaves and serve hot, right from the pan.

VARIATION

After you have completed Step 3, place the pan under the broiler as close to the source of heat as possible, and broil until the surface of the sardines is slightly golden. This should take no more than 1 or 2 minutes. Sprinkle with the remaining thyme leaves and serve immediately.

Pejerreyes Arrebosados
Crispy Fried Smelts

Serves 6 to 8

These tasty little fish—no more than nine inches long—are semi-translucent and have a lovely gold stripe down their body. I often toss them into a cast-iron frying pan, quickly cook them on both sides, and serve them sprinkled with coarse salt and garnished with lemon wedges. That's all you really need to do for a magnificent meal.

I could give you recipe after recipe for smelts; *arrebosados* are one of my favorites. You can bread the fish as in this recipe or dip them in beer batter. (See Variation at end of recipe.)

5 pounds smelts, with heads and tails (7 to 9 inches long)
1½ cups all-purpose flour
1 tablespoon plus 1 teaspoon coarse salt
4 eggs
⅛ teaspoon cayenne
3 cups dried bread crumbs
2½ quarts vegetable oil

GARNISH
3 tablespoons chopped Italian parsley
Lemon wedges
Onion Relish (page 481) (optional)

1. With a sharp paring knife or small scissors, cut along the belly of each smelt, starting from the tail. Remove and discard the guts and gills. Rinse the fish, drain well, and pat dry on paper towels. Pinch the backbone close to the tail to loosen it. Break the backbone at the head and gently pull it out and discard it. Do not remove the heads or tails. Fold each smelt in half and push the tail through the mouth. The smelts will now look like small triangular bags. Set aside.

2. On a tray, mix the flour with the salt. In a bowl, beat the eggs together with the cayenne. On a second tray, spread out the bread crumbs.

3. Dredge the smelts in the flour, shaking off the excess. Then dip them in egg and roll them in bread crumbs.

4. Heat the vegetable oil to 375 degrees. Add the smelts, a few at a time, and deep-fry them until they are golden brown on all sides. Each fish should only take 1 or 2 minutes. Remove from the oil and drain them on towels. Serve the smelts warm, sprinkled with parsley and garnished with lemon wedges and onion relish, if desired.

VARIATION

Mix together 1 cup all-purpose flour, 1½ cups light beer, 1 egg, and 2 teaspoons coarse salt. Let the mixture rest for 3 hours at room temperature or overnight in the refrigerator. Gut, debone, and fold the fish as described in Step 1. Dip the fish in batter; deep-fry and serve as described in Step 4.

Cazuela de Pejerreyes
Smelt Casserole

Serves 6 to 8

This dish is a good candidate for the buffet table as well as for a dinner entrée. It's as good at room temperature as it is piping hot.

5 pounds smelts, with heads and tails (7 to 9 inches long)
¼ cup olive oil
4 cloves garlic, peeled and crushed
2 thin slices ginger, peeled
2 bay leaves
2 tablespoons all-purpose flour
1 tablespoon Spanish paprika
⅛ teaspoon cayenne
1 teaspoon ground cumin
2 cups Chicken Stock (page 461) or Fish Stock (page 466)
1 tablespoon coarse salt
¼ cup chopped Italian parsley

1. Starting in the center, cut an opening along the belly of each smelt, first toward the head and then toward the tail, without breaking into the guts. Discard the guts. Remove and discard the gills. Rinse and drain the smelts and dry them with paper towels. Set aside.

2. Preheat the oven to 400 degrees.

3. In a 15- to 16-inch earthenware casserole, heat the olive oil over high heat. Add the garlic and ginger. Sauté until the garlic is golden. Add the bay leaves. Quickly stir in the flour, paprika, cayenne, and cumin and cook for 1 to 2 minutes, stirring constantly. Add the stock, still stirring, and then the salt. Cook until the sauce has thickened and the spoon leaves a track on the bottom of the casserole, 6 to 8 minutes.

4. Remove the casserole from the heat. Arrange the smelts, slightly overlapping, in the thick sauce. Tightly cover the casserole, first with wax paper and then with aluminum foil or a heavy lid.

5. Bake for 20 minutes. Remove from the oven and serve right from the casserole, sprinkled with parsley.

SHELLFISH

Parihuela Salvaje

Serves 8 to 10

Parihuela salvaje is a wonderfully satisfying combination of fish and shellfish with a spicy sausage in a rich tomato sauce. This *criollo,* or creole, dish is a colorful example of Spanish and Portuguese influences on the cuisines of the New World.

40 littleneck clams
40 mussels
1 pound medium shrimp (16 to 20 per pound)
1 pound freshwater prawns or crayfish or small lobster tails, cut in half
1 pound squid
½ pound skinless and boneless swordfish or tuna or grouper

TOMATO SAUCE
2 tablespoons olive oil
2 tablespoons Achiote Oil (page 472) or olive oil
3 cloves garlic, peeled and chopped
½-inch piece fresh ginger, peeled and chopped
1 chorizo sausage, finely chopped (about 4 ounces)
3 medium onions, peeled and finely chopped (about 3 cups)
1 bay leaf
2 or 3 fresh or dried hot peppers, chopped or crumbled
1 tablespoon coarse salt
1 carrot, peeled and finely chopped
2 stalks celery, washed, strings removed, and finely chopped
2 cups dry white wine or dry vermouth
8 cups canned plum tomatoes, (2 28-ounce cans plus 1 15-ounce can)
6 to 8 sprigs fresh thyme

4 medium-firm tomatoes
2 tablespoons olive oil
2 large cloves garlic, peeled and finely chopped
½ cup green peas, fresh or frozen

(Continued)

1. Wash and brush the clams under cold running water. Place them on a tray, cover them with a damp cloth, and set aside until ready to use. Discard any that do not close when tapped or are broken or damaged.

2. Clean the mussels as described on page 486. Cover with a damp cloth and set aside until ready to use.

3. Peel the shrimp, leaving the last segment of the shell attached, and devein them. Rinse and set aside to drain.

4. Rinse the prawns under cold running water and set aside to drain.

5. Clean the squid as described on page 487. Drain and pat them dry. Slice the squid bodies and tentacles on the diagonal, ¼ inch thick. Set aside.

6. Wipe the swordfish with a damp cloth; cut it into ½-inch cubes and set aside.

7. In a large straight-edged saucepan, heat the 2 tablespoons of olive oil and the 2 tablespoons of achiote oil over medium heat. Stir in the 3 cloves of garlic, ginger, and chorizo and sauté for just a second. Do not burn the garlic. Add the onions, bay leaf, hot peppers, and salt and continue cooking for 4 to 5 minutes, or until the onions are totally translucent. Add the carrot and celery and cook for a minute longer, stirring. Add the white wine and simmer, stirring now and then, for 15 minutes, or until the wine has reduced by half. Add the canned tomatoes and thyme and continue cooking, stirring now and then, until the sauce is very thick and the spoon leaves a track on the bottom of the pan, about 45 minutes.

8. Discard the bay leaf and remove from the heat. Pass the sauce through a food mill with the fine disk, or force the sauce through a strainer, discarding the skins and seeds left in the food mill or strainer. Set the tomato sauce aside.

9. Cut the fresh tomatoes in half crosswise. Remove and discard all the seeds and juices and cut each tomato half into 4 pieces.

10. In an earthenware casserole or saucepan large enough to hold all the shellfish and fish, heat the 2 tablespoons of olive oil over medium heat. Add the 2 cloves of garlic and stir; mix in the tomato sauce and bring to a boil. Lower the heat and stir in the fresh tomato pieces. Put in the clams, cover the saucepan with a tight-fitting lid, and cook for 5 minutes. Add the mussels and continue cooking, covered, for a few minutes longer. Stir in the shrimp, prawns, squid, and swordfish, sprinkle the peas on top, cover the pot again, and cook for another 5 minutes, or until the shells of the clams and mussels have opened and the shrimp are done. Serve hot, right from the earthenware casserole.

VARIATION

Mix 1 teaspoon of saffron threads into the tomato sauce after it has been passed through the food mill in Step 8. Let it rest for 5 minutes, then proceed with the recipe.

Mariscada

Serves 6 to 8

There are as many mariscadas as there are fish in the sea; each time this dish is prepared, it seems to be different. The beauty of it is that you can go to the market with an open mind and select the freshest and best-looking seafood you find there. I have suggested using four kinds of shellfish in this recipe, but you should feel free to substitute or add others. Besides shellfish, chunks of any firm-fleshed fish can be used.

You can prepare mariscada two ways. One is to cook your selection of seafood quickly in a little fish broth without much fuss; the other is to make an *aderezo* and add the seafood to it. (An *aderezo* is a mixture of aromatic vegetables, herbs, and spices that is cooked or sautéed.) I find both ways to be excellent, though in this recipe I happened to use the *aderezo* technique.

24 littleneck clams
24 mussels
6 to 8 crayfish or 1 pound medium shrimp (16 to 20 per pound)
1 pound sea scallops
4½ cups canned plum tomatoes (3 14-ounce cans)
¼ cup olive oil
1 large clove garlic, peeled and finely chopped
1 medium onion, peeled and finely chopped (1 cup)
1-inch piece fresh ginger, peeled and finely chopped
1 jalapeño or serrano pepper, seeded and finely chopped
2 tablespoons chopped fresh thyme leaves or ½ teaspoon
*   dried thyme*
1 bay leaf
1 carrot, peeled and cut into ⅛-inch dice
2 stalks celery, washed, strings removed, and cut into ⅛-inch dice
½ cup dry white wine
½ teaspoon sugar
2 teaspoons coarse salt
2 large fresh tomatoes, cut into 8 pieces (about 1¼ pounds)
2 tablespoons grated lemon rind

1. Scrub the clams in cold water to remove the sand; place them in a container, cover with cold water, and set aside.

2. Clean the mussels as described on page 486. Cover them generously with cold water and set aside.

3. Rinse the crayfish under cold running water, drain, and refrigerate. If shrimp are used instead, peel them, leaving the last segment of the shell attached. Devein the shrimp, rinse under cold running water, pat dry with a cloth or paper towels, and refrigerate.

4. Place the scallops in a strainer, dip into a bowl of cold water, and shake to remove any particles of sand or shell. Drain well, gently pat dry, and refrigerate until ready to use.

5. Pour the canned tomatoes through a food mill or strainer and force the pulp through, removing and discarding the seeds. Set aside.

6. In a sauté pan, heat the olive oil over medium heat. Add the garlic, onion, ginger, and hot pepper and sauté for about 5 to 10 minutes, or until the onion is translucent, stirring occasionally. Add the thyme, bay leaf, carrot, and celery and continue sautéing for another 5 minutes, or until the carrot pieces have softened slightly. Add the wine and cook until most of the liquid has evaporated. Add the tomato pulp and the sugar. Cook over medium heat, stirring now and then, for about 10 minutes, or until the tomato sauce has thickened and a spoon leaves a track on the bottom of the pan. Stir in the salt. Drain the clams and mussels and arrange them in the pan. Add the fresh tomato pieces and the crayfish or shrimp.

7. Cover the pan tightly and cook for 5 minutes. Add the scallops and continue cooking for another 3 to 5 minutes, or until the shellfish have opened. Remove from the heat. Transfer to a large bowl or earthenware casserole, sprinkle with grated lemon peel, and serve.

Migas de Camarones
Shrimp Migas

Serves 6 to 8

—

Migas is a dish based on crumbled bread, which is the exact translation of the word. The Peruvians have mastered this dish to perfection. They use several kinds of hot peppers to create layers of flavors.

It's important, when preparing migas, to use a plain white bread that is neutral enough to carry the sauce's flavorings. For the right satiny quality, the bread must be fresh and have good texture; all the crust should be removed.

You should feel free to substitute squid, crayfish, cubes of chicken, or even small boiled potatoes for the shrimp in this recipe. You will get fantastic results.

2 to 2½ pounds medium shrimp (16 to 20 per pound)
1 or 2 fresh poblano or cayenne or Anaheim peppers
2 dried mirasol or ancho peppers
1 cup light beer
1 tablespoon coarse salt

BREAD SAUCE
¼ cup Rendered Bacon Fat (page 476)
3 tablespoons Achiote Oil (page 472)
2 large cloves garlic, peeled and finely chopped
2-inch piece fresh ginger, peeled and finely chopped
1 large onion, peeled and coarsely chopped (1½ cups)
4 large tomatoes, peeled, seeded (juices saved), and chopped
2 cups fresh white bread crumbs
½ cup chopped walnuts
1 cup Fish Stock (page 466) or Chicken Stock (page 461) or water

¼ cup chopped Italian parsley or fresh cilantro leaves
    or fresh basil leaves

1. Peel the shrimp, leaving the last segment of the shell attached. Devein, rinse, and drain well. Set aside.

2. Roast 1 of the fresh peppers and 1 of the dried peppers as described on page 483. Seed all of the peppers, including the roasted ones.

Place all the hot peppers in a small bowl. Add the beer and salt and let them soak until quite soft, at least 30 minutes. Blend the peppers with the beer in a blender or food processor at high speed until the mixture is very smooth. You should have about 1 cup. Set aside.

3. In a skillet or earthenware casserole, heat the bacon fat and achiote oil over medium heat. Add the garlic and ginger and sauté for a few seconds. Do not let the garlic brown. Add the onion and continue sautéing for about 5 minutes, stirring, until the onion is translucent. Add the blended peppers and cook for another 5 minutes, until the liquid has evaporated and only a slight film of fat or oil remains in the bottom of the skillet. Add the tomatoes with juices, lower the heat, and continue cooking until the tomatoes are quite soft and all the liquid has evaporated, stirring and scraping the bottom of the skillet occasionally.

4. Blend in the bread crumbs and walnuts and cook for about 1 minute, then add the stock. Continue cooking and stirring for another 2 to 3 minutes, or until the sauce has thickened. Add the shrimp to the skillet. Mix well and simmer, stirring now and then, for about 8 minutes, or until the shrimp are firm, but not overcooked. Serve immediately, garnished with chopped parsley.

Picante de Camarones
Shrimp in a Picante Sauce

Serves 6 to 8

The degree of heat generated by the peppers in this dish can be adjusted to your taste. The best way to determine the heat of a chili pepper is to taste a tiny bit before using it. Jalapeño peppers in particular can be very temperamental—generally they are relatively mild or have no heat at all, but sometimes you get one that blows the lid off the pan. So adjust accordingly, adding a few extra or using one instead of two jalapeños, without changing anything else in the recipe.

The mirasol pepper is among the most widely used in Peruvian cooking; it is appreciated for its fine aromatic flavor. Mirasol, literally "looking at the sun" in Spanish, is also known as *ají amarillo,* a name that

(Continued)

alludes to its beautiful bright yellow color. It can be used fresh or dried, and there is even a paste made from it. But don't feel you can't make this dish if you can't get mirasol peppers. Just substitute dried Anaheims or anchos or any of your favorite dried chili peppers.

3 pounds large shrimp (8 to 10 per pound)
1 or 2 dried mirasol peppers, seeded
1 dried red chili pepper, seeded
1 cup dry white wine or Shrimp Stock (page 468) or light beer
3 tablespoons peanut oil
2 tablespoons Achiote Oil (page 472)
3 large cloves garlic, peeled and finely chopped
2 roasted jalapeño peppers (page 483), seeded and finely chopped
5 large tomatoes, peeled, seeded, and chopped
¼ cup fresh bread crumbs
1 cup Shrimp Stock (page 468) or Chicken Stock (page 461) or water
1 tablespoon coarse salt
2 tablespoons chopped Italian parsley or fresh dill

1. Peel the shrimp, leaving the last segment of shell attached. Save the shells for stock. Devein and rinse the shrimp and set aside to drain.

2. In a small bowl, combine the mirasol and red chili peppers with the white wine and let soak for about 15 minutes. Drain the peppers, reserving the liquid. Chop the peppers and set them aside.

3. In an earthenware casserole, heat the peanut and achiote oils over medium heat. Add the garlic, the soaked peppers, and the roasted peppers and sauté for 1 minute, stirring. Do not burn the garlic or the peppers. Add the chopped tomatoes and let them cook until they are totally soft, about 4 minutes, stirring. Mix in the bread crumbs, cook for a few seconds longer, and add the reserved soaking liquid from the hot peppers, 1 cup of shrimp stock, and salt.

4. Bring the sauce to a boil. Lower the heat and simmer for 10 to 15 minutes, or until most of the liquid has evaporated and the spoon leaves a track on the bottom of the casserole. Stir in the shrimp, cover the casserole, and cook for about 8 minutes, or until the shrimp are barely done. Remove from the heat, stir, sprinkle with chopped parsley, and serve right from the casserole.

Camarão con Coco
Shrimp in Coconut Sauce

Serves 8 as an appetizer or 6 as a main course

Brazilian fish cookery is very versatile; it incorporates many flavorings, including coconut, which is a favorite. Coconut works particularly well in this recipe, because it emphasizes the sweet flavor of the shrimp. This dish can be served as an appetizer or as a main course, accompanied by white rice.

2 pounds small shrimp (21 to 25 per pound)
1 heavy coconut
2½ cups milk
2 tablespoons butter
1 medium onion, peeled and finely chopped (about 1 cup)
⅛ teaspoon cayenne
1 jalapeño pepper, cut in half lengthwise and seeded
4 tablespoons coconut or pear or kirsch liqueur
2 tablespoons all-purpose flour
1 teaspoon coarse salt
2 teaspoons cornstarch
¼ cup chopped fresh dill or Italian parsley

1. Peel the shrimp, leaving the last segment of the shell attached. Devein and rinse the shrimp. Set aside.

2. With a pointed instrument, such as an ice pick, pierce two of the three soft "eyes" of the coconut. Shake the liquid into a large measuring cup and add just enough milk to make 3 cups. Remove the coconut meat and peel it. Coarsely chop all the coconut meat and place half of it, with half of the liquid, in the jar of an electric blender or the work bowl of a food processor and blend or process thoroughly. Repeat with the remaining coconut meat and liquid. Set aside.

3. In a large enameled saucepan, melt the butter over medium heat. Add the onion, cayenne, and hot pepper and sauté until the onion is translucent, about 4 minutes. Do not brown the onion. Stir in the liqueur

(Continued)

and continue cooking until all of the liqueur has evaporated, about 1 minute. Mix in the flour and cook, stirring constantly, for a few seconds, or just long enough for all the flour to be absorbed. Add the blended coconut and salt and bring to a boil, stirring. Lower the heat and gently simmer for 10 minutes, stirring now and then.

4. Remove from the heat and set aside to cool for 5 to 10 minutes. Take out and discard the pepper and blend thoroughly in two batches in the jar of an electric blender or the work bowl of a food processor. Force the coconut mixture through a fine sieve or through a strainer lined with a layer of cheesecloth and squeeze out all the liquid, discarding the pulp. This will yield about 4 cups of sauce. Stir in the cornstarch and let sit for about 5 minutes.

5. Stir the strained coconut mixture and pour it into an earthenware casserole or enameled saucepan just large enough to hold all the shrimp. Bring to a gentle simmer, stirring, over medium heat. Continue to cook, stirring now and then, for 10 to 15 minutes longer, or until the sauce is thick enough to coat the back of a spoon.

6. Add the shrimp, stir, cover the casserole, and cook over low heat for another 2 to 3 minutes, or until the shrimp are barely cooked. Remove from the heat and correct the seasoning with salt to taste. Serve right from the casserole, garnished with chopped dill.

VARIATION

Open an additional coconut, as described in the recipe, saving the liquid. (You can add it to the rest of the coconut liquid and use less milk to make up the 3 cups of liquid needed in Step 2.) Peel the coconut and cut the meat into ¼-inch cubes. Add the cubes just after the sauce has come to the simmer in Step 5. Continue with the recipe.

Salpicón de Cangrejo
Crabmeat Salpicón

—

Serves 8 as an appetizer or 6 as a main course

Salpicón is a saladlike dish, refreshing as well as colorful, made with cooked meat, fish, or shellfish. There are many kinds of salpicóns; this one, prepared with crabmeat, is outstanding. It is perfect as an appetizer to start any meal or as a main course for a summer luncheon, accompanied by a good crusty bread and a glass of chilled white wine or beer.

1½ pounds fresh jumbo lump crabmeat
2 tablespoons fresh lemon juice
1 clove garlic, peeled and crushed
½ yellow bell pepper, seeded, deveined, and thinly julienned
½ red bell pepper, seeded, deveined, and thinly julienned
½ stalk celery, washed, strings removed, and thinly julienned
4 to 6 scallions, white parts only, thinly julienned
2 tablespoons olive oil
1-inch piece fresh ginger, peeled and thinly julienned
1 jalapeño or arbol pepper, seeded and thinly julienned
1 tablespoon chopped fresh dill
Coarse salt
Freshly ground white pepper
6 to 8 Boston lettuce leaves

GARNISH
Kalamata olives
1 ear cooked corn, sliced into 8 rounds

1. Check and remove any pieces of shell and cartilage from the crabmeat and set aside.

2. In a bowl large enough to hold all the ingredients, combine the lemon juice and garlic and let rest, undisturbed, for about 15 minutes. With the back of a fork, squeeze the garlic clove into the lemon juice to release its juices. Discard the garlic and set the flavored lemon juice aside.

(Continued)

3. In a large bowl of ice water, combine the julienned bell peppers, celery, and scallions and leave until crisp, about 10 minutes. Drain well and set aside.

4. With a wire whisk, mix the olive oil with the flavored lemon juice. Stir in the ginger, hot pepper, and dill. Add the crabmeat and the drained julienned vegetables and toss well but gently, taking care not to break up the crabmeat. Correct the seasoning with salt and pepper to taste. To serve, place each portion on a Boston lettuce leaf and garnish with black olives and rounds of corn.

Tortillas de Cangrejo
Crab Cakes

Serves 6 as an appetizer

Crabmeat is absolutely delicious when served hot as in these *tortillas de cangrejo,* or crab cakes. The best kind to use is what is called *jumbo lump crabmeat,* which comes from the back fin of the crab.

Crab cakes can be deep-fried as well as sautéed, as suggested in this recipe. Fry them just long enough to get a golden color all around.

1 pound fresh jumbo lump crabmeat
3 tablespoons butter
3 tablespoons all-purpose flour
1 cup Fish Stock (page 466) or Chicken Stock (page 461) or milk
Zest of 1 lemon
⅛ teaspoon white pepper
6 scallions, white parts only, washed and finely chopped
1 teaspoon chopped fresh dill
Coarse salt
¾ cup all-purpose flour
2 eggs, slightly beaten
2 to 2½ cups bread crumbs
8 tablespoons (1 stick) butter, clarified (page 476)
3 tablespoons olive oil
Lemon wedges

1. Check the crabmeat for any pieces of shell and cartilage and remove them; set the crabmeat aside.

2. In a small enameled saucepan, melt the butter over medium heat. When sizzling, mix in the 3 tablespoons of flour and cook, stirring constantly, for 1 to 2 minutes. Do no let the flour brown. With a wire whisk, beat in the stock and cook, constantly stirring and scraping to prevent the sauce from sticking to the pan, until the sauce is thick and a spoon leaves a track on the bottom, about 15 minutes. Remove from the heat, let cool for a few minutes, and add the lemon zest and white pepper. Mix in the scallion and dill.

3. Scrape the sauce into a bowl and gently but thoroughly mix in half the crabmeat. Add the remaining half and mix in carefully so that the lumps of meat do not fall apart. Correct the seasoning with salt and white pepper to taste. Divide the crabmeat mixture and shape into 6 patties, about 2½ to 3 inches in diameter, dipping the palms of your hands into a little bit of cold water each time for easier handling.

4. Place the ¾ cup of flour on a plate, the eggs in a shallow dish, and the bread crumbs on a second plate. Dredge each patty in flour, gently shaking off the excess, then dip into the beaten eggs. Then "bury" the patty in bread crumbs. Gently pat the crumbs onto the patty, brushing off the excess.

5. In a skillet large enough to hold the patties in one layer, heat the butter and oil over medium-high heat. Add the crab cakes and sauté them on one side for about 3 minutes; then turn them with a spatula and sauté on the other side for 3 minutes more, or until golden. Transfer them from the skillet to individual plates or a platter and serve, garnished with lemon wedges.

Almejas con Quinua
Clams with Quinoa

—

Serves 6 to 8

This flavorful dish of Peruvian origin captures the essence of clams. In Peru *machas,* or razor clams, would be used, but *almejas* encompasses clams in general. For this hearty dish, I have used two sizes of quahogs (a term used in the eastern United States for hard-shell clams): cherrystones for chopping, to give the dish richness and substance, and littlenecks in the shell for charm and contrast.

18 to 24 littleneck clams
1 quart shucked cherrystone clams, with their liquor (see Note)
Clam juice or clam broth or water
1 cup quinoa
3 tablespoons olive oil
2 cloves garlic, peeled and finely chopped
1 medium onion, peeled and finely chopped (1 cup)
1 or 2 fresh jalapeño or Anaheim or mirasol peppers,
    seeded and chopped
1 bay leaf
1 teaspoon ground cumin
¼ teaspoon ground white pepper
1 tablespoon tomato paste
3 large potatoes, peeled and cut into ½-inch cubes (about 2 cups)
¼ cup chopped Italian parsley or fresh cilantro leaves

1. Wash and brush the littleneck clams under cold running water, place them on a tray, cover with a damp cloth, and set aside until ready to use. Chop the shucked cherrystone clams and set aside. Pour the liquor through a strainer lined with a double layer of cheesecloth to remove any sand and discard; or let the liquor rest for about 10 minutes, undisturbed, until the sand settles at the bottom and then carefully pour off the liquor, leaving the debris in the container. You should have 3 cups of liquor. If not, add enough clam juice to make 3 cups. Set aside.

2. Place the quinoa in a bowl, add enough cold water to cover by about 2 inches, and let soak for a few minutes. Then massage the grain between the palms of your hands for a moment. Pour through a strainer and rinse under running cold water. Repeat this operation once and set aside to drain.

3. In a large pot or earthenware casserole, heat the oil over medium heat. Add the garlic, onion, hot pepper, bay leaf, cumin, and white pepper and sauté until the onion is totally translucent but not browned. Mix in the tomato paste, add the chopped clams, and cook for a few minutes longer, stirring frequently. Pour in the 3 cups of clam liquor and simmer for 10 to 15 minutes.

4. Add the potatoes, cover the pot, and continue cooking for 10 minutes. Mix in the quinoa and cook for 25 minutes. Stir in the whole clams and continue cooking, covered, for 10 to 15 minutes, or until the clams are barely open, gently stirring once. Correct seasoning with salt to taste, garnish with chopped parsley, and serve.

NOTE   When shucking your own clams, open the clams over a bowl or container to collect all the liquor, and drain them.

Mejillones con Hinojo
Mussel Salad with Fresh Fennel

Serves 8 as an appetizer or 6 as a main dish

The simplest way to enjoy mussels is to steam them open and serve them on the half shell topped with a sauce, such as mayonnaise flavored with fresh herbs, or salsa. This dish which, pairs mussels and fennel, is a bit more complex. It makes a great appetizer or a main dish for a summer lunch.

5½ pounds mussels
½ cup olive oil
¼ cup sherry vinegar
1 tablespoon lemon juice
1 clove garlic, peeled and finely chopped
1 serrano or jalapeño pepper, seeded and finely chopped
½ teaspoon ground fennel
1 teaspoon coarse salt
1 medium red onion, peeled and thinly sliced
2 medium fennel bulbs, thinly sliced
½ cup finely chopped Italian parsley
1 teaspoon finely chopped fresh dill

1. Clean the mussels as described on page 486 and set aside until ready to use.

2. In a skillet or sauté pan with a tight-fitting lid, combine the mussels and 1 cup of water. Cover the saucepan and steam the mussels open over high heat, about 5 minutes. Discard any mussels that have not opened. Remove the mussels with a slotted spoon to a bowl. Save the liquid for another purpose or discard it. When the mussels are cool enough to handle, gently pull off any remaining bits of beard and remove the mussels, intact, from their shells. Discard the shells.

3. In a large bowl, combine the olive oil, vinegar, lemon juice, garlic, hot pepper, ground fennel, salt, sliced onion, sliced fennel, and parsley. Toss and correct the seasoning with salt to taste. Add the mussels, toss again, and transfer to a serving dish. Sprinkle with chopped dill and serve.

NOTE You can save the juice released by the mussels when you cook them open in Step 2 and use it in place of fish stock. The juice will keep well, tightly covered, in the refrigerator for a few days or in the freezer for up to 3 months.

Seco de Choros
Mussel Seco

Serves 6 to 8

When shopping for mussels, buy only those with intact, tightly closed shells. Pick up a mussel to check its weight: it should feel full and heavy no matter what the size.

4 pounds mussels
2 tablespoons olive oil
1 large clove garlic, peeled and chopped
1 jalapeño pepper, seeded and finely chopped
2 medium onions, peeled and finely chopped (2 cups)
1 cup light beer
2 cups rice
3 cups Fish Stock (page 466) or Chicken Stock (page 461) or water
1½ tablespoons coarse salt
1 dried red chili pepper, seeded, crumbled, and chopped
2 cups tightly packed chopped fresh cilantro leaves
½ cup frozen peas, thawed and drained

1. Clean the mussels as described on page 486 and set aside.

2. In a heavy 3-quart saucepan, heat the olive oil over medium heat. Add the garlic and hot pepper and sauté for about 1 minute. Add the onions and sauté until translucent and the edges are slightly golden. Add the beer and cook until most of the liquid has evaporated. Add the rice with the stock. Stir in the salt and the dried pepper. Bring to a boil, cover the saucepan, and cook over medium heat for about 20 to 25 minutes, or until all the liquid is absorbed and the rice is tender. Stir the rice, scraping the bottom of the saucepan.

(Continued)

3. Fold in 1¾ cups of the cilantro and the peas. Bury the mussels in the rice, cover, and cook for about 8 minutes, or until the shells have opened, shaking the pan from time to time. Transfer to a serving platter, sprinkle with the remaining cilantro, and serve.

VARIATION

Substitute 5 pounds of cherrystone or littleneck clams for the mussels. Clean the clams as described on page 486 and proceed with the recipe, starting with Step 2.

Choros a La Perricholi
Mussels à La Perricholi
—
Serves 8 as an appetizer or 6 as a main course

This cinnamon-colored and wonderfully rich mussel dish is named after La Perricholi, a famous beauty and mistress of Amat, a viceroy who governed Peru for thirteen years during the Spanish colonial period.

The dish can be served as an appetizer or as a main course, accompanied by plainly cooked white rice.

5½ to 6 pounds mussels
1½ pounds potatoes
1 tablespoon coarse salt
1 cup dry white wine
½ cup olive oil
1 clove garlic, peeled and finely chopped
3 medium onions, peeled and finely chopped (3 cups)
1 leek, white part only, washed and finely chopped
¾ cup sweet vermouth
4 tablespoons browned flour (see Note)
1 cup Beef Stock (page 462) or Veal Stock (page 464) or Chicken
  Stock (page 461)
½ cup chopped fresh dill

1. Clean the mussels as described on page 486 and set aside.

2. Scrub the potatoes and place them in a pot. Add 6 to 8 cups of water and the salt and bring to a boil. Lower the heat and simmer for 20 minutes, or until the potatoes are tender. When cool enough to handle, peel and set aside.

3. In a large sauté pan with a tight-fitting lid, combine the mussels and wine. Cover the saucepan and steam the mussels open over high heat, about 5 minutes. Discard any that have not opened. With a slotted spoon, transfer the mussels to a bowl and strain the juice through a strainer lined with a double layer of cheesecloth. You should have 3 cups. If not, add stock or water to make 3 cups and set aside. Discard the cheesecloth.

4. When the mussels are cool enough to handle, gently pull off any remaining bits of beard and remove the mussels from their shells. Set aside. Discard the shells.

5. In an earthenware casserole, sauté pan, or large skillet, heat the olive oil. Add the garlic, onions, and leek and sauté until the onions and leek are translucent. Add the vermouth and cook until it has evaporated, about 10 minutes.

6. Sprinkle in the browned flour and stir. Add the 3 cups of reserved mussel juice and the 1 cup of stock and cook, stirring, for 15 minutes, or until the sauce has thickened enough to coat a spoon lightly. Stir in the mussels. With your hands, crumble the potatoes over the mussels, or cut them into bite-size pieces and mix them in. Continue cooking, stirring, over medium heat, until the potatoes and mussels have heated through, about 1 minute. Correct the seasoning with salt to taste, sprinkle with dill, and serve.

NOTE   To brown the flour, put ½ cup all-purpose flour in a small skillet, preferably cast-iron, and cook over medium heat, constantly scraping and stirring the flour to prevent it from sticking to the bottom of the skillet, until the flour turns light brown. Remove the skillet from the heat and pass the flour through a fine sieve. You will have about ⅓ cup.

VARIATION

Substitute 5½ to 6 pounds cherrystone or littleneck clams for the mussels. Clean the clams as described on page 486 and proceed with the recipe, starting with Step 2.

Picante de Calamares
Squid in a Picante Sauce

Serves 6 to 8

*P*icante means "with heat," and that heat comes from hot peppers. One, two, or even more hot peppers are used in a picante sauce to achieve the proper taste.

4½ to 5 pounds small squid
2 dried mirasol peppers, seeded
1 dried ancho pepper, seeded
½ cup pisco (Peruvian brandy) or light rum
3 tablespoons olive oil
2 tablespoons Achiote Oil (page 472)
3 cloves garlic, peeled and finely chopped
3 stalks celery, washed, strings removed, and finely minced
3 sweet red pimientos, drained and finely chopped (about 1 cup)
3 large onions, peeled and finely chopped (4 cups)
1 teaspoon sugar
6 large tomatoes, peeled, seeded (juices saved), and chopped
2 tablespoons coarse salt
½ cup coarsely chopped Italian parsley

1. Clean the squid as described on page 487. Drain and pat them dry with a cloth or paper towels. Slice the squid bodies and tentacles on the diagonal ⅛ inch thick. Set aside.

2. Soak all the dried peppers in the pisco for about 20 minutes. Place the softened peppers with the pisco in the jar of a blender and blend at high speed for a few seconds, or until very smooth.

3. In a medium earthenware casserole, heat the olive and achiote oils over medium heat. Add the garlic and celery and sauté for a few minutes, or until the celery is soft. Add the chopped pimientos, stir, and add the onions. Continue cooking for about 2 minutes, or until the onions are translucent. Add the blended pepper mixture and lower the heat. Add the sugar, chopped tomatoes, and salt. Measure the juices from the tomatoes and add enough water to make 2 cups. Add this liquid to the casserole and bring to a boil. Cover the casserole, lower the heat, and simmer for about 20 minutes, or until all of the liquid has evaporated and the spoon leaves a track on the bottom of the casserole.

4. Remove the lid from the casserole and move the tomato sauce toward the sides, making a well in the middle. Add the squid and sauté over high heat for a few seconds. Mix all of the ingredients together, lower the heat, and cook for another 3 minutes. Correct the seasoning with salt to taste. Sprinkle with parsley and serve in the earthenware casserole.

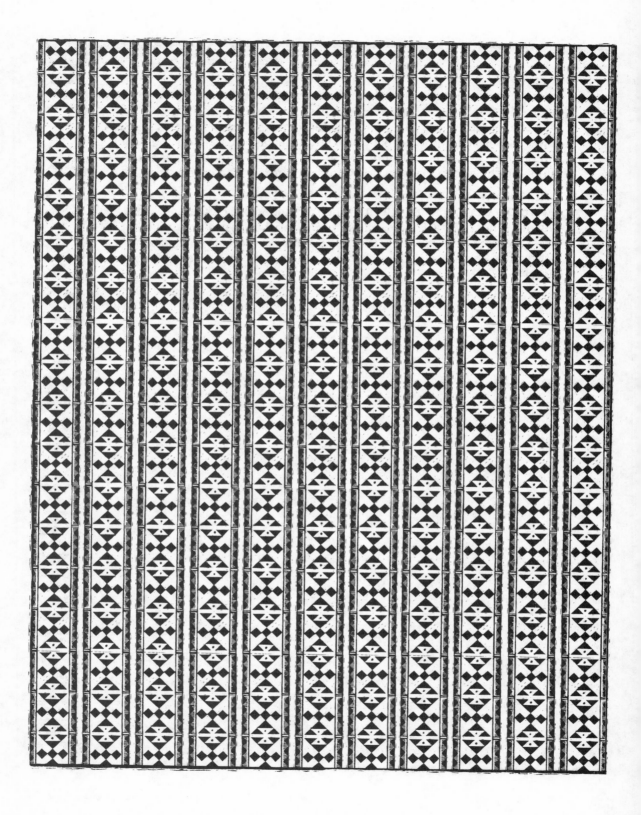

POULTRY & RABBIT

CHICKEN

Pollo al Ajo
Roast Chicken with Garlic and Thyme

Ají de Gallina
Chicken in Hot Pepper and Walnut Sauce

Pollo al Palillo
Chicken in Palillo Sauce

Pollo a la Chinita
Chicken à la Chinita

Salpicón de Pollo con Col
Chicken and Cabbage Salpicón

DUCK

Seco de Pato
Duck Seco

Pato Asado de Panela
Braised Duck with Ginger

Arroz con Pato
Duck and Rice

Pato con Higos
Duck with Figs

GOOSE

Enrollado de Ganso
Roulade of Goose

TURKEY

Pavo Asado
Roasted Wild Turkey

SQUAB

Aguadito de Pichón
Squab Aguadito

QUAIL

Codorniz con Trigo
Quail and Barley

RABBIT

Conejo Frito
Honeyed Fried Rabbit

Conejo con Lentejas
Rabbit and Lentils

Conejo en Salsa de Chocolate
Braised Rabbit in Chocolate Sauce

Aguadito de Conejo
Rabbit Aguadito

Birds play an important part in the diet of all South Americans. Duck, squab, turkey, and chicken top the list. The duck is native to the Americas; the Quechuas developed methods to preserve its meat for long periods by freeze-drying it, as they did potatoes.

Like duck, squab is a red-meat bird that tastes best on the rare side. It should be quickly broiled or grilled or roasted in an extremely hot oven, just long enough to crisp the skin and firm the flesh. Another way to enjoy red-meat birds is to cook the meat slowly to tenderize it and allow its good flavor to fuse with other ingredients, as in aguadito and seco stews.

Quail, or *codorniz*, as it is called in Spanish, is usually braised or chopped, bones and all, and added to a tomato sauce as it cooks; such a sauce is typically used for pasta. Pheasant, or *faisán* in Spanish, has a good flavor, although it has a tendency to be dry and slightly tough. When properly cooked, though, by either quick roasting or slow braising, pheasant is a magnificent treat.

Turkey is the bird usually served at family festivities. The South American domestic turkey is not white but has bluish-black feathers, with a lump of "hair" on its chest that looks like a tassel, and a fiery red head. This turkey looks wild, but its large bony body is filled with more meat than a wild turkey; its thighs are plump, its breast full and voluptuous. Before this magnificent bird appears on the table, it is treated like a king for several weeks, being fed large quantities of chopped red onions, plenty of dried corn and walnuts, and a healthy shot of pisco before it is invited to stroll into the kitchen.

The origins of the domestic chicken go back thousands of years. It is believed that all our barnyard chickens originated in southeast Asia. There are many theories as to how chickens made their way to the New World, but we do know that the chicken was already well established in pre-Columbian times. Chicken has always had, and still has, universal appeal. It lends itself to all types of preparation in the kitchen: from the grill to the oven, to the frying pan, the soup pot, the casserole, and the salad bowl.

Chickens can be categorized by age, which also determines the method of cooking. The best to grill, roast, or broil are squab chickens (¾ pound to 1 pound) and broilers (1½ to 2½ pounds). Next in age and size come the fryers (2½ to 3½ pounds) and roasters (4 to 6½ pounds). Then come the capons and stewing chickens (or fowl), and last, what are called old hens and cocks (or roosters). The latter are more than a year old and usually weigh more than 4 pounds; they are good for stews and soup stocks.

When selecting a chicken, whether whole or cut up, be sure the breast and thighs are full and the skin is creamy white, moist, and free of bruises or soft spots. The inside of the cavity should look rosy and smell fresh. If by any chance you can obtain a chicken with the feet, neck and head, use them or save them, along with the giblets, for the stockpot. The head, neck, feet, gizzard, and heart from any bird will contribute flavor and rich texture to soup stock.

When I was growing up in Lima, chickens were not so easy to get as they are today, and we looked forward to the day when a chicken would appear on the dinner table. We were always glad to see Clopoldo, the chicken farmer, stopping by on his way to the market. He came about twice a month carrying a big bunch of chickens, which he dropped straight onto the kitchen table for Doña Judita, as he called my mother, to make her selection. She would inspect each chicken very carefully. She would press and poke the breast of one of them, asking, "What happened here? Skinny, oh, were you training it to be a model?" She would feel the thighs of another: "And this one? The thighs are too skimpy, they have to exercise, you should let them run free!" She would smell the cavity of each chicken and check its age by inspecting the feet, remarking, "Where did you get this one from, a retirement home?" While this conversation was going on, she would quietly put aside the ones she felt were the best of the lot. Clopoldo would pick up the remaining chickens and leave the house, muttering to himself as always but with a big smile on his face.

Rabbit

Rabbit, especially young ones, the *cuy,* and *viscacha* all enjoy a prominent place in the South American kitchen. The *cuy,* a guinea pig native
to the Andes, is raised for meat in virtually every household. The *cuy*
(pronounced "coo-EE," like its cry) is quite a different animal from the
North American guinea pig. As a domesticated animal raised for food,
it's fat and sassy, often weighing three, four, even five pounds. The *viscacha,* or hare, thrives in the wild, particularly in Argentina.

Rabbit, on the other hand, is bought in the market, usually whole and
in the fur. Rabbit is a superb white-meat animal, extremely versatile.
South Americans are crazy about the taste of rabbit and prepare it in a
variety of ways, from simply frying it to featuring it in the most laborious
and complex of dishes.

CHICKEN

Pollo al Ajo
Roast Chicken with Garlic and Thyme

—

Serves 6 to 8

A garlic-herb paste spread under the skin of a roasting chicken flavors the meat and keeps it moist. Filling the cavity of the chicken with whole hot peppers adds to the flavor, without making the chicken hot. Serve the peppers as a condiment with the chicken.

> To roast a chicken, pick one that is plump and heavy-breasted and weighs between 3½ and 6 pounds. Bring it to room temperature and wipe it inside and out with a damp cloth. Then rub the inside with a cut lime or lemon, a sprinkling of salt, and a generous amount of freshly ground black pepper. For best results, roast it at 375 degrees, allowing 20 minutes to the pound. Baste frequently with a flavorful fat, oil, or butter. Let it sit for at least 8 to 10 minutes before carving.

1 roasting chicken (about 5½ pounds)
1 lime

GARLIC–HERB PASTE
8 tablespoons (1 stick) Clarified Butter (page 476)
24 large cloves garlic, peeled
1-inch piece fresh ginger, peeled and sliced lengthwise into
    4 or 5 slices
1 teaspoon coarse salt
½ cup fresh bread crumbs
3 tablespoons fresh thyme or cilantro or tarragon or dill leaves
8 jalapeño peppers or other small hot peppers

1. Wipe the chicken inside and out with a damp cloth. Cut the lime in half and squeeze and rub it into the skin and cavity.

2. In the top of a small double boiler, combine the clarified butter, garlic, ginger, and salt. Cover tightly and cook over hot water on low heat for 25 minutes, or until the garlic is soft to the touch of a fork. Remove the garlic to a plate and set the butter and ginger aside. With a fork, mash the garlic to a smooth paste; continue to mash while adding the bread crumbs. Mash until all the bread crumbs have been absorbed by the garlic. Add 4 tablespoons of the clarified butter, 1 tablespoon at a time, and mix until all of the butter has been added. Place this mixture in the refrigerator for a few minutes to solidify the butter slightly. (Do not let it get hard.) Remove from the refrigerator, add the thyme leaves, and mash and mix thoroughly to a smooth, pastelike consistency.

3. Preheat the oven to 375 degrees.

4. Run your fingers between the skin and the flesh of the chicken on both sides of the breast and the thighs and legs to separate and loosen the skin. Using a teaspoon, distribute the garlic-herb paste evenly under the skin of the breast, legs, and thighs. Place the hot peppers in a bowl and toss them with 1 teaspoon of the remaining clarified butter. Remove the ginger slices from the clarified butter and place them in the cavity of the chicken. Then fill the cavity with all of the buttered hot peppers.

5. Truss the chicken or tie the legs together and fold the wings under the back. Place the chicken on a rack in a roasting pan. Brush with some of the remaining clarified butter and roast the chicken for about 2 hours, basting after 1 hour with the leftover clarified butter.

6. Remove the chicken from the oven, cut and discard the trussing strings and ginger, transfer to a serving platter, and let sit for 8 to 10 minutes before carving. Serve, garnishing each plate with the peppers.

To truss a chicken or any other bird, place the bird on the work surface on its back, with the legs facing away from you. Take a length of kitchen string and lay the center across the tips of both drumsticks. Wind the sides of the string around the tips and pull both ends of the string toward you so that the legs are tied together. Bring each end of the string through the thighs to the back and flip the bird over so that it is on its breast and the legs are in front of you. Bring the ends of the string around the wing joints. Pull the ends of the string, securing the neck skin under the strings. Pull the ends of the string tightly and tie with a knot so that the whole bird is compactly tied. Fold the wings back under the bird.

Ají de Gallina
Chicken in Hot Pepper and Walnut Sauce

Serves 6 to 8

*A*jí means "hot pepper," but it also refers to a category of dishes in which hot peppers are the star, providing flavor, color, and heat. There are many *ají* dishes, including *ají de camarones* (with shrimp). But *ajíes* are also made with humbler ingredients, such as potatoes *(ají de papas)*, chayote or squash *(ají de calabaza)*, eggs *(ají de huevos)*, cheese *(ají de queso)*, and even avocados, as in *ají de aguacate,* which is quite common in Venezuela. *Ají de mondongo* (with tripe) and *ají de conejo* or *cuy* (with rabbit or Andean guinea pig) have a special place in many South American kitchens. But of all the *ajíes, ají de gallina* is the most spectacular.

1 large frying chicken, with giblets, neck, head, and feet, if available
    (about 4½ pounds)

CHICKEN STOCK
1 large onion, peeled and cut into 8 wedges
1 large carrot, peeled and sliced
2 stalks celery, chopped
½-inch piece fresh ginger, peeled and sliced
8 sprigs fresh thyme or 3 sprigs Italian parsley
2 bay leaves
8 to 10 cloves
1 tablespoon coarse salt

1 cup orange juice
3 tablespoons lime juice
4 to 6 dried mirasol peppers, seeded, or ancho peppers
6 tablespoons olive oil
3 large onions, peeled and finely chopped (about 4 cups)
½ teaspoon ground turmeric (or 1 teaspoon Spanish paprika, if you
    use ancho peppers)
4 slices white bread, crusts removed
1 cup milk
1 cup finely chopped walnuts

2 tablespoons grated parmesan
6 to 8 small potatoes, boiled and peeled

GARNISH
2 hard-boiled eggs, sliced
6 to 8 alfonso or Kalamata olives
2 tablespoons chopped Italian parsley or fresh cilantro leaves

1. Wipe the chicken inside and out with a damp cloth and truss for easy handling, if desired (page 257).

2. Place the giblets and neck in a stockpot. Add the onion wedges, carrot, celery, ginger, thyme, bay leaves, cloves, salt, and 3 quarts of water and bring to a boil over high heat. Lower the heat, cover, and let simmer for 15 minutes.

3. Add the chicken and cook, covered, for 45 minutes, or until the chicken is done. Test by pressing the flesh; it should feel soft but springy. Remove the chicken from the stock and when cool enough to handle, remove the skin and put it back into the simmering stock. Remove all the meat from the bones and put the bones back in the pot. With your fingers, shred the meat. Set aside.

4. Continue simmering the stock over medium heat for about 40 minutes, or until it has reduced to about 5 cups. Strain the stock through a fine sieve or through a strainer lined with a double layer of cheesecloth. Degrease thoroughly. You should have 4 cups of clear chicken stock. If not, add enough water to make 4 cups. Set aside.

5. Combine the orange and lime juice in a bowl. Crumble or break the mirasol peppers into small pieces and soak them in the juice for 20 minutes. Pour into a blender jar and blend until smooth. Set aside.

6. In a sauté pan, heat the olive oil, add the chopped onions and turmeric, and cook over medium heat, stirring, until the onions are totally translucent, about 8 minutes. Add the blended pepper mixture and continue cooking and stirring until all the liquid has evaporated, about 10 minutes.

7. Meanwhile, soak the bread in the milk. Add the soaked bread to the onion-pepper mixture and cook for a few seconds, stirring. Add 2 cups of the chicken stock and continue cooking, stirring now and then, until the sauce has thickened considerably and a spoon leaves a track on the bottom of the pan, about 25 minutes.

(Continued)

8. Add the shredded chicken and the remaining 2 cups of chicken stock. Stir, bring to a boil, lower the heat to the minimum, and gently simmer for 25 minutes. Add the walnuts and cheese, stir, and cook for about 5 minutes, or until the mixture has thickened slightly. Correct seasoning with salt to taste and serve with boiled potatoes. Garnish with hard-boiled eggs and black olives and sprinkle with chopped parsley.

Pollo al Palillo
Chicken in Palillo Sauce

—

Serves 6 to 8

In this dish, chicken is marinated in *palillo* and lime juice, then cooked with yuca. It is always served with a grain, usually rice, though quinoa or even pasta may be used.

Instead of cutting up a whole chicken, you could use chicken parts, particularly drumsticks and thighs, which can withstand the slow stewing process.

1 small frying chicken, cut into 8 or 10 pieces (about 3½ pounds)
3 large cloves garlic, peeled
1 tablespoon coarse salt
2 teaspoons palillo or 2 teaspoons ground turmeric mixed with
    1 teaspoon ground cumin
2 tablespoons fresh lime juice
4 tablespoons olive oil
3 medium onions, peeled and finely chopped (4 cups)
2 tablespoons all-purpose flour
2 teaspoons coarse salt
2 cups Chicken Stock (page 461)
2 pounds yuca, peeled, core removed, and cut into 1½-inch cubes
2 tablespoons chopped fresh cilantro or Italian parsley

1. Wipe the chicken pieces with a damp cloth and place them in a stainless-steel bowl. Set aside.

2. In a mortar with a pestle, pound the garlic, salt, and *palillo* to a smooth paste. Add the lime juice and mix well. Pour this mixture over the chicken pieces in a stainless-steel or glass bowl and mix thoroughly. Let marinate for 2 hours at room temperature or overnight in the refrigerator.

3. In a heavy casserole, heat the oil and over low heat, add the chicken pieces. Gently sauté them until barely golden all around, about 5 to 8 minutes. Transfer the chicken to a plate and set aside. To the same casserole, add the onion and sauté, while stirring, until the onion is translucent, about 5 to 8 minutes. Do not brown. Sprinkle with the flour and the salt and continue cooking, stirring, for 1 minute longer. Add the stock and, while stirring, bring to a boil.

4. Add the yuca, the chicken, and all the juices left on the plate. Lower the heat, cover tightly, and let simmer gently, stirring now and then, for 1 hour to 1 hour and 15 minutes, or until the yuca is tender. Correct seasoning with salt to taste and garnish with chopped fresh cilantro.

Pollo a la Chinita
Chicken à la Chinita

—

Serves 10 to 12

What makes Peru's creole cooking unusual is the contribution of the Chinese settlers along with that of the indigenous Quechua Indians and the Africans brought over as slaves in colonial times. This mixed ethnic cuisine is very colorful—full of unexpected tones and surprises.

The Chinese came to Peru in the mid-nineteenth century. There were open quotas then—that is, no papers were needed to enter the country. Now Lima has one of the largest Chinatowns in the world.

4 or 5 whole chicken breasts, skinless and boneless (about 3½ pounds)

MARINADE
1 large clove garlic, peeled
1 tablespoon coarse salt
1 teaspoon ground turmeric
1 teaspoon ground cumin
3 tablespoons dry sherry
1 tablespoon balsamic vinegar

5 tablespoons peanut oil
2 large cloves garlic, peeled and crushed
12 scallions, white parts only, thinly sliced and placed in ice water
4 medium carrots, peeled, julienned, and placed in ice water
2 large leeks, white parts only, julienned and place in ice water
5 or 6 stalks celery, strings removed, julienned, and placed in ice water
½ pound snow peas, strings removed, julienned, and placed in ice water
1 large green bell pepper, seeded, veins removed, julienned, and placed in ice water
4 large red bell peppers, seeded, veins removed, julienned, and placed in ice water
3 large yellow bell peppers, seeded, veins removed, julienned, and placed in ice water
2-inch piece fresh ginger, peeled and julienned
1 or 2 jalapeño peppers, seeded and julienned

¼ cup coarsely chopped peanuts
1 recipe Sesame Noodles (recipe follows)
3 tablespoons fresh thyme leaves

1. Wipe the chicken breasts with a damp cloth and slice them on the diagonal into ¼-inch strips. Place them in a stainless-steel or glass bowl and set aside.

2. In a mortar with a pestle, pound the garlic, salt, turmeric, and cumin to a smooth paste. Add the sherry and the balsamic vinegar. Mix well. Coat the chicken strips well with this mixture and let marinate for at least 15 to 20 minutes, or until ready to use.

3. In a large skillet over high heat, heat 3 tablespoons of the peanut oil; add the crushed garlic cloves and sauté until the garlic is soft and golden on all sides. Remove the garlic and discard. Add the marinated chicken strips with any leftover marinade and sauté them, over high heat, until most of the liquid has evaporated, 8 to 10 minutes. Transfer the chicken to a bowl and set aside in a warm spot.

4. Drain the scallions, carrots, leeks, celery, snow peas, green pepper, red peppers, and yellow peppers, keeping each vegetable separate.

5. In the same skillet in which you sauté the chicken, heat the remaining 2 tablespoons of peanut oil over high heat and sauté the ginger and jalapeño pepper for a few seconds. Add the scallions, stir; add the carrots, stir; add the leeks and celery, toss gently. Add the snow peas and the green peppers, toss; add the red and yellow peppers, toss. Sauté until all the vegetables are heated through. Push the vegetables aside, forming a well in the center; add the chicken strips and the chopped peanuts. Let heat through, then mix gently. Correct the seasoning with salt to taste. Serve on a nest of sesame noodles garnished with thyme leaves.

(Continued)

Fideos con Ajonjoli
Sesame Noodles

Serves 8 to 10

1 tablespoon coarse salt
1 pound dried fettuccine
10 tablespoons (1¼ sticks) unsalted butter
1 tablespoon olive oil
3 large cloves garlic, peeled and crushed
1 jalapeño pepper, seeded and coarsely chopped
¼ cup white sesame seeds

1. In a large pot, bring 6 quarts of water with the salt to a boil. Add the fettuccine and cook for 8 to 10 minutes, or until barely tender. Remove from the heat, drain, and add 2 tablespoons of the butter and the olive oil. Mix well and set aside, covered, in a warm spot.

2. In a saucepan, heat the remaining butter with the garlic and jalapeño pepper. Cook until the garlic is soft and golden on all sides. Remove from heat and let cool slightly. Strain the flavored butter through a fine sieve, pressing out all the juices, and pour over the pasta. Mix gently, cover, and set aside in a warm spot.

3. In a large skillet, lightly roast the sesame seeds over high heat without butter or oil for a few minutes, until slightly golden. Remove the seeds from the skillet. Just before serving, mix half the seeds with the noodles and sprinkle the remaining seeds on top.

Salpicón de Pollo con Col
Chicken and Cabbage Salpicón

Serves 8 as an appetizer or 6 as a main course

In South America the word *salpicón* refers to a wide range of saladlike dishes. The convenient aspect of these dishes is that the meat can be cooked in advance; as a matter of fact, it really is better to do so, and leftover chicken or turkey is ideal.

3 whole chicken breasts, with skin and bones (about 3 pounds)
1 teaspoon Spanish paprika

LEMON-OIL DRESSING
¼ cup fresh lemon or lime juice
2 teaspoons coarse salt
1 tablespoon Dijon mustard
¼ teaspoon white pepper
¾ cup olive oil

About 1 pound Savoy cabbage, thinly shredded (6 cups)
1 tablespoon coarse salt
1 small sweet onion, peeled and thinly sliced
2 red bell peppers, seeded and julienned
1 carrot, peeled and julienned
2 tablespoons finely chopped fresh dill or Italian parsley

GARNISH
1 large sweet potato, baked and sliced into 6 to 8 pieces (page 390)
18 to 24 alfonso or Kalamata olives
½ pound feta, cut into ½-inch cubes

1. Preheat the oven to 450 degrees.

2. With a damp cloth, wipe the chicken breasts and place them, skin side up, on a rack in a roasting pan. Sprinkle the entire surface with paprika. Roast for about 20 to 25 minutes, or until done. Test by pressing the meat; it should feel firm but springy to the touch. Remove from the oven and let cool thoroughly, undisturbed. Remove and discard the bones and skin. With your fingers, thinly shred the chicken breasts along the grain; place the meat in a stainless-steel bowl and set aside.

3. In a small bowl, mix the lemon juice, salt, Dijon mustard, and white pepper. Add the olive oil and mix thoroughly with a wire whisk until emulsified. Pour this dressing over the shredded chicken; mix well.

4. Place the cabbage in a bowl and sprinkle with salt; toss well and let sit for 10 to 15 minutes. Transfer the cabbage to a strainer or colander, rinse well under cold running water, and drain thoroughly.

5. Add the cabbage, onion, bell peppers, carrot, and dill to the chicken mixture. Toss and correct the seasoning with salt and freshly ground white pepper to taste. Arrange the salpicón in a serving bowl or on a platter and surround it with sweet-potato slices, olives, and feta.

DUCK

Seco de Pato
Duck Seco

—

Serves 6 to 8

Seco is one of the many very popular stewlike dishes of South America. As the name indicates, a seco should be dry—but not too dry. There must be some heady juices for the potato and rice to soak up.

1 duck (5½ to 6 pounds)

MARINADE
4 cloves garlic, peeled
1 tablespoon coarse salt
1 teaspoon ground cumin
¼ teaspoon white pepper
⅓ cup red-wine vinegar

2 large onions, peeled and finely chopped (about 2½ cups)
2 jalapeño peppers, seeded and finely chopped
1 cup light beer
1 tablespoon coarse salt
2 cups Beef Stock (page 462) or Chicken Stock (page 461) or water
2 large potatoes, peeled and quartered
1 cup well packed, finely chopped fresh cilantro leaves
1 cup peas, fresh or frozen (see Note)

1. Wipe the duck inside and out with a damp cloth. Cut the duck into 6 serving pieces: 2 breasts, 2 thighs, and 2 drumsticks. Remove the skin from the breasts and thighs. Place the duck pieces in a stainless-steel or glass bowl and set aside. Cut the skin into strips about ¼ inch wide.

2. Place the skin in a saucepan, add ½ cup water, and bring to a boil. Lower the heat and let simmer, stirring now and then, until all the water has evaporated and the skin has released its fat and is golden in color, about 20 minutes. Drain through a fine sieve. Reserve the skin and the fat. Set aside.

3. In a mortar with a pestle, pound the garlic, salt, cumin, and white pepper to a paste. Add the vinegar and mix well. Pour this mixture over the duck pieces and mix thoroughly. Let marinate at room temperature for 1 to 2 hours or covered in the refrigerator overnight.

4. In a sauté pan, heat ¼ cup of the duck fat. Add the duck pieces and sauté over medium heat until lightly browned on all sides, about 15 to 20 minutes. Transfer the duck from the pan to a plate and discard all but 2 tablespoons of the fat. Add the onions to the remaining fat and sauté, stirring, until barely golden around the edges, about 10 to 15 minutes.

5. Add the jalapeño peppers, beer, and salt and cook over very low heat for 10 minutes, stirring now and then. Add the stock, the duck pieces, and the accumulated juices from the plate. Stir, cover, and simmer for 20 minutes, skimming off any excess fat that rises to the surface. Add the potatoes and continue cooking for about 25 minutes, or until the potatoes are tender.

6. Add the cilantro and fresh peas, stir, and cook for 4 to 5 minutes. Correct the seasoning with salt to taste. Transfer to a serving dish, sprinkle with the reserved golden duck skin, and serve.

NOTE   If frozen peas are used, thaw them in a strainer under cold running water and drain well. Add them to the stew 1 minute before correcting the seasoning.

Pato Asado de Panela
Braised Duck with Ginger

Serves 6 to 8

Ginger was brought to South America by the Spanish and Portuguese settlers so long ago that it has come to be regarded as native to the continent. Ginger is greatly appreciated in two major cuisines: the Peruvian and the Brazilian. In Peru, fresh ginger is used both in small amounts as a flavoring and in quantity as a component of many dishes.

In Brazil, ginger is greatly favored in the south, especially in the regions of São Paulo, Santa Catalina, Rio Grande do Sul, and Paraná. One of the best southern Brazilian dishes is this one, in which duck is braised with a good amount of ginger.

2 ducks (5 to 6 pounds each)

VINEGAR MARINADE
1 cup red-wine vinegar
2 tablespoons ground cumin
1 tablespoon coarse salt
1 tablespoon freshly ground black pepper

DUCK STOCK
1 large onion, peeled and chopped (about 1½ cups)
1 or 2 jalapeño or serrano peppers, seeded and chopped,
  or 1 dried red chili pepper
1 small carrot, washed and chopped
3 leeks, white parts only, washed and chopped
4 stalks celery with leafy tops, washed and chopped
1 bay leaf
1 small bunch fresh thyme
1½ teaspoons juniper berries, slightly crushed, or ¼ cup gin
8 cloves
6 cups Chicken Stock (page 461) or water
1 orange, peeled and thinly sliced
1½-inch piece fresh ginger, peeled and julienned
2 tablespoons chopped Italian parsley

1. Cut each duck into 4 serving pieces: cut away the thighs and legs in one piece, cut off the breast, removing the wings and wishbone, and cut each breast in half. Remove all the skin from the breasts and some of the fatty skin from the thighs. Place all the duck pieces in a stainless-steel or glass bowl and set aside. Cut the skin into strips ¼ inch wide and set aside. Cut the backbones into smaller pieces; cut the wings in half and save, along with the necks, giblets, and heads, if available. Do not use the livers, if any.

2. In a small bowl, combine the vinegar, cumin, salt, and pepper; mix and pour over the duck pieces. Toss until all the pieces are well coated and set aside to marinate at room temperature for 2 hours.

3. In a saucepan, combine the strips of duck skin with ½ cup water. Bring to the boil, lower the heat, and let simmer for about 20 minutes, or until the skin has released all its fat and is crisp and brown. Drain and reserve the fat. Spread the crackling (as the skin is now called) on paper towels and set aside.

4. In a large saucepan, heat ¼ cup of the reserved duck fat; add the wings, necks, backbones, and giblets and sauté over medium heat, stirring now and then, until well browned on all sides. With a slotted spoon, transfer the bones and giblets to a plate.

5. Pour off all but 2 tablespoons of the fat from the saucepan. Add the onion, pepper, carrot, leeks, and celery and sauté, stirring, until all the vegetables are lightly browned, about 15 minutes.

6. Return all the browned bones and gizzards with their accumulated juices to the saucepan. Add the bay leaf, thyme, juniper berries or gin, cloves, chicken stock, and orange slices, while scraping the bottom of the saucepan, and bring to a boil. Lower the heat and simmer gently for 1 hour, uncovered, or until the stock has reduced by half.

7. Remove from heat and pour through a fine sieve, or a strainer lined with a double layer of cheesecloth, into a bowl, pressing out all the juices from the bones and vegetables. Discard the contents of the strainer. Let the stock sit for about 10 minutes, undisturbed, to allow the fat to rise to the surface. Degrease thoroughly. You should have 3 cups of stock. If not, add enough water to make 3 cups.

8. In a sauté pan or casserole large enough to hold all the duck pieces in a single layer, heat 3 tablespoons of the duck fat. Add the duck pieces with all the marinating juices and sauté over medium-high heat,

(Continued)

turning, until the duck pieces are golden on all sides, about 15 minutes. Add the ginger and stir; add the stock and bring to a boil. Lower the heat, cover, and simmer for 1 hour, or until the duck pieces are tender, stirring now and then. Correct the seasoning with salt and black pepper to taste. To serve, sprinkle the strips of crackling on top of the duck and garnish with chopped parsley.

Arroz con Pato
Duck and Rice
—
Serves 8 to 10

2 ducks (5 to 6 pounds each)
2 large onions, unpeeled and quartered
1 carrot, washed and chopped
1 leek, white part only, washed and chopped
1 whole head garlic (not peeled or separated), cut in half horizontally
1 or 2 jalapeño peppers, seeded and sliced twice lengthwise
10 sprigs Italian parsley
1 sprig fresh rosemary
1 bay leaf
2 teaspoons cumin
10 cloves
1 teaspoon black peppercorns
1 large clove garlic, peeled and minced
3 very large onions, peeled and finely chopped (5 cups)
2 tablespoons coarse salt
3 cups rice
½ cup fresh or frozen peas

1. Wipe the ducks inside and out with a damp cloth. Cut each of the ducks into 4 serving pieces: cut away the thighs and legs in one piece; cut off the breasts and cut them in half. Trim off and discard all the excess fat; reserve the backbones, necks, and giblets (but not the livers). Score the skin of the breasts and set aside, skin side up, together with the legs.

2. In a sauté pan, sauté the backbones, necks, and giblets over medium heat for 20 minutes, or until they are brown all over, stirring now and then. Transfer all the bones to a stockpot. Strain the fat through a sieve and reserve. You should have about 1 cup. Deglaze the pan with 2 cups of water by placing the pan over high heat and scraping the bottom to loosen any stuck bits; pour into the stockpot containing the browned bones. Set aside.

3. In the same sauté pan, heat 2 tablespoons of the duck fat; add the onions, carrot, leek, and head of garlic. Sauté the vegetables over medium-high heat for 8 minutes, stirring now and then.

4. Transfer the vegetables from the pan to the stockpot with the deglazing liquid and the bones. Add 10 cups of cold water, the jalapeño pepper, parsley, rosemary, bay leaf, cumin seed, cloves, and peppercorns. Bring to a boil, lower the heat, and simmer, uncovered, for 1 hour.

5. Strain the stock through a fine sieve or through a strainer lined with a double layer of cheesecloth, pressing out all the juices; discard the contents of the sieve or strainer. Let the stock sit, undisturbed, for 10 to 15 minutes, to allow the fat to rise to the surface. Remove and discard the fat.

6. In a sauté pan, heat 3 tablespoons of duck fat. Add the duck pieces, skin side down, and sauté over very low heat for 30 minutes. Shake the pan from time to time. Turn the pieces over and sauté for 5 minutes. Transfer the duck pieces to a plate and set aside. Discard all the fat.

7. In a casserole, heat 3 tablespoons of duck fat; add the minced garlic and chopped onion. Sauté over medium heat, stirring now and then, until the onions start to get golden around the edges, about 8 to 10 minutes. Add the salt and mix well. Arrange the duck pieces on top of the onion and add the accumulated juices. Add the rice and 6 cups of duck stock.

8. Bring to a boil, lower the heat to the minimum, cover tightly, and let cook for 20 minutes, or until all the liquid has been absorbed by the rice and the duck is tender. Fold in the peas and let them heat through for about 3 minutes. Correct seasoning with salt to taste. Serve right from the casserole.

(Continued)

Arroz Con Pato y Culantro
Duck and Rice with Cilantro

—

Finely chop 1 cup well-packed fresh cilantro leaves. Fold them into the duck and rice when you add the peas in Step 8. Continue to cook until the peas are heated through and the rice has turned green from the cilantro.

Pato con Higos
Duck with Figs

—

Serves 6 to 8

Fig trees grow just about everywhere in Lima. Several huge fig trees surrounded one corner of the backyard of my house in Lima, and their large, bright green leaves formed a canopy shadowing a good part of the garden. Those old trees produced such an overwhelming abundance of fruit that we could have fed the whole neighborhood with figs.

When selecting fresh figs for cooking, whether they are big or small, black or green, pick ones that are hard and slightly unripe so that they will soften yet hold their shape during the cooking process. When using dried figs, pick large, moist ones with soft skin.

2 ducks (5 to 6 pounds each)
5 pounds veal knuckle bones or calves' feet
3 medium onions, unpeeled and quartered
2 carrots, washed and sliced
12 dried Turkish figs (about 8 ounces)
1 large sweet potato, washed and cut into large pieces
2 oranges, peeled and quartered
1 lemon, washed and quartered
1 lime, washed and quartered
½ pineapple, unpeeled and cut into small pieces (about 1¼ pounds)
2½ cups grapes, washed (about 1 pound)

3 green apples, such as Granny Smiths, unpeeled and quartered
   (1½ pounds)
1 large sprig fresh rosemary
8 cups red wine
2 cups honey or sugar
2 3-inch cinnamon sticks
8 cloves
12 juniper berries
1 bay leaf
1 dried red chili pepper
4 sweet potatoes, baked and cut in half (page 390)

1. Wipe the ducks inside and out with a damp cloth. Cut each of them into 4 serving pieces: cut away the thighs and legs in one piece; cut off the breasts and cut them in half. With a sharp knife, score the skin in a crisscross pattern. Place the duck pieces on a tray, skin side up, and allow them to sit at room temperature for several hours, or until ready to use.

2. Preheat the oven to 475 degrees.

3. Remove and discard most of the skin and fat from the backbones, wings, necks, and giblets (but not the livers) and chop the bones into small pieces. Place the duck bones in a roasting pan with the giblets, veal bones, onions, and carrots and roast for 1 hour. Remove from the oven, strain all the fat from the roasting pan into a bowl or cup, and reserve. Set the bones and vegetables aside.

4. In a large stockpot, heat 2 tablespoons of duck fat over medium heat and add 4 of the figs, the cut-up sweet potato, the oranges, lemon, lime, pineapple, grapes, and apples. Sauté, stirring now and then, until all the fruit is soft, about 20 minutes.

5. Add the roasted bones and vegetables, 8 quarts of cold water, and the rosemary sprig. Bring to a boil, lower the heat, and simmer for 4 hours, stirring now and then.

6. Strain the fruit stock through a fine sieve or a strainer lined with a double layer of cheesecloth, pressing out all the juices. Discard the contents of the sieve or strainer and let the stock sit, undisturbed, for 10 to 15 minutes to allow all the fat to rise to the surface. Remove and discard the fat. You should have about 4 cups of duck-fruit stock.

(Continued)

7. Meanwhile, in a saucepan, combine the wine, honey, cinnamon sticks, cloves, juniper berries, bay leaf, and dried chili pepper. Bring to a boil, lower the heat, and simmer for 40 minutes; add the remaining 8 figs and simmer for 15 to 20 minutes longer. Do not allow the figs to burst. (If the figs are getting soft too soon, remove them). Transfer the figs to a plate and set aside. Strain the syrup through a fine sieve. Discard the contents of the sieve. You should have about 4 cups of wine sauce.

8. Preheat the oven to 475 degrees.

9. In a sauté pan, combine the fruit stock and the wine sauce. Bring to a boil, lower the heat to medium-low, and simmer gently for 2 hours, or until the combined sauces have reduced to 3 cups. Skim every time foam rises to the surface. Place the sauce and the figs in the top of a double boiler, with hot water in the bottom pan, and let heat through for about 15 minutes before serving.

10. Place the duck legs on a rack in a roasting pan and roast them for 15 minutes. Prick the surface of the skin without touching the flesh of the thigh section and continue to roast for another 10 to 15 minutes, or until golden. Remove from the oven and set aside in a warm spot.

11. Place the duck breasts, skin side down, in a cast-iron skillet. Over very low heat, sauté them for 10 minutes, or until the skin is crisp. Turn the breasts over and sauté for 4 minutes longer.

12. Pour some of the sauce from the double boiler onto a serving dish or platter. Arrange the 8 duck pieces and the 8 figs on top. Garnish with sweet-potato halves and serve with duck-fig sauce on the side.

GOOSE

Enrollado de Ganso
Roulade of Goose
—
Serves 8 to 10

Almost every part of a goose can be used to make something delicious. The fat, for example, is one of the most flavorful there is and enhances any food you cook with it. In my kitchen, goose fat is appreciated as much as the goose itself; we collect every drop of it.

Goose, like most birds, is easy to prepare. It's just a matter of putting it into a hot oven and quickly roasting it to obtain a crisp skin and meat as rare and juicy as possible. In this recipe, however, the goose is boned and some of the meat is used to make a nice sweet filling; then it is rolled and tightly tied, and roasted or braised. The result is extremely flavorful—and easy to carve. There will be plenty of goose for everybody, since the number of servings is more than double that of goose roasted on the bone, which yields rather modest portions. You can serve this goose hot or cold.

1 goose, with giblets, liver, and some fat from the cavity, boned
    (about 8 to 9 pounds)
1 cup loosely packed fresh bread crumbs
3 large cloves garlic, peeled and minced
10 dried figs, preferably California (Calimyrna) jumbo figs,
    coarsely chopped (about 1½ cups)
1½ cups black walnuts, coarsely chopped, or about 2 cups walnuts,
    coarsely chopped
1 tablespoon chopped fresh sage or ½ teaspoon dried sage
¼ teaspoon white pepper
⅛ teaspoon cayenne
¼ teaspoon ground allspice
1 tablespoon coarse salt
⅓ cup raisins, soaked in ½ cup pisco or light rum for
    10 to 15 minutes

(Continued)

1. Lay the boned goose flat, skin side down, on a cutting board. Remove about 1 pound of the meat from the thickest layers of the breast and thighs and grind. Clean and coarsely chop the giblets and liver.

2. In a bowl, combine the ground meat and chopped giblets and liver with about 4 tablespoons of goose fat and the remaining ingredients. Mix thoroughly.

3. Preheat the oven to 350 degrees.

4. Place the flattened goose, skin side down, horizontally in front of you. Spread the filling evenly over the half of the goose nearest to you. Fold the sides in, lift the near edge, and roll the goose evenly until you reach the opposite end. Secure the roll by tying with kitchen string: first tie the roll in the center, then tie both ends. Continue tying between the strings, alternating sides, until the roll is evenly tied at about ½-inch intervals.

5. Place the roulade on a rack in a roasting pan and mount for about 1 hour 45 minutes, turning once halfway through cooking. (If the skin gets brown too quickly, cover with a piece of well-buttered brown paper or oiled aluminum foil; remove the paper or foil 10 minutes before the roulade is done.)

6. Remove from oven and let cool for 20 minutes in a warm spot. Remove the strings, transfer to a cutting board or serving platter, slice, and serve.

To bone a goose, remove the skin with the flesh from the carcass without piercing the skin or slashing the flesh. Remove the wings at the second joint. Lift up the skin from the neck to expose the flesh and with a sharp paring knife, slit and cut around the wishbone. Release, remove, and discard the wishbone. Place the goose, breast side down, on the work surface, with the legs facing you. With a sharp knife, cut open the whole length of the bird along the center of the backbone from the neck to the tail, scraping and cutting the meat away from the bone, thus exposing the entire clean backbone. Then cut right through the thigh joints, separating them from the rest of the carcass. Cut the joints at the shoulders. Cut on top and around the breastbone and down the other side, separating the meat from the bone as you go along. Pull and remove the carcass in one piece.

Slit the skin open from the second joint of the wings; scrape and cut away the meat; remove the bones. Cut around the bone of the thigh to free it of the meat. Holding the tip in one hand, scrape with the knife, pushing and cutting the meat away from the bone. Continue to scrape all the way down to release the thigh and drumstick bones. Repeat the same operation with the other thigh and drumstick. At this point the goose is boned in its entirety and ready to be used.

This method of boning can be used for all birds.

TURKEY

Pavo Asado
Roasted Wild Turkey

Serves 8 to 10

I remember one Christmas in Peru, when turkey was to be the center-piece of the meal. It was ordered several weeks ahead, as was typical. The turkey arrived, feathers and all, and walked proudly into the house, making loud noises so that everyone would know it had arrived! It was nursed and cared for and fed a daily diet of dry cracked corn, chunks of red onion, quantities of greens, and a ration of walnuts—starting with one and increasing by one more every day for fifteen days, at which time he was given a healthy double shot of pisco. That turkey never knew what hit him. He had so much pisco he was walking into the walls! I imagine he was a very happy bird by the time he fulfilled his destiny. Turkeys prepared in this fashion were always plump, moist, and tender, and I have never tasted better.

1 wild turkey, with giblets (about 8½ pounds)
½ lemon

BREAD STUFFING
4 thin slices bacon, chopped
10 tablespoons (1¼ sticks) unsalted butter
2 large onions, peeled and finely chopped (about 3 cups)
1 or 2 jalapeño peppers, seeded and finely chopped,
*   or ⅛ teaspoon cayenne (optional)*
¼ teaspoon ground cardamom
¼ teaspoon ground cloves
2 stalks celery, washed, strings removed, and finely chopped (½ cup)
½ cup raisins soaked in ½ cup pisco, calvados, or gin for
*   10 to 15 minutes*
¾ cup coarsely chopped pecans or walnuts
6 cups finely crumbled fresh cornbread or corn muffins or crumbled
*   black bread (without crust) or crumbled soft white bread*
1 tablespoon chopped fresh thyme leaves
¼ cup chopped Italian parsley

2 eggs
¼ cup milk
2 teaspoons coarse salt
6 tablespoons unsalted butter or Rendered Bacon Fat (page 476)
¼ cup dry white wine or vermouth

1. Wipe the inside and outside of the turkey with a damp cloth. Rub the cavity thoroughly with the lemon. Trim, clean, and chop the giblets; set both aside.

2. Place the bacon in a skillet and sauté over low heat until it has released most of its fat, about 3 to 4 minutes, stirring. Add the butter and when it has melted, add the onions, giblets, jalapeño, if using, cardamom, cloves, and celery and sauté over moderate heat until the onions are translucent, about 5 to 6 minutes, stirring occasionally. Add the raisins with the pisco and cook until all the liqueur has evaporated, about 4 minutes. Stir in the nuts and bread crumbs and continue sautéing, while stirring, for 3 minutes or until the bread crumbs have absorbed all the liquid and are well mixed.

3. Remove from heat, correct the seasoning with salt to taste, and fold in the thyme and parsley. Beat the eggs, milk, and salt together and add to the stuffing, mixing thoroughly. Correct seasoning with salt to taste.

4. Fill and tightly pack the cavity and neck of the turkey with the stuffing. Close with skewers or sew with a butcher needle and kitchen string.

5. Preheat the oven to 350 degrees.

6. In a small saucepan over moderate heat, combine the butter and wine. Bring to a boil, remove from heat, and set aside in a warm spot.

7. Tie the tips of the drumsticks together and fold the wings to the back, or truss the bird (page 257). Place the bird, breast side up, in a roasting pan and brush thoroughly with the butter-wine mixture. Roast the turkey for about 2 hours, basting frequently with the butter-wine mixture. When done, the skin should be golden brown all around and the thigh joint should move easily up and down. You can also test by puncturing the thigh with a fork: the juices should run clear not red. (If the skin starts to get too brown too soon, cover it with a piece of buttered

(Continued)

brown paper or aluminum foil. Discard the brown paper or foil 10 minutes before the bird is done.)

8. Remove the turkey from the oven and let the bird sit for 10 to 15 minutes before carving. Remove and discard any strings. Place the bird on a platter or cutting board and serve.

NOTE   Rather than stuff the bird, you can serve the stuffing separately alongside it. Add the juices from the cavity and/or deglaze the roasting pan and add this sauce to the stuffing to enhance its flavor. Keep the stuffing warm in a double boiler or reheat it if necessary.

VARIATION

Bring a domestic turkey, weighing between 10 and 15 pounds, to room temperature and wipe it inside and out with a damp cloth. Preheat the oven to 350 degrees. Rub the inside of the turkey with a cut lemon, salt, and freshly ground black pepper. Place in a roasting pan and roast for 15 to 20 minutes per pound, basting frequently with a flavorful fat. Cover, if necessary, as in Step 7. Test for doneness as in Step 7. Remove from the oven and allow the turkey to rest for about 15 minutes before carving. If a stuffing is desired, use the one for wild turkey.

SQUAB

Aguadito de Pichón
Squab Aguadito

Serves 6 to 8

I always looked forward to going to the *palomar,* or dovecote, with my grandfather. He knew every individual bird, its habits, its virtues, its faults. I loved to hear him talk about his doves and their offspring. He spoke with such precision and detail that I could almost visualize each one. He checked the birds every morning and thus came to know them intimately.

After my grandfather had examined all the nests, he would select a bird for the kitchen. He would tell my grandmother how this particular bird should be cooked, whether grilled or stewed. There was really no difference between one or the other: it was how he wanted it to be prepared for his dinner that day.

But he had a point. There are only two ways to cook squab. One is to sear it and cook it briefly so that the meat is as rare as possible. The other is to cook it slowly to tenderize the meat and develop its maximum flavor, as in aguadito, a thick, full-bodied stew.

4 squab, including giblets, necks, heads, and feet, if available (about 1 to 1¼ pounds each)

SQUAB STOCK (see Note)
3 tablespoons olive or vegetable oil
2 carrots, peeled and coarsely chopped (2 cups)
1 large onion, unpeeled and cut into 8 wedges
3 stalks celery with leafy tops, washed and chopped (1 cup)
1-inch slice fresh ginger, unpeeled and cut in half lengthwise
4 cloves garlic, peeled
1½ cups light beer

3 tablespoons olive oil
1 medium onion, peeled and finely chopped (1 cup)
2 cloves garlic, peeled and minced
2 jalapeño peppers, seeded and minced
1 cup long-grain rice
2 teaspoons coarse salt
½ cup chopped fresh cilantro leaves

1. Wipe each squab inside and out with a damp cloth. Cut off the wings, necks, heads, and feet, if available, and set aside with the giblets. With a sharp knife or kitchen shears, cut along both sides of each backbone; remove it and set aside with the giblets. Cut each bird in half crosswise and set aside.

2. In a 3-quart stockpot, heat the olive or vegetable oil and sauté the necks, heads, feet, wings, and backbones together with the giblets, carrots, onion, celery, ginger, and garlic for 5 minutes, stirring frequently. Add the beer and bring to a boil, while scraping the bottom of the pan. Continue cooking until the beer has reduced to half or less. Add 7 cups of water and bring to a boil. Lower the heat and simmer for about 1 hour, skimming the foam as it rises to the surface, until the stock has reduced to about half.

(Continued)

3. Strain through a fine sieve or through a strainer lined with a double layer of cheesecloth. Degrease the stock. You should have about 4 cups; if not, add enough water to make 4 cups.

4. In a sauté pan, heat the olive oil and quickly sauté the squab pieces until they are evenly browned on all sides. Push the browned pieces to the side and add the onion, garlic, and jalapeños to the center of the pan; sauté, stirring, for 3 to 4 minutes, or until the onion is translucent. Add 3 cups of stock, the rice, and the salt. Bring to a boil, stir, lower the heat to a minimum, and gently simmer, tightly covered, for 15 to 20 minutes, or until the rice is done.

5. Stir in the fresh cilantro and correct the seasoning with salt to taste. The rice should be quite moist. If it is dry, add some of the remaining stock and allow to cook, covered, for 1 or 2 minutes. To serve, ladle a generous amount of rice into a soup plate and garnish with a piece of squab.

NOTE   Four cups of Chicken Stock (page 461) can be used instead of squab stock.

VARIATION

Substitute about 3 pounds of boneless chicken breasts for the squab. Cut each one into 8 equal strips and proceed with the recipe, starting with Step 4. Use Chicken Stock (page 461) instead of squab stock.

QUAIL

Codorniz con Trigo
Quail and Barley

Serves 6 to 8

Barley is a nutritious grain with a rich, nutty flavor. It can be used in soups and stews or as an accompaniment to poultry, meat, or fish. A refreshing cold drink called *fresco de trigo* is also made from barley.

6 to 8 quail (about 5½ ounces each)
2 teaspoons ground cumin
¼ teaspoon ground allspice
¼ teaspoon ground white pepper
2 tablespoons coarse salt
8 sprigs fresh sage or rosemary or 1 small bunch thyme (½ ounce)
3¼ cups barley (1 pound)
2 dried mirasol or red chili peppers, seeded
2 large cloves garlic, peeled
½ cup lard or vegetable oil
¼ cup Rendered Bacon Fat (page 476), Rendered Duck Fat
    (page 475), or olive oil
2 large onions, peeled and finely chopped
1 teaspoon ground turmeric
4 cups Chicken Stock (page 461) or Veal Stock (page 464) or water

1. Wipe the quail dry inside and out with a cloth and tuck the necks, if any, inside the neck cavities. Combine the cumin, allspice, white pepper, and 1 tablespoon of salt and sprinkle each quail inside and out with this mixture. Place a sprig of sage or rosemary or a few sprigs of thyme into each cavity and with a short piece of kitchen string, tie the birds' legs together at the tips. Set aside.

2. Place the barley in a sieve and rinse under cold running water. Set aside to drain thoroughly.

3. Finely chop the hot peppers and garlic together.

4. In a large skillet, heat the lard. Add the quail and sauté over medium heat until they are golden on all sides, about 10 to 12 minutes. Remove the birds to a plate, discarding the lard.

5. In an earthenware casserole, heat the bacon fat. Add the pepper-garlic mixture and stir. Add the onions, turmeric, and the remaining tablespoon of salt and sauté until the onions are translucent, about 5 minutes. Mix in the drained barley, add the stock, and bring to a boil. Lower the heat, cover the casserole, and simmer for 20 minutes, stirring now and then.

6. Arrange the browned quail with the accumulated juices in the barley, cover the casserole, and continue cooking for 20 to 25 minutes,

(Continued)

shaking the casserole from time to time to prevent the contents from sticking to the bottom. Remove from heat and serve piping hot, right from the casserole.

RABBIT

Conejo Frito
Honeyed Fried Rabbit

Serves 6 to 8

When I think of the Barrios Altos, the old section of Lima, what comes to my mind is not so much the incredible old colonial houses with their huge patios or inner courtyards but one particular street corner filled with the intoxicating smell of *chicharrones de conejo,* or fried rabbit. I always found a reason to pass by this corner and stop for some fried rabbit and sweet-potato chips.

Preparing fried rabbit is simply a matter of dropping the rabbit pieces into piping-hot oil and letting the heat do the rest, but there are interesting ways to add extra flavor. One way is to fry the rabbit in a flavorful fat. Another way is to coat the rabbit with a flavorful marinade before frying it. Many kinds of marinade can be used, from a simple sprinkling of salt, pepper, paprika, other spices, and herbs to more unusual combinations, such as the spicy honey marinade in this recipe, which accentuates the wonderful sweet taste of the meat. Yuca Straws (page 396) or Sweet-Potato Chips (page 390) would be perfect accompaniments.

2 small rabbits (about 1½ pounds each)

HONEY MARINADE
¼ teaspoon ground white pepper
1 teaspoon ground fennel
1 teaspoon dried oregano, crumbled
⅛ teaspoon cayenne
1 tablespoon coarse salt
2 tablespoons lemon juice
¼ cup honey

2 quarts vegetable oil, for frying
Coarse salt

1. Wipe the rabbits inside and out with a damp towel and remove any excess fat. Cut each rabbit into 3 pieces: the hind legs, the front legs, and the loin. Then separate the 2 hind legs and the 2 front legs, leaving the loin in 1 piece. You will have 5 serving pieces. Repeat this procedure with the second rabbit. Place in a stainless-steel or glass bowl and set aside.

2. In a small bowl, combine the pepper, fennel, oregano, cayenne, and salt. Add the lemon juice, mix well, and let stand for 10 to 15 minutes. Add the honey and mix thoroughly. Pour this mixture over the rabbit pieces and toss, making sure that each piece is well coated. Let marinate at room temperature for about 1 hour.

3. Remove the rabbit pieces from the marinade and gently pat dry with cloth towels.

4. In a fryer or a large sauté pan, heat the oil to about 350 degrees. Add all the rabbit pieces, turn the temperature down to 325 degrees, and fry for about 12 to 15 minutes, turning often. Remove the rabbit pieces from the oil, sprinkle with coarse salt, and serve hot.

NOTE   To fry rabbit, you would normally heat the fat or oil to 375 degrees, as for other fried foods, in order to sear the outside, forming a crisp, golden envelope that seals all the moisture inside. When the marinade is sweetened, however, the temperature must be lower: heat the oil to 350 degrees, then lower it to 325 degrees when you add the rabbit pieces.

Conejo con Lentejas
Rabbit and Lentils

Serves 6 to 8

Rabbits always arrived fresh and in full fur in my grandmother's kitchen. They had to be of a certain size and plumpness, and even the quality of the fur was inspected to see if the animal had been raised and

(Continued)

fed properly. Skinning the rabbit was always an event for me. As soon as it was time, I would run and get my bicycle pump. First I would open a little hole in the skin by the back leg of the rabbit and put my finger between the flesh and the skin to loosen it. Then I would take the point of the hose and hold it tight under the skin so the air could not escape through the hole. I would start pumping, forcing air through the whole body of the rabbit. Soon it would become totally inflated, like a balloon ready to take off. The rest was easy. I just cut around the legs, cut open the skin from tail to head, and undressed the rabbit, taking off its furry little coat with ease.

Rabbit meat, delicate and white, can be prepared in every conceivable way. Rabbit with beans is a very common dish in the South American kitchen. I adore rabbit cooked with lentils. I find their rich flavor brings out the subtle taste of the rabbit.

This dish is good for lunch, great for dinner, and ideal for entertaining. If you are entertaining a South American, don't forget to prepare some white rice to go with it!

1 rabbit (about 3½ pounds)

RABBIT STOCK
¼ cup Rendered Bacon Fat (page 476) or olive oil
4 stalks celery with leafy tops, washed and coarsely chopped
2 medium carrots, washed and coarsely chopped
1 head garlic, unpeeled, cut in half horizontally
2 large onions, unpeeled and coarsely chopped
1 or 2 dried red chili peppers
1 small bunch fresh thyme
12 sprigs Italian parsley
1 bay leaf
12 to 16 allspice berries
6 cloves
1 teaspoon fennel seed
1 tablespoon coarse salt
4 medium tomatoes, peeled and chopped (seeds and juice saved)

LENTILS
3 tablespoons Rendered Bacon Fat (page 476)
3 cloves garlic, peeled and minced
2 medium onions, peeled and minced (2 cups)
⅓ cup marsala

2½ cups (1 pound) lentils, rinsed in a strainer under cold
  running water and drained
1 tablespoon coarse salt
3 tablespoons chopped Italian parsley

1. Wipe the rabbit with a damp cloth inside and out; remove and discard any fat. Remove and set aside the kidneys and heart. Cut the rabbit into 3 sections: the hind legs, the loin, and the front legs. Then separate the 2 hind legs and the 2 front legs; leave the loin in 1 piece. You will have 5 pieces. Set aside.

2. In a stockpot, heat the ¼ cup of bacon fat over high heat; add the rabbit pieces and quickly brown them lightly on all sides, about 5 minutes. (If all the pieces do not fit, brown them in batches.) Transfer the rabbit pieces to a plate and set aside.

3. To the same stockpot add the celery, carrots, garlic, onions, and chili peppers and sauté for 5 to 8 minutes, stirring now and then. Add the thyme, parsley, bay leaf, allspice berries, cloves, fennel seed, salt, and the reserved kidney and heart. Pour in 8 cups of water and the juice and seeds from the tomatoes. Bring to a boil, lower the heat, and simmer for 10 minutes. Add the rabbit pieces with the accumulated juices from the plate and simmer over low heat for 45 minutes to 1 hour, or until the rabbit pieces are tender.

4. Using tongs, remove the rabbit pieces from the stock and when cool enough to handle, carefully cut them into 10 smaller serving pieces: cut the hind legs in half, the loin in half, and the front legs in half; set aside.

5. Strain the stock through a strainer lined with 2 layers of cheesecloth, pressing out all the juices from the vegetables, herbs, and spices. Discard the cheesecloth and its contents, reserving the stock. You will have about 7 cups. Let the stock sit for a few minutes and degrease. Set the stock aside.

6. In a large sauté pan, heat the 3 tablespoons bacon fat over high heat. Add the minced garlic and onions and sauté for about 4 minutes, stirring. Add the marsala and cook, stirring constantly, until the wine has evaporated, about 2 minutes. Add the tomatoes and sauté, stirring now and then, for about 5 minutes. Add 1 cup of the reserved stock and continue cooking until all the liquid has evaporated and the tomatoes

(Continued)

are soft, about 3 minutes. Add the lentils, salt, and 4 cups of stock, stir, and arrange the 10 rabbit pieces on top of the lentils. Pour any accumulated juices from the plate into the saucepan, cover, and simmer over very low heat, shaking the pan from time to time to prevent the lentils from sticking to the bottom, for 35 to 40 minutes, or until the lentils are tender. (If the lentils dry out too fast, add a little more of the remaining stock.)

7. To serve, transfer the lentils to a serving dish or earthenware casserole, arrange the rabbit pieces on top, and sprinkle with parsley.

Conejo en Salsa de Chocolate

Braised Rabbit in Chocolate Sauce

Serves 6 to 8

Rabbit or hare braised in a dark, velvety sauce flavored and enriched with chocolate makes a superb dish. In my kitchen, I use chocolate not only for sweets but for savory dishes. I add a little bit of pure chocolate to many dishes, using it just as I would a spice. Chocolate's bitter and punchy quality brings out the hidden flavors of meat, especially game.

2 rabbits (about 2½ pounds each)
1 cup olive oil or Rendered Bacon Fat (page 476)
2 large cloves garlic, peeled and minced
2 large onions, peeled and finely chopped (3 cups)
4 stalks celery, washed, strings removed, and finely chopped (1 cup)
1 carrot, peeled and grated (½ cup)
¼ teaspoon ground cloves
½ teaspoon ground cardamom
⅛ teaspoon cayenne
1 cup port or sweet wine
3 morcilla sausages, peeled and chopped
2 ounces unsweetened chocolate, finely chopped
¼ cup all-purpose flour
8 cups Chicken Stock (page 461) or Veal Stock (page 464) or water

1 tablespoon coarse salt
3 tablespoons chopped fresh cilantro or Italian parsley

1. Wipe the rabbits inside and out with a damp cloth. Remove and set aside the kidneys and hearts. Cut each rabbit into 3 sections: the hind legs, the loin, and the front legs. Then separate the 2 hind legs and the 2 front legs, leaving the loin in 1 piece. You will have 10 pieces, total.

2. In a sauté pan, heat the olive oil and sauté the rabbit pieces over medium heat for 20 minutes, or until they are quite brown on all sides. Turn the rabbit pieces frequently during this process. Transfer the rabbit from the saucepan to a plate and set aside.

3. Pour off all but ¼ cup of the oil from the saucepan. Add the garlic and onions and sauté over medium heat, stirring, until the onions start to get golden around the edges, about 10 minutes. Add the celery, carrot, cloves, cardamom, and cayenne. Add the port, stir, and cook until all of the wine has evaporated. Add the morcilla sausages and cook for 1 minute longer. Add the chocolate, stir, sprinkle the flour on top, and continue cooking for another minute, stirring. Add 3 cups of the stock and the salt; bring to a boil, stirring constantly. Lower the heat and simmer for about 25 minutes, or until the sauce has thickened, stirring now and then. Add the remaining 5 cups of stock and while stirring, bring to a boil over medium heat.

4. Add the rabbit pieces and the giblets. Lower the heat to the minimum, cover tightly, and cook for 1 hour 10 minutes, stirring now and then and scraping the bottom of the pan, or until the rabbit is tender and the sauce is enriched and has thickened again. Transfer to a serving platter, sprinkle with fresh cilantro, and serve.

VARIATION

Liebre en Salsa de Chocolate
Hare in Chocolate Sauce

—

Use a hare weighing about 5 pounds instead of 2 rabbits. Rub the entire hare clean with lemon juice or red-wine vinegar. Then wipe it with a towel and allow it to air for several hours, undisturbed, before cooking. Cut the hare in 3 sections: the hind legs, the loin, and the front legs. Cut the loin in half and cut the thighs from the legs. You will have 8 pieces. Proceed as for rabbit, adding the hare in Step 4, along with an additional

(Continued)

4 cups of stock. Cook for 2 hours, or until the hare is tender and the sauce has thickened slightly. If the sauce gets too thick, add more stock or water to maintain the right coating thickness.

Aguadito de Conejo
Rabbit Aguadito

—

Serves 6 to 8

Aguadito, as the name suggests, is a moist dish, and it is very popular in Peru. The main ingredient is a grain, such as rice or quinoa, beans, or even fine pasta. This is mixed with chunks of meat or seafood and vegetables and cooked in plenty of well-flavored stock or in water.

One of the best aguaditos combines rabbit and orzo. This rice-shaped pasta behaves differently from any other kind of pasta during cooking. For one thing, it is hard enough to hold its shape while it absorbs liquid. In this lusty dish, it soaks up the flavorful rabbit essences from the stock and becomes extremely rich.

1 rabbit (about 3½ pounds)

SPICY RABBIT STOCK
8 cups Chicken Stock (page 461)
1 pound onions, unpeeled, coarsely sliced
1 medium carrot, washed and coarsely sliced
4 stalks celery, with leafy tops, washed and cut into large pieces
1 leek, white part only, cut in half and washed
1½-inch piece fresh ginger, unpeeled and sliced
2 heads garlic, unpeeled, cut in half horizontally
6 sprigs fresh tarragon or cilantro
8 sprigs Italian parsley
1 or 2 jalapeño peppers
1 tablespoon annatto seeds
16 to 18 juniper berries
20 black peppercorns
1 tablespoon coarse salt

¼ cup Rendered Bacon Fat (page 476) or olive oil

1 tablespoon Achiote Oil (page 472)
2 large cloves garlic, peeled and minced
1 medium onion, peeled and minced (1 cup)
1 tablespoon Spanish paprika
1 tablespoon coarse salt
2¼ cups orzo (1 pound)
½ cup peas, fresh or frozen
3 tablespoons chopped Italian parsley

1. Wipe the rabbit inside and out with a damp cloth, remove and discard any fat, and set aside. Remove and set aside the kidneys and heart, if available.

2. In a large stockpot, combine the chicken stock and 4 cups of water with the onions, carrot, celery, leek, ginger, garlic, tarragon, parsley, jalapeño peppers, annatto seeds, juniper berries, peppercorns, salt, and the rabbit kidneys and heart. Bring to a boil over high heat; lower the heat and let simmer for 15 minutes. Place the rabbit in the simmering stock and continue to simmer, stirring and turning the rabbit now and then, for 45 minutes to 1 hour, or until the rabbit is tender. Using tongs, remove the rabbit from the stock. When cool enough to handle, remove all the meat from the bones, cut it into large chunks, and set aside. Discard the bones.

3. Strain the stock through a strainer lined with 2 layers of cheesecloth, pressing out all the juices from the vegetables, herbs, and spices. Discard the cheesecloth and its contents, reserving the stock. You should have 8 cups of strained stock. If not, add enough water to make 8 cups.

4. In a sauté pan or casserole, heat the bacon fat and achiote oil. Add the garlic, onion, paprika, and salt and sauté over medium heat, stirring constantly, until the onion is totally translucent, about 4 minutes. Add the 8 cups of stock, stir, and bring to a boil; lower the heat and simmer for 5 minutes. Stir in the orzo and continue cooking, stirring now and then, for 10 minutes.

5. Add the rabbit meat with all the accumulated juices from the plate. Cook for 20 minutes over low heat, stirring now and then and scraping the bottom of the pan to prevent the orzo from sticking. Add the fresh peas, stir, and cook 5 minutes longer. (If frozen peas are used, mix in just before serving.) Correct seasoning with salt to taste, garnish with chopped Italian parsley, and serve.

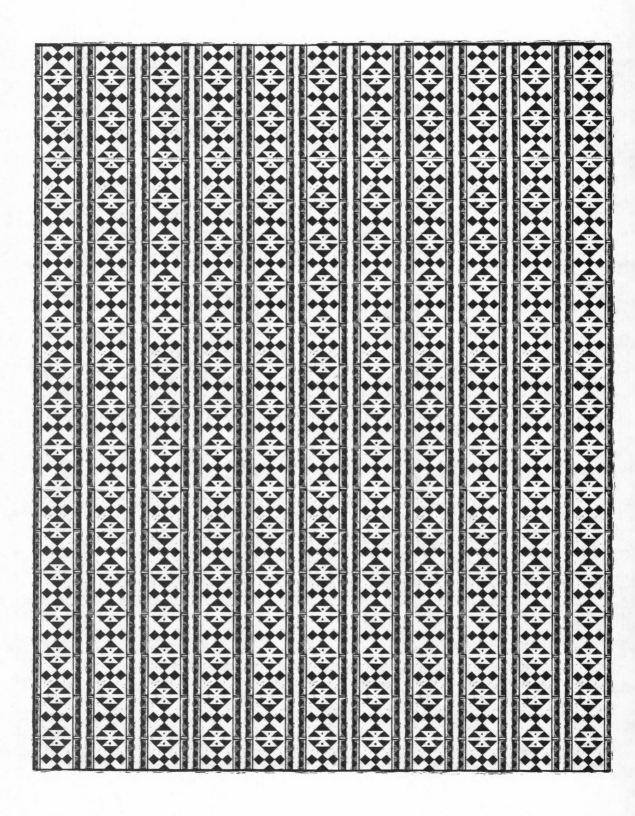

MEAT

BEEF

Bistek al Ajiaco
Flank Steak Ajiaco
—

Matahambre
Flank Steak Filled with Spinach and Pistachios
—

Salpicón de Carne
Meat Salpicón
—

Ropa Vieja
Beef and Cabbage Salad
—

Asado con Pimienta Negra
Roast Beef in a Black-Pepper Crust
—

Costillas a la Brasa
Grilled Short Ribs
—

Tuco de Tallarines con Asado
Braised Beef with Pasta and Tomato Sauce
—

Arroz Tapado
Beef and Rice Cake

VEAL

Lomo de Ternera al Horno
Roast Loin of Veal
—

Ternera con Anchoas y Tomillo
Roast Veal with Anchovies and Fresh Thyme
—

Ternera con Salsa de Cerveza
Veal Tenderloin in Beer Sauce
—

Pierna de Ternera al Horno
Roast Veal Shanks
—

Chuletas al Limón
Lemon Veal Chops
—

Ternera en los Manzanos
Double Veal Chops with Apple Filling

PORK

Lechón Asado
Roast Suckling Pig
—

Lomo Horneado con Camote y Cebollas
Roast Loin of Pork with Sweet Potatoes and Onions
—

Jamón del País
Poached Fresh Ham
—

Atamalado de Cerdo con Quinua
Pork and Quinoa Atamalado
—

Carapulcra
—

Feijoada

LAMB

Cordero Asado con Menta
Roast Leg of Lamb with Mint
—

Cordero a la Parrilla con Culantro
Broiled Butterflied Leg of Lamb with Cilantro
—

Pierna de Cordero con Pistachos
Roast Leg of Lamb with Pistachios
—

Costillas de Cordero a la Brasa
Broiled Rack of Lamb
—

Brochetas de Cordero
Lamb Brochettes
—

Estofado de Cordero con Cebollas de Perla
Lamb Estofado with Pearl Onions
—

Seco de Cordero
Lamb Seco
—

Atamalado de Cordero con Quinua
Lamb and Quinoa Atamalado

VENISON

Venado a la Parrilla
Grilled Venison

—

Estofado de Venado y Mote
Venison and Hominy Estofado

VARIETY MEATS

Anticuchos

Estofado de Lengua
Braised Tongue in Tomato-Raisin Sauce

Mondongito a la Jardinera
Sautéed Tripe with Peppers

Riñoncitos de Ternera con Romero
Kidneys with Fennel on Rosemary Skewers

Migas de Ternera con Encebollado
Sautéed Calves' Liver Smothered in Onions

Lechecillas con Hongos
Sweetbreads with Mushrooms

The early cultures of South America confined themselves to agriculture with very little thought given to meat. It was not until the rise of the Inca Empire that an interest in meat as a food source started to develop. The Quechuas, led by their emperor, the Inca, understood the delicate ecological balance of the region and realized that the stock of animals whose meat could be used as food was limited.

Llamas, vicuñas, alpacas, and guanacos—the camels of the Andes—abounded. The Quechuas domesticated them and carefully managed their growth and distribution. Vicuñas, alpacas, and guanacos were appreciated more for their wool and their droppings than for their meat. Besides transportation, the llama provided fuel in the form of dried excrement, wool for weaving and braiding rope, hide for sandals, fat for candles, and meat.

Llama meat was rarely eaten fresh. Originally, it was air-dried high in the Andes, where the air is cool and extremely dry. The method was simple. Cleaned llama meat was thinly sliced and placed between several layers of cloth. The juices of the meat were extracted by trampling on top of the cloth. Then the meat was removed, salted, and hung in the shade to dry. Dried llama meat was called *charqui,* and it kept very well for long periods of time. The very same process is used today, and you will find *charqui* in the markets of Peru and Bolivia. *Charqui* is also found in Chile, but there it is made from mule or donkey meat rather than llama. Today llama meat is also made into a delicious cured ham, *jamón llamero. Chalona* and *salpresa* are other common types of air-dried meat. *Chalona* is somewhat softer and lighter in color than *charqui* and is made from lamb; *salpresa* is made from beef.

Wild animals were the Quechuas' other main source of meat. One of the most widely hunted animals was *jabalí,* or boar, including *chacoan,* and the collared and the white-lipped peccary, the latter two having the greatest range, from the southwestern United States all the way down to central Argentina. *Saíno* was and still is the most appreciated of the wild boars from a culinary standpoint. It is small, and it roams freely through South American forests, as does the *huangana,* another type of boar that is far less desirable because of its strong musky odor.

Venados, or deer, graze freely around the edges of the forests where the foothills of the Andes meet the jungle, from the northern part of Colombia and Venezuela as far south as southwestern Argentina. There are several kinds of deer, including the marsh deer, pampas deer, brocket deer, and the smallest of all, the *pudu.*

In the same regions you can find the *carachupa,* or armadillo, from the Spanish word referring to its flexible armorlike covering. Even today the meat of this animal is used as food and is considered delicious; the valuable shell is transformed into musical instruments and baskets.

It was not until colonial times that the cow, pig, lamb, goat, and sheep were introduced into South America. These animals had a great impact on the food culture of South America. Today, pork is extremely popular and is cooked in every conceivable way in every corner of the continent. Who can forget the intoxicating aroma of *chicharrones* that wafts through the streets of Lima in the early morning hours? These are morsels of pork cooked in their own fat and served with thin slices of sweet potato fried in the pork fat. What a breakfast!

The vast plains of green grasses that are so characteristic of Argentina became the natural home for cattle. Today, production of beef in Argentina ranks among the highest in the world, and the country supplies all its neighbors with beef. For the people of Argentina and Uruguay, meat is so much a part of their food culture that a meal without it is unthinkable. Grilled meats and *asados,* or roasted beef, are extremely popular, to the point that there are eating establishments, *churrasquerias,* that specialize in grilled meats.

Beef, pork, lamb, mutton, and goat are sold in every market in South America, and are prepared in a variety of ways. *Cabrito,* or kid, is always reserved for special occasions, such as birthdays or weddings. Just about every part of the animal is utilized. Nothing is wasted. Walking into my grandmother's house, you knew immediately what was on the stove by the appetizing aroma of her *choncholi* (chitterling) soup. *Mondongo,* or tripe, is quite common, and in each country there are hundreds of ways to prepare it. Beef heart is one of the most popular dishes in Lima—*anticuchos,* or chunks of marinated beef heart skewered and quickly cooked over an open fire. Pigs' feet are the main ingredient of another well-known traditional dish, this one from Ecuador, *patita con maní.* It is a stewlike dish that also contains peanuts. Tongue, liver, sweetbreads, brains, ears, cheeks, tails—all have found their way into the South American kitchen. In the famous Brazilian dish *feijoada,* several parts of the pig—hocks, snouts, tails, and ears—as well as blood sausage are cooked with black beans.

One of my grandmother's great meals was her roasted veal shins. She would rub a paste of garlic, salt, and hot peppers into the meat and let it stand overnight. The next day she laid the two shins on a bed of sliced onions, brushed the meat with achiote oil, and placed the pan in the oven of her wood stove. She roasted the shins until they had just the right rich color and a bouquet that would make your stomach growl. She put the shins on big serving platters and brought them to the table, and there she would carve them in front of the entire family. I don't remember that there was ever anything left but bones. And that was not the end of it. Those bones would be found the following morning simmering away in a pot, the starting point of the next meal. My grandmother, like all good South American cooks, wasted absolutely nothing.

Lamb was one of the meats my mother cooked often. Some nights she would make it into a tasty seco, a stewlike dish with chunks of lamb and potatoes in an aromatic herbal sauce, that even my grandmother acknowledged was good. Usually, though, she would prepare the lamb in a very quick and simple way. She might massage a leg of lamb with a mixture of garlic and anchovies and then briefly roast it in a very hot oven. More often she would butterfly the leg and press lots of chopped fresh cilantro into the meat, then quickly grill it as close to the flame as possible, burning the surface and creating a charred, black crust. The inside remained pink, and the meat was always extremely juicy and tender. Other times she used fresh mint, which she gathered in the backyard, where it grew in great profusion.

Mutton, lamb and baby lamb, goat and kid—all have a prominent place on the South American table, and with good reason. They have character and they are delicious—and we South Americans do have a passion for tasty foods.

BEEF

Bistek al Ajiaco
Flank Steak Ajiaco

Serves 8 as an appetizer or 6 as a main course

Of all Brazil's *panelas,* delicious stewlike dishes, the most popular is made with flank steak; they call it *panela de carne.* Flank steak appears on the Venezuelan table so often that it should be one of the national dishes. This cut is also used in Argentina, Uruguay, and Chile.

Peruvians call flank steak *bistek,* and they prepare it in many ways. Ajiaco, which is seasoned with a combination of hot peppers, is one they are particularly fond of. It is served for lunch and dinner and in smaller portions as an appetizer.

3 cloves garlic, unpeeled
1 medium onion, unpeeled, quartered
3 stalks celery with leafy tops, washed and cut into 3 pieces each
3 cloves
1 tablespoon coarse salt
1 bay leaf
12 black peppercorns
1 flank steak, trimmed (about 1½ pounds)

4 to 6 dried mirasol or ancho or mulatto or poblano peppers, seeded, soaked in warm water for 1 hour, and drained
1 jalapeño or serrano or arbol pepper, seeded and finely chopped
¼ cup olive oil
1 large clove garlic, peeled and finely chopped
3 medium onions, peeled and finely chopped (about 2½ cups)
¼ teaspoon turmeric
2 teaspoons coarse salt
3 or 4 potatoes, boiled, peeled, and cut into 1-inch cubes (about 1 pound)
1 tablespoon lemon juice

GARNISH
3 or 4 tablespoons chopped Italian parsley
7 or 8 alfonso or Kalamata olives

(Continued)

1. In a large pot, combine the garlic, onion, celery, cloves, salt, bay leaf, peppercorns, and 3 quarts of cold water. Bring to a boil, lower the heat, and simmer for 10 minutes. Add the flank steak, bring to a boil again, lower the heat, and simmer for 1½ hours, or until the meat is totally tender. Remove the flank steak. When cool enough to handle, shred the meat along the grain. Set aside. Strain the cooking liquid through a fine sieve or through a strainer lined with several layers of cheesecloth; degrease and reserve ½ cup.

2. In the jar of a blender, combine the drained dried pepper and the fresh hot pepper and blend with the ½ cup of reserved cooking liquid until totally smooth. Set aside.

3. In an earthenware casserole or a sauté pan, heat the olive oil over low heat. Add the garlic and onions and sauté, stirring now and then, until the onions begin to turn lightly golden around the edges. Add the blended hot peppers, turmeric, and salt and continue cooking, stirring now and then, for 1 to 2 minutes. Add the shredded meat, stir, and cook over low heat for 5 minutes. Add the boiled potatoes, stir gently, and cook long enough for the potatoes to heat through and absorb some of the juices. Add the lemon juice, stir, correct the seasoning with salt to taste, and remove from heat. Garnish with chopped parsley and olives and serve hot, right from the casserole, or transfer to a serving platter.

Matahambre
Flank Steak Filled with Spinach and Pistachios

Serves 6 to 8

*M*atahambre (literally, "kill-the-hunger") is a stuffed piece of meat, usually flank steak, sometimes breast of veal. The filling might consist of one or more well-seasoned meats combined with vegetables, eggs, and nuts. Every home has its own special recipe. I particularly like a combination of pork, veal or calves' brains, and spinach. The brains give it good texture.

Although *matahambre* can be sliced and served as soon as it has cooled, it is usually kept in the refrigerator and used over several days. The taste seems to improve with age.

1 large flank steak (about 2½ pounds)

FILLING
1 pound ground pork
½ pound ground veal
2 ounces salt pork, rinsed, rind removed, and chopped
1 large clove garlic, peeled and minced
¼ teaspoon ground cloves
½ teaspoon ground white pepper
¼ teaspoon ground nutmeg
1½ teaspoons ground fennel
1 tablespoon coarse salt
¼ cup amontillado sherry
¾ cup frozen leaf spinach, thawed, stems removed, squeezed dry, and finely chopped (1 10-ounce package)
¼ cup peeled pistachios or pignolis or chopped hazelnuts
1 long, thin carrot, peeled and blanched in boiling salted water for 5 to 8 minutes

6 quarts Beef Stock (page 462) or Chicken Stock (page 461)
2 bay leaves
2 sprigs fresh rosemary
4 tablespoons coarse salt

1. Wipe the flank steak all around with a damp cloth and trim off any excess fat. If you have an untrimmed flank steak, pull off the thin membrane on one side and then the thicker one on the other. Place the steak in front of you on the work surface with one of the long sides facing you. Holding the steak flat with one hand, cut a 2-inch slit in the narrowest and thickest end with a sharp paring knife and start to make a pocket for the filling. Lift up the upper lip and with a long sharp slicing knife, the blade kept horizontal, cut in a fanlike manner deeper into the flesh, leaving a border of about 2 inches on the remaining three sides. Be careful not to pierce the steak, or the filling will spill out during the cooking process. Set aside.

(Continued)

2. In a stainless-steel bowl, combine the pork, veal, salt pork, garlic, cloves, pepper, nutmeg, fennel, salt, and sherry. Mix thoroughly. Fold in the chopped spinach and the pistachios. Push this mixture into the pocket of the flank steak, making sure that all the corners are filled. When the entire mixture has been pushed into the cavity, stick the blanched carrot in the middle. Close the opening by sewing it together with a trussing needle and kitchen string.

3. In a large stockpot, combine the stock, the filled flank steak, bay leaves, rosemary sprigs, and salt. When the stock beings to boil, lower the heat, cover, and simmer for 1 hour, turning the flank steak from time to time.

4. Remove the stockpot from the heat and let the flank steak sit in the cooking liquid for 30 minutes. Remove the meat to a tray and place a light weight on top (about 4 to 6 pounds; a medium cast-iron pan is ideal). When thoroughly cold, slice and serve. Serve the poaching liquid for soup.

STORAGE NOTE   *Matahambre* will keep, well wrapped, in the refrigerator for up to 5 days.

VARIATIONS

Calves' brains may be substituted for the veal. Use 1 small brain or half a large one (10 ounces or less). Clean the brain thoroughly by pulling the thin membrane from the surface and crevices. Add to the ground pork and with your hands, mash the brain and mix it well into the pork. Continue with the recipe.

After you have completed step 2, preheat the oven to 400 degrees. In a mortar with a pestle, pound a clove of garlic with a pinch of salt and mix in a few drops of olive oil. Rub the steak with this paste and place it on a rack in a roasting pan. Lower the oven temperature to 375 degrees, place the meat in the oven, and roast for 1 hour, turning once. Remove from the oven and allow to cool thoroughly with a light weight on top (about 4 to 6 pounds). Slice the matahambre and serve at room temperature or store it in the refrigerator, with the weight, until ready to use.

Salpicón de Carne
Meat Salpicón

—

Serves 6 to 8

1 flank steak (about 2 pounds)

SPICE RUB
4 large cloves garlic, peeled
1 tablespoon coarse salt
1 teaspoon ground cumin
½ teaspoon freshly ground black pepper
¼ teaspoon cayenne

3 tablespoons olive oil
2 medium onions, cut into 8 pieces
1 bay leaf
6 to 8 sprigs fresh thyme or cilantro or Italian parsley
2 tablespoons coarse salt
6 scallions, white parts only, julienned
3 stalks celery, washed, strings removed, and julienned
1 large carrot, peeled and julienned
1 red bell pepper, seeded and julienned

VINAIGRETTE SAUCE
2 tablespoons red-wine vinegar (see Note)
1 teaspoon coarse salt
¼ teaspoon ground black pepper
⅓ cup olive oil

GARNISH
6 to 8 Boston or romaine lettuce leaves, washed and well drained
3 ounces feta, cubed
1 ear cooked corn, cut into ½-inch-thick slices

1. Trim the excess fat from the flank steak and wipe both sides with a damp cloth. Set aside.

2. In a mortar with a pestle, pound the garlic and salt to a paste. Add the cumin, black pepper, and cayenne and continue pounding until well blended. Rub this mixture into the flank steak and marinate for several hours at room temperature, or overnight, covered, in the refrigerator.

(Continued)

3. In a large pot, heat the olive oil over medium heat. Add the flank steak and brown it thoroughly on both sides. Remove the meat to a plate and set aside. In the same pot, combine the onion pieces, bay leaf, thyme, salt, and 3 quarts of water. Bring to a boil, lower the heat, stir, and simmer for 15 minutes. Add the flank steak, reserving the juices left in the plate, and bring to a boil again. Lower the heat and simmer, covered, for 1½ to 2 hours, or until the meat is tender. Remove the pot from the heat and cool the meat in the broth. Remove the meat and pat dry with a clean cloth.

4. With your fingers, shred the meat along the grain into a stainless-steel bowl. Add the julienned scallions, celery, carrot, and bell pepper and set aside.

5. In a small stainless-steel or glass bowl, combine the reserved meat juices with the vinegar, salt, and pepper. Mix well and blend in the oil. Pour the vinaigrette over the meat and vegetables, toss, and correct the seasoning with salt and freshly ground black pepper to taste. Place a lettuce leaf on each plate, spoon a serving of salpicón on top, garnish with cubes of feta and slices of corn, and serve. Or line a serving bowl or platter with the lettuce leaves, arrange the salpicón on top, garnish with the feta and corn, and serve.

NOTE   You can blend 1 tablespoon Dijon mustard with the vinegar if you like.

Ropa Vieja
Beef and Cabbage Salad

Serves 6 to 8

I have often wondered if this dish is called *ropa vieja,* literally "old clothes," because it's so colorful. Some people believe the name comes from the fact that the salad can be made with leftover meat. But in my estimation the dish is so good that I cook a flank steak with the sole purpose of making *ropa vieja.* Although brisket or eye of round may be used, I prefer flank steak for its leanness and fine flavor.

1 flank steak (about 2 pounds)

SPICY BROTH
1 head garlic, unpeeled and cut in half horizontally
1 large onion, unpeeled and quartered
1 large carrot, washed and sliced
4 stalks celery with leafy tops, washed and cut into pieces
2-inch piece fresh ginger, sliced
2 or 3 jalapeño peppers or dried red chili peppers
10 black peppercorns
10 to 15 juniper berries
6 to 8 sprigs fresh thyme or Italian parsley
1 tablespoon coarse salt

VINAIGRETTE DRESSING
¼ cup red-wine vinegar
2 teaspoons coarse salt
¼ teaspoon ground white pepper
⅔ cup olive oil

1 large red onion, peeled and thinly sliced
1 small Savoy cabbage, cut in half, core removed, and shredded
1 red bell pepper, seeded and julienned

GARNISH
¼ cup finely chopped fresh dill or Italian parsley
Alfonso or Kalamata olives

1. Trim any excess fat from the flank steak and wipe it with a damp cloth on both sides. Set aside.

2. In a large stockpot, combine the broth ingredients with 4 quarts of water. Bring to a boil and simmer for 10 to 15 minutes. Add the flank steak and continue cooking for ½ to 2 hours, or until the meat is tender.

3. Remove from the heat and allow the meat to cool in the broth. When cool, remove the meat and drain thoroughly. (The stock can be strained, degreased, and reserved for another purpose.) Trim any fat from the meat and shred it finely along the grain with your fingers, putting the shredded meat in a large bowl.

4. In a small bowl, combine the vinegar, salt, white pepper, and olive oil and blend thoroughly. Pour the dressing over the meat and toss. Add the onion, cabbage, and red pepper. Toss well and adjust the seasonings.

5. Transfer to a serving platter and sprinkle with chopped dill. Garnish with olives and serve at room temperature.

Asado con Pimienta Negra
Roast Beef in a Black-Pepper Crust

Serves about 16

Every time I cook an *asado,* I get a delectable reminder of those countries where beef is the star of the kitchen: Argentina, Paraguay, and Uruguay. This culinary term means different things in different places. For Argentinians, *asado* refers to grilling over an open flame, and indeed they are masters of this—they barbecue practically everything. In the rest of the continent, *asado* usually means oven-roasted meat, both what North Americans call roast beef and pot roast. The best cuts for *asados* are top round, bottom round, and rump.

1 top round, most of the fat trimmed off (10 pounds)
⅓ cup black peppercorns
1 teaspoon ground cardamom

1. Wipe the meat on all sides and tie with 5 pieces of thick kitchen string. Tie first in the center, then on both ends, and then again between the ties.

2. Place the peppercorns on a piece of wax paper, about 25 inches long. Fold the paper in half lengthwise to cover the pepper, fold in about 2 inches on the 3 open sides, and with a rolling pin or a meat mallet, crack the peppercorns. Mix the cracked pepper with the cardamom and press this mixture into the roast beef, covering the entire surface. Place on a rack in a roasting pan and let sit at room temperature for 30 minutes before roasting.

3. Preheat the oven to 500 degrees.

4. Place the pan on the middle rack of the oven and roast the beef for 1 hour 15 minutes for rare, 1 hour 40 minutes for medium-rare. Remove from the oven and let stand in a warm spot for 20 minutes before carving. Remove the strings, place the meat on a cutting board, and carve the meat as thin as possible.

STORAGE NOTE   The roast will keep, tightly wrapped, for about 10 days in the refrigerator.

Costillas a la Brasa
Grilled Short Ribs

Serves 6 to 8

Short ribs are cut from the end of the rib roast. The bones are flat and the meat is lean, with a layer of fat. At first glance there seems to be a lot of fat, but it is easily trimmed away since most of it is on the surface. Leave a little bit of the fat, though: it will baste the ribs as it melts away during cooking.

6 strips short ribs, about 10 × 2½ inches each (7½ pounds)
1 tablespoon black peppercorns
1 tablespoon coarse salt

1. Place the meat, bone side down, on a work surface and with a sharp paring knife, remove most of the fat. Turn the meat, bone side up, and score to make a diamond pattern. Set aside.

2. Place the peppercorns on a 20-inch piece of wax paper. Fold the paper in half lengthwise to cover the pepper, fold in about 2 inches on all 3 sides, and with a rolling pin or a meat mallet, crush the peppercorns.

3. Preheat the broiler.

4. Sprinkle the crushed pepper on all sides of the short ribs and arrange them comfortably on a rack in a roasting pan. Broil the meat, bone side up, for 8 minutes as close to the source of heat as possible (ideally about 2½ inches). Turn the ribs and continue to broil for 6 minutes more. At this point the meat should be rare in the center and quite crusty and charred on the outside. Remove from the broiler. Sprinkle with salt, place on a cutting board, cut the meat between the ribs, and serve.

Tuco de Tallarines con Asado
Braised Beef with Pasta and Tomato Sauce

Serves 8 to 10

One of the most satisfying foods in the world is pasta. South Americans like to embellish their pasta with rich, tasty sauces. *Tuco* is one of them. It is a tomato-based sauce that gets its strength from the meat that is braised in it.

1 eye of round, trimmed of all fat (about 3½ pounds)
6 large cloves garlic, peeled
1 tablespoon coarse salt
2 teaspoons ground cumin
1 teaspoon dried oregano, crumbled
¼ teaspoon ground white pepper
1 small carrot, peeled and cut into 16 sticks, 3 × ⅛ inch

TOMATO SAUCE
¼ cup olive oil
1 or 2 dried red chili peppers, seeded
3 cloves garlic, peeled and minced
5 large onions, peeled and finely chopped (8 cups)
1 bay leaf
1 teaspoon dried oregano
1 carrot, peeled and grated
4 stalks celery, strings removed and finely chopped
7 large tomatoes, peeled, seeded, and finely chopped
12 cups canned Italian plum tomatoes, put through a food mill
    and seeds discarded (3 35-ounce cans)

¼ cup olive oil
2 tablespoons Achiote Oil (page 472)
2 cups Beef Stock (page 462)
2 pounds linguine or penne rigate or ziti, cooked
Grated parmesan

1. Wipe the beef on all sides with a damp cloth. Set aside.

2. In a mortar with a pestle, pound the garlic, salt, cumin, oregano, and white pepper to a smooth paste.

3. With a sharp paring knife, cut on a slant to make a 1½- to 2-inch-deep slit in the meat. Fill with a bit of the garlic paste; insert 1 carrot stick and cut off the end so that it is flush with the meat. Keep doing this at 1½- to 2-inch intervals all around the meat until all the carrot sticks are used up. Rub the meat all around with any remaining garlic paste. Set aside.

4. In a large sauté pan, heat the oil over medium heat. Add the hot peppers and stir. Add the garlic, onions, bay leaf, and oregano and sauté, stirring now and then, for 15 minutes, or until the onions start to get golden around the edges. Add the carrot and celery and continue cooking and stirring for 2 minutes. Add the fresh tomatoes, stir, and cook until the mixture has thickened, about 15 minutes. Add the canned tomatoes, stir, bring to the boil, lower the heat, and continue cooking for 1 hour, stirring now and then. The sauce is ready when it is quite thick. Remove from the heat. You should have about 6 cups of rich tomato sauce.

5. While the sauce is cooking, braise the beef. In a large sauté pan, heat the olive and achiote oils over low heat. Add the beef and braise, covered, for 1 hour, turning the meat every 8 to 10 minutes until evenly browned on all sides. Transfer the meat to a pot large enough to hold it. Deglaze the sauté pan: add the stock and boil for about 2 minutes over high heat, while scraping the bottom of the pan.

6. Strain the stock through a fine sieve or through a strainer lined with a double layer of cheesecloth into a small bowl. Let it sit for a few minutes to allow the fat to rise to the surface. Remove and discard all the fat.

7. Pour the stock into the pot containing the beef. Add the tomato sauce, stir, cover, and simmer gently over very low heat for 2 hours, stirring and turning the meat from time to time. Remove from the heat and let rest in a warm spot, undisturbed, for 20 to 30 minutes before serving.

8. Transfer the meat from the sauce to a serving platter. Thinly slice the beef. Correct the seasoning of the sauce with salt to taste. Toss the cooked pasta with some or all of the tomato sauce, arrange on a platter, sprinkle with grated parmesan, and serve with the sliced beef.

Arroz Tapado
Beef and Rice Cake

Serves 8 to 10

—

Arroz *tapado,* an easy dish to prepare, consists of a meat filling between two layers of rice. Leftover rice is generally used, but the filling, what the Chileans call *pino,* is prepared especially for this dish.

Although *arroz tapado* is usually served at room temperature, I find it more attractive to sprinkle some cheese on top for color and run it under the broiler. It can also be baked. Either way, it is a good dish for dinner, lunch, or the buffet table.

4 large cloves garlic, peeled and chopped

1-inch piece fresh ginger, peeled and chopped

1 or 2 jalapeño peppers, seeded and chopped

1 or 2 dried mirasol peppers, seeded, or 1 dried red chili pepper, seeded (optional)

3 tablespoons Achiote Oil (page 472)

3 tablespoons olive oil

4 medium onions, peeled and finely chopped (4 cups)

1 teaspoon dried oregano

¼ teaspoon ground cloves

3 teaspoons ground cumin

2 bay leaves

2 teaspoons coarse salt

4 inner stalks celery, strings removed and finely chopped

3 tablespoons tomato paste

2 pounds coarsely ground beef

¼ cup raisins

½ cup pisco (Peruvian brandy) or light rum or sherry

2 cups Beef Stock (page 462) or Chicken Stock (page 461), or 1 cup water plus 1 cup red or white wine

¼ cup coarsely chopped walnuts

10 Kalamata olives, seeded and sliced

2 tablespoons fresh thyme leaves

¼ cup chopped Italian parsley

Freshly ground black pepper

10 cups Steamed Rice (page 423)
2 hard-boiled eggs, sliced
½ cup grated jarlsberg

1. On a cutting board, combine the garlic, ginger, and fresh hot peppers. Crumble the dried hot peppers over them and mince everything together.

2. In a large sauté pan, heat the achiote and olive oils over medium heat. Add the minced garlic mixture and stir; add the onions, oregano, cloves, cumin, bay leaves, and salt. Sauté, stirring now and then, until the onions are translucent, about 5 minutes. Add the celery and tomato paste and cook, stirring, for 1 minute longer. Push the onion mixture to the side and place the ground beef in the center of the pan. Cook the beef, stirring, for 10 minutes over medium-low heat.

3. Meanwhile, in a cup, soak the raisins in the pisco for 10 minutes.

4. Add the stock to the beef mixture. Stir, bring to a boil, and cook over medium heat until all the stock has evaporated, about 8 minutes. Add the raisins with the pisco and continue cooking until the pisco has evaporated. Stir in the walnuts, olives, thyme, and parsley and remove from the heat. Correct the seasoning with salt and black pepper.

5. Preheat the broiler.

6. Press 5 cups of the cooked rice into the bottom of a 3-quart round baking dish about 3 inches high. Spread all of the beef filling over the rice, arrange the hard-boiled egg slices on top, and cover with the remaining 5 cups of rice, pressing down gently with the back of a spoon to smooth the surface. Sprinkle with the grated jarlsberg and broil just long enough for the cheese to melt and turn golden. Remove the dish from the broiler and serve.

VARIATIONS

Substitute the same amount of ground lamb or ground chicken for the ground beef and proceed with the recipe.

After you have completed Step 4, preheat the oven to 375 degrees. Beat 2 eggs with ¾ cup beef or chicken stock and pour over the top layer of rice. Sprinkle with the grated jarlsberg, cover tightly, and bake for about 35 minutes. Remove from the oven and serve hot or warm.

(Continued)

After you have completed Step 4, preheat the oven to 375 degrees. Mix the rice thoroughly with 2 pounds grated or finely chopped fresh mozzarella, assemble the dish, and pour ¾ cup beef or chicken stock over the entire surface. Cover tightly and bake for 35 minutes. Remove from the oven and serve hot or warm.

VEAL

Lomo de Ternera al Horno
Roast Loin of Veal

—

Serves 8 as an appetizer or 6 as a main course

Loin of veal is delicious when it is freshly roasted, and it is equally wonderful cold, sliced as thin as possible by hand or with a meat slicer and served as an appetizer with various garnishes, including Onion Relish (page 481). Thin slices of veal can also be served on lettuce leaves with a sauce, such as Salsa Cruda (page 480) or an herbal sauce made with cilantro or parsley (pages 477–479)—even mustard is good. Hot or cold, this roast is perfect for the buffet table. Thinly sliced, it will provide a generous number of servings.

*1 boneless veal loin, with the flank or flap, excess fat removed,
    15 × 11 inches (about 4½ pounds)*
2 large cloves garlic, peeled
1 tablespoon coarse salt
⅛ teaspoon ground cloves
¼ teaspoon ground cinnamon
*1 tablespoon green peppercorns in brine, rinsed and drained,
    or freeze-dried green peppercorns*
6 tablespoons butter, softened
1 tablespoon fresh thyme leaves

1. Wipe the meat with a damp cloth and place it on the work surface. Cover the flank with a piece of wax paper or plastic wrap and pound the flank (not the loin) with a meat mallet to gain about 2 inches in length and width. Set aside.

2. In a mortar with a pestle, pound the garlic, salt, cloves, cinnamon, and green peppercorns to a smooth paste. Add the butter and blend well.

3. Preheat the oven to 475 degrees.

4. Spread all but 2 tablespoons of the butter mixture over the flap, sprinkle with thyme leaves, and roll, starting from the loin, to the opposite end. Tie with kitchen string, first in the center of the roll, then alternating from one side to the other, at ¾-inch intervals. At this point, the saddle should be about 14 inches long and 3½ inches wide.

5. Rub all around with the remaining butter mixture and roast for 45 minutes. Remove from the oven and let sit in a warm spot for 15 to 20 minutes. Remove the strings, place the meat on a cutting board, slice, and serve.

STORAGE NOTE   This roast stores extremely well, tightly wrapped, in the refrigerator for up to 1 week. Serve at room temperature as an appetizer or as a dish for the buffet table.

Ternera con Anchoas y Tomillo
Roast Veal with Anchovies and Fresh Thyme

Serves 6 to 8

I prefer to cook veal quickly in a very hot oven, searing it and preserving all of the juices trapped inside. A loin of veal takes only a very short time in a hot oven, about thirty-five minutes. Remember to let the meat relax for ten to fifteen minutes after roasting.

1 boneless veal loin, excess fat removed, about 12 × 5 × 2 inches
(3 pounds)
2 cloves garlic, peeled
1 tablespoon coarse salt
1 teaspoon ground cumin
¼ teaspoon ground cinnamon
¼ teaspoon ground white pepper
6 anchovy fillets, drained
1 tablespoon red-wine vinegar
¼ cup fresh thyme leaves
8 pieces thin fatback, 5 × 6 inches each (½ pound)

1. Wipe the meat with a damp cloth and set aside.

2. In a mortar with a pestle, pound the garlic, salt, cumin, cinnamon, and white pepper to a smooth paste. Add the anchovies and continue pounding until the anchovies are well incorporated. Add the vinegar, mix well, and let sit for a few minutes. Rub this mixture into the veal and marinate for 1 hour, or until ready to use.

3. Preheat the oven to 500 degrees.

4. Sprinkle and press the thyme leaves evenly all around the meat. Cut 7 pieces of kitchen string, each about 16 inches long. Place the strings on the work surface, running vertically, at 1½-inch intervals. Place 4 pieces of the fatback, horizontally overlapping one another, over the middle of the strings. Place the veal over the fatback and cover with the remaining 4 pieces of fatback, also overlapping. First tie the string in the middle; continue tying, alternating from one side to the other.

5. Place the meat on a rack in a shallow roasting pan. Put the pan in the middle level of the oven and lower the heat to 475 degrees. After 10 minutes, turn the meat to the opposite side and continue roasting for 20 minutes. (The total roasting time should be 30 to 35 minutes.) Remove the roast from the oven to a warm spot for 10 minutes, or until ready to serve. Remove and discard the strings, place the roast on a cutting board or serving platter, and serve.

Ternera con Salsa de Cerveza
Veal Tenderloin in Beer Sauce

Serves 6 to 8

2 boneless veal tenderloins, excess fat removed, each about 12 inches long (1¾ pounds each)
3 large cloves garlic, peeled
2 tablespoons coarse salt
2 teaspoons ground coriander
2 teaspoons ground fennel
½ teaspoon ground white pepper
Grated rind of 1 lime or lemon
2 tablespoons dry vermouth
10 thin slices bacon
1-inch piece fresh ginger, peeled and chopped
½ cup safflower oil or vegetable oil
1 cup light beer
6 sprigs plus 1 small bunch fresh tarragon
3 tablespoons all-purpose flour
2 cups Chicken Stock (page 461)
1 teaspoon sugar
2 tablespoons chopped fresh cilantro leaves or Italian parsley

(Continued)

1. Tie each veal loin with kitchen string into a neat roll. First tie the middle, then tie the ends, then between one end and the middle, between the other end and the middle, and so on, until the loin is tied at ½-inch intervals. Each roll should measure 12 × 2½ inches. Set aside.

2. In a mortar with a pestle, pound the garlic, salt, coriander, fennel, and pepper to a smooth paste. Mix in the lime rind and add the vermouth. Blend well and let sit for a few minutes. Rub this mixture all around both rolls and marinate for 10 to 15 minutes at room temperature.

3. Layer the bottom of a large skillet or earthenware casserole with the bacon slices. Add the ginger, safflower oil, beer, 1 cup of water, and 6 sprigs tarragon. Cook over medium heat for about 8 minutes, or until all the liquid has evaporated.

4. Place the veal loins in the skillet or casserole and cook the meat for 10 minutes on one side, 10 minutes on the second side, and 5 minutes each on the remaining sides. If the bacon and tarragon get too brown, remove and discard them. Transfer the meat from the skillet to a pan and set aside in a warm spot, or place in a warm oven.

5. While the meat is resting, prepare the sauce. Remove all but ¼ cup of the fat from the skillet or casserole. Add the flour and cook over medium-high heat, scraping the bottom of the skillet, for about 1 minute. Stir in the stock, sugar, and the bunch of tarragon and simmer, stirring, for about 6 minutes, or until the mixture is thick and coats the back of a spoon. Strain the sauce through a fine sieve, pressing out all the juices. Correct the seasoning with salt and white pepper to taste. You should have about 1½ cups of sauce.

6. Cover the bottom of a large serving platter with a thin layer of sauce. Remove and discard the strings and slice both loins about ¼ inch thick. Arrange the slices on top of the sauce and serve, sprinkled with chopped cilantro. Pass the remaining sauce in a sauceboat. Or cover the bottom of individual dinner plates with a thin layer of sauce and place a few slices of meat on top. Sprinkle with chopped cilantro and serve.

Pierna de Ternera al Horno
Roast Veal Shanks
—

Serves 6 to 8

Veal shanks are so flavorful, very little is needed to make a great dish. The shanks also look great when cooked whole and presented that way. I like to serve them on a buffet table at parties.

2 veal shanks (about 5 pounds each)
3 large cloves garlic, peeled and minced
2 or 3 jalapeño peppers, seeded and minced, or 1/8 teaspoon cayenne
1-inch piece fresh ginger, peeled and grated
4 teaspoons coarse salt
1 teaspoon coarsely ground black pepper
2 medium onions, peeled and sliced
2 carrots, peeled and coarsely julienned
8 stalks celery, strings removed and thinly sliced
2 large bunches fresh thyme (about 2 ounces, total)
1 tablespoon olive oil
3 tablespoons all-purpose flour
4 cups Veal Stock (page 464) or Chicken Stock (page 461) or water
3 tablespoons amontillado sherry
Ground white pepper

1. Wipe the veal shanks with a damp cloth. Set aside.

2. In a small stainless-steel bowl, combine the garlic, hot peppers, ginger, and 2 teaspoons of the salt. Place the veal shanks on a tray and rub them thoroughly with the garlic-ginger mixture. Sprinkle with the black pepper and marinate, covered, for 8 hours at room temperature, or overnight in the refrigerator.

3. Preheat the oven to 400 degrees.

4. Spread the onions, carrots, celery, and thyme sprigs on the bottom of a roasting pan. Coat the shanks with the olive oil and place them

(Continued)

on top. Place the roasting pan in the oven, lower the temperature to 375 degrees, and roast the shanks with the vegetables for 1 hour 15 minutes, or until golden all around, turning the shanks once after 35 minutes.

5. Remove the shanks from the oven, transfer to a serving platter, and set aside in a warm spot. Remove all the vegetables and thyme from the roasting pan, place them in a saucepan, sprinkle with the flour, and set aside.

6. Drain all the fat from the roasting pan and deglaze the pan with 1 cup of stock, constantly scraping the bottom of the pan. After the pan is thoroughly deglazed, pour all the juices into the saucepan containing the vegetables. Add the remaining 3 cups of stock, stirring, the remaining 2 teaspoons of salt, and the sherry and bring to a boil. Lower the heat and gently simmer for 10 to 15 minutes, stirring now and then.

7. Strain the sauce through a fine sieve, squeezing the vegetables to remove all the juices. Correct the seasoning with salt and white pepper to taste. You will have 1½ to 2 cups of sauce. Pour the sauce over the veal shanks and serve.

Chuletas al Limón
Lemon Veal Chops

Serves 8

—

Veal chops seasoned with lemon rind, ground coriander, and cracked white pepper and then quickly sautéed are quick, extremely simple, and delicious.

8 veal rib chops, 1 inch thick, frenched (3½ pounds) (see Note)
3 tablespoons grated lemon rind
2 teaspoons ground white pepper
2 teaspoons ground coriander
2 teaspoons coarse salt
Vegetable oil for sautéing

GARNISH
2 tablespoons fresh thyme leaves or chopped Italian parsley
3 or 4 lemons, white skin peeled off, thinly sliced and seeded

1. Pound the veal chops until they are as thin as possible and have doubled in size. To do this, place the meat between two pieces of wax paper and pound with a meat mallet in all directions, moving away from the bone. Make sure that when you pound the chop, you hit it with the mallet absolutely flat. Peel away the wax paper after a couple of strokes, turn the chop, and continue pounding. Keep doing this until the chops have stretched quite thin. Change wax paper if necessary.

2. Press the lemon rind with the palm of your hand into each side of each veal chop. Sprinkle each side with white pepper, coriander, and salt. Set aside until ready to use.

3. In a large skillet, heat the oil over high heat. Sauté the chops, 2 or 3 at a time, until golden in color, about 2 to 3 minutes. Turn the chops and continue cooking for 2 to 3 minutes more, or until golden. Repeat until all the chops are sautéed. Arrange the chops on a serving platter, sprinkled with the thyme leaves and garnished with peeled lemon slices.

NOTE   To french the chops, cut and scrape away all the meat from the bones.

Ternera en los Manzanos
Double Veal Chops with Apple Filling

Serves 6

6 double veal chops, each 1½ inches thick with a single bone
 (about ¾ pound each)

APPLE FILLING
1 tablespoon freeze-dried green peppercorns
1 teaspoon dried cardamom
¼ teaspoon ground cinnamon
⅛ teaspoon ground allspice
1 tablespoon coarse salt
2 tablespoons olive oil
5 slices bacon, minced
1 medium onion, peeled and finely chopped (1 cup)
1½-inch piece fresh ginger, peeled and grated
3½ pounds tart green apples, peeled, cored, and finely chopped
 (6 cups)

½ cup Rendered Bacon Fat (page 476) or olive oil
1½ cups safflower oil
Coarse salt
3 tablespoons chopped Italian parsley

1. Wipe the veal chops with a damp cloth on all sides. Hold one chop flat against the work surface and with a sharp paring knife, make a small cut in the top part of the chop closest to the bone. Make the opening as small as possible. Insert the knife into the middle of the chop with the blade facing the bone. With a circular motion, open a pocket, cutting toward the bone without making any tears in the meat. Repeat with the remaining chops.

2. In a mortar with a pestle, pound the green peppercorns, cardamom, cinnamon, allspice, and salt until the peppercorns are crushed and mixed to a fine powder. Set aside.

3. In a large skillet, heat the olive oil and the bacon. Sauté for about 1 minute to release the fat. Do not brown the bacon. Add the onion and ginger and cook for 1 minute. Add 3 teaspoons of the spice mixture and

½ cup of water. Stir and cook over low heat until all the liquid has evaporated, about 5 minutes. Add the apples and continue cooking, stirring and scraping the bottom of the skillet from time to time, for about 55 minutes, or until the apples have softened to a smooth puree-like consistency. Correct the seasoning with salt to taste. Remove the skillet from the heat and let the filling cool.

4. Insert a circular #4 pastry tube in a large pastry bag and fill with the apple mixture. Insert the pastry tube inside the slit of each chop and squeeze to fill the pockets generously with the apple mixture. If you do not have a pastry tube, spoon the mixture into the pockets. Sprinkle the chops on both sides with the remaining spice mixture.

5. In a large skillet, heat the bacon fat and safflower oil over high heat. Reduce the heat to medium-high and place the chops, cut side down, in the hot fat. Sauté for about 5 minutes to seal the openings. Lay the chops flat on one side and sauté for 5 minutes, then turn over to the opposite side and sauté for 5 minutes longer. Repeat, turning the chops every 5 minutes on each side for a total cooking time of 30 minutes, or until light golden on both sides. Sprinkle the chops with salt to taste and chopped parsley. Transfer to a platter and serve.

VARIATION

Substitute the same amount of Bartlett, Anjou, or Comice pears for the apples and proceed with the recipe.

PORK

Lechón Asado
Roast Suckling Pig

—

Serves 8

Back in Peru, I knew there was going to be a celebration as soon as I walked into the kitchen and saw a little pig resting on the kitchen counter.

A crisp skin is the key to making a suckling pig a smashing success. I find this skin so irresistible that I have to stop myself from picking on it, or the pig will arrive at the table without any. For ideal crispness, never baste the pig with liquid of any kind before, during, or after roasting. Instead, wipe the skin dry and let the pig sit on the kitchen counter—as it did back home in my mother's kitchen—for several hours before cooking so the skin will dry out. Another method is to apply lard or a flavored colored oil to the skin; this should be done once at the beginning of the roasting. To keep the skin crisp after the pig has been roasted, be sure not to pour any liquid over it. Never cover the pig to keep it warm or for any other reason. If you need to keep the pig warm, place it in a warm oven with the door slightly ajar.

A suckling pig weighing between ten and fifteen pounds will serve about eight people as a main course. For a buffet, where portions are smaller, you can get twice that many servings from it.

1 suckling pig (12 to 15 pounds)

MARINADE
18 cloves garlic, peeled and finely chopped
1 tablespoon dried oregano
2 teaspoons ground cumin
½ teaspoon ground cloves
1 tablespoon ground white pepper
½ cup lime or lemon juice
½ cup orange juice
¼ cup Achiote Oil (page 472)

2 medium onions, peeled and sliced
3 large carrots, peeled and thinly sliced
1 bunch celery, strings removed and sliced

1. Wipe the pig inside and out with a damp cloth. Butterfly the pig by placing it, cavity up, on the work surface. Open the cavity. With a cleaver, crack the ribs on both sides of the backbone and press down on both sides of the rib cage to flatten. Set aside.

2. In a small bowl, combine the garlic, oregano, cumin, cloves, pepper, lime juice, and orange juice. Mix well and let sit for 1 hour at room temperature. Add the oil and blend thoroughly.

3. Rub the pig thoroughly inside and out with the garlic-oil mixture, and let marinate for 12 hours at room temperature or, preferably, 24 to 48 hours in the refrigerator.

4. In a roasting pan large enough to hold the pig, mix the onions, carrots, and celery and arrange them in the middle of the rack. Place the pig, cavity down, over the vegetables, making sure that all the vegetables are inside the cavity and the feet and head are inside the roasting pan (see Note).

5. Loosely cover the ears, snout, and tail with small pieces of oiled aluminum foil to protect them from burning. With a clean dry cloth, wipe off the marinade from the surface of the skin and let the pig air-dry, undisturbed, for 4 to 6 hours.

6. Preheat the oven to 475 degrees.

7. Place the roasting pan in the oven, lower the heat to 450 degrees, and roast the pig for 1½ to 2 hours, or until golden and crisp. Do not baste. Remove the pig from the oven and let sit in a warm spot for 8 to 10 minutes before carving. Do not cover. Transfer the pig with the vegetables to a large serving platter and serve.

NOTE   To make sure that the legs of the pig stay inside the pan while roasting, tie the front right hoof, bring the string over the pig to the front left hoof, and tie so that both front hooves are inside the roasting pan. Bring the string down to the back left hoof and tie it, then bring the string over the pig to the back right hoof, and tie it tightly so that both back legs stay inside the roasting pan. Bring the string around to the front right hoof and tie tightly.

Lomo Horneado con Camote y Cebollas

Roast Loin of Pork with Sweet Potatoes and Onions

Serves 6 to 8

What I like best about this dish is the crust on the meat that is formed by the spices and sugar in the marinade. It gives the roast an appetizing color and unusual flavor and seals in all the wonderful juices.

When roasting a loin of pork with the bone, ask your butcher to free it from the meat for easy carving.

1 pork loin, with bones (5 to 6 pounds)

MARINADE
2 large cloves garlic, peeled
2 teaspoons coarse salt
½ teaspoon ground cinnamon
¼ teaspoon ground cloves
⅛ teaspoon cayenne
3 tablespoons brown sugar
1 tablespoon red-wine vinegar
20 to 24 fresh sage leaves, minced (1½ tablespoons)
*   or 1 teaspoon dried and ground sage*

3 tablespoons olive oil
6 to 8 medium sweet potatoes (about 3½ pounds)
6 to 8 medium Bermuda onions (about 2½ pounds)
Freshly ground black pepper

1. Wipe the loin with a damp cloth. Split the back and scrape or feather the bones for easy carving. Set aside.

2. In a mortar with a pestle, pound the garlic, salt, cinnamon, cloves, and cayenne to a smooth paste. Blend in the sugar, vinegar, and sage and mix well. Rub this mixture over the entire surface of pork loin. Place the loin on a rack in a roasting pan large enough to hold the meat, sweet potatoes, and onion and let sit at room temperature for 1 to 2 hours.

3. Preheat the oven to 400 degrees.

4. Rub the meat with 1 tablespoon of the oil. Rub the sweet potatoes with another tablespoon of the oil and arrange them around the loin. Cut a cross on top of each onion, going halfway through. Rub the onions with the remaining oil and arrange them on the roasting rack around the loin and the sweet potatoes. Roast in the middle level of the oven for 1 hour 20 minutes.

5. Remove and let sit in a warm spot for about 10 minutes. Transfer the loin to a serving platter, sprinkle salt and freshly ground black pepper to taste in the middle of the opened onions, arrange them and the sweet potatoes around the roast, and serve.

Jamón del País
Poached Fresh Ham

Serves about 25

At noon outside the open-air restaurants around the markets in Lima, men with long knives slice *jamón del país* nonstop, making mountains and mountains of sliced fresh ham. Their assistants feverishly open up the warm, crusty *pan francés,* or Peruvian hard rolls, and stuff each one with ham, onion relish, and a lettuce leaf. They can barely keep pace with the customers, who grab the sandwiches almost faster than they can be made.

1 fresh ham, with bone (about 16 pounds)

MARINADE
6 large cloves garlic, peeled
¼ cup coarse salt
¼ teaspoon cayenne
1 tablespoon ground white pepper
1 tablespoon ground cumin
3 tablespoons ground turmeric
¼ cup red-wine vinegar
3 tablespoons lemon juice
1 cup Achiote Oil (page 472)

STOCK
5 pounds pigs' feet or veal bones, chopped
4 medium onions, unpeeled and quartered
4 carrots, washed and chopped
8 stalks celery with leafy tops, washed and coarsely chopped
2 heads garlic, unpeeled and cut in half horizontally
5 or 6 jalapeño peppers or dried red chili peppers
3 bay leaves
10 cloves
6 juniper berries
8 to 10 sprigs fresh cilantro or Italian parsley
10 black peppercorns
12 sprigs fresh thyme or ½ teaspoon dried thyme
6 tablespoons coarse salt

3 cups red-wine vinegar
Onion Relish (page 481)

1. Remove the fat, gristle, and bone from the ham. Reserve the bone for the stock and place the ham in a shallow stainless-steel pan. Set aside.

2. In a mortar with a pestle, pound the garlic, salt, cayenne, white pepper, cumin, and turmeric to a smooth paste. Add the vinegar and lemon juice. Mix well and let sit for a few minutes to dissolve the spices; then blend in the oil. Pour this mixture over the ham and rub it well all around. Cover the ham tightly with plastic wrap and let marinate overnight in the refrigerator, preferably 24 to 48 hours. After the ham has been marinated, wrap it in a double layer of cheesecloth in such a way as to simulate the original shape; secure and tie it tightly with kitchen string.

3. Meanwhile, make the stock. In a large stockpot combine the ham bone, pigs' feet, onions, carrots, celery, garlic, hot peppers, bay leaves, cloves, juniper berries, cilantro, peppercorns, thyme, salt, and 16 quarts of water. Bring to a boil, lower the heat, and simmer, uncovered, for 3 hours, skimming the foam as it rises to the surface. Remove the stockpot from the heat and let cool for 2 hours. Strain the stock through a fine sieve or several layers of cheesecloth, discarding the bones, vegetables, spices, and herbs. Degrease the stock thoroughly. You should have 10 quarts of stock.

4. Add the vinegar to the stock and bring to a boil. Gently submerge the wrapped ham in the stock, lower the heat, and simmer for 3½ hours. Do not boil.

5. Remove from the heat and let the ham cool in the stock for at least 2 hours. Remove the ham from the stock and let cool at room temperature. Remove the cheesecloth, place the ham on a wooden cutting board or serving platter, slice, and serve, garnished with onion relish.

NOTE   If the ham is not served the same day as it is cooked, leave it in the stock and refrigerate it overnight. Remove the ham from the stock and serve cold.

STORAGE NOTE   The ham, if well wrapped or tightly covered, will keep in perfect condition for up to 2 weeks in the refrigerator.

Atamalado de Cerdo con Quinua
Pork and Quinoa Atamalado

Serves 6 to 8

Atamalados are stews that feature meat, chicken, or seafood with a grain, such as quinoa, rice, or barley, or a small pasta like orzo.

2 pounds lean pork, from the loin, leg, or shoulder

MARINADE
2 cloves garlic, peeled
2 teaspoons coarse salt
½ teaspoon ground white pepper
½ teaspoon ground cumin
1 tablespoon red-wine vinegar

2 dried ancho peppers, seeded
1 fresh or dried mirasol pepper or dried red chili pepper, seeded
1 fresh jalapeño or arbol or serrano pepper, seeded and roasted (page 483)
⅓ cup vegetable oil
2 tablespoons Achiote Oil (page 472)
2 medium onions, peeled and finely chopped (2 cups)
1 clove garlic, peeled and minced
2 teaspoons coarse salt
6 cups cooked quinoa with 3 cups of the cooking liquid or 3 cups water (page 419)
2 tablespoons chopped fresh cilantro leaves

1. Wipe the pork with a damp cloth, cut it into 2-inch cubes, and place in a stainless-steel bowl. Set aside.

2. In a mortar with a pestle, pound the garlic, salt, white pepper, and cumin to a smooth paste. Add the vinegar and mix well. Pour this mixture over the cubed pork and mix thoroughly. Cover the bowl and set aside to marinate for 3 to 4 hours at room temperature or overnight in the refrigerator.

3. In a bowl, crumble all the dried peppers and soak them in ½ cup of warm water for 15 minutes. Place the soaked peppers with the liquid and the fresh peppers in the jar of a blender or the work bowl of a food processor and puree.

4. Drain the pork and pat the cubes dry. In a large heavy saucepan, heat the vegetable and achiote oils over high heat. Add the pork cubes and quickly brown them evenly on all sides, stirring. Transfer to a plate and set aside.

5. Add the onions, minced garlic, and salt to the saucepan. Cook over high heat, stirring frequently, until the onions are golden around the edges, about 8 minutes. Add the pureed peppers and cook 5 minutes more, stirring constantly, until all the liquid has evaporated.

6. Add the reserved quinoa cooking liquid or water, blend thoroughly, and bring to a boil. Add the pork with any juices left on the plate and the cooked quinoa, stir, lower the heat, and gently simmer for 30 minutes, or until the pork is tender. If the pork is not tender after 30 minutes and the quinoa has dried out too much, add additional water and continue cooking until the pork is tender. The quinoa should be moist. Correct the seasoning with salt to taste, sprinkle with chopped cilantro, and serve hot.

Carapulcra

Serves 6 to 8

Carapulcra is *the* Peruvian meat-and-potato dish. The pepper used in this dish is *qjí amarillo,* or mirasol, a hot yellow pepper that lends its distinctive golden color, in addition to its special taste and character. If dried mirasol peppers are not available, you can use other types of peppers, such as anchos; the dish won't have that golden color or quite the same flavor, but it will be equally tasty.

1 pound papa seca. *(about 2½ cups) (see Note)*

MARINADE
1 clove garlic, peeled and finely chopped
1 tablespoon coarse salt
2 teaspoons ground cumin
⅛ teaspoon ground cloves
¼ cup amontillado sherry
1 tablespoon Achiote Oil (page 472) or olive oil

2½ to 3 pounds boneless pork, cut into 8 to 12 equal chunks
4 or 5 dried mirasol peppers, seeded
1 carrot, peeled and chopped
2 to 4 tablespoons lard or Rendered Bacon Fat (page 476),
    Rendered Duck Fat (page 475), or olive oil
2 tablespoons Achiote Oil (page 472)
1 large clove garlic, finely chopped
3 medium red or yellow onions, peeled and finely chopped (3 cups)
1 bay leaf
1 tablespoon coarse salt
6 cups Chicken Stock (page 461) or Beef Stock (page 462)
    or Veal Stock (page 464) or water
1 cup coarsely chopped peanuts

1. Place the *papa seca* in a dry skillet over high heat and roast constantly, shaking the skillet and stirring the potatoes, for about 5 minutes. Do not let them get too brown. Remove from the heat and place the roasted potatoes in a strainer, shaking to remove and discard the excess potato powder. Place the potatoes in a bowl, add 6 to 8 cups of cold water, and let soak for at least 4 to 5 hours or overnight. Drain the potatoes through a strainer, discarding the soaking water.

2. In a mortar with a pestle, pound the garlic, salt, cumin, and cloves to a paste. Stir in the sherry and let stand for a few minutes. Thoroughly mix in 1 tablespoon of the oil. Rub the meat with this mixture and let marinate for 1 hour at room temperature or overnight in the refrigerator, covered.

3. In a small bowl, combine the mirasol peppers and 1 cup of warm water. Let soak for about 20 minutes. Pour the soaked peppers with the liquid into a blender or food processor and blend or process at top speed. With the machine running, add the chopped carrot and continue blending for a second longer. Set aside.

4. In a casserole or saucepan, heat 2 tablespoons of lard and 2 tablespoons of achiote oil (or 4 tablespoons lard) over medium heat. Add the pork pieces and lightly brown them on all sides, about 15 minutes. Transfer the meat from the saucepan to a plate.

5. Add the chopped garlic, onions, and bay leaf to the fat remaining in the saucepan and sauté until the onions are translucent, about 4 to 5 minutes. Add the blended pepper-and-carrot mixture and the salt and continue cooking until all the liquid has evaporated, about 10 minutes. Add the browned meat with the accumulated juices and 6 cups of stock or water. Bring to a boil, lower the heat, cover, and gently simmer for 1 hour, stirring now and then.

6. Add the potatoes and ¾ cup of the peanuts, stir, and continue cooking for 45 minutes to 1 hour, or until the meat is tender, stirring from time to time. If the meat is not tender and all the liquid has been absorbed, add extra stock or water and continue cooking. Correct the seasoning with salt to taste. Remove from the heat, garnish with the remaining peanuts, and serve.

NOTE   *Papa seca* are available in food specialty shops.

VARIATION

Substitute a 3½-pound chicken, cut into 8 serving pieces, for the pork. Marinate it as you would the pork in Step 2 and proceed with the recipe. Add only 3 cups of stock or water instead of 6 at the end of Step 5. Immediately add the chicken with the potatoes and peanuts in Step 6. Cook over low heat for 40 to 45 minutes, or until the chicken is tender.

Feijoada

Serves 10 to 12

Feijoada, a rich concoction of beans (usually black beans) cooked with an assortment of pork cuts, is the ceremonial dish of Brazil. A true feijoada has at least five different cuts of pork. Although the choice of meat rests very much on the individual cook (each one has his or her own idea of what is right), certain cuts are a must, including snouts, ears, tails, ham hocks or pigs' feet, and blood sausages. These cuts give the dish its identity. Cuts of fresh pork are dominant, but it is not unusual to find a piece of smoked pork or a chunk of cured beef in a feijoada.

The choice of garnishes offered with the feijoada depends pretty much on the locale. The most standard are slices of orange, thin rounds of onion, and vegetables like kale or collards and pumpkin. Feijoada is always served with rice.

2 pounds dried black beans
3 ham hocks (about 3½ pounds)
1 pig's snout, cut into 1-inch cubes
1 pig's tail, whole
10 cups Beef Stock (page 462)
1 pig's ear, sliced into ½-inch strips
3 tablespoons Rendered Bacon Fat (page 476) or olive oil
3 dried red chili peppers, seeded
3 cloves garlic, peeled and finely chopped
3 large onions, peeled and finely chopped (4½ cups)
⅓ cup amontillado sherry
2 morcilla sausages, peeled and chopped (about ½ pound)
24 sprigs fresh cilantro
3 tablespoons chopped Italian parsley

1. Wash the black beans thoroughly under cold running water. Place them in a container or bowl, add 8 cups of cold water, and let soak overnight.

2. In a stockpot, combine the ham hocks, snout, and tail and the stock. Bring to a boil, skimming the foam as it rises to the surface. Lower the heat and simmer for 2 hours, stirring now and then.

3. Remove the ham hocks from the stock; remove the meat from the bones and cut into 2 pieces. Cover the meat and set aside. Put the bones back into the simmering stock. Add the pig's ear, stir, and continue cooking until the stock has reduced considerably, about 35 minutes. Discard the bones, transfer the tail to a plate, cover, and set aside. Remove the stock from the heat and set aside. You should have 4 cups of stock, with pieces of snout and ear.

4. In a large pot, combine the beans and their soaking water with 6 cups of cold water. Bring to a boil, lower the heat, and simmer for 1 hour 45 minutes to 2 hours. When the beans are cooked, drain, reserving both the beans and their cooking liquid.

5. In a large saucepan or casserole, heat the bacon fat and peppers. Add the garlic and onions and sauté over medium heat until the onions start to get golden around the edges, about 15 minutes. Add the sherry and continue cooking and stirring until the sherry has evaporated. Add the sausages and sauté for a minute longer, stirring. Add all of the reserved cooking liquid from the beans and the reserved stock with snout and ear and stir. Bring to a boil, lower the heat, and simmer for 20 minutes.

6. Add the beans and the cilantro, stir, and cook over low heat for 45 minutes, stirring now and then. If the beans are too dry, add a little extra water. Add the reserved pieces of ham hock and the tail, stir, cover, and continue cooking for 20 minutes. Remove and discard the cilantro.

7. Serve directly from the casserole, or transfer the pieces of ham hock to a plate and transfer the beans to a serving dish. Arrange the tail in the middle of the beans and surround them with the pieces of ham hocks. Sprinkle with chopped parsley and serve.

LAMB

Cordero Asado con Menta
Roast Leg of Lamb with Mint

Serves 6 to 8

Mint is a plant that offers refreshing flavor to the cook but can be a terror for the gardener. I will never forget the time my grandfather was experimenting with mint and planted different varieties of it in my grandmother's geranium pots and around the edges of her garden. My grandmother was furious with him as she stood by and watched the mint take over and choke out all her beautiful flowers. The mint eventually found its way into the kitchen, and my inventive grandmother found a million ways to cook with it, including this dish.

1 whole leg of lamb, "H" (hip) bone removed (page 335) (about 8 pounds)
3 large cloves garlic, peeled
2 tablespoons coarse salt
1 tablespoon ground cumin
⅛ teaspoon cayenne
⅛ teaspoon ground bay leaf
⅛ teaspoon ground cloves
3 tablespoons aguardiente or pisco (Peruvian brandy) or light rum, or 2 tablespoons red-wine vinegar
2 tablespoons olive oil
1 cup chopped fresh mint

1. Trim off most of the fat from the leg of lamb and wipe it with a damp cloth. Set aside.

2. In a mortar with a pestle, pound the garlic and the salt to a paste. Add the cumin, cayenne, bay leaf, and cloves and continue pounding. Add the aguardiente and let sit for about 10 minutes. Blend in the olive oil.

3. Rub the meat all around with the garlic mixture and marinate for 8 hours at room temperature or overnight, covered, in the refrigerator.

4. Preheat the oven to 500 degrees.

5. Just before roasting, press the chopped mint with the palm of your hand all around the leg of lamb and place on a roasting rack in a shallow roasting pan. Put the pan in the oven, lower the temperature to 475 degrees, and roast the leg of lamb, undisturbed, for 45 minutes for rare, 1 hour for medium-rare. The leg of lamb is ready when it looks plump, the meat around the shank bone has shrunk exposing some of the bone, and the meat is fairly firm when pressed with your finger in the thickest part. Remove from the oven and let rest for about 10 minutes in a warm spot. Transfer to a serving platter, slice, and serve.

To prepare a leg of lamb for roasting, trim away the fat and fell (membrane) and remove the "H" (hip) bone. With a sharp knife, cut, loosen, and pull the fell away, being careful not to tear the meat. Trim off the fat, leaving only a very thin layer. (It will give some moisture to the meat while roasting and will disappear by the time it has finished cooking.) To remove the "H" bone, place the leg on its back on the work surface. Insert a thin, sharp, sturdy knife along the "H" bone. Follow the bone as closely as possible, cutting toward the bone. Cut around and inside the socket of the joint. Remove and discard the bone in one piece.

Cordero a la Parrilla con Culantro
Broiled Butterflied Leg of Lamb with Cilantro

—

Serves 6 to 8

1 whole leg of lamb (7½ to 8 pounds)
3 large cloves garlic, peeled
1 tablespoon coarse salt
1 teaspoon ground cumin
6 anchovy fillets, drained
2 tablespoons balsamic vinegar
2 tablespoons olive oil
1 teaspoon coarsely ground black pepper
⅔ cup finely chopped fresh cilantro leaves

1. Butterfly the lamb and score it (page 337). Set aside.

2. In a mortar with a pestle, pound the garlic, salt, and cumin to a paste. Add the anchovy fillets and continue pounding until smooth. Pour in the vinegar, mix well, and let sit for a few minutes. Blend in the olive oil. Rub the lamb with this mixture, sprinkle with the pepper and cilantro leaves, and let marinate at room temperature in a stainless-steel bowl or tray for 2 to 3 hours.

3. Preheat the broiler.

4. Place the lamb on a roasting rack in a shallow roasting pan, scored side down, and broil for 6 to 10 minutes, about 2 inches from the heat source. Turn the lamb and broil for 5 to 6 minutes on the other side. Transfer the lamb to a warm serving platter or a cutting board, let rest in a warm spot for about 5 minutes, slice, and serve.

NOTE   The lamb may also be grilled.

Pierna de Cordero con Pistachos

Roast Leg of Lamb with Pistachios

Serves 6 to 8

A leg of lamb needs very little seasoning. I often roll it in freshly cracked black pepper, then roast it in a very hot oven for a short time. I particularly like to use nuts with lamb, as in this recipe. You can substitute roasted hazelnuts, cashews, pignolis, or even peanuts for the pistachios.

1 whole leg of lamb, "H" (hip) bone removed (page 335)
(about 7½ pounds)
¼ cup Achiote Oil (page 472)
3 tablespoons red-wine vinegar
3 dried mirasol peppers or 4 dried red chili peppers, seeded
3 large cloves garlic, peeled
2 tablespoons coarse salt
2 teaspoons ground cumin
16 to 18 pistachios, skins removed (page 485)

1. Trim off most of the fat from the leg of lamb and wipe with a damp cloth. Set aside.

(Continued)

2. In the jar of a blender, combine the oil and vinegar; crunch the hot peppers into the jar and blend until smooth. Set aside. In a mortar with a pestle, pound the garlic, salt, and cumin to a smooth paste. Add the pepper mixture and mix well. Set aside.

3. With a sharp paring knife, make a cut at an angle about ½ inch deep in the leg of lamb and insert 1 pistachio in the slit. Keep doing this at equal intervals all around the leg of lamb until all the nuts have been used. Place the meat on a jelly-roll pan or lipped tray. Pour the pepper-and-garlic mixture over the meat and rub it thoroughly all around. Let marinate at room temperature for about 4 hours, or until ready to roast.

4. Preheat the oven to 500 degrees.

5. Place the marinated leg of lamb on a rack in a shallow roasting pan, put the roasting pan in the oven, lower the temperature to 475 degrees, and roast the leg of lamb, undisturbed, for 45 minutes for rare, 1 hour for medium-rare. The lamb is ready when the leg looks plump, the meat has shrunk away from the shank bone, and the meat is fairly firm when pressed with your finger in the thickest part. Remove from the oven and let rest for about 10 minutes in a warm spot. Transfer the leg of lamb to a serving platter or cutting board, slice, and serve.

Costillas de Cordero a la Brasa
Broiled Rack of Lamb

Serves 6 to 8

Both the saddle and the rack of lamb are extremely flavorful, and very little seasoning is required. When cooking a rack of lamb, remove most of the deckel, or cap of fat, leaving only a very thin layer on top of the meat.

6 to 8 racks of lamb, 5 rib bones each, backbone and deckel removed, trimmed of most of their fat (about 1 pound each, dressed weight)

MARINADE
4 large cloves garlic, peeled
1 tablespoon coarse salt
2 teaspoons ground cumin
¼ teaspoon ground cloves
½ teaspoon freshly ground black pepper
3 tablespoons red-wine vinegar
⅔ cup Chinese oyster sauce
¼ cup olive oil

*2 cups chopped fresh mint leaves or a combination of Italian parsley
    and fresh cilantro leaves, or ½ cup dried spearmint, crumbled*
Sprigs fresh mint

1. From each of the racks, remove 1 bone from each side, leaving 3 of them. French the racks by making a shallow cut on the back of the rack about 2½ inches from the top of the bone and scraping off the fat, membrane, and meat around and between each of the bones.

2. In a mortar with a pestle, pound the garlic, salt, cumin, cloves, and pepper to a smooth paste. Add the vinegar and mix well. Stir in the oyster sauce and blend in the oil. Rub the racks of lamb with this mixture and let them sit at room temperature for about 2 hours, or until ready to cook (or overnight, well covered, in the refrigerator).

3. Preheat the broiler.

4. Wrap the exposed bones with aluminum foil to protect them. Place the chopped fresh mint leaves on a small tray or dish and press each of the racks into the herb to coat the meat totally. If using dried mint, sprinkle it over the racks before grilling.

5. Broil the racks, bone side up, as close to the source of heat as possible for 8 to 10 minutes. Turn the racks and continue to broil for 10 minutes, or until the racks have an even and slightly charred crust and are still ruby-red in the center. Remove and discard the foil from the bones, garnish with sprigs of fresh mint, and serve.

NOTE   The lamb may also be grilled.

Brochetas de Cordero
Lamb Brochettes

—

Serves 6 (makes 6 brochettes)

There are really no set rules regarding what to place on brochettes. Different vegetables can be substituted for those called for in this recipe. Try, for example, young leek bulbs, mushrooms, baby eggplants, or any combination of small vegetables.

3½ pounds boneless leg of lamb

MARINADE
3 large cloves garlic, peeled
1 tablespoon coarse salt
2 teaspoons ground cumin
1 teaspoon dried spearmint, crumbled
⅛ teaspoon cayenne
2 tablespoons red-wine vinegar
5 tablespoons olive oil

12 large mushroom caps, wiped or brushed clean (about 1 pound)
4 red bell peppers, seeded and cut into 2-inch pieces
6 jalapeño peppers, cut in half lengthwise and seeded
2 tablespoons chopped fresh mint or Italian parsley

1. Wipe the lamb clean with a damp cloth and cut into 18 equal cubes. Place them in a stainless-steel bowl and set aside.

2. In a mortar with a pestle, pound the garlic and salt to a paste. Add the cumin, spearmint, and cayenne and continue pounding. Add the vinegar, mix, and let sit for 10 to 15 minutes. Add 3 tablespoons of the olive oil and blend well. Pour the mixture over the lamb cubes and mix well, making sure that each cube is coated. Let marinate at room temperature for 1 hour, or overnight in the refrigerator. Remove the lamb, saving any leftover marinade. Add the remaining 2 tablespoons of olive oil, mix well, and set aside for basting.

3. Thread a 10-inch skewer with 1 mushroom cap, followed by 1 piece of bell pepper, ½ hot pepper, 1 piece bell pepper, 1 lamb cube, 1 piece bell pepper, 1 lamb cube, 1 piece bell pepper, 1 lamb cube, ½ hot pepper, and ending with 1 mushroom cap. Repeat with 5 additional skewers. (Each skewer should have 2 mushrooms caps, 2 halves of hot peppers, 3 lamb cubes, and 4 pieces of bell peppers.)

4. Preheat the broiler.

5. Place the brochettes in a roasting pan and broil them about 3 to 4 inches from the heat source. After 5 minutes, brush the brochettes with the marinade. Continue broiling for 5 minutes more, then turn the brochettes over, brush again with the marinade, and broil for 10 minutes, or until the lamb is tender. The total broiling time is about 20 minutes. Sprinkle with chopped mint and serve.

NOTE   The brochettes may also be grilled.

Estofado de Cordero con Cebollas de Perla
Lamb Estofado with Pearl Onions

Serves 6 to 8

Terms like stew, ragout, and fricassee, even when they are translated accurately, mean nothing to most South Americans. They have their own names for stews: there is the seco, which literally means "dry," the aguadito, literally "moist" or "liquidy," as well as the guiso, the atamalado, and the estofado, in which meat is braised in a flavorful stock, as in this recipe. Serve the dish with something to absorb the sauce, like rice or quinoa.

1 leg of lamb (about 7 pounds)

MARINADE
1 or 2 dried mirasol peppers, seeded and minced, or 2 or 3 dried
    red chili peppers
2 tablespoons white vinegar
3 large cloves garlic, peeled
1 tablespoon coarse salt
1 teaspoon ground turmeric
2 teaspoons ground cumin
1/8 teaspoon ground cloves
1 tablespoon sesame oil
1 tablespoon olive oil

5 tablespoons olive oil
1½ to 2 pounds pearl onions, peeled (page 484)
¼ cup flour
8 cups Lamb Stock (page 465) or Beef Stock (page 462), or
    3 cups Corn Beer (page 470) and 5 cups water
1 tablespoon coarse salt
2 large yuca, peeled, cut into 1-inch pieces, and cored
    (about 3½ pounds)
3 tablespoons chopped fresh mint or Italian parsley

1. Remove the fell or membrane and all the fat from the lamb. Remove the bone and save for stock. Cut the meat into 3-inch cubes and place them in a stainless-steel bowl. Set aside.

2. In a cup, soak the pepper in the vinegar for about 15 minutes. Set aside.

3. In a mortar with a pestle, pound the garlic, salt, turmeric, cumin, and cloves to a paste. Add the vinegar with the peppers and continue pounding. Blend in the sesame oil and olive oils. Pour this mixture over the lamb pieces and mix thoroughly, making sure that every piece is well coated. Marinate for 6 to 8 hours at room temperature, or overnight, covered, in the refrigerator.

4. In a large sauté pan, heat 3 tablespoons of olive oil over high heat. Add the lamb pieces and quickly sear them until golden brown on all sides, about 25 minutes. With a slotted spoon, transfer the meat to a casserole and set aside in a warm spot.

5. In the same sauté pan, sauté the pearl onions until light golden all around. Transfer the onions to a plate and set aside. In the same pan, heat the remaining 2 tablespoons of olive oil. Stir in the flour and cook for 1 minute. Add 3 cups of stock and continue cooking, stirring constantly with a wire whisk, for about 10 minutes, or until the stock has reduced by half and has thickened slightly. Mix in the remaining stock and 1 tablespoon salt and continue cooking over medium heat, stirring now and then, for about 20 minutes.

6. Remove from the heat and pour into the casserole containing the lamb. Place the casserole over low heat, cover, and cook for 40 minutes, stirring now and then. Add the yuca and continue cooking for 45 minutes, or until the yuca is tender.

7. Add the pearl onions, mix, and cook for 5 to 8 minutes. Correct the seasoning with salt to taste. Sprinkle with chopped mint and serve right from the casserole.

Seco de Cordero
Lamb Seco

Serves 6 to 8

—

Among the most popular stewlike dishes in Peru are secos, which, as the name suggests, are rather dry. They should never be too dry, though: there should be enough sauce to moisten the starches that are served with it. Two starches are traditionally used in a seco. Potatoes are most common as the first starch, but yuca is also quite popular. The second starch, usually rice, is served as an accompaniment.

1 leg of lamb (about 7½ pounds)

MARINADE
4 large cloves garlic, peeled
1 tablespoon coarse salt
1 teaspoon ground cumin
½ teaspoon freshly ground black pepper
½ cup red-wine vinegar
2 tablespoons olive oil

3⅓ tablespoons olive oil
2 or 3 jalapeño peppers, seeded and finely chopped, or 2 dried mirasol peppers, seeded and crumbled, or 2 dried red chili peppers
4 medium onions, peeled and finely chopped (about 5 cups)
1 tablespoon coarse salt
1½ cups light beer (1 12-ounce bottle)
6 cups Lamb Stock (page 465) or Beef Stock (page 462) or Chicken Stock (page 461) or water
4 large potatoes, peeled and quartered
2 cups tightly packed fresh cilantro leaves, washed, drained, and finely chopped

1. Remove the fell or membrane and all the fat from the lamb. Remove the bone and set aside for stock. Cut the meat into 2½- to 3-inch cubes, place them in a stainless-steel bowl, and set aside.

2. In a mortar with a pestle, pound the garlic, salt, cumin, and black pepper to a smooth paste. Add the vinegar, mix, and blend in the 2 tablespoons of olive oil. Pour this mixture over the lamb, making sure that all pieces are well coated, and marinate at room temperature for 2 to 3 hours.

3. In a casserole or sauté pan, heat the 3⅓ tablespoons olive oil over high heat. Quickly brown the meat thoroughly on all sides, turning frequently, for about 20 minutes. (If the lamb does not fit in one layer in the casserole all at once, brown in two batches.) With a slotted spoon, transfer the lamb pieces to a plate and set aside.

4. In the same casserole, combine the hot peppers, onions, and salt and sauté, stirring, until the onions are golden around the edges, about 15 minutes. Add the beer, lower the heat, and cook until all of the beer has evaporated, about 15 minutes. Add the browned lamb together with the accumulated juices from the plate. Add the stock and stir. Bring to a boil, lower the heat, cover the casserole, and cook for about 1 hour, or until the meat is tender.

5. Add the potatoes, cover, and continue cooking for 20 minutes, or until the potatoes are cooked, adding more stock or water, if necessary. Add the cilantro, mix well, and cook for a few minutes longer. Serve hot, right from the casserole.

Atamalado de Cordero con Quinua
Lamb and Quinoa Atamalado

Serves 6 to 8

Atamalados, stewlike meat dishes found throughout South America, are always cooked on top of the stove and require very little watching. They can be prepared ahead of time and reheated without any loss of flavor. In fact, the flavor often improves.

2½ pounds boneless lamb (leg or shoulder)

MARINADE
2 dried mirasol or ancho or red chili peppers, seeded
1 cup light beer
1 jalapeño pepper, seeded and chopped
2 cloves garlic, peeled
1 tablespoon coarse salt
1 teaspoon ground cumin
8 to 10 anchovy fillets, drained
⅛ teaspoon ground cloves
⅓ cup red-wine vinegar

3 tablespoons olive oil
2 medium onions, peeled and finely chopped (2 cups)
*5 cups Chicken Stock (page 461) or water or quinoa cooking liquid
    and water*
6 cups Boiled Quinoa (page 419)
¼ cup chopped fresh cilantro leaves

1. Wipe the lamb with a damp cloth, remove any excess fat, and cut into 2-inch cubes. Place in a stainless-steel bowl and set aside.

2. Soak the dried peppers in the beer for 15 minutes, or until soft. Place the jalapeño pepper and the soaked peppers with the beer in the jar of a blender and blend until smooth. Set aside.

3. In a mortar with a pestle, pound the garlic and salt to a paste. Add the cumin, anchovies, and cloves and pound until smooth. Add the vinegar, mix, and pour over the lamb pieces. Mix thoroughly and marinate for about 20 minutes.

4. In a sauté pan or earthenware casserole, heat the oil over high heat. Add the marinated lamb pieces and quickly cook them, stirring, until they are slightly brown on all sides. Add the onions and continue to sauté until the onions are translucent. Add the pepper-beer mixture and cook until the liquid has almost evaporated. Add the stock and stir. Bring to a boil, cover, lower the heat, and simmer gently for 20 to 25 minutes, or until the lamb is tender.

5. Add the quinoa and continue cooking, stirring now and then, for 10 to 15 minutes, or until the liquid had reduced to half or less. Stirring now and then to prevent the lamb and quinoa from sticking to the bottom of the pan, cook, uncovered, over very low heat for 20 to 25 minutes. Remove from the heat. Correct the seasoning with salt to taste, add the chopped cilantro, mix, and serve.

VENISON

Venado a la Parrilla
Grilled Venison

—

Serves 6 (makes 6 brochettes)

1 boneless venison loin (about 3½ pounds)

MARINADE
4 cloves garlic, peeled
1 tablespoon coarse salt
1 teaspoon ground cumin
⅛ teaspoon ground cloves
3 tablespoons amontillado sherry or marsala
3 tablespoons olive oil
3 tablespoons fresh thyme leaves

Freshly cracked black pepper
½ cup Rendered Bacon Fat (page 476) or olive oil

1. Wipe the meat with a damp cloth and cut it into 1½- to 2-inch cubes. Place the cubes in a stainless-steel bowl and set aside.

2. In a mortar with a pestle, pound the garlic, salt, cumin, and cloves to a fine paste. Add the sherry, mix thoroughly, and blend in the olive oil. Pour this mixture over the venison cubes, making sure that all the pieces of meat are coated. Sprinkle on the thyme leaves and toss. Let the meat marinate at room temperature for 1 to 2 hours, or until ready to use.

3. Thread a skewer with 3 venison cubes and sprinkle with pepper. Continue until all the meat is on skewers. Grill over an open fire, brushing frequently with bacon fat. Or broil under a hot broiler about 2½ inches from the heat source, about 4 minutes on each side, brushing with bacon fat when turning. Or cook on top of the stove in a large cast-iron frying pan: heat the bacon fat and quickly sauté the meat on all sides for about 6 minutes. No matter how the brochettes are cooked, the meat should be crusty on the outside and juicy and rare in the middle. Serve the brochettes as soon as they are done.

Estofado de Venado y Mote
Venison and Hominy Estofado
—

Serves 6 to 8

Venison always reminds me of llama meat. They resemble each other very much in color, leanness, and taste.

1 saddle of venison, boned and trimmed of fat (6 pounds)

MARINADE
3 large cloves garlic, peeled
2 tablespoons coarse salt
1 tablespoon ground cumin
¼ teaspoon ground cloves
¼ teaspoon cayenne
3 tablespoons red-wine vinegar
1 tablespoon sweet vermouth

BOUQUET GARNI
5 or 6 celery tops
1 large bunch fresh thyme (1 ounce)
6 sprigs Italian parsley
10 juniper berries, slightly crushed

3 tablespoons Achiote Oil (page 472)
6 tablespoons Rendered Bacon Fat (page 476) or olive oil
2 pounds mushrooms, wiped clean, stems cut flat with the caps
1 large onion, peeled and cut into 6 wedges
3 tablespoons all-purpose flour
*3 cups Beef Stock (page 462) or 1 cup Corn Beer (page 470)
   and 2 cups water*
4 cups canned hominy, rinsed and well drained (2 16-ounce cans)

1. Wipe the meat with a damp cloth, cut into 2-inch cubes, and place in a stainless-steel bowl. Set aside.

2. In a mortar with a pestle, pound the garlic, salt, cumin, cloves, and cayenne to a paste. Add the vinegar and mix; add the vermouth and blend well. Pour this mixture over the venison cubes and mix thor-

(Continued)

oughly, making sure that all the pieces of meat are coated. Marinate at room temperature for 2 to 3 hours.

3. Wrap the celery tops, thyme, parsley, and juniper berries in a piece of cheesecloth and tie with kitchen string. Set aside.

4. In a large casserole, heat the oil and bacon fat. Add the meat and quickly sear and brown on all sides. This should take about 15 minutes. With a slotted spoon, transfer the meat to a plate. Set aside.

5. In the same casserole, quickly sauté the mushroom caps until all their liquid has evaporated and they start to get barely golden. Add the onion and sauté until light golden. Sprinkle with the flour and add the stock, stirring. Bring to a boil, stirring frequently. Add the venison and accumulated juices from the plate and the bouquet garni and gently simmer, covered, for 1 hour.

6. Add the mushroom caps and accumulated juices from the plate and continue cooking for 45 minutes, or until the meat is tender. Add the hominy and cook, covered, for 15 minutes longer. Correct seasoning with salt to taste. Serve hot, right from the casserole.

VARIATIONS

Substitute 6 pounds of goat meat, preferably from the leg, for the venison. Be sure to trim the meat of all fat. Proceed as for venison.

Substitute 6 pounds of lean beef for the venison. Use only 1½ cups of beef stock. Omit Step 4. Add the beef with the sautéed mushroom caps in Step 5 and simmer for 1½ hours, or until the beef is tender.

VARIETY MEATS

Anticuchos

Serves 6 to 8

Walking through the streets of Lima, you are bound to see barbecue grills with flames shooting up between skewers of anticuchos. The air is filled with an aromatic smoke that draws you to them. This is street food at its best, and you can make it easily at home, on the grill or under the broiler or in a heavy cast-iron skillet.

1 beef heart (about 4 pounds)
3 large cloves garlic, peeled
1½ tablespoons coarse salt
⅛ teaspoon freshly ground black pepper
2 teaspoons ground cumin
3 dried mirasol or red chili peppers, seeded
1 dried ancho pepper, seeded
¾ cup red-wine vinegar
⅓ cup Achiote Oil (page 472)
2 or 3 strips bacon

1. Soak 8 bamboo skewers, about 8 to 10 inches long, in cold water overnight, or use metal skewers.

2. Trim any fat from the heart and remove veins and membranes. Cut into 24 cubes. Place in a bowl and set aside.

3. In a mortar with a pestle, pound the garlic, salt, pepper, and cumin to a paste. Set aside.

4. In a bowl, combine the mirasol and ancho peppers with the red-wine vinegar. Let soak for about 15 minutes, or until the peppers are soft.

5. Place the peppers and vinegar in the jar of a blender or work bowl of a food processor and blend or process at high speed until liquidized. Add this mixture to the garlic paste and mix thoroughly. Allow to sit for

(Continued)

10 minutes. Add the oil, stir, and pour this mixture over the cubed beef heart. Mix well. Let marinate, covered, at room temperature for 10 to 12 hours, or overnight, covered, in the refrigerator.

6. Prepare the grill or preheat the broiler.

7. Thread 3 cubes of heart on each of the skewers, reserving the marinating juices, and set aside. In a saucepan, heat ¼ cup of the reserved marinating juices with the bacon over medium heat until all the liquid has evaporated and only the oil and the fat from the bacon remain. Discard the bacon. Brush the skewered cubes of heart with the flavored oil. Grill over white-hot coals, brushing them constantly with the oil and turning them once. They should cook for only 1 to 2 minutes on each side so that the outside is red and the inside medium to rare. To broil the anticuchos, place the skewers about 2 to 3 inches from the heat source. Brush generously with flavored oil and broil for 1 or 2 minutes on one side. Turn the skewers, brush again with flavored oil, and broil for 1 or 2 minutes. Serve at once.

VARIATION

Prepare the beef heart through the end of Step 5. Do not place on skewers. Heat ¼ cup of the reserved marinating juices in a 12-inch cast-iron skillet, add the bacon, and sauté the bacon until golden. Discard the bacon. Place the beef heart cubes in the skillet and cook quickly over high heat while turning, until the meat is seared on all sides, about 5 minutes. Serve at once.

Estofado de Lengua
Braised Tongue in Tomato-Raisin Sauce
—
Serves 6 to 8

Fresh tongue is much appreciated in South America and is usually found in the refrigerator already cooked and waiting to be served in a variety of ways. It is ideal as a fiambre, or cold cut, for sandwiches, salads, and *entremeses* and *bocaditos,* or "finger foods."

Tongue is also often served as an *entrada,* or appetizer. It is thinly sliced and presented on a small plate by itself or on a bed of lettuce leaves or thinly sliced cooked potatoes, with mustard, ground hot peppers, and a gutsy sauce like aioli, an aromatic herbal sauce, or Salsa Cruda (page 480) on the side. This recipe is for a main-course dish.

1 fresh beef tongue (about 4½ pounds)
15 sprigs fresh cilantro
¼ cup Achiote Oil (page 472)
2 tablespoons olive oil
4 large cloves garlic, peeled and minced
2 or 3 jalapeño or serrano peppers, seeded and minced,
  or ¼ teaspoon cayenne
6 medium onions, peeled and finely chopped (6 to 8 cups)
1 cup amontillado sherry
3 inner stalks celery, strings removed and finely chopped
1 carrot, peeled and grated
5 large red bell peppers, roasted and peeled (page 484), seeded,
  and finely chopped, or 1 cup canned sweet red peppers,
  drained (1 13¾-ounce can)
12 large tomatoes, peeled, seeded (juices saved), and finely chopped
2 tablespoons coarse salt

BOUQUET GARNI
1 large bunch fresh basil, chopped with stems (6 ounces)
1 small bunch fresh thyme, chopped with stems (½ ounce)
8 cloves

2 cups Chicken Stock (page 461)
½ cup seedless raisins
2 tablespoons chopped Italian parsley

1. Wash the tongue under cold running water. Place in a large stockpot and add 7 quarts of water and the cilantro. Bring to a boil. Lower the heat and simmer, covered, for 2 to 2½ hours, turning the tongue now and then. Transfer the tongue from the cooking liquid to a tray and when cool enough to handle, pull and peel off the skin. To do this, pierce the skin in a corner and pull it off with your fingers. It should be very easy. If not, put the tongue back in the water and cook a little longer. Trim and discard all bones, cartilage, and fat from the base of the tongue.

(Continued)

2. In a large sauté pan, heat the achiote and olive oils over high heat. Add the garlic, hot peppers, and onions and sauté, stirring, until the onions are totally translucent, 10 to 15 minutes. Add the sherry and continue to sauté for 4 to 5 minutes, stirring. Add the celery, carrot, and peppers, stir, and sauté over medium heat for 5 minutes. Add the tomatoes with juices and the salt and continue cooking over medium heat, stirring now and then, for 50 minutes to 1 hour. Remove from the heat and set aside. You should have about 8 cups of tomato mixture.

3. Wrap the chopped basil and thyme and the cloves in a piece of cheesecloth and tie with kitchen string. Set aside.

4. In a large heavy casserole, preferably enameled, combine the tongue, tomato mixture, stock, raisins, and bouquet garni. Bring to a boil, lower the heat, cover, and simmer gently over very low heat for 45 minutes, stirring now and then. Remove from the heat and correct the seasoning with salt to taste.

5. Pour the sauce into a rimmed serving platter. Thinly slice the tongue and arrange over the sauce. Sprinkle with parsley and serve hot.

STORAGE NOTE   Cooked tongue will keep, well wrapped, in the refrigerator for up to 8 days.

Mondongito a la Jardinera
Sautéed Tripe with Peppers

Serves 8 as an appetizer or 6 as a main course

No matter how tripe is to be prepared, it must be precooked. In this recipe the precooking water is flavored with ginger, herbs, and hot peppers, which clean the tripe and give it an appetizing bouquet. It is important to keep the tripe as white as possible, so avoid using whole fresh herbs, which may tinge it green. Instead, use just the stems of the herbs without the leaves.

1 head garlic, unpeeled and cut in half horizontally
3-inch piece fresh ginger, sliced
1 jalapeño pepper, sliced in half

2 tablespoons coarse salt
5 pounds tripe

5 tablespoons olive oil
2 large cloves garlic, peeled and crushed
2 jalapeño peppers, seeded and julienned
1 tablespoon coarse salt
2 large carrots, peeled, cores removed, and cut into 3 × ⅛-inch strips
3 medium green bell peppers, seeded and julienned
2 medium red bell peppers, seeded and julienned
2 medium yellow bell peppers, seeded and julienned
8 stalks celery, strings removed, and cut into 3 × ⅛-inch strips
8 scallions, white parts only, cut in half horizontally and julienned
   (2 cups)
Freshly ground black pepper
3 tablespoons chopped Italian parsley

1. In a stockpot, combine the garlic, ginger, hot pepper, salt, and 5 quarts of water. Bring to a boil, add the tripe, and cook, uncovered, for 40 to 45 minutes, or until the tripe is tender when pierced with a fork. Remove the tripe to a colander and let drain. When it is cool enough to handle, remove and discard any fat and slice the tripe into 3 × ½-inch strips.

2. In a large sauté pan, heat the olive oil, add the garlic, and sauté until lightly golden. Do not brown. Remove and discard the garlic. Add the tripe and jalapeños, sprinkle with the salt, and sauté, stirring, for 1 to 2 minutes. Add the carrot strips and continue sautéing for 3 minutes. While stirring, add all the bell peppers and the celery and continue cooking, stirring, for about 1 minute, just long enough to warm the peppers through. Add the scallions, toss, correct the seasoning with salt and pepper to taste, sprinkle with chopped parsley, and serve.

Riñoncitos de Ternera con Romero

Kidneys with Fennel on Rosemary Skewers

Serves 6 to 8 (makes 18 skewers)

Back home, when a sprig of rosemary was needed in the kitchen, it was just a matter of running to the door and clipping some from the hedges out front. *Romero,* or rosemary, is found in Lima in the form of neatly trimmed garden hedges rather than as a garden herb. Its use in the kitchen is casual—usually just a matter of dropping a sprig into the poaching liquid for fish or meat. Sometimes a branch of rosemary takes the place of a basting brush or thick stalks form a rack under a roast of lamb or kid, giving the meat a nice perfume—and filling the house with appetizing odors that drive everyone crazy!

I like to substitute branches of rosemary for bamboo or other types of skewers. They not only hold the meat and vegetables in place as any skewer would do, they also add a subtle aroma and taste without overwhelming the natural flavor of the meat and vegetables. The skewers should be thick and stiff enough to hold a sharp point for piercing the meat when threading it and not to bend or break while cooking.

3 veal kidneys (about 14 ounces each)
3 tablespoons coarse salt
3 fennel bulbs, tops and bottoms trimmed, washed, and cut into
    72 1-inch-square pieces (about 1½ pounds)
18 sprigs fresh rosemary
1 cup Rendered Bacon Fat (page 476) or olive oil

1. Clean the kidneys by removing and discarding the outer membranes and any fat around them. Cut the kidneys open and cut out and discard the central cores. Cut them up following their natural formations, into 54 1½-inch cubes. Soak the pieces in 4 cups of water with the salt for 15 minutes.

2. Remove the kidney pieces from the water and dry them on a cloth towel. Meanwhile, prepare the rosemary sprigs by stripping the leaves about 5 inches from the base of the sprig and sharpening the tip of the base to a point. Thread each skewer, starting with 1 piece of fennel and 1 piece of kidney. Alternate pieces of fennel and pieces of kidney until you have 4 pieces of fennel and 3 pieces of kidney on a skewer. Repeat until all the skewers are done.

3. In a large cast-iron skillet, heat the bacon fat over high heat. Add 9 of the skewers and sauté for a total of 4 minutes, turning them frequently. Remove from the pan and set aside in a warm place. Sauté the second batch in the same bacon fat. The kidneys should be pinkish to rare in the inside and quite juicy. Serve immediately.

VARIATION

Substitute lamb kidneys for veal kidneys. Allow 2 lamb kidneys per serving. Remove the membrane and fat from the surface. Butterfly each kidney: starting at the curved side, cut through the middle about three-quarters of the way down and open the kidney up to form a circle with the core exposed. You can also simply cut each kidney in half starting at the curved side. Proceed with the recipe.

Migas de Ternera con Encebollado
Sautéed Calves' Liver Smothered in Onions

—

Serves 6 to 8

The South American passion and hunger for onions is beautifully expressed in a single term, *encebollado*, literally "enveloped in onions." When preparing an *encebollado*, a great deal of precision and attention goes into cooking the onions. They are sliced thin—but not too thin— then quickly sautéed over high heat while you constantly shake and toss the pan.

An *encebollado* usually accompanies crisp fried fish or grilled meats; it is also superb with liver, as in this recipe.

2 cups all-purpose flour

2 teaspoons ground cumin

½ teaspoon ground white pepper

1 tablespoon coarse salt

2 tablespoons Achiote Oil (page 472) or Curry Oil (page 473)

1 piece slab bacon, rind removed and thinly sliced (10 to 12 ounces)

6 to 8 slices calves' liver, about ¾ inch thick

ENCEBOLLADO

2 cloves garlic, peeled and finely chopped

2 or 3 jalapeño peppers, or any other fresh hot peppers, seeded and julienned

3 pounds red onions, peeled, root cores removed, and thinly sliced (about 8 cups)

¼ cup fresh thyme leaves

Freshly ground black pepper

Coarse salt

1. On a tray, combine the flour, cumin, pepper, and salt. Mix well and set aside.

2. In a large skillet, heat the oil and bacon over low heat. Sauté for about 8 minutes, or until the bacon is crisp. Transfer the bacon to a plate and set aside.

3. Dip each slice of liver into the flour mixture, shaking off any excess, and place immediately in the fat in the skillet. Sauté the liver over medium heat for 5 minutes on each side, shaking the skillet to prevent sticking. Transfer the liver to a warm platter or serving dish and keep in a warm spot.

4. Put the garlic and hot peppers in the same skillet and stir. Add the onions and 3 tablespoons of the thyme leaves and sauté over high heat, stirring, shaking, and tossing frequently, for about 2 minutes. Sprinkle with freshly ground black pepper and salt to taste. With a slotted spoon, remove the onions and arrange around the liver. Serve hot, garnished with the reserved bacon slices and sprinkled with the remaining thyme leaves.

Lechecillas con Hongos
Sweetbreads with Mushrooms

Serves 6 to 8

3½ pounds sweetbreads (6 pieces)
2-inch piece fresh ginger, unpeeled and sliced
3 dried red chili peppers
2 pounds mushrooms
¼ cup olive oil
2 medium onions, peeled and cut into 8 wedges
2 tablespoons unsalted butter
3 large cloves garlic, peeled and minced
2 dried mirasol peppers, seeded and crumbled,
    or ⅛ teaspoon cayenne
¼ cup all-purpose flour
2 teaspoons ground turmeric
1 teaspoon ground cumin
⅛ teaspoon ground nutmeg
1 tablespoon coarse salt
3 cups Chicken Stock (page 461)
4 sprigs fresh mint
7 sprigs Italian parsley
5 celery tops, washed and chopped
1 bay leaf
⅔ cup fresh or frozen peas (thawed, rinsed, and drained)
2 tablespoons chopped Italian parsley

1. Place the sweetbreads in a bowl and add enough cold water to cover. Set aside until ready to use.

2. In a large pot, bring 3 quarts of water, together with the ginger and hot peppers, to a boil. Lower the heat and simmer, covered, for 10 minutes. Add the sweetbreads, bring to a boil, and cook over high heat, uncovered, for about 5 minutes, or until the sweetbreads are firm. Remove them from the poaching liquid and drop them into ice-cold water, leaving them just long enough to cool them. Remove and wipe dry with cloth towels. Pull off and discard the membranes that encase the sweetbreads without damaging the meat.

3. Line a baking tray or jelly-roll pan with several layers of clean towels or cloth napkins. Arrange the sweetbreads in one layer close to one another and cover them with more layers of cloth towels. Cover with another tray and place a 6- to 8-pound weight on top (see Note). Let stand for several hours or overnight in the refrigerator.

4. Wipe the mushrooms clean, cut the stems flush with the caps, and clean and chop the stems. Set aside.

5. In a skillet, heat the olive oil over high heat. Add the onions and sauté, gently turning, until light golden on all sides, about 6 to 8 minutes. Transfer the onions to a plate and set aside. Put the mushroom caps in the same skillet and sauté for about 6 minutes, stirring. With a slotted spoon, add them to the plate with the onions.

6. In the same skillet, melt the butter over medium heat. Add the garlic and mirasol peppers. Blend in the flour and cook, stirring, until the butter and flour froth together for a few seconds. Do not brown. Add the mushroom stems and stir. Add the turmeric, cumin, nutmeg, and salt and mix well. Add 2 cups of the stock, stirring with a wire whisk. Bring to a boil and continue cooking, stirring, for about 5 minutes, or until the liquid has thickened slightly. Whisk in the remaining cup of chicken stock, bring to a boil, and add the mint, parsley sprigs, celery tops, and bay leaf. Lower the heat and simmer for 15 minutes, stirring now and then, or until the sauce has thickened enough to coat the back of a spoon.

7. Remove from the heat and strain the sauce through a fine sieve into a casserole or flameproof earthenware dish, pressing out all the juices from the mushroom stems and herbs. Discard the contents of the sieve.

8. Remove the sweetbreads from under the weights and cut them into large bite-size pieces. Add the sweetbreads to the sauce and cook gently over low heat, stirring now and then, for 8 minutes. Add the onions and mushrooms with their accumulated juices from the plate, and fresh peas, if using. Stir, cover, and cook for 5 minutes longer. Correct the seasoning with salt to taste. If using frozen peas, gently toss them in just before serving. Sprinkle with chopped parsley and serve right from the casserole.

NOTE   You can use kitchen weights, large canned goods, bricks, stones, or a pan filled with several quarts of water.

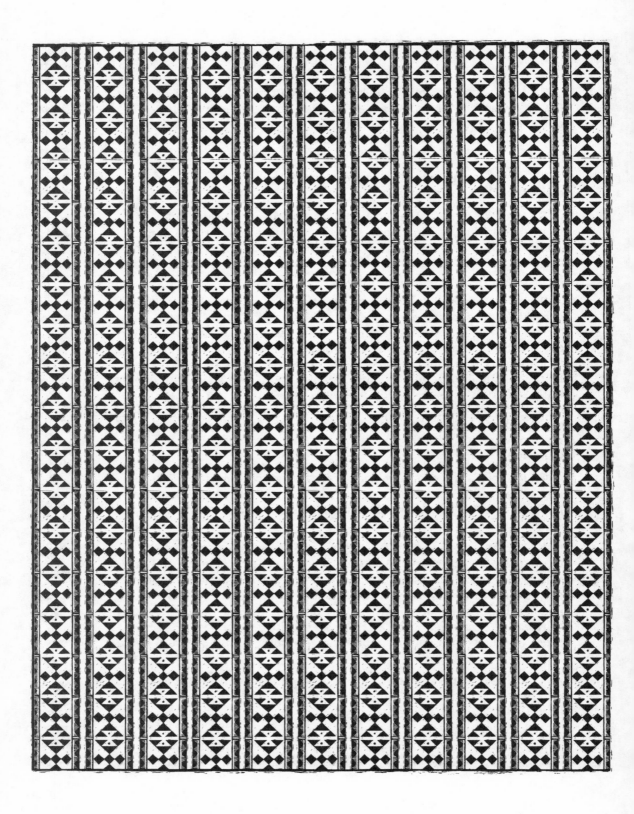

VEGETABLES & GRAINS

POTATOES

Ocopa

Papas Sancochadas con Salsa de Avellanas
Potatoes with a Sweet Pepper and Hazelnut Sauce

Guiso de Papas con Pimientos
Braised Potatoes with Sweet Peppers

Picante de Papas
Potatoes in a Picante Sauce

Ensalada de Papas
Blue-Potato Salad

Causa a la Limeña
Causa in Gold

Papas a la Arequipeña
Arequipeña Potatoes

Causa Azulada
Causa in Blue

Tortilla de Papas
Potato Tortilla

Entomatado de Papas
Potato Casserole

Papas Rellenas
Stuffed Potatoes

Guiso de Papa Seca
Andean Potatoes

SWEET POTATOES

Camotes Asados
Baked Sweet Potatoes

Camote Frito
Sweet-Potato Chips

Camote en Salsa de Dátiles
Sweet Potatoes in Date Sauce

Puré de Batata y Jengibre
Sweet-Potato and Ginger Puree

YUCA

Yuca Sancochada
Boiled Yuca

Yuca Arrebosada
Sautéed Yuca

Yuca Frita
Yuca Straws

ONIONS

Cebollas y Ajos Asados
Roasted Onions and Garlic

PEPPERS

Pimientos Rellenos
Roasted Sweet Peppers with Goat Cheese

Ajíes Rellenos
Hot Peppers Filled with Ham and Cheese

TOMATOES

Tomates Rellenos
Tomatoes Filled with Tomatoes and Almonds
—

Huevos Tripados
Tomatoes and Peruvian Egg Noodles
—

SQUASH

Locro
—

Zapallo Horneado
Braised Butternut Squash
—

Calabazas Rellenas
Acorn Squash Stuffed with Quinoa
—

LIMA BEANS

Habas Frescas Dorados en Limón
Baby Lima Beans Braised in Lemon
—

Habas en Salsa de Aceittunas
Lima Beans in Olive Sauce
—

CORN

Choclo Sancochado
Corn on the Cob
—

Picante de Choclo
Corn in a Picante Sauce
—

Pepian de Choclo
Corn Pepian
—

Salpicón de Mote
Hominy Salpicón
—

QUINOA

Quinua Sancochada
Boiled Quinoa
—

Quinua a la Jardinera
Quinoa à la Jardinière
—

Salpicón de Quinua
Quinoa Salpicón
—

Frituras de Quinua
Quinoa Croquettes
—

RICE

Arroz Cocido
Steamed Rice

Vegetables in South America are not viewed as a side dish but as an integral part of the meal. They are honored in soups, stews, and even desserts, and they are used in combination with meat and seafood. But most often they are served by themselves.

Potatoes

Potatoes are one of the most important vegetables and are among the world's largest food crops. The rich variety of potatoes that exists today started with species cultivated in the Andes eight thousand years ago. Various strains evolved to meet local needs and conditions along South America's mountainous backbone. This selection process resulted in thousands of distinct types of potatoes; the Quechuas sometimes grew as many as two hundred different kinds in a single field. Unlike those familiar to us in North America, potatoes found in the Andes often have brilliantly colored skins and flesh. Some are bright yellow, deep purple, or black; some have eye-catching shapes, from long, thin, and smooth to wrinkled with deep eyes. Most have a rich potato flavor and wonderful texture, and all have high nutritional value.

To ward off hunger and famine, the people of the early cultures of South America who relied on potatoes as a staple food found ingenious techniques of preserving them. There were two ways of freeze-drying, a method that took advantage of the climate of the Andes, where nights are cold and days dry. One was to leave raw potatoes, covered with a cloth to keep off the dew, out in the open for a few days and nights. At night they froze, and the next day they were trampled to press out the water from the previous night's freezing. These potatoes were called *chuño*. In the other method, the potatoes were boiled before freezing and were not trampled; these were called *papa seca*.

This natural freeze-drying technique is very much alive today. The taste of these potatoes, especially the *papa seca*, is indescribable. They have a wonderful crunchy texture and nutty flavor and, once reconstituted, they are cooked in many ways. I have included a few recipes using *chuño* and *papa seca*, even though they are sometimes difficult to find in North America.

Sweet Potatoes

Another root vegetable popular in South America is the sweet potato, which is actually a tuber, not a potato. Though it is of uncertain origin, the sweet potato is known to have been cultivated extensively by the early Peruvians; it was called *apichu* in Quechua. It is more commonly known as *camote, batata,* or *batata dulce,* and there are two kinds: the *amarillo* and the somewhat larger *morado,* which has a purplish skin. They are used interchangeably in everything from soups to desserts.

Yuca

Yuca, also called cassava or manioc, from the Indian name for it, *manihot,* is widely cultivated throughout the tropical regions of South America. It is a starchy vegetable with a distinctly sweet taste and dense texture. You can prepare it just about any way you would potatoes, and then some.

A handsome root of Amazon origins, yuca is a staple of Brazilian cuisine. The Brazilians call it *mandioca.* They make it into *biju,* a crisp flat bread, and *farofa,* which is coarsely ground yuca flour roasted on top of the stove with a bit of oil. *Farofa* can be found on every tabletop in Brazil; it is sprinkled vigorously over practically any food that has the slightest hint of moisture. Yuca is also used to make tapioca.

Other Edible Roots

Besides potatoes, sweet potatoes, and yuca, which are virtually universal foodstuffs in South America, there are many other edible roots that are popular where they are grown. I have not given any recipes for these vegetables because they are not available in North America, but I did want to mention a few of the more interesting among them.

One is the *arracacha,* which is quite common in Colombia. It resembles the parsnip in form and color and has a mild flavor with an undertone of celery. Another similarly shaped root is the *maca.* A low-growing plant that can survive the harsh conditions of high altitudes, it grows abundantly around lakes and rivers in Peru. Also from high altitudes is the *mashua,* which resembles the tropical yuca.

Among the lesser known South American edible roots are *ahipa,* succulent and crisp like an apple, and *mauka,* which some call the cassava of the highlands.

Yacon, a distant relative of the sunflower, is grown not for its seed but for its root. It can be eaten raw, and because of its crunchy texture and sweet taste, it is often called the apple of the earth.

Peppers

Peppers were cultivated in South America as far back as seven thousand years ago. There are still many peppers growing in the wild that are gathered and eaten. Whether wild or cultivated, the pepper has long played a major role in the diet of South Americans; in fact, it is often the only vegetable and flavoring available for the people of the Andes.

The typical meal of the Quechuas is remarkably simple yet tasty and nutritious: a boiled potato and a hot pepper. Corn and other foods are often accompanied with a hot pepper and nothing else.

Peppers give personality, flavor, texture, and heat to South American food. It is customary to choose a specific type of pepper for its flavor, color, size, and the thickness of its flesh. The spicy, thick-fleshed *rocoto,* for example, is usually stuffed with meat; it is also one of the peppers of choice for pickling. The sweet bell pepper, with its sturdy, thick flesh, also lends itself to stuffing; a bell pepper filled with cheese makes a wonderful yet simple meal.

The *ají amarillo,* or mirasol pepper, is one of the most popular of the hot peppers, fresh or dried. Fresh, it has a somewhat lemony flavor; dried, it has a deeper taste and a slightly smoky bouquet. The mirasol is also ground and used as a condiment. So is *ají colorado,* marketed in the United States as the Colorado or New Mexico chili, another popular variety of hot pepper.

Peppers, whether they are hot or sweet, fresh or dried, tiny or immense, red, yellow, green, or brown, have been embraced by every cuisine of note. In the form of paprika, cayenne, and chili powder, they are the most widely used spice in the world. In addition, peppers are eaten as vegetables, both in combination with other vegetables or on their own, as in *chiles rellenos,* or stuffed peppers, and as the base for countless condiments and sauces. Peppers bring food alive, not only in South America but virtually everywhere in the world.

Tomatoes

The tomato was one of the many fruits native to the Andes, but it was not cultivated there. It was more like a berry—green, red, orange, or yellow, from currant to cherry size—that was gathered in the wild and eaten. The tomato was first cultivated in what is now Mexico; the word *tomato* comes from *tomatl,* a Nahuatl word. Over time it developed in size and shape until it became what we know as a tomato today.

Squash

The squash is one of the most versatile vegetables on earth. It can be used for its flesh and for its seeds, as food for man and fodder for animals; its hard shell can be used as a vessel. As a crop, squash offers high yield with little labor and is highly resistant to pests and heat. Of the foods native to South America, squash is among the most nutritious.

Of all the indigenous varieties of squash in South America, the most popular is the *zapallo,* a hard-shelled or winter squash that resembles the North American butternut squash in taste and texture though not in color or shape. It is grown in Colombia, Ecuador, Peru, Bolivia, northern Argentina, and northern Chile. It is a standard item in every market and is found in every size, some weighing as much as eighty pounds; these are sold in chunks.

Lima Beans

The lima bean, which was named after the city of Lima, was well known to the Incas and their predecessors. This legume, and others that grew wild in the Andes of Peru and part of Argentina, came to be cultivated by the ancient peoples of the Andes because the common bean did not perform well at high elevations. Slow growth and poor yield, coupled with the large quantities of precious fuel needed to cook it (since water boils at a lower temperature at high altitudes than at sea level), doomed the common bean. In addition to the lima bean, which does indeed cook quickly, the peoples of the Andes developed the *basul, tarwi,* and *nuña.*

These curious beans burst open upon heating and require very brief cooking.

Corn

The birds did a fabulous job of spreading corn throughout the Americas, even to the most remote parts. This wonderful grain has long been an integral part of the diet of South Americans. It is grown extensively, and there are countless varieties with different-colored kernels and varying textures. Hominy, which is a variety of corn with large white kernels, is called *mote* by the Quechuas.

Quinoa

A similar but more significant offering was traditionally made with quinoa. On certain holidays, especially around harvest time, the Inca himself filled a golden goblet with quinoa and made an offering to the Inti. Quinoa was a precious grain, not because it was rare but because it thrives where corn does not.

For the sake of simplicity, quinoa is usually referred to as a grain, though technically it is not. It is the seed of an annual herb of the *Chenopodium* family. The plant grows three to six feet high and has leaves shaped like a goose foot. The seeds are large and are found in clusters at the ends of the stalks. In its native lands, all parts of the plant are utilized: the seeds and the young leaves as food, the plant, after harvest, as animal fodder, the woody stalks as fuel, and the saponin-rich wash water as shampoo.

Quinoa is extremely hardy. It thrives under conditions few other crops can tolerate: low rainfall; high altitudes with thin, cold air and a hot sun; subfreezing temperatures; and poor, sandy soil. This ability to thrive has made quinoa as strong a staple food crop today as it was for millions of people of the Inca Empire centuries ago.

Quinoa has a good nutritional profile, high in protein and other nutrients, and takes very little time to prepare. It does have to be washed, though, since the seeds are covered with saponin, a bitter substance that acts as a natural pesticide. Commercially available quinoa has already been washed, but I like to rinse it again before cooking.

POTATOES

Ocopa

Serves 6 to 8 (makes 2¼ cups sauce)

It is the sauce that makes this dish. This sauce is also good with cold meats and with shrimp, in which case the dish is called *ocopa de camarones.*

2 pounds new potatoes, scrubbed (see Note)
3 tablespoons coarse salt
6 to 8 dried mirasol or ancho or serrano peppers, or a combination of any of these
1 cup plus 2 tablespoons olive oil
2 medium cloves garlic, peeled and chopped
1 small onion, peeled and finely chopped (¼ cup)
¼ teaspoon ground turmeric
2 slices crustless white bread, soaked in ¼ cup milk
1 cup milk
1 tablespoon fresh lemon juice
4 ounces feta, mashed
Ground white pepper

GARNISH
6 to 8 Boston or romaine lettuce leaves
3 heaping tablespoons coarsely chopped walnuts
2 hard-boiled eggs

1. Place the potatoes in a 2½-quart saucepan with enough water to cover by 2 inches. Add the salt. Bring to a boil and cook until the potatoes are done, about 45 minutes. Drain, peel, and set aside.

2. Using tongs, sear 2 of the peppers over an open flame. Remove the seeds from all of the hot peppers, including the seared ones. Soak all the peppers in 1½ cups warm water for about 30 minutes, or until the peppers are soft. Place the peppers in a blender jar with ½ cup of the soaking liquid, discarding the rest of the liquid, and blend into a paste. Set aside.

(Continued)

3. In a skillet, heat 2 tablespoons of the oil. Add the garlic, onion, and turmeric and sauté until the onion is lightly golden around the edges, 2 to 3 minutes. Add the pepper mixture and continue cooking, stirring now and then, until all of the liquid has evaporated, 4 to 5 minutes. Remove from the heat.

4. Transfer the onion-pepper mixture to a blender jar, add the soaked bread and the additional cup of milk, and blend for a second. With the blender at full speed, pour in the remaining 1 cup of oil in a thin stream; the sauce will thicken as it blends. Mix in the lemon juice. Transfer the sauce to a bowl and mix in the crumbled feta. The texture should remain somewhat coarse. Correct seasoning with salt and white pepper to taste.

5. Place 1 or 2 potatoes, whole or sliced, on a lettuce leaf and spoon the sauce liberally over the potatoes. Sprinkle with some chopped walnuts, garnish the plate with a slice of hard-boiled egg, and serve.

NOTE   Allow 1 large or 2 small potatoes per serving.

STORAGE NOTE   If the sauce is not used immediately, pour it into a jar, pour a thin layer of olive oil over the surface, cover tightly, and store in the refrigerator. It will keep for up to 1 week.

Papas Sancochadas con Salsa de Avellanas

Potatoes with a Sweet Pepper and Hazelnut Sauce

—

Serves 8 as an appetizer or 6 as a main course

This red pepper-and-hazelnut sauce is a great partner for the potato. Together they make an elegant appetizer or a main course for lunch accompanied by some good crusty bread and, of course, a glass of ice-cold beer. On a hot summer day, there is nothing better.

Any type of potato is fine for this dish, although I have suggested all-purpose potatoes. Pasta, hot or cold, also lends itself to this sauce, especially twisted shapes like fusilli, rotelle, or radiatore that trap plenty of sauce.

8 large all-purpose potatoes, scrubbed
¾ cup olive oil
4 to 6 dried red chili peppers, seeded
8 large red bell peppers, roasted (page 484) and seeded, or
  2 13¾-ounce cans canned sweet red pimientos, well drained
¼ cup red-wine vinegar
2 cloves garlic, peeled
½ Granny Smith apple, peeled, cored, and coarsely chopped
1 teaspoon coarse salt
¾ to 1 cup blanched hazelnuts or almonds, roasted (page 485)

GARNISH
8 lettuce leaves or shredded lettuce
1 ear cooked corn, sliced into 8 rounds

1. Place the potatoes in a large pot with enough water to cover generously. Bring to a boil, lower the heat, and simmer until the potatoes are cooked, about 45 minutes. Drain, peel, and cover the potatoes with a cloth. Set aside in a warm spot.

2. In a small skillet, heat 1 tablespoon of the olive oil over high heat and quickly toast the hot peppers for less than 1 minute. Do not let the peppers burn. Remove from the heat and set aside to cool.

(Continued)

3. In the jar of an electric blender, combine the roasted bell peppers, the remaining oil, and the wine vinegar and blend at top speed until smooth. With the motor running, add the garlic, the roasted hot peppers and the oil from the skillet, the apple pieces, and salt and continue blending until the mixture is totally smooth. Slowly start adding the hazelnuts and blend until the mixture has thickened. Transfer the sauce to a bowl and correct the seasoning with salt to taste.

4. Arrange the warm potatoes, whole or sliced, over lettuce leaves or shredded lettuce and coat the potatoes generously with the sauce. Garnish with the rounds of cooked corn and serve.

STORAGE NOTE   If the sauce is not used immediately, pour it into a jar, pour a thin layer of olive oil over the surface, cover tightly, and store in the refrigerator. It will keep for up to 1 week.

Guiso de Papas con Pimientos
Braised Potatoes with Sweet Peppers

Serves 6 to 8

5 pounds large all-purpose potatoes
½ cup olive oil
3 large cloves garlic, peeled and crushed
3 or 4 jalapeño peppers
2 large onions, peeled and cut into 1½-inch squares
3 large green bell peppers, seeded, ribs removed, and cut into
*   1½-inch squares*
4 large red bell peppers, seeded, ribs removed, and cut into
*   1½-inch squares*
3 large yellow bell peppers, seeded, ribs removed, and cut into
*   1½-inch squares*
1 tablespoon ground fennel or cumin
2 tablespoons coarse salt
1 sprig fresh sage or rosemary or a few sprigs fresh oregano
*   or thyme*
1 tablespoon chopped Italian parsley

1. Peel the potatoes. Cut each in half lengthwise and then into 1½-inch pieces. Place in cold water to cover. Set aside until ready to use.

2. In a large sauté pan, heat the olive oil with the crushed garlic and hot peppers over low heat and sauté until the garlic is brown all around, about 4 minutes. Do not burn the garlic. Discard the garlic, leaving the peppers in the saucepan. Add the onions and sauté, stirring constantly, over high heat to brown them lightly, about 3 minutes. With a large slotted spoon, transfer the onions and hot peppers to a bowl. In the remaining hot oil in the pan, sauté the green, red, and yellow bell pepper pieces for 1 or 2 minutes, stirring constantly. With a slotted spoon, remove the peppers and add them to the vegetables in the bowl. Set aside.

3. Drain the potatoes and add them to the hot oil in the sauté pan. Sauté over medium heat for 5 minutes, stirring constantly. Sprinkle the potatoes with the ground fennel and salt. Stir in water to cover and add the sage. Cover the sauté pan, lower the heat, and cook for 20 minutes, stirring the potatoes now and then and adding more water as necessary.

4. Gently mix in the reserved vegetables. Cover and continue cooking, shaking the sauté pan from time to time to prevent the potatoes from sticking to the bottom of the pan, for 15 minutes, or until the potatoes are done. Remove from the heat, sprinkle with parsley, and serve.

VARIATION

Trim off the feathery tops of 1 or 2 small fennel bulbs and cut the bulbs into 1½-inch squares. Braise the fennel with the onion in Step 2 and proceed with the recipe.

Picante de Papas
Potatoes in a Picante Sauce

Serves 6 to 8

Cook the potatoes in an earthenware or other casserole that can be brought to the table. It makes a nice presentation and prevents overhandling (the potatoes are very delicate after they are cooked). The dish should be served piping hot, alone or accompanied by plain boiled rice.

5 pounds large all-purpose potatoes
4 tablespoons olive oil
2 large cloves garlic, peeled and minced
3 stalks celery, washed, strings removed, and minced
2 large onions, peeled and finely chopped
*3 dried mirasol peppers or dried red chili peppers, seeded and
    crumbled or ground*
1 teaspoon ground turmeric
2 tablespoons coarse salt
1 or 2 tablespoons chopped fresh cilantro leaves

1. Peel all the potatoes. Place one of the peeled potatoes in cold water to cover and set aside. Cut all the other potatoes in half lengthwise and then into 1½-inch cubes and keep them covered with cold water until ready to use.

2. In a casserole, heat the olive oil over medium heat. Add the garlic and celery and sauté for a few seconds. Do not burn the garlic. Add the onions, peppers, turmeric, and salt. Sauté, stirring, until the onion is soft, about 12 minutes.

3. Drain the cubed potatoes and stir them into the casserole. Add 1 cup cold water, cover, and cook for 35 to 40 minutes, stirring now and then.

4. Drain and grate the reserved potato and gently mix into the casserole. Cover the casserole again and continue cooking over low heat for 15 minutes, or until all the potatoes are done, shaking the casserole to prevent the vegetables from sticking to the bottom of the pan. Remove from the heat. Correct the seasoning with salt to taste, sprinkle with chopped cilantro leaves, and serve.

Ensalada de Papas
Blue-Potato Salad
—

Serves 6 to 8

A spectacular potato salad can be made with blue potatoes, which have a rich flavor and an extraordinary color.

3 to 3½ pounds blue potatoes, Yellow Finns, or new potatoes, scrubbed
¼ cup red-wine or raspberry vinegar
1 large clove garlic, peeled and crushed
8 to 10 anchovy fillets, drained and minced
¾ cup olive oil
2 or 3 jalapeño peppers, seeded and finely chopped
8 scallions, trimmed, washed, and thinly sliced
1 cup chopped fresh mint leaves
1 cup chopped Italian parsley

1. Place the potatoes in a 2½-quart pot. Add 8 cups of water and cook, covered, for 20 minutes, or until the potatoes are done. Remove from the heat, drain off all the water, and place the potatoes on a rack to let the moisture evaporate as they cool. When the potatoes are cool, peel them. Cut them lengthwise and then crosswise into ½-inch slices. Set aside.

2. Pour the vinegar into a cup and drop in the crushed garlic. With the tines of a fork, mash the garlic and let soak for 10 to 15 minutes, or until ready to use. Remove and discard the garlic. On a plate, mash the anchovy fillets thoroughly with a fork. Mash in 1 tablespoon of the garlic-flavored vinegar and add this to the vinegar in the cup. Mix well.

3. In a bowl large enough to hold the potatoes, combine the garlic-flavored anchovy vinegar and the olive oil. Whisk thoroughly. Stir in the hot peppers and scallions. Add the sliced potatoes and toss gently. Add the mint and parsley and toss again. Correct the seasoning and serve.

STORAGE NOTE   This salad will keep well, tightly covered, in the refrigerator for a few days.

Causa a la Limeña
Causa in Gold

—

Serves 8 to 10

A causa is a potato cake with a flavorful filling, such as cooked meat or seafood or, as in this recipe, an array of blanched vegetables. The quality of the potato is essential to the success of a causa. In its land of origin, Peru, the *papa amarilla*, a yellow-fleshed potato, is used.

To serve a causa, cut it into wedges, place each one on whole or shredded lettuce leaves, and garnish it with hard-boiled eggs, olives, tiny feta cubes, corn-on-the-cob slices, roasted pepper strips, onion rings, caperberries, pickles, walnuts, and/or anchovies.

Except for those filled with seafood, causas can be made a day or two in advance and refrigerated. They can be served as an appetizer or main course and are ideal for the buffet table.

3 pounds baking potatoes, scrubbed
2 pounds new or all-purpose potatoes, scrubbed
4 dried mirasol or red chili peppers, crumbled
2 bay leaves
3 tablespoons coarse salt

FILLING
1 small fennel bulb, trimmed and cut into ¼-inch dice (1 cup)
3 stalks celery, washed, strings removed, and cut into
*   ¼-inch dice (1 cup)*
1 turnip, peeled and cut into ¼-inch dice (1 cup)
1 carrot, peeled and cut into ¼-inch dice (1 cup)
1 small red beet, peeled and cut into ¼-inch dice (1 cup)
1 red bell pepper, seeded, ribs removed, and cut into ¼-inch dice
*   (1 cup)*
½ cup blanched fresh peas or frozen peas, thawed
5 to 6 scallions, white parts only, thinly sliced (about ½ cup)
2 cups mayonnaise
1 tablespoon Dijon mustard
¼ cup olive oil

1 large clove garlic, peeled and crushed
Juice of 1 lemon or lime
3 tablespoons Achiote Oil (page 472) or Paprika Oil (page 474)

GARNISH
2 teaspoons olive oil
½ teaspoon white-wine vinegar or lemon or lime juice
1 or 2 hard-boiled eggs, sliced or quartered (optional)

1. Place all the potatoes in a large pot with enough water to cover by about 2 inches. Add the crumbled peppers, bay leaves, and 2 tablespoons salt and boil, covered, until the potatoes are done, 45 minutes to 1 hour. As soon as the potatoes are done, remove them from the water and place them on a rack to cool, discarding the water.

2. When the potatoes are cool enough to handle, peel them and mash by pressing them with the back of a large spoon or your fingers through a strainer into a bowl. Set aside.

3. In a small pot, bring 4 cups of water to a full boil. Blanch the fennel and celery for about 1 minute. Transfer the vegetables with a large slotted spoon or a small scoop strainer to a bowl. In the same boiling water, blanch the turnip and carrot for about 4 minutes. Drain and add to the other cooked vegetables. Cook the beet in the same water for about 20 minutes, or until tender. Drain, add to the bowl, and let all the vegetables cool. When cool, mix in the bell pepper, blanched or thawed peas, and scallions.

4. In a bowl, mix 1 cup of the mayonnaise with the mustard. Fold in 3 cups of the vegetables, reserving the rest for garnish. Correct the seasoning with salt and set aside.

5. In a small skillet, heat the olive oil with the crushed garlic. Immediately remove from the heat; do not let the garlic brown. Let the oil cool with the garlic, then discard the garlic and save the oil.

6. In a cup, dissolve the remaining tablespoon of salt with the lemon or lime juice.

7. Stir the achiote oil, garlic-flavored oil, and the salted lemon juice into the mashed potatoes. Correct the seasoning with salt to taste.

(Continued)

8. Oil the ring (but not the bottom) of an 8-inch springform pan and place it on a serving platter with the groove that runs around the rim facing up. Press half the mashed potatoes into the pan. Make a rim 1 inch high and 1 inch wide with some of the potatoes, pressing against the sides of the pan to create a well. Spoon the vegetables mixed with the mayonnaise and mustard evenly into the well and gently press to smooth the surface. Gently press in the remaining mashed potatoes to cover the vegetables. Smooth the surface and spread the remaining cup of mayonnaise evenly over the potatoes. Carefully remove the springform ring, leaving the causa on the bottom.

9. Prepare the garnish by mixing the reserved vegetables with the olive oil, vinegar, and salt and white pepper to taste. Surround the causa with the vegetables, garnish the top with sliced or quartered hard-boiled eggs, if desired, and serve.

VARIATIONS

Substitute 3 cups shredded cooked chicken, turkey or other poultry for the vegetables in Step 4 and proceed with the recipe through Step 8. Garnish the causa with hard-boiled eggs, if desired, and serve.

Substitute 3 cups of flaked cooked fish (or 2 6½-ounce cans of white tuna, packed in oil or water, drained) for the vegetables. Mix with ½ cup sliced scallions, 1 or 2 tablespoons chopped fresh herbs, and the mayonnaise and mustard in Step 4 and proceed with the recipe through Step 8. Garnish with hard-boiled eggs, if desired, and serve.

Substitute 1½ pounds cooked small shrimp and 1½ pounds blanched bay scallops for the vegetables. Mix with ½ cup sliced scallions, 1 or 2 tablespoons chopped fresh herbs, and the mayonnaise and mustard in Step 4 and proceed with the recipe through Step 8 and serve immediately.

Papas a la Arequipeña
Arequipeña Potatoes

—

Serves 6 to 8

The colonial city of Arequipa in southern Peru is famed for its white volcanic-brick buildings and for this unique dish. A mirasol pepper set among the potatoes is filled with olive oil, which is spooned over the dish before serving.

2½ to 3 pounds all-purpose potatoes
½ pound feta or Muenster, cut into ¼-inch dice
¼ pound mozzarella, cut into ¼-inch dice
1½ teaspoons coarse salt
4 tablespoons olive oil
½ cup heavy cream or milk or water
1 fresh or dried mirasol or ancho pepper

1. Peel and cut the potatoes into ¼-inch dice. Keep covered with cold water until ready to use.

2. In a bowl, combine the potatoes, feta, mozzarella, salt, and 1 tablespoon of the oil, and toss. Distribute evenly in a shallow ovenproof earthenware or glass baking dish and pour the cream over the potatoes.

3. Preheat the oven to 350 degrees.

4. Remove the seeds from the pepper by cutting it open lengthwise so the pepper forms a small receptacle. Push the pepper deep into the middle of the potato mixture, cut side up, and fill with the remaining olive oil. Bake for 1 to 1½ hours, or until the potatoes are tender. Remove from the oven, spoon the hot olive oil from the pepper over the potatoes, and serve piping hot.

Causa Azulada
Causa in Blue

Serves 8 to 10

The stunning, almost electrifying color of blue potatoes, as well as their natural, sweet flavor and velvety texture, make them ideal for a causa. This causa can be prepared one or two days in advance. In fact, the color of the potatoes seems to intensify under refrigeration, making the causa even more attractive.

5 pounds blue potatoes, scrubbed
1 head garlic, unpeeled and cut in half horizontally
5-inch piece fresh ginger, sliced
2 or 3 branches fresh rosemary or sage or sprigs of tarragon
3 tablespoons plus 2 teaspoons coarse salt
2 tablespoons sherry, raspberry, or red-wine vinegar
6 tablespoons olive oil
1 clove garlic, peeled and minced
2 or 3 jalapeño peppers, seeded and minced
2 to 2½ pounds Swiss chard, washed and drained
1 cup mayonnaise
½ cup pitted and sliced alfonso or Kalamata olives

GARNISH (optional)
Roasted red bell pepper (page 484), cut into strips
Hard-boiled eggs
Pitted alfonso or Kalamata olives

1. Place the potatoes in a large pot with enough water to cover by about 2 inches. Add the garlic, ginger, rosemary, and 1 tablespoon of the salt and cook over medium heat until done, about 35 to 40 minutes. As soon as the potatoes are cooked, remove them from the water and place them on a rack to cool, discarding the water.

2. When the potatoes are cool enough to handle, peel them and mash them by pressing them with the back of a large spoon or your fingers through a strainer into a bowl. Add 2 more tablespoons of the salt, 1 tablespoon of the vinegar, and 2 tablespoons of the olive oil. Using your hands, mix well. Set aside.

3. Separate the stems from the leaves of the Swiss chard, reserving the stems. Blanch the leaves quickly in boiling water for a few seconds and drain thoroughly. Coarsely chop them, place in a clean napkin or cloth, and twist to squeeze out all the water

4. In a skillet, combine 2 tablespoons of the oil, the minced garlic, and the hot pepper and stir for a second over high heat (do not let the garlic brown or burn). Add the chopped Swiss chard and sauté, stirring, for 4 to 5 minutes. Mix in 1 teaspoon of salt and the remaining tablespoon of vinegar. Remove from the heat and set aside to cool.

5. Oil the ring (but not the bottom) of a 9-inch springform pan and place the pan on a serving platter with the groove that runs around the rim facing up. Press half the mashed potatoes into the pan. Spread the Swiss chard evenly over the potatoes and put the remaining mashed potatoes on top, pressing to shape and smoothing out the surface. With a large spatula, spread the mayonnaise uniformly over the surface of the potatoes. Remove the springform by carefully lifting it, leaving the causa on the plate.

6. Cut the reserved Swiss chard stems on the diagonal into 1-inch pieces. In a skillet, heat the remaining 2 tablespoons of oil over high heat. Add the stems and sauté for 5 minutes. Mix in the remaining teaspoon of salt and the sliced olives. Remove from the heat and let cool. Surround the bottom of the causa with the braised stems. Serve as is or garnish the top with roasted pepper, hard-boiled eggs, and/or olives.

VARIATION

Substitute 3 pounds of baking potatoes and 2 pounds of all-purpose potatoes for the 5 pounds of blue potatoes.

Tortilla de Papas
Potato Tortilla

Serves 6 to 8

This potato tortilla can be transformed with very little effort by adding seafood, chorizo sausage, artichokes, or Jerusalem artichokes. (See Variations at end of recipe.)

3½ pounds all-purpose potatoes
½ cup plus 1 tablespoon olive oil
1 tablespoon coarse salt
1 large onion, peeled and thinly sliced (2 cups)
8 medium eggs

1. Peel the potatoes and place them in a bowl, with cold water to cover, until ready to use. Just before using, cut them into quarters and thinly slice them.

2. In a large skillet, heat ½ cup olive oil over medium heat. Add the sliced potatoes and cook, covered, turning with a spatula occasionally until the potatoes are half-done, 10 to 15 minutes. Mix in the salt and sliced onion and continue cooking until the onion slices are wilted and the potatoes are tender, but not collapsing, 10 to 15 minutes. Remove the skillet from the heat and transfer the potatoes and onion to a bowl; set aside to cool slightly. Some of the vegetables will stick to the bottom of the skillet; do not scrape them off.

3. In a small bowl, beat the eggs and thoroughly fold them into the cooked potatoes and onions.

4. Heat a 10½-inch nonstick omelet pan. Add the remaining tablespoon of olive oil and continue to heat, almost to the point of smoking. Carefully coat the sides and bottom of the pan with the hot oil. Pour the potato mixture into the pan and leave over high heat for 1 or 2 minutes. Lower the heat as much as possible and let cook until the potato mixture has set enough to be turned, about 15 minutes.

5. Place a cover of a pot or a large plate over the pan and carefully flip the potato mixture over onto it. Slide the mixture back into the pan, cooked side up, and continue cooking over very low heat for about 15 to 20 minutes longer, or until the mixture has set. The tortilla should feel firm when pressed. Place a serving platter over the pan and gently flip the tortilla onto it. Serve hot or at room temperature.

STORAGE NOTE   Tortillas keep well, tightly covered, for up to 1 week in the refrigerator. Do not store tortillas made with seafood.

VARIATIONS

Add 1 pound bay scallops, sliced sea scallops, tiny shrimp, or crabmeat to the cooked potatoes and onions in Step 2 and proceed with the recipe.

Thinly slice a 4-ounce chorizo sausage and add with the onions in Step 2. Proceed with the recipe.

Cook 2 artichokes, scrape the flesh off the base of the leaves, and thinly slice the hearts. Add the flesh and hearts to the beaten eggs in Step 3 and proceed with the recipe.

Peel and thinly slice 1½ pounds Jerusalem artichokes. Using only 2½ pounds potatoes, proceed with the recipe to the end of Step 2. Add the Jerusalem artichokes to the cooked potatoes and onions just before folding in the eggs in Step 3.

Entomatado de Papas
Potato Casserole

—

Serves 6 to 8

3½ pounds California or Florida White potatoes or baking potatoes
1 clove garlic, peeled and minced
1 large onion, peeled and sliced (about 2 cups)
1 tablespoon coarse salt
½ cup loosely packed fresh thyme leaves
1 to 1¼ pounds fresh mozzarella, shredded (3½ cups)
3 jalapeño peppers, seeded and julienned
1½ pounds tomatoes, cut into ¼-inch slices
½ cup slivered almonds
2 tablespoons olive oil

1. Peel the potatoes and slice ⅛ inch thick. Keep covered with cold water until ready to use.

2. Preheat the oven to 375 degrees.

3. Sprinkle the bottom of a 12 × 2½-inch round earthenware casserole or baking dish with the minced garlic. Cover the bottom of the casserole with the onion slices and sprinkle with 1 teaspoon of the salt and one-third of the thyme leaves. Spread half the potato slices evenly over the onions. Sprinkle with 1 cup of shredded cheese and another third of the thyme leaves. Distribute half the julienned hot peppers and then overlap with slices of tomato. Sprinkle with another teaspoon of salt and the remaining thyme leaves, hot peppers, and another cup of cheese. Arrange the remaining potato slices on top, overlapping one another. Sprinkle with the remaining 1½ cups of cheese, the last teaspoon of salt, and the almonds; dot with olive oil.

4. Place a piece of oiled parchment paper over the casserole, cover tightly with aluminum foil, and bake for 1 hour. Remove the foil and parchment paper and continue to cook until the surface is barely golden, about 10 minutes longer. Remove from the oven and serve.

Papas Rellenas
Stuffed Potatoes

—

Serves 10 as an appetizer or 5 as a main course

A single stuffed potato served on a lettuce leaf and garnished with onion relish makes a substantial appetizer. For a main course, serve two and garnish them with slices of corn-on-the-cob, black olives, and cubes of feta in addition to the onion relish.

3 pounds new potatoes, scrubbed
1 tablespoon coarse salt

FILLING
2 tablespoons Achiote Oil (page 472) or Paprika Oil (page 474) or
*   olive oil*
1 medium onion, peeled and chopped (about 1 cup)
2 jalapeño or serrano peppers or 1 dried red chili pepper,
*   seeded and chopped*
½ teaspoon ground cumin
¼ teaspoon sugar
⅛ teaspoon ground white pepper
1 teaspoon coarse salt
1 teaspoon finely chopped fresh oregano or ⅛ teaspoon
*   dried oregano*
½ pound lean ground beef
1 tablespoon dark seedless raisins
3 large alfonso or Kalamata olives, pitted and julienned
1 hard-boiled egg, coarsely chopped

1 cup all-purpose flour
3 eggs, lightly beaten
4 cups fresh bread crumbs
6 to 8 cups vegetable oil
Lemon wedges or Onion Relish (page 481)

1. Place the potatoes in a 2½-quart pot with enough water to cover by about 2 inches. Add 1 tablespoon of salt and bring to a gentle boil. Cook the potatoes until done, about 40 to 45 minutes. Drain, let cool

(Continued)

slightly, and peel them. With a fork or your fingers, crumble the potatoes into small pieces and place them in a strainer. With the back of a soup spoon, force the potatoes through the strainer over a bowl. Correct the seasoning with salt to taste and set aside.

2. In a skillet, heat the oil. Add the onion and sauté until it is translucent and the edges are golden, about 5 minutes. Add the hot peppers, cumin, sugar, white pepper, 1 teaspoon of salt, and the oregano and continue cooking for 1 minute. Add the meat and cook over medium-low heat until all the liquid from the meat has evaporated, about 5 to 6 minutes. Add the raisins and continue cooking for 2 minutes, stirring frequently. Stir in the olives. Remove from the heat and set aside until the mixture is cool. Stir in the hard-boiled egg and correct the seasoning with salt to taste.

3. Divide the mashed potatoes into 10 equal portions. When forming the stuffed potatoes, dip your hands into cold water to prevent the potatoes from sticking. Flatten one portion of mashed potatoes between the palms of your hands into a circle measuring 3½ to 4 inches in diameter. Make a slight well in the center and fill it with a rounded tablespoon of meat filling. Fold the potato circle to close. Press the edges together to seal and with both hands, shape the stuffed potato to resemble a large egg. Repeat until all the potatoes have been assembled.

4. Dredge the stuffed potatoes in the flour, gently shaking off the excess. Dip them into the beaten eggs and roll them in the bread crumbs until they are well coated.

5. In a deep saucepan or deep-fat fryer, heat the vegetable oil to 375 degrees. Slip the potatoes into the hot oil and deep-fry them until golden all around, about 1 minute. With a slotted spoon or the fryer basket, lift the potatoes from the oil; drain on towels or paper towels. Serve at once, garnished with lemon wedges or onion relish.

VARIATIONS

Substitute a combination of all-purpose potatoes and yuca for the new potatoes. Prepare 2 pounds of all-purpose potatoes as described in Step 1. Meanwhile, peel and rinse 1 pound of yuca and cook in unsalted water for 25 minutes, or until done. Mash the yuca with the potatoes in Step 1 and proceed with the recipe.

Substitute ½ pound ground, pork, veal, or chicken for the ground beef.

Guiso de Papa Seca
Andean Potatoes

—

Serves 6 to 8

*P*apa seca, or freeze-dried potatoes, are still made the ancient way. (see page 366 for a description of the method). The potatoes are quick to prepare.

1 pound papa seca
3 dried ancho peppers, seeded and cut into pieces
3 tablespoons Paprika Oil (page 474), Achiote Oil (page 472),
   or olive oil
2 large cloves garlic, peeled and minced
1 large onion, peeled and finely chopped (1½ cups)
1 tablespoon coarse salt
½ cup unsalted peanuts, finely chopped

1. Place the *papa seca* in a colander and shake to remove any powder. Transfer to a bowl, cover with a generous amount of water, then drain, discarding the water along with anything that floats on the surface. Add 6 cups of cold water to the washed potatoes and let soak overnight at room temperature or in the refrigerator. Drain and set aside.

2. In a small bowl, soak the ancho peppers in 1½ cups warm water for about 15 minutes, or until they are soft. Pour the softened peppers with their soaking liquid into the jar of an electric blender or the work bowl of a food processor and blend or process until smooth. Set aside.

3. In a sauté pan, heat the oil and the garlic for 1 or 2 seconds. Do not burn the garlic. Mix in the onion and sauté over medium heat for 5 minutes. Add the blended pepper mixture and the salt, mix well, and cook, stirring now and then, until most of the liquid has evaporated and the spoon leaves a track on the bottom of the pan, about 20 to 25 minutes. Add the peanuts and stir for 1 minute. Add the drained *papa seca,* folding in half at a time. Mix well and heat over very low heat, stirring and scraping from time to time to prevent the potatoes from sticking to the bottom of the pan, until they are hot and fluffy, about 25 minutes. Correct the seasoning with salt to taste and serve hot.

SWEET POTATOES

Camotes Asados
Baked Sweet Potatoes

—

Sweet potatoes are used extensively in the South American kitchen, both the bright orange ones with reddish brown skin that are mistakenly called yams and the paler orange ones, as well as *batatas blancas,* which have white flesh and reddish purple skin.

Preheat the oven to 400 degrees. Wash and scrub the sweet potatoes well and wipe dry. Rub with oil and arrange in a roasting pan. Bake for 45 minutes to 1 hour, or until they are soft when pressed or pierce easy with a fork. Serve at once.

Camote Frito
Sweet-Potato Chips

—

Serves 6 to 8

These chips traditionally accompany the *chicharrones,* or morsels of pork fried in their own fat, that are sold at breakfast time in the streets of Lima. Sweet-potato chips go with just about any fried, grilled, or roasted meat, and they make a wonderful snack.

4 to 6 sweet potatoes, peeled or unpeeled
5 to 6 cups vegetable oil or Rendered Duck Fat (page 475) or
    Rendered Bacon Fat (page 476)
1 tablespoon coarse salt (optional)

1. Wash and dry the sweet potatoes and cut them crosswise into slices no more than ⅛ inch thick.

2. In a deep-fat fryer or large pot, heat the oil to 365 to 375 degrees. Drop in the sweet-potato slices all at once or in several batches, depending on the size of the fryer or pot used, and fry them until they are barely golden, about 1 minute. Remove them from the oil, drain, and serve, sprinkled with salt, if desired.

Camote en Salsa de Dátiles
Sweet Potatoes in Date Sauce

—

Serves 6 to 8

8 sweet potatoes (about 6 pounds)
1 unripe pineapple
15 juniper berries, crushed
1 3-inch cinnamon stick
8 to 10 cloves
1 or 2 dried red chili peppers (optional)
1 pound pitted dates, chopped
¼ cup Clarified Butter (page 476)
4 to 6 ounces dried apricots
¼ cup chopped walnuts

1. Peel the sweet potatoes and cut them into 1½-inch cubes. Keep covered with cold water until ready to use.

2. Cut off and discard the top of the pineapple. Wash and dry the fruit. Cut off the bottom and trim off the skin all around. Put the bottom and skin in a small stockpot. Cut the pineapple lengthwise into quarters; remove the core and add to the skin in the stockpot. Cut the pineapple into 1½-inch cubes and set aside.

3. In the pot containing the skin, bottom, and core of the pineapple, combine the juniper berries, cinnamon stick, cloves, hot peppers, if using, and 8 cups cold water. Bring to a boil, lower the heat, and simmer, covered, for 45 minutes to 1 hour.

4. Remove from the heat and strain through a fine sieve or strainer. Press the skin against the walls of the sieve or strainer to squeeze out

(Continued)

all the juices. Discard the skin. You should have 6 cups of stock. If not, add enough water to make 6 cups.

5. Pour 2 cups of the fruit stock into the jar of an electric blender or the work bowl of a food processor. Add half the chopped dates and blend thoroughly. Add 2 more cups of the stock and the remaining dates and blend until the mixture is totally smooth.

6. In a sauté pan large enough to hold the sweet potato cubes comfortably, heat the clarified butter over high heat. Add the pineapple cubes and cook them until they are golden brown all around. With a slotted spoon, remove them to a plate. Set aside.

7. Add the blended dates to the same pan and cook for 5 minutes, stirring. Add the remaining 2 cups of fruit stock and stir. Drain the sweet potato cubes, add them to the sauce, and cook over medium heat, tightly covered, stirring gently now and then, for about 30 minutes.

8. Gently mix in the reserved pineapple and the dried apricots and continue cooking, covered, for about 15 minutes, or until the sweet potatoes are tender, shaking the pan from time to time to prevent the potatoes from sticking to the bottom. Remove from heat and serve piping hot, garnished with chopped walnuts.

NOTE   To reheat this dish, add ½ cup water, cover tightly, and warm in a preheated 300-degree oven for about 20 minutes.

Puré de Batata y Jengibre
Sweet-Potato and Ginger Puree

—

Serves 6 to 8

8 sweet potatoes, baked in a 400-degree oven for 45 to 60 minutes
1 tablespoon butter, softened
½ cup sliced almonds
5-inch piece fresh ginger, peeled and grated
¼ teaspoon ground allspice
3 eggs, separated
1 tablespoon butter, melted
¼ teaspoon ground cinnamon
1 teaspoon sugar

1. When the sweet potatoes are cool enough to handle, peel them and mash them by forcing them through a strainer into a bowl. You should have 5 to 6 cups of mashed sweet potatoes. Set aside.

2. Grease a 10½ × 8 × 2-inch baking dish with the softened butter. Sprinkle about 5 tablespoons of the sliced almonds on the bottom and sides and set aside until ready to use.

3. In a small bowl, mix the grated ginger with the allspice and set aside until ready to use.

4. With a wire whisk or an electric mixer, beat the egg yolks until frothy and lemony in color. Stir in the ginger-allspice mixture and mix this, together with the melted butter, into the mashed sweet potatoes. Mix thoroughly and spread evenly in the prepared baking dish.

5. Preheat the oven to 375 degrees.

6. Beat the egg whites until soft dry peaks are formed. Sprinkle the cinnamon into the egg whites and fold in 2 tablespoons of the sliced almonds. Spread the egg whites evenly on top of the sweet-potato mixture in the baking dish and sprinkle with the sugar and the remaining almonds. Bake for 20 to 25 minutes, or until the surface is golden brown. Remove from the oven and serve at once.

YUCA

Yuca Sancochada
Boiled Yuca
—

The quality of the yuca root is more important than the cooking method when it comes to preparing yuca. A good root smells clean and fresh, with no sour or ammonialike odor. The bark should be free of mold, soft spots, or cracks. Even when the bark appears to be in perfect condition, though, the flesh may not be all right. The only way to be sure is to cut the yuca open: the flesh should be chalk-white all the way through, without any grayish-blue fibers or other discoloration.

Fresh yuca does not store well, so it is best to buy it when you need it. If you must store it, keep it in the coolest place possible. Cooked yuca, however, does store well. When buying yuca, allow half a pound per person.

Cut the roots of the yuca crosswise into 3-inch sections. Remove the bark: slit it lengthwise with a sharp knife, then place a knife with a rounded point under the pinkish underskin to loosen and peel off the bark and skin. Rinse the pieces and keep them in cold water to cover until ready to cook.

In a large pot, combine the yuca with enough cold water to cover by at least 2 inches. Bring to a boil, lower the heat, and gently simmer for 20 to 25 minutes, or until the yuca is tender to the touch of a fork. Check individual pieces for doneness: some may cook faster than others. Drain immediately in a colander and let cool. When cool enough to handle, break or cut the yuca in half or quarters lengthwise and with a paring knife, remove and discard the fibrous cores. Serve as is, use in another recipe, or store.

STORAGE NOTE Drain and cool the yuca, place in a container, cover with a moist towel, and cover tightly; refrigerate for up to 1 week. Or place the cooked yuca in an airtight container and freeze for up to 6 months.

Yuca Arrebosada
Sautéed Yuca
—

Serves 6 to 8

3 to 4 pounds yuca, boiled (page 394)
8 tablespoons (1 stick) butter or Clarified Butter (page 476)
1 tablespoon olive oil
1 large clove garlic, peeled and slightly crushed
2 teaspoons coarse salt
2 tablespoons chopped Italian parsley

1. After the yuca is done, gently remove the pieces from the hot water and let drain. When cool, cut them into quarters lengthwise and cut out and discard the fibrous core.

2. In a large skillet, combine the butter, oil, and garlic over low heat. Sauté the garlic for just 1 or 2 seconds. Add the yuca pieces, sprinkle them with 1 teaspoon of salt, and cook them on one side for about 8 minutes. If the garlic gets too brown, remove and discard it. Sprinkle the yuca with the remaining teaspoon of salt; turn with tongs and continue cooking for about 8 minutes longer, or until the yuca is pale golden all around. Remove, correct the seasoning with salt to taste, sprinkle with chopped parsley, and serve.

Yuca Frita
Yuca Straws

Serves 6 to 8

Yuca straws offer stiff competition to French fries. They are irresistible as a snack or with cocktails, and they make a great garnish or side dish with grilled or roast meat or fish.

4 pounds yuca, boiled (page 394)
6 cups vegetable oil
1 to 2 tablespoons coarse salt

1. After the yuca is done, gently remove the pieces from the hot water and let drain. When thoroughly cool, cut them into quarters lengthwise and cut out and discard the fibrous core. Cut the pieces in half again and then cut them in ¼-inch-thick sticks. Set aside.

2. In a deep-fat fryer or large pot, heat the oil to 365 to 375 degrees. Deep-fry the yuca in several batches until light golden, about 10 minutes. Remove them from the oil, drain, and sprinkle with salt. Toss well and serve.

ONIONS

Cebollas y Ajos Asados
Roasted Onions and Garlic

—

Serves 6 to 8

Roasted onions and garlic are a good accompaniment for roasts.

6 1-pound Bermuda onions, unpeeled
6 large whole heads garlic, unpeeled
4 tablespoons olive or vegetable oil

GARNISH
Coarse salt
Freshly ground black pepper
Butter or olive oil

1. Preheat the oven to 475 degrees.

2. Trim but do not cut off the root ends of the onions. Cut a cross about 1 inch deep on the top of each onion. Rub them all around with 1 tablespoon of oil and arrange them, cut side up, in a roasting pan. Place in the oven and roast for 1 hour 20 minutes. Remove the pan from the oven and spoon 1 teaspoon of oil into the opening of each onion.

3. Rub the heads of garlic with the remaining oil. Place them in the roasting pan with the onions. Return the pan to the oven and roast for 25 to 30 minutes, or until the onions are totally tender when pierced with a fork through the center. The garlic heads are done when they feel soft to the touch.

4. Remove the roasting pan from the oven, sprinkle the openings of the onions with coarse salt and freshly ground black pepper, and top with a lump of butter or a few drops of olive oil. With a towel, hold each head of garlic down on its side and with a fork, pull out, remove, and discard the root end. Serve hot.

PEPPERS

Pimientos Rellenos
Roasted Sweet Peppers with Goat Cheese

—

Serves 8 as an appetizer or 4 as a main course

When selecting peppers for this dish, choose the largest and firmest you can find, with an even, fiery red color and thick flesh. If the flesh is thin or if you want more of a pepper flavor, use two peppers. Place the filling in the smaller of the two, then wrap the filled pepper in the larger one. Double-wrapping is also necessary to keep the cheese from leaking out if the peppers break when roasted.

8 large red bell peppers, roasted (page 484)
1 log montrachet goat cheese (11 to 12 ounces)
1 tablespoon fresh thyme leaves
1 tablespoon chopped Italian parsley
2 tablespoons olive oil
1 teaspoon toasted sesame seeds
8 romaine lettuce leaves

GARNISH (optional)
½ small red cabbage, shredded as thinly as possible
¼ cup raspberry vinaigrette (see Note)
½ red bell pepper, cut into ¼-inch dice

1. Roast and peel the peppers as described on page 484 but keep the peppers in one piece. Using a paring knife, cut one side of each pepper open. Unfold it carefully and remove and discard the seeds.

2. Place the cheese, thyme leaves, and parsley on a plate and mash until all the ingredients are well incorporated. Divide this mixture into 8 equal portions and press to shape each portion into an oval.

3. Preheat the broiler.

4. Place one portion of the cheese mixture close to the bottom end of an opened pepper; fold one side of the pepper over to enclose the cheese totally. Then fold the other side over, tucking in the top end of the pepper. Shape with your hands to simulate a whole pepper. Repeat until all the peppers are done.

5. Lightly brush an enameled gratin dish with some of the olive oil. Arrange the peppers in the dish, brush each pepper generously with the remaining oil, and sprinkle with sesame seeds. Broil on the lowest level of the preheated broiler until the surface of the peppers starts to show a scattering of small charred spots, 8 to 10 minutes.

6. Remove the peppers from the broiler, place each one on a romaine lettuce leaf, and pour some of the pan drippings over each of the peppers. Place a handful of shredded red cabbage around the peppers, if desired, sprinkle the cabbage with raspberry vinaigrette, garnish with diced red bell pepper, and serve.

NOTE   To make the raspberry vinaigrette, combine 1 tablespoon raspberry vinegar with 3 tablespoons olive oil and blend well.

VARIATION

Preheat the oven to 375 degrees, put the dish of peppers in the upper level of the oven, and bake for about 10 minutes. Remove from the oven and serve as described in Step 6.

Ajíes Rellenos
Hot Peppers Filled with Ham and Cheese

Serves 8

I have suggested ancho peppers in this recipe, but you can use other dried hot peppers as long as they are broad and long enough to hold a generous amount of filling. They should not be overwhelmingly hot. If the peppers are too hot for your taste, soak them in salt water rather than plain water to lower their potency.

8 dried ancho peppers
1¼ pounds fresh mozzarella
½ pound serrano or prosciutto ham, thinly sliced
1 cup fresh bread crumbs
¼ cup fresh thyme leaves
¼ cup chopped Italian parsley
¼ cup ground almonds (about 1 ounce)
¼ cup capers
1 teaspoon coarse salt
2 medium onions, peeled and thinly sliced
1 tablespoon olive oil
¼ cup dry white wine

1. Place the peppers in a bowl and add enough water to cover generously. Soak them overnight (or 4 to 8 hours for freshly dried anchos). Drain them thoroughly. Using scissors, cut the peppers open lengthwise, starting at the stem. Remove and discard the seeds with a teaspoon and set the peppers aside.

2. Grate 1 pound of the mozzarella and cut ¼ pound into ¼-inch dice. Set aside.

3. Finely chop half of the ham. Set aside.

4. Preheat the oven to 400 degrees.

5. In a small bowl, combine the grated and cubed mozzarella, the bread crumbs, thyme, parsley, almonds, capers, salt, and chopped ham, and mix well. Divide this mixture into 8 equal portions. Line each pepper with a slice of ham, add a portion of the mozzarella mixture, and place another slice of ham on top. Close the pepper as tightly as possible. Repeat until all the peppers have been filled.

6. Cover the bottom of a baking dish or earthenware casserole with the onion slices. Arrange the filled peppers on top, packing them as close as possible to one another. Brush each pepper with oil and sprinkle with wine. Cover the dish with a sheet of oiled parchment paper and seal with a piece of aluminum foil. Bake in the middle level of the oven for 25 to 30 minutes. Serve piping hot, right from the baking dish.

TOMATOES

Tomates Rellenos
Tomatoes Filled with Tomatoes and Almonds

Serves 8

8 large tomatoes (about 10 to 12 ounces each)
4 medium tomatoes (about ½ pound each)
3 tablespoons Paprika Oil (page 474) or olive oil
½ cup blanched whole almonds
2 large cloves garlic, peeled and minced
1-inch piece fresh ginger, peeled and minced
3 jalapeño peppers, seeded and finely chopped
1 stalk celery, washed, strings removed, and finely chopped
1 medium onion, peeled and finely chopped (1 cup)
⅛ teaspoon ground cloves
1 tablespoon coarse salt
8 slices lightly toasted bread, buttered (optional)
1 tablespoon olive oil

1. Prepare the 8 large tomatoes for filling: with a sharp paring knife, cut a conical plug about 1 inch away from the stem end of each tomato. With the paring knife or a grapefruit knife, loosen the pulp all around the sides of the tomato, being careful not to pierce the shell. With a teaspoon, force and scoop out the pulp and set it aside. Scrape out all the seeds over a strainer into a bowl. Place the empty tomato shell, cut side down, on a towel or paper towels, keeping its conical plug beside it. Repeat with remaining tomatoes. Set aside. Save the pulp to be minced.

2. In a pot containing boiling water, blanch 2 of the 4 smaller tomatoes for a few seconds. With a slotted spoon, remove them from the water and when cool enough to handle, peel them and remove conical plugs (as you did with the large tomatoes) as close to the stem ends as possible. Cut the tomatoes in half crosswise and add the seeds to the strainer containing the seeds from the 8 large tomatoes. Mince the pulp from the 4 tomatoes with the pulp from the 8 large tomatoes.

3. Cut the remaining 2 tomatoes in half crosswise, cut out and discard conical plugs, add the seeds to the strainer, and cut the pulp into ½-inch chunks. Set aside. With your hands or a soup spoon, rub the seeds against the wall of the strainer to extract all the juices. Set aside, discarding the seeds.

4. In a sauté pan, heat the paprika oil with the almonds over medium heat; sauté for about 1 minute. Stir in the garlic, ginger, hot peppers, and celery and sauté for 2 to 3 minutes. Mix in the onion, cloves, and salt; cook, stirring, for about 1 minute. Add all of the chopped tomato pulp. Bring to a boil, stirring. Lower the heat and simmer, stirring now and then, for about 20 minutes, or until most of the liquid has evaporated.

5. Add the reserved juice from the tomatoes and simmer over medium heat, stirring, until the sauce is thick enough for the spoon to leave a light track at the bottom of the pan, about 15 minutes. Remove from the heat and gently stir in the fresh tomato chunks. You should have about 4 cups of tomato filling.

6. Preheat the oven to 450 degrees.

7. Turn the tomatoes over, cut side up, and divide the filling evenly among them. Cover each tomato with its corresponding top. If toast is used, place 1 slice on the bottom of each of 8 gratin dishes and set the filled tomato on top. If not, simply transfer the filled tomatoes to 8 individual porcelain or earthenware gratin dishes and place them on a baking tray. Brush each of the tomatoes generously with olive oil and place the tray in the middle level of the oven for 10 to 12 minutes. Remove from the oven and serve hot.

Huevos Tripados
Tomatoes and Peruvian Egg Noodles

—

Serves 6 to 8

The delicate sauce in this recipe is perfect with many foods, including meat, fish, vegetables, and pasta, but true justice is done when it is served with *huevos tripados,* or noodles made with eggs.

This sweet fragrant dish always reminds me of home. It was something my mother made on the days when she said she didn't feel like cooking. We all loved it. I will never forget my baby sister toddling into the kitchen, pulling on my mother's dress, and part-asking, part-telling her, "Mama, today you don't feel like cooking, right?"—implying that it might, just possibly, be a good day for her favorite food, *huevos tripados.*

NOODLES
24 eggs
1 teaspoon coarse salt
¼ teaspoon ground white pepper
1 cup grated parmesan
⅓ cup finely crushed English water biscuits or soda crackers
2 tablespoons Clarified Butter (page 476)

TOMATO SAUCE
9 tomatoes (4 to 4½ pounds)
3 tablespoons Paprika Oil (page 474) or olive oil
1 large clove garlic, peeled and minced
1 medium onion, peeled and minced
1 bay leaf
2 teaspoons ground fennel
1 tablespoon coarse salt
1 small carrot, peeled and grated

1 cup chopped fresh basil leaves (optional)

1. Break the eggs into a large bowl; add ½ cup cold water, the salt, and the white pepper. With a wire whisk, blend the ingredients together. Stir in the grated cheese and the crushed soda crackers.

2. Place a 10-inch nonstick skillet or omelet pan over medium heat. Lightly brush the bottom with clarified butter and pour ½ cup of the thoroughly stirred egg mixture in the middle of the pan, quickly tilting the skillet in all directions so that the egg mixture evenly coats the entire bottom of the pan before setting. Let cook until the mixture has set, 1 to 1½ minutes. Using a long, wide spatula, carefully lift and turn the omelet to cook for a few seconds on the other side. Remove from the heat, tilting the skillet so that the omelet slides easily onto a large plate or tray. Repeat until all the egg mixture has been used. You should have about 12 omelets stacked on top of one another. Cover and keep warm.

3. Blanch 7 of the tomatoes for a few seconds in rapidly boiling water. With a slotted spoon, remove them from the water and when cool enough to handle, peel and cut out their conical plugs. Cut the tomatoes in half crosswise and squeeze the seeds into a strainer over a bowl. Finely chop the tomato pulp. You should have about 3½ cups. Set aside.

4. Cut the 2 remaining tomatoes in half crosswise. Remove the seeds and add them to the strainer. Coarsely grate the pulp and set aside. With your hands or a soup spoon, press and rub the seeds against the wall of the strainer to squeeze out all the tomato juices. Save the juice and discard the seeds.

5. In an earthenware casserole or any cooking dish that can be brought to the table, heat the paprika oil and garlic over medium heat. Do not burn the garlic. When the oil starts to bubble, stir in the onion, bay leaf, fennel, and salt; sauté for about 5 minutes. Add the grated carrot and the juice from the tomatoes and cook, stirring, over high heat, until all the liquid has evaporated, about 8 minutes. Add the chopped tomato and simmer for 10 minutes, stirring now and then. Mix in the grated tomato and cook just to heat through, about 1 minute. Remove from the heat and set aside.

6. Stack 4 of the warm omelets on top of one another. Roll them tightly together and cut the roll across, either straight down or at an angle, into ¼-inch-wide noodles, keeping the sections rolled up. Repeat this until all the omelets are rolled and cut. Arrange all the rolls of noodles, overlapping one another, on top of the hot tomato sauce and garnish with basil, if desired. To serve, use 2 forks to toss the egg noodles gently with the tomato sauce.

NOTE This dish tastes best when served hot, but if necessary, it can be reheated. Cover the casserole tightly with oiled parchment paper and a sheet of aluminum foil and place it in the lower part of a preheated 375-degree oven for about 20 to 25 minutes, or until the sauce is hot.

SQUASH

Locro

Serves 6 to 8

Locro is a vegetable stew that varies from country to country. In the highlands of Ecuador, for example, *locro* is made with potatoes, milk, cheese, and eggs; on rare occasions a piece of firm white fish or some shellfish is dropped in. In Argentina, *locro* is made with squash; sometimes corn is added. This is also true for the *locros* of Peru, of which there are several varieties.

No matter what its country of origin, *locro* is always served hot as a main course and accompanied with rice. In Peru they garnish *locro* with onion relish, which gives a piquant touch to this very satisfying dish.

3 medium butternut squash (about 4 pounds)
¼ cup olive oil
2 cloves garlic, peeled and chopped
2 medium onions, peeled and finely chopped (about 2½ cups)
2 large tomatoes, peeled, seeded, and chopped
1½ tablespoons chopped fresh oregano or 1 teaspoon dried oregano
1 tablespoon coarse salt
¼ teaspoon ground white pepper
2 ears corn, husks and silks removed, and kernels cut off the cobs
1 cup fresh or frozen and thawed peas

GARNISH
*1 ear corn, husk and silk removed, cut crosswise into ½-inch slices,
    and blanched (see Note)*
Onion Relish (page 481)

1. Remove and discard the skin and seeds from the squash and cut into 1-inch cubes. You should have about 10 cups. Set aside.

2. In a sauté pan, heat the olive oil over low heat. Add the garlic and sauté for 1 minute. Do not burn the garlic. Add the onions and continue to sauté until the onions are lightly golden, about 8 minutes. Mix in the squash, chopped tomatoes, oregano, salt, pepper, and ½ cup of water and cook, stirring now and then, for 25 minutes, or until the squash is barely tender.

3. Stir in the corn kernels, cover the sauté pan, and continue cooking for 5 minutes longer. Add the peas, stir, and cook for another 3 to 5 minutes. Remove from the heat, correct the seasoning with salt and white pepper to taste, and serve, garnished with 1 slice of corn per serving and some onion relish.

NOTE   To blanch the corn for garnish, bring a pot of salted water to a boil, add the corn slices, and bring back to a boil. Remove from heat, cover, and let sit for 3 to 5 minutes. With a slotted spoon, remove the corn slices from the water and drain. The corn may also be blanched whole and then sliced.

VARIATIONS

Substitute ½ cup milk or half-and-half for the water in Step 2. Proceed with the recipe.

Add 1 cup of ¼-inch cubes of feta with the corn in Step 3. Proceed with the recipe. When using feta, do not add salt until the very end. Then taste and add salt as needed.

Zapallo Horneado
Braised Butternut Squash

—

Serves 6 to 8

3 large butternut squash (about 6 pounds)
4 tablespoons butter, melted
3 tablespoons chopped fresh dill
2 teaspoons coarse salt
1 clove garlic, peeled and minced (optional)
¼ cup chopped fresh mint leaves

1. Rinse and dry the squash. Cut each squash crosswise into 1½-inch-wide circles, starting from the top. Stop when the squash gets broader than 1½ inches and the seeds are exposed. Set the slices aside. With a soup spoon, scrape out and discard the seeds. With a potato peeler, remove the skin and discard. Cut this part of the squash into 1½-inch cubes and place them in a bowl. Add 2 tablespoons of the melted butter and 2 tablespoons of the dill; toss well while sprinkling in 1 teaspoon of the salt. Set aside.

2. Preheat the oven to 375 degrees.

3. Butter the bottom of an earthenware or glass baking dish large enough to hold all the pieces of squash with 1 tablespoon of the melted butter and sprinkle with the garlic, if using, and the chopped mint. Arrange the squash circles around the sides of the baking dish. Brush the surface of the squash circles with the remaining melted butter and sprinkle with the remaining teaspoon of salt. Fill the center of the dish with the squash cubes and tightly cover with aluminum foil. Bake for 45 minutes, or until tender. Remove from the oven, take off the foil, sprinkle the cubes with the remaining chopped dill, and serve hot.

VARIATION

Slice the unpeeled butternut or acorn squash onto 1½-inch circles, removing and discarding the seeds. Butter the bottom of a baking dish and sprinkle with garlic, if using, and herbs. Arrange the squash in the dish, overlapping the pieces. Brush generously with melted butter, sprinkle with salt, cover, and bake in a preheated 375-degree oven for 45 minutes, or until tender.

Calabazas Rellenas
Acorn Squash Stuffed with Quinoa

Serves 16 as an appetizer or 8 as a main course

—

A whole acorn squash filled with quinoa is spectacular as a main dish. You can also serve it as an appetizer or side dish, but then you would have to cut it in half.

This flavorful quinoa filling can be used for other kinds of squash, both winter and summer varieties.

8 acorn squashes (about 1 pound each)
½ pound (2 sticks) butter, melted
Coarse salt
2 cups raw quinoa
½ cup dark rum
1 cup seedless golden raisins
4 stalks lemon grass or grated rind of 2 lemons
12 scallions, tops and roots trimmed and discarded, finely chopped
⅛ teaspoon ground cloves
⅛ teaspoon ground nutmeg or mace
¼ teaspoon ground white pepper
1 cup chopped blanched hazelnuts or almonds or walnuts
1 tablespoon olive oil

1. Wipe the squash with a damp cloth. Cut off a piece about 1 inch from the top of each squash and save to serve as a lid. (Keep each lid with its corresponding bottom.) With a soup spoon, scoop out and discard the seeds. Trim the base just enough for the squash to stand upright. Brush the inside and the lid of each squash generously with some of the melted butter, sprinkle them all with about 2 teaspoons of salt, and set aside.

2. Prepare the quinoa as described on page 419, using 8 cups of cold water. Set aside.

3. Combine the rum and the raisins in a cup and let soak for about 15 minutes, or until ready to use.

(Continued)

4. Remove and discard the upper leaves and the tough outer layers of the lemon grass and mince the rest.

5. Preheat the oven to 375 degrees.

6. In a sauté pan, heat the remaining melted butter over medium heat. Stir in the lemon grass, scallions, cloves, nutmeg, pepper, and 1 tablespoon salt; sauté for 2 minutes. Add the raisins and soaking liquid and cook, stirring from time to time, until all the alcohol has evaporated, about 6 minutes. Add the chopped nuts, mix in the cooked quinoa, and continue to cook, stirring, for 5 minutes longer. Remove from the heat. Stir in the grated lemon rind, if using.

7. Fill and tightly pack the cavity of each squash with the quinoa mixture and fit its lid on top. Arrange the squash in a baking pan. Brush well all around with olive oil, add 2 cups of water, cover with aluminum foil, and bake for 30 minutes. Remove the foil and continue baking for 40 to 50 minutes, or until the squash is soft. Serve hot.

NOTE   The quinoa filling can be prepared in advance and stored in the refrigerator, tightly covered, for a few days. The squash may also be filled and refrigerated one day prior to cooking. Simply remove it from the refrigerator a few hours before baking, brush with olive oil, and bake as directed.

LIMA BEANS

Habas Frescas Dorados en Limón
Baby Lima Beans Braised in Lemon

Serves 6 to 8

Lima beans are excellent fresh, but they are not at all bad frozen. Fresh limas take a little longer to cook and absorb more water than frozen ones.

8 cups fresh or frozen baby lima beans (2½ pounds or 2 20-ounce packages)
8 tablespoons (1 stick) butter
Grated rind of 1 lemon (2 teaspoons)
3 tablespoons olive or vegetable oil
1 or 2 jalapeño peppers, seeded and finely chopped
1 cup pignolis, roasted (page 485)
Juice of 1 lemon
1 tablespoon coarse salt
12 scallions, roots and tops trimmed, thinly sliced
1 cup shredded or coarsely chopped fresh mint leaves

1. If fresh beans are used, rinse them. Place frozen beans in a strainer, rinse under cold running water, and drain.

2. With a fork, mash 4 tablespoons of the butter with the lemon rind.

3. In a sauté pan, melt the remaining 4 tablespoons of butter with the oil over medium heat. Stir in the hot pepper, pignolis, beans, 1½ cups water, the lemon juice, and salt. Bring to a boil, stirring. Lower the heat and simmer, stirring now and then, until the beans are barely tender and have absorbed all the liquid, about 8 minutes. If the beans are not tender and have absorbed all the water, add extra water and continue cooking. When the beans are done, mix in the scallions and remove from heat. Stir in the lemon butter and correct the seasoning with salt to taste. Garnish with the shredded mint leaves and serve.

Habas en Salsa de Aceittunas
Lima Beans in Olive Sauce

Serves 6 to 8

This dish of Peruvian origin is made with dried lima beans and those wonderful purple-black *aceittunas de botija*, which are called alfonso olives outside Peru. If they are unavailable, you can use Kalamatas or any other black olive with good flavor, such as lugano, gaeta, salona, royal (royal victoria), or morocco olives. The quality and flavor of the olive will determine the final personality of this dish.

2 pounds dried large lima beans (see Note)
2 dried ancho peppers, 1 roasted (page 483)
1 dried mirasol pepper, roasted (page 483)
½-inch piece fresh ginger, peeled and chopped
1 pound alfonso or Kalamata olives, pitted
3 tablespoons olive oil
3 large cloves garlic, peeled and minced

GARNISH
10 to 12 scallions, white parts only, julienned
*   and placed in ice water*
3 stalks celery, washed, strings removed, julienned,
*   and placed in ice water*

1. Rinse the lima beans under cold running water and place in a large container. Add 12 cups of water and let soak overnight.

2. Drain the beans, place them in a pot with 12 cups of water, and cook for 35 to 40 minutes. Remove from the heat and drain, discarding the cooking liquid. Remove 3 cups of hot beans and force them through a food mill or strainer until all the beans are mashed. Discard the skins and set the mashed beans aside. Set aside the whole beans.

3. Remove and discard the seeds from all the hot peppers and break them into small pieces into 1 cup of warm water. Add the chopped ginger and soak for 15 minutes.

4. Place the softened peppers and ginger with the soaking liquid in the jar of an electric blender and blend at top speed until smooth. Pour the mixture out and set aside. Put the pitted olives and 2 cups of water in the same jar and blend thoroughly until smooth. Set aside.

5. In a saucepan or an earthenware casserole, heat the olive oil over medium heat. Stir in the garlic; do not let it burn. Add the pepper-ginger mixture and cook, stirring now and then, for 10 minutes, or until most of the liquid has evaporated. Mix in the blended olives and cook, stirring now and then, for 3 minutes. Stir in the mashed beans, lower the heat, and continue to cook for 5 minutes. Add the whole beans and cook for 20 minutes, stirring gently from time to time. Remove from the heat. Combine and drain the julienned scallions and celery. Serve the beans hot, garnished with the julienned vegetables.

NOTE   Dried baby lima, Great Northern, or canary beans may be substituted for dried large lima beans.

CORN

Choclo Sancochado
Corn on the Cob
—

Corn is best when cooked right after picking. Next best is farm-fresh corn from a roadside stand or the market. Open the husks a bit to make sure that the kernels are small and milky inside and check for firmness by pressing them with your fingertips. If you must store corn, wrap the husks in a damp cloth or plastic bag and place in the refrigerator. When cooking corn, use plenty of water. Do not add salt while boiling; this will toughen the kernels.

In a large kettle bring to a boil enough water to cover the ears of corn. While the water is coming to a boil, husk the ears and remove and discard the silk. Drop the ears in the boiling water, let it return to a boil, and cook for 3 to 5 minutes. Do not overcook. Drain and serve immediately.

Another way to cook corn is to steam it over a bed of husks. Husk the ears and cover the bottom of a large pot with husks. Add enough water to come halfway up the bed of husks. Bring to a boil. Arrange the cobs on the bed, tightly cover the pot, and steam the corn for 3 to 5 minutes.

Picante de Choclo
Corn in a Picante Sauce

Serves 6 to 8

Hot peppers are the major flavoring in this interesting dish.

15 ears corn
3 or 4 dried mirasol or pasilla or ancho or New Mexico peppers,
*   seeded and cut into thirds*
2 tablespoons Achiote Oil (page 472) or Paprika Oil (page 474)
*   or olive oil*
1 tablespoon olive oil
1 clove garlic, minced
1 large onion, peeled and minced (about 1½ cups)
½ teaspoon ground cumin
½ teaspoon ground turmeric
1½ tablespoons coarse salt
1 egg at room temperature, lightly beaten
2 tablespoons chopped fresh cilantro leaves or dill or Italian parsley

GARNISH
1 tablespoon chopped fresh cilantro leaves or dill or Italian parsley
Boiled potatoes

1. Husk the corn and remove and discard the silk. Set aside 3 of the ears and cook the remaining 12 for 3 to 5 minutes. When cool enough to handle, slice off all the kernels, discarding the cobs. You should have about 8 cups. Set aside.

2. In a small bowl, soak the hot peppers in 2 cups of warm water for 15 to 20 minutes.

3. Slice off the kernels from the 3 reserved ears of corn. Place the kernels in the jar of an electric blender with 1 cup of cold water and blend thoroughly. Strain the blended corn into a bowl, pressing against the sieve to squeeze out all the juices. Discard the skins. Pour half the blended and strained corn back into the jar of the blender. Drain the hot peppers, discarding the water. Add them to the strained corn and

(Continued)

blend until smooth. Pour this mixture into the bowl containing the remaining blended corn. Set aside.

4. In a sauté pan, heat the achiote oil, olive oil, and minced garlic over medium heat. Do not burn the garlic. Stir in the onion, cumin, and turmeric and sauté for 2 minutes. Pour in the corn-pepper mixture, 1 cup of water, and salt and gently simmer for 20 to 25 minutes, stirring now and then.

5. Thoroughly mix in the cooked corn kernels and ½ cup of water and cook for 1 hour, stirring now and then.

6. Remove from the heat and stir in the beaten egg. Correct the seasoning with salt to taste and stir in the 2 tablespoons chopped herbs. Serve hot, garnished with the 1 tablespoon of chopped herbs, over warm boiled potatoes, sliced or whole.

Pepian de Choclo
Corn Pepian

Serves 6 to 8

This delicious corn dish is native to Peru. For a variety of textures, some of the corn is grated, some is pureed, and some is left whole. Sometimes pork or chicken is added. Cheese is not customarily used in a pepian, but I find it balances the overwhelming sweetness of most North American corn.

20 ears corn
2 large cloves garlic, peeled
1 tablespoon coarse salt
1 tablespoon ground cumin
¼ teaspoon ground white pepper
¼ cup red-wine vinegar
3 tablespoons Rendered Bacon Fat (page 476) or Rendered Duck Fat
    (page 475) or olive oil
2 medium onions, peeled and finely chopped
3 jalapeño peppers, seeded and finely chopped

6 to 8 ounces feta, cut into ⅛-inch dice
2 or 3 tablespoons butter (optional)
1 tablespoon chopped Italian parsley or fresh dill

1. Husk the corn and remove and discard the silk. Separate 6 ears and slice off all the kernels; you should have about 4½ cups. Set aside. Separate 7 ears and grate off all the kernels; you should have 2 cups.

2. Slice the kernels from the remaining 7 cobs. Place them in the jar of an electric blender, add 2 cups of cold water, and blend until smooth. Pour the blended corn through a strainer, pressing against the sides to squeeze out all the juices. Discard the skins. Mix the grated and blended corn together. You should have about 7½ cups. Set aside.

3. In a mortar with a pestle, pound the garlic, salt, cumin, and pepper to a smooth paste. Mix in the vinegar.

4. In an enameled saucepan, heat the fat. Add the onions and the pounded garlic mixture and sauté until the onions have wilted and all the liquid has evaporated, about 6 minutes. Stir in the hot peppers, and cook for 2 minutes. Add the 4½ cups of corn kernels and continue cooking for 5 minutes longer, stirring. Add the 7½ cups of grated and blended corn and cook over very low heat for 1 hour 30 minutes, stirring and scraping every 5 to 10 minutes to prevent the corn from sticking to the bottom of the pan.

5. Gently mix in the feta and continue cooking for 5 minutes. Remove from the heat, stir in the butter, if using, and correct the seasoning with salt to taste. Sprinkle with parsley and serve.

VARIATION

Cut up about 2 pounds of pork shoulder or chicken, preferably a stewing hen, into 1½-inch cubes. Proceed with the recipe through Step 3. Then marinate the cubes for several hours in the pounded garlic mixture. Transfer the meat with the marinating juices to the saucepan with hot fat at the beginning of Step 4 and brown all around. Transfer to a plate, sauté the onions, and proceed with the recipe. Return the meat with any accumulated juices to the saucepan with the grated and blended corn, stir, and cook until the meat is done.

Salpicón de Mote
Hominy Salpicón

Serves 6 to 8

Mote, or hominy, is cooked white corn. A staple food throughout the Andes, it is usually carried by the Quechuas in a little bag hanging from the shoulders and nibbled as a snack during the day.

9 cups canned hominy (6 16-ounce cans)
Juice of 1 lemon
1 large clove garlic, peeled
1 tablespoon coarse salt
1 tablespoon Pernod or fresh lemon or lime juice
2 teaspoons grated lemon rind
2 cups Mayonnaise Made with Milk (page 482) (without lemon juice or vinegar)
2 or 3 fresh jalapeño peppers, seeded, julienned, and placed in ice water
1 large carrot, peeled, cored, julienned, and placed in ice water
12 scallions, trimmed, julienned, and placed in ice water
6 celery stalks, washed, julienned, and placed in ice water
8 leaves Boston lettuce or radicchio (for lettuce-leaf cups) (optional)

1. Drain the hominy and rinse under cold running water. Toss with the lemon juice and drain thoroughly. Spread and roll the hominy in a large towel, pressing slightly to absorb all the moisture. Transfer to a large bowl and chill thoroughly in the refrigerator for about 1 hour, or until ready to use.

2. In a mortar with a pestle, pound the garlic and salt to a smooth paste. Add the Pernod and the lemon zest, mix well, and with a wire whisk, blend this mixture into the mayonnaise.

3. Combine all the julienned vegetables and drain them well, or use a salad spinner to remove all the water.

4. Remove the chilled hominy from the refrigerator, mix in the flavored mayonnaise, and correct the seasoning with salt to taste. Gently toss in all the vegetables and serve immediately in lettuce-leaf cups, if desired.

QUINOA

Quinua Sancochada
Boiled Quinoa
—

Cooked quinoa has almost limitless uses in the kitchen. Just a handful in a chowder, soup, stew, salad, or dessert will impart an interesting taste and added texture. Quinoa can also be served as an accompaniment to meat, seafood, or vegetables, or enjoyed on its own. All that's needed to bring out its flavor is salt. Some butter or olive oil and pepper will emphasize its nutty taste.

Commercially sold quinoa has been prewashed to remove the bitter saponin that coats it, but you should still rinse it under cold running water before cooking. It is best to boil quinoa in plain water and add seasonings after it has cooked. Allow about one-third cup raw quinoa per serving.

Pour 1 pound (about 2⅓ cups) of quinoa into a bowl of cold water and wash it, rubbing it between your hands. Drain. Repeat until the water is clear; it usually takes two washings. In a saucepan, combine the quinoa with 8 to 10 cups cold water. Bring to a boil, stirring now and then. Lower the heat and simmer for about 10 minutes, or until barely cooked. The quinoa is done when all the grains have turned translucent. Remove from the heat and pour through a strainer, draining well. Do not rinse. To help the quinoa cool faster, fluff it with a fork or spread it out on towels to cool. You should have about 7 cups of cooked quinoa. Serve or store in a tightly covered container in the refrigerator until ready to use.

Quinua a la Jardinera
Quinoa à la Jardinière

Serves 6 to 8

In this dish an array of uniformly diced vegetables emphasizes the texture of the quinoa. A far greater variety of vegetables can be used, or some of those suggested can be replaced; try fresh or frozen peas, cooked corn kernels, or beans. (Black beans, in particular, would give a nice touch of extra color.) You could also add some chopped roasted nuts—almonds, walnuts, black walnuts, or pecans—for contrast. Fresh herbs are a must: you could use mint, cilantro, oregano, basil, or even tarragon instead of thyme, dill, or parsley.

2 cups raw quinoa
3 or 4 tablespoons olive oil or butter
1-inch piece fresh ginger, peeled and minced
1 medium carrot, peeled, cored, and cut into ⅛-inch dice
1 small red onion, peeled and cut into ⅛-inch dice, or 6 scallions,
  roots and tops trimmed, thinly sliced
1 stalk celery, washed, strings removed, and cut into ⅛-inch dice
1 red bell pepper, seeded and cut into ⅛-inch dice
1 green bell pepper, seeded and cut into ⅛-inch dice
1 tablespoon coarse salt
¼ teaspoon ground white pepper
1 tablespoon fresh thyme leaves or chopped fresh dill or
  Italian parsley (optional)

1. Prepare the quinoa as described on page 419.

2. Meanwhile, in a saucepan, heat the olive oil with the ginger over medium heat. Add the carrot and sauté for 1 minute. Stir in the onion and cook, stirring, for 1 minute more. Add the celery, stir, then add the red and green peppers, salt, and white pepper. Sauté for about 2 minutes, or just long enough for the peppers to heat through. Stir in the hot quinoa and correct the seasoning with salt and white pepper to taste. Remove from the heat, sprinkle with the thyme leaves, if desired, and serve.

Salpicón de Quinua
Quinoa Salpicón

—

Serves 6 to 8

This salpicón is wonderful for a summer lunch.

1 pound raw quinoa (about 2⅓ cups)
¼ cup fresh lime juice
¼ teaspoon ground white pepper
1 teaspoon coarse salt
1 jalapeño or serrano pepper, seeded and finely chopped
½ cup olive oil
1 medium cucumber, peeled, seeded, and finely diced
1 medium tomato, seeded and finely diced
6 to 8 scallions, white parts only, finely sliced
⅓ cup chopped Italian parsley
⅓ cup chopped fresh mint leaves or dill

GARNISH
Radicchio or Boston lettuce leaves (or shredded radicchio
*   or Boston lettuce)*
Cornichons
Capers
Hard-boiled quail eggs
Rounds of corn on the cob
Feta cubes
Black olives

1. Prepare the quinoa as described on page 419. Let cool.

2. In a small bowl, combine the lime juice, white pepper, salt, and hot pepper. Gradually blend in the olive oil. Set aside.

3. In a large bowl, combine the cold quinoa with the cucumber, tomato, scallions, parsley, and mint. Toss gently. Add the lime juice-and-olive oil mixture and toss again. Correct the seasoning with salt and white pepper to taste. Serve in radicchio-leaf cups or in a nest of shredded radicchio and garnish as desired.

Frituras de Quinua
Quinoa Croquettes

Serves 6 to 8

⅔ cup raw quinoa
¼ cup all-purpose flour
3 tablespoons grated parmesan
2 teaspoons coarse salt
⅛ teaspoon ground white pepper
4 or 5 scallions, trimmed and finely chopped
3 tablespoons chopped Italian parsley
1 egg
1 egg yolk
¾ cup vegetable oil
Lemon wedges

1. In a strainer, rinse the quinoa under cold running water. Drain well. In a skillet, toast the quinoa over high heat, stirring constantly and scraping the bottom of the pan, for 5 minutes. Remove from the heat, transfer the grain to a 1½-quart saucepan, and add 1⅓ cups cold water. Bring to a boil, lower the heat, cover, and cook for 10 minutes, or until all the water has been absorbed. Remove from the heat and let cool.

2. In a bowl, combine the quinoa, flour, parmesan, salt, and pepper. Mix thoroughly. Add the scallions, parsley, egg, and egg yolk and blend until the mixture has the consistency of a soft dough.

3. In a sauté pan, heat the vegetable oil over medium heat. With a soup spoon, shape the mixture into egg shapes. Drop them gently into the hot oil and cook them until they are golden all around. Remove from the oil, drain on towels or paper towels, and serve hot or warm, garnished with lemon wedges.

RICE

Arroz Cocido
Steamed Rice
—

Rice can be boiled or steamed in plain water or stock, or steamed after sautéing it in a bit of oil, butter, or Rendered Duck Fat or Bacon Fat (pages 475–476). To give rice an interesting nutty flavor, immerse a quarter of an artichoke, choke removed, in the middle of the rice right after the water has been added. When the rice is done, remove and discard the artichoke.

In a saucepan, heat 1 tablespoon olive oil over low heat. Add 1 or 2 peeled and crushed garlic cloves and sauté, stirring, until the garlic is lightly brown on all sides, about 4 minutes. Do not burn the garlic. Remove and discard the garlic. Add 2 cups long-grain rice and sauté, stirring, for about 5 minutes. Add 4 cups of water. Bring to a boil over high heat, cover the saucepan tightly, and simmer over very low heat for 10 to 12 minutes, or until the rice has absorbed all the liquid. Fluff the rice with a fork, season with salt, and serve.

VARIATION

Substitute 1 small peeled and finely chopped onion for the garlic. Sauté in 2 tablespoons oil or fat until it starts to turn golden around the edges, about 5 minutes. Proceed with the recipe.

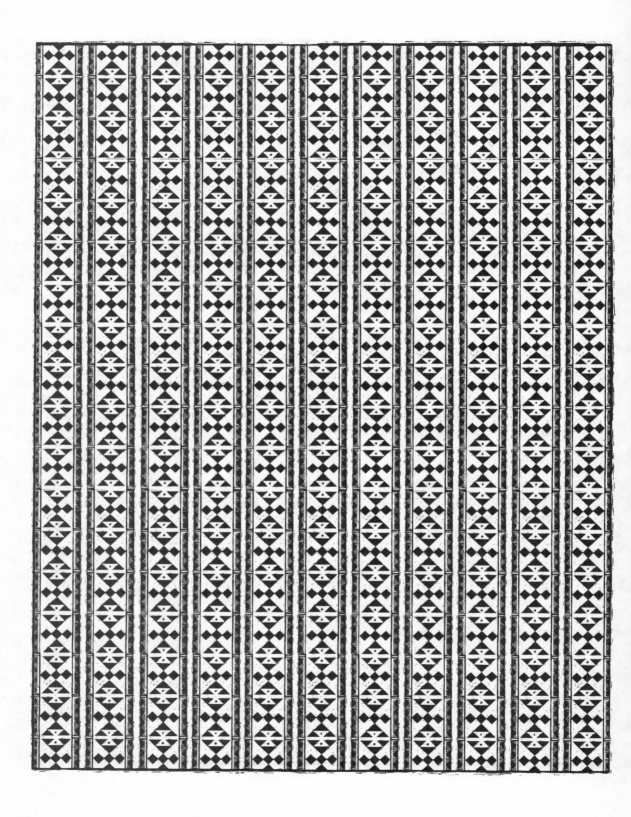

DESSERTS

FRUITS

Higos en Almibar
Poached Figs
—

Peritas en Champán
Pears in Champagne
—

Piña a la Parrilla en Salsa de Ron
Grilled Pineapple in Rum Sauce
—

Tomatitos en Salsa de Jengibre
Tomatoes Posing as Strawberries
—

Melocotones en Azafrán
Peaches in Saffron

PUDDINGS

Mazamorra Morada
Purple Pudding
—

Frijol Colado
Bean Pudding
—

Manjar de Quinua
Quinoa Pudding
—

Pudín de Coco
Coconut Pudding
—

Leche Asada con Laurel
Bay Leaf Pudding
—

Budín de Santa Rosa
Farina and Almond Pudding with
Blackberry Sauce

CAKES, PASTRIES, AND COOKIES

Keke de Quinua
Quinoa Cake
—

Alfajores
—

Turrón de Doña Pepa
—

Picarones
—

Maná
Manna

ICE CREAM

Helado de Camote
Mock Lucuma Ice Cream

A bowl laden with fruit and draped with clusters of grapes sitting in the middle of the table waiting for the meal to be finished—this is dessert for all South Americans. *Buñuelos*, puddings, pastries, pastelitos, poached fruit, and a host of other sweets play a role, but not as part of a meal. Rather, they are eaten in the morning with coffee, in the afternoon with tea, or as a snack, especially before bedtime.

There are many fine modern commercial pastry shops in South America, but traditionally the best *golosinas*, or sweets, are made in and sold by convents, which at one time had a monopoly on producing sweets. This tradition dates back to colonial times and is very much alive today. The convents have always taken great pride in their sweets and competed furiously with one another both to create the finest sweets and to attract customers. It is said that when nuns from different convents would meet and begin to discuss sweets, the discussion sometimes got so heated they would pull off one another's headdresses and start hitting each other!

FRUITS

Higos en Almibar
Poached Figs

—

Serves 6 to 8

In addition to their great taste and texture, fresh figs have a wonderful aromatic bouquet provided by the leaves. You can add a few to the poaching liquid with the spices, even omitting the spices altogether. Once the syrup has been reduced, discard the leaves or use them as a garnish.

12 fresh unripe figs, preferably Canadria or Kadota
2 cups sugar
12 to 15 juniper berries
6 to 8 allspice berries
1 3-inch cinnamon stick

1. With a damp cloth, gently wipe the figs and set them aside.

2. In an enameled or stainless-steel pot, combine the sugar, juniper berries, allspice berries, cinnamon, and 8 cups of water. Bring to a boil, lower the heat, and simmer for 15 to 20 minutes. Add the figs and continue to simmer for 20 to 25 minutes. With a wooden spoon, transfer the figs to a serving bowl and set aside.

3. Continue to cook the poaching liquid over medium heat until it has reduced to 2 to 2½ cups. Strain the liquid over the figs in the bowl and garnish with the cinnamon stick and a few of the juniper berries, discarding the rest of the juniper berries and the allspice berries. Serve chilled.

Peritas en Champán
Pears in Champagne

Serves 6 to 8

The final flavor of these poached pears depends on the quality of the champagne. It need not be the finest or the most expensive, just of decent quality. This principle, of course, applies to any wine used in cooking. In this recipe, white wine may be used in place of the champagne.

18 to 24 Seckel pears or 6 to 8 large unripe pears
6 cups dry champagne
1 cup sugar
2 3-inch cinnamon sticks
8 to 12 juniper berries
1 dried red chili pepper

1. With a vegetable peeler, carefully peel each pear, leaving the stem attached. Place the pears in an enameled or stainless-steel pot containing the champagne, sugar, cinnamon, juniper berries, and hot pepper. Bring to a boil, lower the heat, and gently simmer for about 35 minutes, or until the pears are tender.

2. With a wooden spoon, transfer the pears to a serving bowl. Continue to cook the poaching liquid over medium heat until reduced to 2 to 2½ cups, about 25 minutes. Pour the hot syrup over the pears in the bowl, along with the cinnamon sticks, hot pepper, and a few of the juniper berries (discard the rest). Serve chilled.

VARIATIONS

Substitute 18 to 24 tiny lady apples for the pears. Peel them, leaving the stems attached, and proceed with the recipe. Cook the apples for only 20 minutes, or until barely tender.

Add ½ cup cassis to the champagne in Step 1.

Peras en Vino Tinto
Poached Pears in Red Wine

—

Peel 8 unripe pears, leaving the stems attached. Combine with 6 cups red wine, 1 cup sugar, 3 3-inch cinnamon sticks, and 1 dried red chili pepper (omit the juniper berries). Cook for about 1 hour, testing from time to time after the first 20 minutes with a thin skewer or cake tester, until the pears are tender. Continue as in Step 2.

You may also poach the pears in a combination of 4 cups red wine and 2 cups port.

Piña a la Parrilla en Salsa de Ron
Grilled Pineapple in Rum Sauce

—

Serves 6

The pineapple, native to South America, has gained tremendous respect outside its homeland. Quite possibly it was called "pineapple" in English because it resembles a pine cone. In some other languages it is called *ananas,* from the word for it in the Tupi-Guaraní language of the Brazilian Indians.

A perfectly ripe pineapple is fantastically fragrant, and you can simply slice off the skin and enjoy it as is. Or you can sprinkle the slices with sugar and cinnamon and let them stand for a while to bring out the juice.

An even better way to present pineapple is to grill it. For this purpose, the pineapple must be hard and unripe and should be cut into rather thick slices. This recipe calls for one large pineapple to serve six; for eight servings, use two smaller pineapples cut into four slices each.

1 large unripe pineapple (about 4 pounds)
1 cup sugar
½ teaspoon ground cinnamon
¼ teaspoon ground cloves
½ cup dark rum

1. Cut off about 1 inch at the base and crown top of the pineapple, reserving the top for garnish. Stand the fruit up on the work table and with a large, sharp kitchen knife, slice off strips of skin, cutting down along the contours of the pineapple. Cut away any remaining eyes. Slice the pineapple crosswise into 6 even slices. With a corer or a sharp paring knife, remove and discard the core from each slice. Place the slices on a jelly-roll pan.

2. Preheat the broiler.

3. In a small bowl, combine the sugar, cinnamon, and cloves. Sprinkle half the mixture evenly over the pineapple slices. Place them in the broiler, as close as possible to the heat source, and quickly broil them until they are lightly golden, about 8 minutes. Remove the pan from the broiler, turn the slices, sprinkle them with the remaining sugar mixture, and continue broiling for another 5 minutes, or until golden.

4. Arrange the grilled slices on a serving platter. Add the rum and ¼ cup cold water and thoroughly deglaze the pan over low heat, scraping to loosen any bits of caramelized sugar. Pour the mixture through a strainer and over the pineapple slices. Garnish the platter with the reserved crown top and serve.

Tomatitos en Salsa de Jengibre
Tomatoes Posing as Strawberries

Serves 6 to 8

Tomatoes are absolutely delicious prepared as a dessert. In this dish, cherry tomatoes are treated like berries. They must be ripe yet firm enough to survive blanching. Handle them gently when peeling to keep them whole without damaging them.

You can also use the little yellow tomatoes that are shaped like teardrops. In many instances they are even sweeter than cherry tomatoes. Or combine the two kinds.

3 1-pint baskets cherry tomatoes (about 2½ pounds)
1 cup sugar
1 3-inch cinnamon stick
2½-inch piece fresh ginger, peeled and cut lengthwise into 3 slices
1 strip lemon rind

1. Blanch the tomatoes in boiling water for about 10 seconds. With a large slotted spoon, remove them from the water and when cool enough to handle, peel them: prick the surface of the skin with the sharp point of a paring knife close to the stem end and gently pull off the skin, being careful not to damage the flesh. Place the tomatoes in a serving bowl and set aside.

2. In an enameled or stainless-steel saucepan, combine the sugar, cinnamon, ginger, lemon rind, and 3 cups cold water. Bring to a boil, lower the heat, and simmer for about 35 minutes, or until the liquid has reduced to 2 cups. With a slotted spoon, remove and discard the ginger and lemon rind and pour the hot syrup over the tomatoes. Serve thoroughly chilled.

Melocotones en Azafrán
Peaches in Saffron

—

Serves 8

Saffron should be as fresh as possible, the stigmas intact, waxy, and soft. Saffron that is dry and crumbly has been stored improperly or been hanging around the grocer's shelves for too long. Powdered saffron is simply unacceptable. If good saffron is not available, poach the peaches without it.

8 large unripe peaches
1 cup sugar
⅛ teaspoon Spanish saffron
1 dried red chili pepper
8 to 12 allspice berries
2 bay leaves
1-inch piece fresh ginger, peeled and cut lengthwise into 3 slices

1. With a vegetable peeler, peel all the peaches and set them aside.

2. In an enameled or stainless-steel pot, combine the sugar, saffron, hot pepper, allspice berries, bay leaves, ginger, and 8 cups cold water. Bring to a boil, lower the heat, and simmer for 10 minutes. Add the peaches and gently simmer for about 30 minutes, or until they are tender. To test, pierce them with a thin wooden skewer or toothpick. When the skewer or toothpick goes halfway through easily, the peaches are done. With a wooden spoon, gently transfer the peaches from the poaching liquid to a serving bowl.

3. Continue to cook the poaching liquid over medium heat until it has reduced to 2 to 2½ cups, about 30 minutes. With a slotted spoon, remove and discard the ginger and all but a few of the allspice berries. Pour the hot syrup over the peaches in the bowl. Serve chilled.

PUDDINGS

Mazamorra Morada
Purple Pudding
—
Serves 6 to 8

Mazamorra morada is a classic pudding, popular throughout Peru and Ecuador. It is distinguished by its appetizing purple color, which comes from purple corn.

Sweet-potato flour, which adds natural sweetness, is the starch customarily used for this pudding. *Chuño* flour, from dried potatoes, is also used. It is similar to cornstarch, which I have used in this recipe.

How thick you make the pudding is pretty much a matter of personal taste. It can range from almost liquid to firm, depending on how much and what kind of starch is used. This recipe makes a rather firm pudding. For a looser texture, use a quarter of a cup less starch; for a firmer texture, a quarter of a cup more.

1½ to 2 pounds dried purple corn on the cob (see Note)
1 small pineapple, washed, top and bottom removed and discarded, and chopped with skin
2 pears, washed and chopped
2 peaches, washed and chopped, pits saved
2 quince or green apples, washed and chopped
1 3-inch cinnamon stick
8 cloves or allspice berries
1 lemon, quartered
1¼ cups sugar
8 dried peaches, cut in half (about 3½ ounces)
2 or 3 ounces dried mirabelles (see Note)
¾ cup cornstarch
Juice of 1 lime or lemon
Ground cinnamon

1. Rinse the corn and remove the kernels by twisting the cobs. Soak both kernels and cobs in 10 cups of cold water overnight.

2. Transfer the kernels and cobs to a large pot. Measure the soaking liquid and add enough water to make 15 cups. Add this to the corn in the pot. Then add the pineapple, pears, peaches, peach pits, quince, cinnamon stick, cloves, lemon, and sugar. Bring to a boil, lower the heat, and simmer for 2 to 2½ hours.

3. Remove from the heat; take out the corn cobs and strain the mixture, pressing against the strainer to extract all juices from the corn kernels, fruits, and spices. You should have 8 cups. If you don't, place the purple corn and the fruit back into the pot and add just enough water to cover the ingredients. Bring to a boil and simmer for 15 to 20 minutes. Remove from the heat, strain through a strainer lined with several layers of cheesecloth, and add the amount needed to make the 8 cups. Strain again through a fine sieve or a strainer lined with several layers of cheesecloth into an enameled saucepan. Add the dried peaches and mirabelles.

4. In a small bowl, combine 1 cup of the strained juice and the cornstarch. With a fork, mix thoroughly until the cornstarch has dissolved. Pour this mixture back into the enameled saucepan containing the juice and dried fruits. Bring to a boil over medium heat, whisking with a wire whisk. Continue cooking and whisking until the mixture is thick, 20 to 25 minutes.

5. Stir in the lime juice and remove from heat. Pour the pudding into a deep 2-quart serving dish, let cool, and serve, dusted with a bit of ground cinnamon.

NOTE Dried purple corn and dried mirabelles are available in food specialty stores.

Frijol Colado
Bean Pudding

—

Serves 6 to 8

*F*rijol colado traces its origins to the ancient towns of Ica and Chincha in southern Peru. There the hot pudding is poured into a *poto* or calabaza, a dry gourd with a thick, woody skin, then it is sprinkled with sesame seeds and left to stand for one or more days. The pudding absorbs the wonderful bouquet of the *poto*. It is served right from the gourd.

The usual bean for this pudding is *frijol canario,* or the yellow canary bean. Red kidney beans, as in this recipe, are also used. Dried white beans, like Great Northerns, would be a good substitute.

2 pounds dried red kidney beans
4-inch piece fresh ginger, cut lengthwise into 4 slices
2 3-inch cinnamon sticks
⅓ cup raw sesame seeds
½ teaspoon plus 2 tablespoons unsalted butter
4 cups whole milk
1 cup firmly packed dark brown sugar (½ pound)
Grated rind of 1 lemon
½ teaspoon ground cinnamon
¼ teaspoon ground cloves
⅛ teaspoon ground nutmeg

1. Rinse and soak the beans overnight in 3 quarts of water. Drain, place the beans in a large pot, and add 4 quarts of water, the ginger, and the cinnamon sticks. Bring to a boil, lower the heat, and cook until the beans are very tender, about 1 hour.

2. While the beans are cooking, place the sesame seeds, without any butter or oil, in a small skillet and lightly roast them over medium heat, constantly shaking the pan and stirring the seeds. This should not take more than a few minutes. Immediately pour the seeds onto a plate and set aside to cool.

3. Butter the bottom and sides of an $11 \times 8 \times 2$-inch baking dish or a 1½-quart serving dish with ½ teaspoon butter and coat with all but 1 tablespoon of the cooled sesame seeds. Place the dish in the refrigerator until ready to use.

4. When the beans are tender, remove them from the heat and drain, discarding the cooking liquid, ginger, and cinnamon sticks. While the beans are still hot, force them through a food mill in several batches into a bowl, adding a bit of the milk from time to time to moisten the pulp, leaving only the skins on the disk of the food mill; discard them. Repeat until all the beans have been forced through and about 2 cups of milk is left.

5. Transfer the pureed beans to an enameled saucepan, blend in the remaining milk, and mix in the brown sugar, grated lemon rind, cinnamon, cloves, and nutmeg. Bring to a boil over medium-low heat, constantly stirring and scraping the bottom of the pan with a wooden spoon. After the mixture has come to a boil, place the saucepan on a "flame tamer" and cook over extremely low heat, stirring now and then, and scraping the bottom of the pan to prevent the mixture from sticking, for 1 hour 20 minutes, or until the spoon leaves a track on the bottom of the pan. Add the 2 remaining tablespoons of butter and beat the pudding vigorously for a few minutes, or until fluffy and lighter in color.

6. Remove the prepared dish from the refrigerator, spoon in the pudding, smooth the surface, and sprinkle the remaining sesame seeds on top. Let cool thoroughly. Serve at room temperature, accompanied by a warm crusty white bread.

Manjar de Quinua
Quinoa Pudding

—

Serves 6 to 8

3 cups raw quinoa
⅓ cup raisins
½ cup dark rum
3 cups whole milk
2 cups heavy cream
2 cups sugar
½ teaspoon coarse salt
1 scant teaspoon ground cinnamon
¼ teaspoon ground cloves
½ cup freshly grated coconut meat or packaged unsweetened
grated coconut (optional)
3 egg yolks

GARNISH
Ground cinnamon
Crème fraîche

1. Place the quinoa in a fine sieve and wash under cold running water. Drain. In a large pot, combine 8 cups of cold water and the quinoa. Bring to a boil, stirring now and then. Lower the heat and simmer for about 10 minutes, or until the quinoa is cooked. (It is done when the grains have turned from white to translucent.) Remove from the heat and pour through a strainer. Do not rinse. Set aside and let drain.

2. In a cup, soak the raisins in the rum for about 10 minutes. Set aside.

3. In an enameled or stainless-steel saucepan, combine the quinoa, milk, cream, sugar, salt, cinnamon, and cloves and bring to a boil over low heat, stirring now and then to prevent sticking and burning. Turn the heat down as low as possible or use a "flame tamer" and cook for 15 to 20 minutes, stirring frequently, until most of the liquid has evaporated and the mixture has a thick puddinglike consistency. Mix in the raisins and rum and the coconut, if using, and continue cooking for 5 to 10 minutes, stirring constantly, until all the moisture has evaporated and the spoon leaves a track when moved across the bottom of the saucepan.

4. Remove the pan from the heat and add the 3 egg yolks, beating continuously and vigorously. Continue beating until the yolks have been thoroughly absorbed. Pour the pudding into a shallow earthenware, porcelain, or glass dish. Sprinkle the surface lightly and evenly with ground cinnamon and let cool to room temperature. Serve, garnished with a dot of crème fraîche.

STORAGE NOTE   After the pudding has cooled to room temperature, it can be stored, tightly covered, in the refrigerator for up to 1 week.

Pudín de Coco
Coconut Pudding
—

Serves 6 to 8

This pudding is glazed with a caramel made with annatto seeds. When the custard is unmolded, the glaze melts into a spectacular orange-amber sauce.

2 coconuts

CARAMEL
1½ cups sugar
8 cloves
1 dried red chili pepper
1 tablespoon annatto seeds

CUSTARD
4 cups milk
1 cup sugar
1 3-inch cinnamon stick
½ cup plus 1 tablespoon manioc flour (see Note)
Grated rind of 1 lemon
18 egg yolks

1. With a pointed instrument, such as an ice pick, pierce two of the three soft "eyes" of the coconuts and pour off the whitish liquid. You should have about 1½ cups from both coconuts. If not, add enough water to make 1½ cups. Set aside. Crack the coconuts open and remove the meat. Peel off and discard the brown skins. Grate half of 1 coconut to make 1 loosely packed cup.

2. In a small pot, combine the sugar, cloves, hot pepper, annatto seeds, and ½ cup of cold water. Bring to a boil over medium heat and cook for 15 to 20 minutes, or until the mixture has reached the consistency of a light caramel (about 295 to 300 degrees on a candy thermometer). Remove from the heat, pour into a 2-quart baking dish, and immediately coat to glaze the bottom and sides of the dish thoroughly. Set aside to cool.

3. Place half of the chopped coconut pieces in the jar of an electric blender. Add half of the milk and blend until smooth. Pour into an enameled or stainless-steel pot. Repeat with the remaining half of the coconut meat and the milk. Rinse the jar of the blender with the reserved coconut liquid and add this to the pot. Mix in the sugar, add the cinnamon stick, and bring to a boil over medium heat, stirring with a wooden spoon. Lower the heat and simmer for 10 to 15 minutes, stirring now and then.

4. Remove from the heat, take out and discard the cinnamon stick, and blend again in several batches while hot. While the blended mixture is still hot, strain it in several batches through a strainer lined with a double layer of cheesecloth into an enameled pot. Gather the ends of the cheesecloth and twist the cloth to squeeze out all the juices from the coconut pulp. Discard the dry pulp. Repeat with the remaining coconut mixture. You should have about 7 cups of coconut milk. If not, add enough milk or cream to make 7 cups.

5. Whisk the manioc flour into the coconut milk. Add ½ cup of the reserved grated coconut and bring to a boil over medium heat, stirring constantly with a wire whisk. Lower the heat and cook, stirring, for 8 to 10 minutes. Remove from the heat and beat the mixture until cool. Add the grated lemon rind and the remaining grated coconut.

6. Preheat the oven to 350 degrees.

7. Place the egg yolks in a bowl and with a wire whisk, beat thoroughly. Then beat in half of the cooled coconut mixture; when incorporated, blend in the other half. Pour the mixture into the prepared baking dish. Place the dish into a larger one containing enough boiling water to reach two-thirds up the sides of the pudding. Bake in the lower level of the oven for 1 hour 45 minutes. Remove from the oven and set aside, without taking the baking dish out of the hot water. Let stand, undisturbed, for 30 minutes.

8. Remove the baking dish from the water. Let cool thoroughly for about 8 hours in a cool spot, or overnight in the refrigerator. Loosen the edges of the pudding by running a sharp paring knife all around the dish. Unmold and serve.

NOTE   Manioc flour is available in food specialty stores.

Leche Asada con Laurel
Bay Leaf Pudding

Serves 6 to 8

The pungent leaves of the bay tree are used mainly as a flavoring for savory dishes. It is quite unusual and exciting to find a bay leaf in a sweet pudding, as in this recipe. The bay leaf lends the pudding a delicate tone.

CARAMEL
1 cup sugar
1 bay leaf

CUSTARD
8 egg yolks
4 whole eggs
1 cup sugar
2 teaspoons vanilla extract
4 cups whole milk
1 cup heavy cream

1 large bay leaf

1. In a small saucepan, combine the sugar, bay leaf, and ¼ cup of water. Cook over medium heat until the sugar turns light amber (295 to 300 degrees on a candy thermometer). Remove the caramelized bay leaf and set aside. Pour the caramel into a 2½-quart baking dish, coating the entire bottom and sides. Immediately invert the dish over wax paper and set aside to cool.

2. In a large bowl, combine the egg yolks, whole eggs, sugar, and vanilla and with a wire whisk, beat until the mixture is pale yellow. Thoroughly mix in the milk and cream.

3. Preheat the oven to 350 degrees.

4. Pour the mixture into the caramel-coated dish and place it in a larger one containing enough boiling water to reach two-thirds up the sides of the pudding. Place in the lower level of the oven. Place the bay leaf in the center of the custard and bake for 50 minutes to 1 hour. Remove from the oven and lift out the baking dish containing the pudding. Let cool thoroughly at room temperature or overnight in the refrigerator. Place the reserved caramelized bay leaf next to and slightly overlapping the baked one and serve.

NOTE   If the pudding is refrigerated, it can be unmolded onto a serving platter. Garnish the center with the reserved caramelized bay leaf and serve.

Budín de Santa Rosa
Farina and Almond Pudding with Blackberry Sauce

—

Serves 8 to 12

8 cups whole milk
1½ cups farina
1 cup sugar
1 heaping cup blanched almonds, ground (6 ounces)
¼ teaspoon orange extract or 1 teaspoon vanilla extract

GARNISH
Blackberry Sauce (recipe follows)
Cranberry Sauce (recipe follows)

1. In an enameled or stainless-steel pot, whisk the milk with a wire whisk as you add the farina in a thin stream. Mix in the sugar and ground almonds. Stir in the orange extract and cook over medium heat, stirring constantly with a wire whisk, until the mixture becomes quite thick and starts to boil, 12 to 15 minutes. Remove from the heat.

2. Pour the pudding into a 2-quart serving dish. Set aside to cool. Serve at room temperature, accompanied by one or both fruit sauces.

VARIATIONS

Pour the pudding into an 8-cup loaf pan or terrine instead of the serving dish in Step 2 and refrigerate. To serve, unmold and slice the pudding.

Soak ½ cup seedless raisins in ½ cup rum for about 10 minutes. Mix the raisins and soaking liquid into the pudding halfway through the cooking.

Salsa de Moras

Blackberry Sauce

—

Makes 5½ cups

5 half-pint containers fresh blackberries (about 7 cups)
1 cup sugar
Juice of 1 lemon
¼ cup light rum (optional)

1. Set aside 1 container of blackberries. In the jar of an electric blender, blend half of the remaining blackberries with half the sugar, lemon juice, and rum, if using, until smooth. Repeat with the remaining berries, sugar, lemon juice, and rum. Force the sauce through a strainer until only the seeds are left. Discard them.

2. With a sharp knife, slice the reserved blackberries in half crosswise and fold them into the strained sauce. Let cool.

VARIATION

Substitute raspberries for the blackberries. Use the same quantity, reserving 1 pint of whole raspberries to fold into the sauce at the end.

Salsa de Cranberry

Cranberry Sauce

—

Makes 5 cups

10 cups fresh or frozen cranberries (3 12-ounce packages)
4 cups sugar
1 3-inch cinnamon stick
2-inch piece fresh ginger, peeled and cut lengthwise into 4 slices

1. Set aside 2 cups of cranberries.

2. In an enameled or stainless-steel saucepan, stir together the sugar, 1 cup cold water, cinnamon, and ginger. Place the saucepan over low heat and cook without stirring until the sugar has caramelized, about 18 minutes. Add the 8 cups of cranberries, mix well, and cook, stirring now and then, for 8 to 10 minutes, or until the berries have totally collapsed.

3. Remove from the heat, take out and reserve the cinnamon stick, and pour the sauce through a strainer or a food mill. Press out all the pulp from the cranberries until only the skins remain in the strainer or food mill. Add ½ cup of warm water to the strainer or food mill and continue to press out all of the remaining pulp from the skins.

4. Pour the sauce back into the saucepan in which it was cooked, add the reserved cinnamon stick, and bring to a gentle boil over low heat. Cook for about 10 minutes. Mix in the reserved whole cranberries and cook for another 5 minutes. Remove from the heat and let cool.

CAKES, PASTRIES, AND COOKIES

Keke de Quinua
Quinoa Cake

—

Serves about 8

1½ cups raw quinoa
6 tablespoons unsalted butter, softened
¾ cup firmly packed dark brown sugar
1 teaspoon ground cinnamon
¼ teaspoon ground cloves
2 teaspoons vanilla extract
1 teaspoon grated lemon rind
¼ cup dark rum
4 large eggs
½ cup milk
½ cup heavy cream
½ cup finely chopped walnuts

GARNISH
½ tablespoon confectioners' sugar
Crème fraîche or whipped cream

1. Place the quinoa in a fine sieve, rinse under cold running water, and drain.

2. In a saucepan, combine the quinoa with 8 cups cold water. Bring to a boil, lower the heat, and simmer for about 10 minutes, or until the quinoa is barely tender. Do not overcook. Remove from the heat, pour the quinoa through a fine strainer, and let drain. Do not rinse.

3. Butter an 8-inch round cake pan with about 1 tablespoon of the butter. Set aside.

4. In a mixing bowl, with a wire whisk, cream together the remaining butter, the sugar, cinnamon, cloves, vanilla, lemon rind, rum, and eggs until the sugar has dissolved. Add the milk and heavy cream and mix thoroughly.

(Continued)

5. Preheat the oven to 350 degrees.

6. In another mixing bowl, combine the quinoa and walnuts. Thoroughly fold in the creamed butter mixture and pour into the prepared baking pan.

7. Bake the cake for 1 hour 30 minutes. Remove from the oven, place on a rack, and allow to cool thoroughly. Unmold the cake by placing a plate over the cake pan and turning the two upside down. Then turn the plate right side up, onto a cake plate or serving platter. Place the confectioners' sugar in a fine sieve and lightly dust over the surface of the cake. Serve with crème fraîche.

VARIATION

The cake may be glazed, when cool. Combine 2 cups sugar, ½ cup water, and 6 to 8 cloves in a small saucepan. Cook over low heat, without stirring, for about 8 minutes, or to the thread stage (230 to 234 degrees on a candy thermometer). Mix in the juice of 1 lemon. Remove and discard the cloves. Place the cake on a rack, pour the syrup onto the center of the cake, and using a rubber spatula, cover the entire surface, letting the syrup drip down the sides.

Alfajores

Makes 28 pastries

Manjar blanco, or milk pudding, is eaten by itself or used as a filling for a variety of sweets. Cooking the pudding is somewhat time-consuming, but once it's made, it keeps for several weeks. Then it can be used as a pudding, a spread for toast, a replacement for jam, or as a snack with a piece of warm crusty white bread.

Manjar blanco, also called *dulce de leche,* is an essential part of many pastries, especially alfajores. The filling of alfajores, made with either fresh or condensed milk, is always the same, more or less, but the pastry varies, depending on where it is made and on personal taste. It can be either a flaky dough resembling puff pastry, or a type of cookie dough. One of the lightest, most delicate, and delicious pastries of all is made with eggs, as in this recipe.

PASTRY
3¼ cups all-purpose flour
½ teaspoon baking powder
5 tablespoons shortening
20 large egg yolks
3 tablespoons pisco (Peruvian brandy) or light rum

MILK PUDDING
8 cups whole milk
2 cups sugar
1 4-inch cinnamon stick

¼ cup confectioners' sugar

1. Sift 3 cups of the flour and the baking powder into a bowl and set aside.

2. In a small saucepan, melt the shortening.

3. In a bowl, beat the egg yolks while slowly adding the melted shortening and pisco. Add the sifted flour with the baking powder and mix well until the dough is smooth.

4. Preheat the oven to 375 degrees.

(Continued)

5. On a pastry board dusted with the remaining flour, roll out the dough about ⅛ to 1/16 inch thick—the thinner the better. With a cookie cutter, cut the dough into 4- to 4½-inch circles. Place the circles on a baking sheet lined with parchment paper, prick them several times with the tines of a fork, and bake them for 15 to 20 minutes, or until barely golden. Remove from the oven and place the pastries on a rack to cool.

6. In an enameled saucepan, combine the milk, sugar, and cinnamon stick and bring to a boil, stirring. Lower the heat as low as possible and simmer for 4½ hours, stirring with a wooden spoon every 5 minutes for the first 2½ hours and then continuously for the remaining time, or until the milk mixture has a puddinglike consistency and the spoon leaves a track on the bottom of the pan (see Note). Remove from heat and beat the pudding for a few minutes with the wooden spoon until smooth and light in color. Let cool. The pudding is now ready to be used.

7. To assemble the pastries, place 2 tablespoons of the cooled milk pudding onto the center of the flat side of a pastry circle and place another pastry circle, flat side down, on top, to resemble a sandwich. Repeat with the remaining pastry circles and filling. Place the confectioners' sugar in a strainer, lightly dust the alfajores, and serve.

NOTE   If the milk sticks or starts to burn on the bottom of the saucepan while simmering, stop stirring and immediately pour the milk through a strainer into a clean enameled saucepan. Add the cinnamon stick and continue simmering.

Manjar Blanco

Quick Milk Pudding

—

Makes 4 cups

5 14-ounce cans sweetened condensed milk (8½ cups)
1 4-inch cinnamon stick

1. Combine the milk and cinnamon stick in an enameled saucepan. Bring to a boil, lower the heat to very low, and let simmer, stirring and scraping the bottom of the pan every 10 to 15 minutes to prevent the pudding from sticking to the pan, for 2½ hours, or until the mixture has a puddinglike consistency and the spoon leaves a track on the bottom of the pan. If the milk sticks or starts to burn while simmering, stop stirring and strain it into a clean enameled saucepan. Add the cinnamon stick and continue simmering.

2. Remove from the heat and beat the pudding for a few minutes with a spoon until light in color. Let cool.

Turrón de Doña Pepa

Serves 8

The October festival in Lima arrives and like magic, peddlers appear everywhere carrying large wooden boards laden with turrón de doña pepa, the traditional holiday pastry. It is the feast of Cristo Morado, also called Señor de los Milagros, or the Gentleman of Miracles, because of the great number of miracles attributed to him.

DOUGH
4¼ cups all-purpose flour
½ teaspoon coarse salt
*1 cup chilled lard or Rendered Bacon Fat (page 476) or Duck Fat
    (page 475) or ½ cup vegetable shortening plus
    ½ cup softened butter*
6 large egg yolks
½ cup anisette (see Note)

SYRUP
1 cup fresh orange juice
Juice of 1 lemon
1½ cups firmly packed dark brown sugar
½ cup white sugar

GARNISH
½ teaspoon tiny multicolored candy sprinkles
1 teaspoon larger colored candy sprinkles

1. Sift 4 cups of the flour and the salt into a bowl. Add the fat and with your fingertips, incorporate quickly until it is distributed through the flour and the mixture has a mealy consistency. Place the egg yolks in a cup, add the anisette, and beat with a fork until well mixed. Make a hollow in the center of the flour-and-fat mixture, pour in the eggs, and work the mixture into a smooth dough. Divide it into 36 equal portions.

2. Preheat the oven to 350 degrees.

3. Place the remaining flour in the corner of a pastry board and use some of it to dredge the board lightly (or use a marble slab, with no additional flour). Take one portion of the dough and with the heel of your hand, flatten it into a 5 × 2-inch strip. Push the sides of the dough toward the center, dip your hand lightly into the flour, pressing against the board or slab, and roll the dough into a 5 × ¼-inch stick, like a cigar. Place the pastry stick on a baking sheet lined with parchment paper. Repeat until all 36 portions of dough have been rolled up.

4. Place the baking sheet in the middle level of the oven and bake for 40 to 45 minutes, or until the sticks are barely golden. Remove from the oven and with a spatula, very gently transfer the sticks to a rack to cool.

5. To make the syrup, combine the orange juice and lemon juice in a small saucepan with the brown and white sugars. Place the saucepan over very low heat and cook, without stirring, for about 1 hour, or until the sugar starts to bubble halfway up the pan (255 to 260 degrees on a candy thermometer). Remove from the heat and let cool for 15 to 20 minutes, or until the syrup starts to thicken and the spoon leaves a light track on the bottom of the pan.

6. To assemble, place 12 of the pastry sticks in an even line (touching one another) on a small cutting board, marble slab, or serving platter. Spoon some of the syrup over the pastry to coat well. Arrange a row of 6 sticks in the opposite direction, close together on top, and then another row of 6 alongside it. Coat with more syrup. Place the remaining 12 sticks in the opposite direction, close together on top. Spoon the remaining syrup over the entire stack to coat well. Garnish the finished pastry by sprinkling with the tiny colored sprinkles and then with the larger ones. Let stand for several hours, then cut into individual portions and serve.

NOTE   You can substitute anise syrup for the anisette. In a small saucepan, combine 2 tablespoons of aniseed, ¼ cup sugar, and 1 cup water and cook over low heat until the mixture has reduced by about half or more. Let cool or chill thoroughly, then strain through a fine sieve. Proceed with the recipe.

STORAGE NOTE   This pastry keeps well, without refrigeration, for a few days. Keep it in a cool spot.

Picarones

Makes 28 picarones

Picarones are always served hot or warm, accompanied by a light, aromatic sugar syrup. It is customary to eat them with your hands: press the picarones against the plate to absorb the syrup, then lick the syrup off your fingers.

1 cup lukewarm milk (100 to 115 degrees)
1 tablespoon sugar
1 tablespoon yeast
2 tablespoons cornstarch
3 pounds baked butternut squash (see Note) or 2½ pounds
  Baked Sweet Potatoes (page 390)
⅛ teaspoon coarse salt
2 cups all-purpose flour

SYRUP
1 cup firmly packed dark brown sugar
1 cup white sugar
2 4-inch cinnamon sticks
1 dried red chili pepper, seeded
4 to 6 cloves

6 cups vegetable oil

1. In a small mixing bowl, combine the milk, sugar, and yeast and let stand in a draft-free place to proof, 10 to 15 minutes. Stir in the cornstarch and let stand a few minutes longer.

2. Peel the squash or sweet potato and pass through a fine sieve. You should have 1 cup. Place in a large bowl, add the salt and the yeast-cornstarch mixture, and blend thoroughly. Fold in the flour and continue to stir vigorously to make a soft, well-blended dough.

3. Place the mixing bowl in a draft-free place, cover with a wet cloth or plastic wrap, and let rise for about 2 hours, or until double in bulk. Punch the dough down with a wooden spoon. At this point the dough should be soft and somewhat elastic.

4. To make the syrup, combine the brown sugar, white sugar, cinnamon sticks, hot pepper, cloves, and 1 cup water in a small saucepan. Slowly cook over low heat for 20 to 25 minutes, stirring occasionally, until the mixture thickens into a syrup. Set aside to cool.

5. In a large sauté pan or deep fryer, heat the oil to 325 degrees. Scoop out 1 tablespoonful of the dough and with another tablespoon, scrape the dough into the hot oil. Fry until golden. Repeat until all the dough is fried. Remove the picarones from the oil with a slotted spoon and drain on paper towels.

6. Pour syrup to taste over the picarones and serve.

NOTE To bake the squash, preheat the oven to 400 degrees. Cut the squash in half, scoop out the seeds, and rub the inside and outside with olive oil. Place the squash in a baking dish with 1 cup of water, cover the dish with aluminum foil, and bake for 20 minutes. Remove the foil and bake for another 35 minutes, or until the squash is soft when pierced with a fork.

Maná
Manna
—
Makes 24 cookies

Manna was the food that fell from heaven to nourish the Israelites as they crossed the desert to the Promised Land. These cookies are among the favorite sweets made in the convents by nuns.

2 cups blanched and roasted hazelnuts (page 485)
Grated rind of 1 lemon
½ cup sugar
2 eggs, separated
1 whole egg
½ cup all-purpose flour
2 cups confectioners' sugar

(Continued)

1. Grind the nuts and place in a bowl. Mix in the grated lemon rind and sugar. Fold in the 2 egg yolks (save the whites in a bowl) and the whole egg and knead until all the ingredients are well incorporated.

2. On a pastry board, divide the flour into two equal portions. Place the hazelnut mixture into the middle of one portion and knead to incorporate the flour until the dough becomes pliable enough to be rolled into an 18 × 1½-inch roll. With a knife, cut the roll crosswise into 24 equal pieces, each about ¾ inch thick.

3. Preheat the oven to 375 degrees.

4. Lightly flour your hands with the remaining flour and form each piece of dough into a ball between the palms of your hands. Place them on a baking sheet lined with parchment paper. Place in the middle level of the oven and lower the heat to 350 degrees. Bake for 12 to 15 minutes, or until still pale but firm to the touch. Remove from the oven and transfer the cookies to a rack to cool.

5. Put the cookies in the bowl containing the egg whites and toss until they are well coated and have absorbed most of the egg whites. Transfer them to another bowl containing the confectioners' sugar. Shake the bowl to coat the cookies all around with a generous amount of sugar. Let the cookies stand for about 1 hour for the sugar to dry. Serve.

ICE CREAM

Helado de Camote
Mock Lucuma Ice Cream

Makes about 2½ quarts

One of the fruits I love best is *lucuma*, which grows in the highlands of Peru, Ecuador, Colombia, and northern Chile. Its firm and perfumed flesh is bright yellow or orange with a rich, starchy texture that resembles perfectly baked sweet potatoes, which I have used in this recipe.

5 to 5½ pounds Baked Sweet Potatoes (page 390)
4 cups heavy cream
1 cup sugar
⅛ teaspoon coarse salt
¼ teaspoon ground mace
1 teaspoon vanilla extract
4 egg yolks
Grated peel of 1 orange
¼ cup chopped walnuts

1. Peel the sweet potatoes, force the pulp through a strainer into a bowl, and let cool. Place the bowl over ice to cool thoroughly. Mix in 1 cup heavy cream, a little at a time, and set aside until ready to use, stirring now and then.

2. In a saucepan, combine the remaining cream, sugar, salt, mace, and vanilla extract and heat over low heat until lukewarm.

3. In a bowl, beat the egg yolks with a wire whisk or an electric beater until pale yellow. Continue to beat as you add the flavored cream in a thin stream.

4. Pour the egg-yolk mixture into the top of a double boiler over simmering water. Add the orange peel and cook, stirring, until the mixture is thick enough to coat the back of a spoon lightly, about 8 minutes. Transfer the custard to a bowl and let it cool, stirring now and then. Place the bowl over ice and let it cool thoroughly by stirring with a wire whisk until the mixture is frothy and very thick.

5. Stir in the chilled sweet-potato mixture a bit at a time until it is all incorporated and place in the freezer or an ice cream machine. If using an ice cream machine, follow the manufacturer's directions. If not, freeze the mixture for several hours until settled and hard. Break into small pieces, transfer to the work bowl of a food processor, and pulse until smooth. Immediately freeze the mixture again for several hours and repeat this operation. Leave the ice cream in the freezer until ready to use. Just before serving, remove the ice cream from the freezer to soften slightly. Serve, sprinkled with the chopped walnuts, if desired.

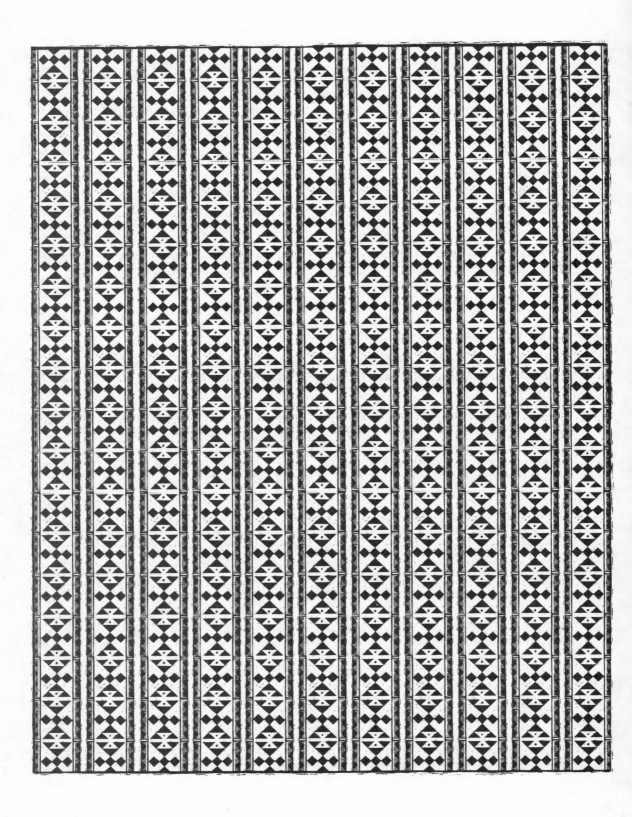

BASICS

STOCKS

Caldo de Pollo
Chicken Stock

Caldo de Carne
Beef Stock

Caldo de Ternera
Veal Stock

Caldo de Cordero
Lamb Stock

Caldo de Pescado
Fish Stock

Caldo de Camarones
Shrimp Stock

Caldo de Vegetales
Vegetable Stock

CORN BEER

Chicha de Jora
Corn Beer

OILS AND FATS

Esencia de Achiote
Achiote Oil

Esencia de Curry
Curry Oil

Esencia de Pimentón
Paprika Oil

Manteca de Pato
Rendered Duck Fat

Manteca de Chancho
Rendered Bacon Fat

Mantequilla Clarificada
Clarified Butter

SAUCES

Salsa de Culantro
Cilantro Sauce

Salsa de Albahaca
Basil Sauce

Salsa de Perejil
Parsley Sauce

Salsa Cruda
—

Encurtido de Cebollas
Onion Relish

Mayonesa de Leche
Mayonnaise Made with Milk

BASIC TECHNIQUES

Asar Ajíes
Roasting Fresh Hot Peppers

Asar Ajísecos
Roasting Dried Hot Peppers

Asar Pimientos
Roasting Bell Peppers

Pelar Cebollas de Perla
Peeling Pearl Onions

Asar Nueces
Roasting Nuts

Pelar Pistachos
Peeling Pistachios

Limpieza de Mejillones
Cleaning Mussels

Limpieza de Almejas
Cleaning Clams

Limpieza de Calamares
Cleaning Squid

Sancochar Pulpo
Blanching Octopus

Sasonar Vinagres
Flavored Vinegars

STOCKS

Caldo de Pollo
Chicken Stock

Makes about 3 quarts

Chicken stock is the most versatile of all the meat stocks: it can be substituted for beef, veal, and other meat stocks, and fish and vegetable stocks as well. Chicken stock is also the quickest of the meat stocks to prepare. To be good, chicken stock must have good bouquet, good flavor, good body, and good color—light amber in hue.

4½ to 5 pounds chicken bones, backs, necks, gizzards, heads, and feet (but no livers)
3 stalks celery with leafy tops, washed and cut into large pieces
1 large carrot, washed and cut into large pieces
2 medium onions, unpeeled and quartered
6 cloves garlic, unpeeled
2-inch piece fresh ginger, sliced (optional)
2 or 3 dried red chili peppers or 8 to 10 black peppercorns
8 to 10 sprigs fresh thyme or 1 or 2 bay leaves
8 to 10 stems Italian parsley
4 to 6 cloves

1. In a 10-quart stockpot, combine all the ingredients with 7 quarts of cold water. Bring to a boil, lower the heat, and simmer, uncovered, for 2 hours, skimming off the foam as it rises to the surface.

2. Remove from the heat and strain through a fine sieve or a strainer lined with 1 or 2 layers of cheesecloth. Discard the bones and vegetables. Degrease by scooping all the fat off with a ladle in a circular motion. The stock is now ready to be used. If it is not used immediately, store it in the refrigerator without degreasing it. Degrease the stock when it is to be used by removing the hardened layer of fat from the surface.

(Continued)

Chicken stock will keep in the refrigerator in perfect condition for up to 5 days if tightly covered. To lengthen the life of the stock after 5 days without freezing, bring it to a full boil, let cool slightly, and return it to the refrigerator, tightly covered. To store the stock for a longer period of time, it must be frozen. Once it has been defrosted, it must be used immediately. Do not refrigerate or refreeze. Always store stock in a nonreactive container, such as plastic, glass, or stainless steel.

Caldo de Carne
Beef Stock

Makes about 8 quarts

4 large onions, unpeeled and cut into eighths (about 3½ pounds)
2 to 3 leeks, trimmed, washed, and cut into 3 pieces each
   (about 1 pound)
1 whole head garlic, unpeeled, cut in half horizontally
8 stalks celery with leafy tops, washed and cut into pieces
2 small carrots, washed and sliced
6 pounds beef bones, preferably marrow and knuckle bones
8 pounds veal bones, preferably shank, knuckle bones, and feet,
   or a combination
1 oxtail, cut into small pieces
8 cloves
2 bay leaves
35 sprigs fresh thyme
24 black peppercorns
2 or 3 jalapeño or arbol peppers or 1 or 2 dried red chili peppers
   (optional)

   1. Preheat the oven to 500 degrees.

   2. Place all the vegetables in a large roasting pan, covering the entire bottom of the pan. Arrange the bones on top of the vegetables. Place the roasting pan in the upper third of the preheated oven and bake for 1 hour.

3. Remove from the oven and transfer all the bones and vegetables to a large stockpot. Pour off and discard all the fat from the roasting pan. Deglaze the pan by adding 4 cups of water to the pan and bringing it to a full boil over high heat, constantly scraping to release all the bits stuck to the pan. Pour this into the stockpot. Add 11 quarts of water, the cloves, bay leaves, thyme, peppercorns, and hot peppers, if using. Bring to a boil, skimming the foam as it rises to the surface. Lower the heat, stir, cover, and simmer for about 5 hours.

4. Remove the stock from the heat and let cool, undisturbed. Strain through a fine sieve or strainer lined with a double layer of cheesecloth. Discard the bones, vegetables, and herbs and let the stock rest, undisturbed, for 10 to 15 minutes to allow the fat to rise to the surface.

5. Degrease the stock by scooping off the fat with a ladle, using a circular motion; discard it. The stock is now ready to be used. If the stock is not to be used immediately, store it in the refrigerator without degreasing it. Degrease before using by removing the hardened layer of fat from the surface.

STORAGE NOTE   This stock keeps very well in the refrigerator for up to 1 week. To ensure the life of the stock, clarify it after 3 days (see below), let it cool, and put it back in the refrigerator. To store the stock for longer periods, freeze it. It is practical to freeze it in several small airtight containers so that only the amount needed for a soup or sauce has to be defrosted. Stock that has been defrosted should never be refrigerated or refrozen. Use it at once.

To clarify 8 quarts of meat stock, add 1½ pounds ground lean beef, veal, or chicken; 8 egg whites and the crushed eggshells; 2 cups vegetables, such as chopped carrots, celery, and leeks; 1 or 2 chopped tomatoes; and a few sprigs of herbs, such as fresh thyme, parsley, or dill. Bring the stock to a full boil. Remove from the heat and let sit, undisturbed, until cool. The impurities that were dispersed in the liquid will settle to the bottom along with the chopped meat, eggs, and vegetables, leaving a clear amber broth on top. Strain through a strainer lined with cheesecloth. Season to taste with salt and use or store.

Caldo de Ternera
Veal Stock

—

Makes about 8 quarts

6 pounds veal bones, preferably knuckle bones
2 veal shanks, cut into 1-inch pieces (10 pounds), or breast of veal
  (about 9 pounds)
2 calves' feet, cut into small pieces
4 large onions, unpeeled, cut into quarters (about 3½ pounds)
1 whole head garlic, unpeeled, cut in half horizontally
8 stalks celery with leafy tops, washed and cut in half
1 parsnip, washed and chopped, or 1 carrot, washed and chopped
1 small turnip, washed and chopped
2 bay leaves
6 to 8 sprigs fresh oregano or fresh thyme, or 1 large sprig
  fresh rosemary
24 black peppercorns
18 allspice berries
1 or 2 dried red chili peppers, seeded

1. Place all the ingredients in a large stockpot, add 12 quarts of water, and bring to a boil. Skim as the foam rises to the surface. Lower the heat, cover, and simmer for 5 hours.

2. Remove the stock from the heat and let cool, undisturbed. Strain through a fine sieve or a strainer lined with a double layer of cheese-cloth. Discard the bones, vegetables, and herbs and let the stock sit, undisturbed, for 10 to 15 minutes to allow the fat to rise to the surface.

3. Degrease by scooping all the fat off with a ladle in a circular motion. Discard the fat. The veal stock is now ready to be used. If it is not used immediately, store it in the refrigerator without degreasing it. Degrease the stock when it is to be used by removing the hardened layer of fat from the surface.

Caldo de Cordero
Lamb Stock

—

Makes about 2 quarts

4 pounds lamb bones, including neck bones
3 large onions, unpeeled, quartered
2 whole heads garlic, unpeeled, cut in half horizontally
6 to 7 stalks celery with leafy tops, washed and sliced
2 carrots, washed and sliced
3 medium tomatoes, quartered (about 1 pound)
1 whole leek, washed and coarsely chopped
1 tablespoon coriander seed
6 to 8 cloves
2 dried red chili peppers
1 small bunch fresh thyme (½ ounce)
8 sprigs fresh mint
8 black peppercorns

1. Preheat the broiler or the oven to 500 degrees.

2. Spread the bones, onions, and garlic in a roasting pan and broil them for 15 to 20 minutes until they are completely brown, or roast them for 30 minutes. Transfer the bones, onions, and garlic to a large stockpot.

3. Pour off and discard all the fat from the roasting pan. Add 2 cups of water to the roasting pan and deglaze by placing the pan over low heat and scraping to release all the drippings that stuck to the bottom. Add the deglazing liquid to the stockpot with 18 cups of water. Add the rest of the ingredients.

4. Bring to a boil, skimming every time foam rises to the surface. Lower the heat and simmer for 2½ to 3 hours, or until the stock has reduced to about 9 cups.

5. Remove from the heat and strain the stock through a fine sieve or a strainer lined with several layers of cheesecloth. Discard the bones, vegetables, herbs, and spices. Let the stock sit for 10 to 15 minutes, undisturbed, to allow all the fat to rise to the surface.

(Continued)

6. Degrease by scooping all the fat off with a ladle or spoon in a circular motion. Discard the fat. The stock is ready to be used. If the stock is not to be used immediately, store it in the refrigerator without degreasing it. Remove the layer of congealed fat when ready to use the stock.

NOTE   You may also make a quick lamb stock with the bones from a leg of lamb. Do not roast the bones. Use about half as many vegetables, herbs, and spices.

STORAGE NOTE   The stock may be refrigerated, tightly covered, for up to 1 week. It may be frozen for up to 6 months. Do not refrigerate or refreeze after defrosting.

Caldo de Pescado
Fish Stock

Makes about 4 quarts

A good fish stock has the delicate taste and refreshing scent of the sea. You need to have lots of fish bones, heads, tails, fins, and skins to get a broth full of flavor and body. The spine bones of the fish are especially good to use. The gills, however, must be discarded or they will tarnish the stock. Fish skins, like the fins and tails, have a natural gelatin that gives the stock substance.

The final taste of the stock will be determined mainly by the type of fish bones and scraps used. The broth of fatty fish, such as salmon, eels, bonito, tuna, and some kinds of trout, will always have the pronounced taste of the fish it was made with. This type of stock is good for the preparation of dishes featuring the same kind of fish with which the stock was made.

A more neutral, delicate flavor is obtained by using leaner types of fish, such as flounder, sole, and all other flatfish, including halibut. Tile, all types of bass, snapper, hake, and especially cod make a beautiful stock that will blend well with vegetables, meat, and poultry, as well as seafood.

Raw shells from shrimp, crayfish, lobster, and other crustaceans add good flavor to fish stock. Save these shells by freezing them so you have them on hand when a fish stock is needed. The shells by themselves—without the addition of any other fish scraps—will produce a good stock with excellent bouquet, provided there are plenty of them.

5 pounds fish heads, bones, tails, fins, and skin
1 large onion, peeled and chopped
2 cloves garlic, peeled and crushed
1-inch piece fresh ginger, peeled and sliced
1 leek, trimmed of most of the green leaves, washed and chopped
1 or 2 jalapeño peppers, cut in half lengthwise and seeded
5 stalks celery with leafy tops, washed and chopped
1 parsnip or small carrot, peeled and chopped
8 to 10 sprigs fresh dill or Italian parsley
6 sprigs fresh thyme or oregano
2 to 3 sprigs cilantro or mint
10 cloves or allspice berries

1. Clean the fish head by removing and discarding the gills. Cut the head in half or quarter it.

2. Place the cleaned heads, bones, tails, fins, and skin in a large stockpot. Add the rest of the ingredients and 16 cups of water. Slowly bring to a boil; reduce the heat and simmer gently over very low heat for about 20 minutes, skimming as the foam rises to the surface.

3. Remove the stockpot from the heat. Let it cool and pour the stock through a fine sieve or a strainer lined with a double layer of cheesecloth. Discard the contents of the sieve or strainer. The fish stock is now ready to be used or stored.

STORAGE NOTE Fresh fish stock will keep, tightly covered, for no more than 3 days in the refrigerator. It can also be frozen for up to 4 months.

Caldo de Camarones
Shrimp Stock

—

Makes about 2½ cups

Reserved shrimp shells, crushed and coarsely chopped
3 cups Chicken Stock (page 461) or 1½ cups white wine mixed with
    1½ cups water or 3 cups water
2 stalks celery with leafy tops, washed and chopped
1 medium onion, peeled and chopped (1 cup)
½-inch piece fresh ginger, thinly sliced (optional)
8 black peppercorns
3 sprigs Italian parsley

1. Place the shrimp shells in a saucepan. Add the stock, celery, onion, ginger, if using, peppercorns, and parsley. Bring to a boil, lower the heat, and simmer, uncovered, for 20 minutes.

2. Pour the stock through a fine sieve, pressing out all the juices from the vegetables and shells.

Caldo de Vegetales
Vegetable Stock

—

Makes about 2 quarts

6 to 8 cups chopped leaves of romaine or Boston or iceberg lettuce,
*   or sorrel, or a combination of any two*
3 leeks, washed and sliced (about 1 pound)
4 stalks celery with leafy tops, washed and coarsely chopped
2 medium onions, peeled and thinly sliced
2 carrots, washed and chopped
1 small fennel bulb, chopped, or 6 to 8 sprigs fresh dill
2 green cabbage leaves, sliced
4 sprigs fresh oregano or mint
8 sprigs fresh thyme
4 sprigs Italian parsley
1 bay leaf
1 or 2 jalapeño peppers, seeded, or red chili peppers (optional)

1. Place all the ingredients in a stockpot, including the hot peppers, if using, with 8 cups of cold water and slowly bring to a boil. Skim the foam as it rises to the surface. Lower the heat and simmer, partly covered, for 40 to 45 minutes.

2. Remove the stock from the heat. Let it cool, then strain it through a fine sieve or a strainer lined with a double layer of cheesecloth. Discard the cheesecloth with the vegetables and herbs, reserving the stock. The stock is now ready to be used or stored.

STORAGE NOTE   This stock can be stored in the refrigerator for up to 10 days, but it is better to make it fresh.

CORN BEER

Chicha de Jora
Corn Beer

Makes about 4 quarts

Chicha de jora, or corn beer, is the beer of the Andes. There are two types of *jora*, or sprouted corn, one yellow and one reddish: *jora blanca* (white *jora*) and *jora negra* (black *jora*). The yellow type is preferred in Ecuador. In Peru, both types are used, often in combination. The proper sweetener for *chicha* is *chancaca*, or raw sugar. It is quite similar in taste to dark brown sugar, which I have used in this recipe.

Though *chicha* is very easy to prepare, it is extremely important to follow the one rule that will determine success or failure: all the materials you use must be made of ceramic, porcelain, glass, stainless steel, wood, or cloth. If not, the *chicha* will turn sour.

Chicha de jora is ready to drink the day it is made, but it is not customary to do so. It is best to let the *chicha* rest for at least five days to give it a chance to develop its full flavor and texture. After that the *chicha* starts fermenting. It will leave a pleasant piquant sensation on your tongue when you drink it.

To quicken the fermentation, you can add a teaspoon of yeast with the sugar. The degree of fermentation is a matter of taste: the longer the *chicha* stands, the higher the alcohol level. A well-fermented *chicha de jora* has a thick foam on the surface, indicating that it is alive and ready for a good party.

1 pound jora
8 allspice berries or cloves
2 cups tightly packed dark brown sugar
Lemon wedges (optional)

1. In a large stainless-steel pot, combine the *jora*, allspice berries, and 8 quarts of cold water. Stir and let soak for about 1 hour.

2. Place the pot over medium heat and bring to a boil, stirring now and then. Lower the heat and gently simmer for 4½ hours, stirring occasionally with a wooden spoon and scraping the bottom of the pot to prevent sticking. If too much liquid evaporates, add enough *boiling water* to compensate. You want to have 3 to 4 quarts at the end. Remove from heat and let sit undisturbed for about 1 hour.

3. Strain through a stainless-steel strainer lined with a double layer of cheesecloth into a ceramic, procelain, or glass container, twisting the cheesecloth to squeeze out all the juices. Discard the contents of the cheesecloth. Drop in the 2 cups of brown sugar; do not stir. Store the container, covered with a piece of cloth, in a dark, draft-free, warm spot, undisturbed, for 5 to 8 days or more, depending on how strong and how thick you want the *chicha* to be. The longer it sits, the higher the alcohol content will be and the thicker it will get.

4. Chill thoroughly, correct the seasoning with sugar to taste, and serve in a beer glass, garnished with lemon wedges, if desired.

To make *jora*, soak dry kernels of yellow or Indian corn for 1 or 2 days in plenty of cold water. Line a baking tray with several sheets of newspaper covered with a double layer of cheesecloth. Spray with water to moisten the paper and cloth thoroughly. Drain the corn kernels and spread them evenly over the cheesecloth. Cover with a double layer of moistened cheesecloth. Place the tray in a dark spot and keep the cloth moist, but not wet, at all times until the corn has sprouted, about eight to ten days. Transfer all the sprouted corn to a dry baking tray and dry it in the sun for a full day. If one day in the sun is not enough, bring the tray in and keep it indoors overnight, then put it out in the sun the next day. When the kernels are thoroughly dry, partially crush them. The *jora* is ready to be used or stored. Store in an airtight container in a dark, dry, cool place. It will keep almost indefinitely.

OILS AND FATS

Esencia de Achiote
Achiote Oil

—

Makes about 1 cup

Annatto or achiote seeds are a beautiful fiery red. Indigenous to tropical America, they are also known as *anatta, aploppas, arnotto, arleana,* and *urucu*—just to mention a few names. The early Amazon tribes used the color from these seeds to adorn their bodies. Later they learned to use them to give color and flavor to foods. This spice is still frequently used in South American cooking. Sometimes the seeds are added directly to the cooking liquid; sometimes they are used in the form of a paste; more commonly, the seeds are infused in lard *(manteca de achiote)* or in oil, as in this recipe. Whichever way it is used, annatto gives an appetizing bright-yellow color to food besides adding a distinctive flavor.

Annatto seeds should be fresh, with a bright-reddish color when you buy them. If the seeds are brown or dark burgundy, you can be sure they have lost not only their color but much of their flavor as well. The smell should be woodsy and aromatic, the flavor slightly punchy and a bit peppery, with a note of nutmeg. The seeds can be kept almost indefinitely when properly stored in a tightly covered jar in a cool, dark, dry place.

1 cup olive or vegetable oil
½ cup annatto (achiote) seeds (see Variation)
1 dried red chili or serrano pepper, crumbled
1 bay leaf

1. In a small saucepan, combine the oil, annatto seeds, hot pepper, and bay leaf. Let sit, stirring now and then, for 30 minutes.

2. Place the saucepan over low heat and bring to a gentle boil while stirring. Immediately remove from the heat and cool thoroughly, stirring now and then.

3. Pour through a fine sieve or through a strainer lined with several layers of cheesecloth. The oil is ready to be used or stored. Discard the pepper and bay leaf and check the seeds (see Note).

NOTE   If the seeds still have a bright color after straining the oil in Step 3, you can use them another time, using ½ cup of oil instead of 1 cup and a fresh pepper and bay leaf. Repeat the entire procedure, discarding the seeds, pepper, and bay leaf.

STORAGE NOTE   The oil can be kept refrigerated in a tightly covered jar for up to 1 year.

VARIATION

Substitute ¼ cup paprika mixed with 1 teaspoon ground turmeric for the annatto seeds.

Esencia de Curry
Curry Oil

Makes about 1 cup

With some simple adjustments you can change the flavor of this curry oil. You could add extra spices, such as a bay leaf, ground fennel, or juniper berries; or replace the cloves with allspice berries or half a teaspoon of mace; or replace the cumin with a teaspoon of cardamom. Turmeric is interchangeable with *palillo,* a South American spice: they are similar in flavor, and both give foods an appetizing yellow color.

1½ cups olive or vegetable oil
½ cup curry powder (about 2 ounces)
2 teaspoons ground cumin
1 tablespoon ground turmeric
6 to 8 cloves
1 to 2 dried mirasol or red chili peppers, crumbled

1. In a small saucepan, combine all of the ingredients. Let sit for 30 minutes, stirring now and then.

(Continued)

2. Place the saucepan over low heat and bring to a gentle boil, stirring. Immediately remove from the heat and let the contents cool thoroughly.

3. Pour through an extra-fine sieve or a strainer lined with several layers of cheesecloth, squeezing the cheesecloth to extract all the oil from the spices. Discard the contents of the sieve or cheesecloth. The oil is ready to be used or stored.

STORAGE NOTE   Curry oil will keep for up to 1 year, either in the refrigerator or in a cool, dark, dry place. Store in a tightly covered jar.

VARIATION

Add 2 or 3 crushed cloves garlic with the spices. If the garlic starts browning too quickly in Step 2, remove and discard it. Garlic-curry oil has a short shelf life: use it within 1 week.

Esencia de Pimentón
Paprika Oil

Makes about 1 cup

There are two types of paprika to choose from: sweet and hot. If you use hot paprika, omit the cayenne in this recipe. There are also two distinct and very different kinds of paprika: Hungarian, which is the more flavorful of the two, and Spanish, which is redder and deeper in color. Sweet or hot, Hungarian or Spanish, all are good for making this flavored oil.

1½ cups olive or vegetable oil
½ cup Spanish paprika
½ teaspoon cayenne
8 to 10 allspice berries, cracked, or juniper berries, crushed

1. In a small saucepan, combine all of the ingredients. Let sit for 30 minutes.

2. Place the saucepan over low heat and bring to a gentle boil while stirring. Immediately remove from the heat. Let sit until thoroughly cool.

3. Pour through a strainer lined with several layers of cheesecloth, squeezing the cheesecloth to extract all the oil from the spices. Discard the cheesecloth. The oil is ready to be used or stored.

STORAGE NOTE   Paprika oil will keep, tightly covered, in the refrigerator for up to 1 year.

Manteca de Pato
Rendered Duck Fat

Makes about 1 quart

All waterfowl have a certain amount of fat, but none has so much as the white Long Island duckling. As a matter of fact, this duck was originally bred by the Chinese for a high yield of fat, not for the meat. The fat is concentrated in the thick skin.

Goose fat is also superb. Remove the big chunk of white fat from the cavity and any excess fat from the neck and thighs and render it the same way as duck fat. The two can be used interchangeably.

Slice the skin and fat of 1 duck into ¼-inch strips and chop any excess fat. In a saucepan, combine the duck skin and extra fat, 1 bay leaf, 8 to 12 juniper berries or allspice berries or cloves, and 1 cup cold water. Bring to a boil. Lower the heat and simmer until all the water has evaporated and most of the fat has been released, about 45 minutes. The skin will cook in its own fat until it is slightly golden and crisp. Remove from the heat and strain through a fine sieve or a strainer lined with a double layer of cheesecloth; let drain well. The fat is ready to use or store.

NOTE   The bits of golden skin, or cracklings, can be used to garnish soups, stews, and salads.

STORAGE NOTE   Duck fat keeps extremely well in the refrigerator, in an airtight container, for up to 3 months. It will keep in the freezer for up to 6 months.

Manteca de Chancho
Rendered Bacon Fat

—

Makes 1 cup

In South America, the most commonly used fat for cooking all meats, fish, and vegetables is rendered pork or bacon fat.

Cut 1 pound slab bacon or fatback into small pieces and place in a saucepan with ½ cup cold water. Cook over medium heat until all the water has evaporated and the bacon has become crisp, about 20 minutes. Strain the fat through a fine sieve or a strainer lined with several layers of cheesecloth. Pour the fat into a jar. It is ready to use or store.

NOTE   The bacon bits can be used as a garnish.

STORAGE NOTE   Rendered bacon fat keeps very well in the refrigerator, in an airtight container, for up to 1 month. You can also freeze the fat for up to 6 months.

Mantequilla Clarificada
Clarified Butter

—

Makes ⅓ cup

To clarify butter is to remove its milky substances, leaving just the fat behind. Clarified butter has a pure taste and does not burn as easily as regular butter. If more than ⅓ cup of butter is needed, simply increase the amount and proceed as directed.

Melt 8 tablespoons (1 stick) unsalted butter in a double boiler or a small heavy saucepan over low heat. Skim the white froth that rises to the top with a spoon and discard. Carefully pour the clear yellow liquid into a jar, leaving the milky residue in the bottom of the pan.

STORAGE NOTE   Clarified butter will keep, tightly covered, in the refrigerator for 2 to 3 weeks.

SAUCES

Salsa de Culantro
Cilantro Sauce

Makes about 1 cup

2 cups tightly packed cilantro leaves
½ cup olive oil
2 cloves garlic, peeled
1-inch piece fresh ginger, peeled and chopped
1 or 2 jalapeño peppers, seeded and chopped
2 teaspoons coarse salt
1 tablespoon fresh lime juice

1. Wash the cilantro leaves and drain well. Dry with paper towels or in a salad spinner.

2. In the jar of a blender or work bowl of a food processor, combine the oil, garlic, ginger, peppers, and salt. Blend or process at high speed for a few seconds, then add the cilantro leaves, little by little. Continue blending until the ingredients are smooth. Add the lime juice, correct the seasoning with salt to taste, and serve.

STORAGE NOTE   To store, cover the surface of the sauce with ¼ cup olive or vegetable oil, pouring the oil over an inverted tablespoon so as not to disturb the surface. Cover tightly and refrigerate for up to 2 weeks.

Salsa de Albahaca
Basil Sauce

Makes about 1½ cups

6 cups tightly packed basil leaves
½ cup olive oil
1 clove garlic, peeled
½-inch piece ginger, peeled and coarsely chopped
1 or 2 fresh jalapeño peppers, seeded and chopped
1 teaspoon coarse salt
2 tablespoons peanuts or pignolis or hazelnuts, roasted (page 485)
1 tablespoon fresh lemon juice
Freshly ground black pepper

1. Wash the basil leaves and drain well. Pat dry with a cloth or paper towels.

2. In the work bowl of a food processor, combine the oil, garlic, ginger, hot pepper, and salt and blend for a few seconds. With the motor running, add the basil leaves, a few at a time, and continue to process until the mixture is quite smooth. Then, while continuously processing, add the nuts and the lemon juice. Correct seasoning with salt and pepper to taste. The sauce is ready to be used or to be stored.

NOTE   To prepare the sauce in the blender, pour 1 cup of olive oil instead of ½ cup into the blender jar. Proceed as above, adding 2 tablespoons of lemon juice instead of 1 tablespoon at the end.

STORAGE NOTE   To store, cover the surface of the sauce with ¼ cup olive oil, pouring it over an inverted tablespoon. Cover tightly and refrigerate for about 2 weeks.

Salsa de Perejil

Parsley Sauce

—

Makes about 1¼ cups

Although either variety of parsley can be used to make this sauce, flat-leaf Italian parsley is preferred because its flavor is so much more pronounced than that of curly parsley.

2 cups tightly packed parsley leaves
3 cloves garlic, peeled and minced
2-inch piece fresh ginger, peeled and minced
2 or 3 jalapeño peppers, seeded and minced
1 stalk celery, strings removed and minced
6 scallions, white parts only, minced
2 teaspoons coarse salt
3 tablespoons lime juice
½ cup olive oil
Freshly cracked black pepper

1. Wash the parsley and drain well. Dry with a cloth, paper towels, or in a salad spinner.

2. On a cutting board, coarsely chop the parsley. Add the minced garlic, ginger, peppers, celery, and scallions and continue to chop the combined ingredients until the parsley is finely chopped. Transfer to a bowl; add the salt, lime juice, and olive oil. Blend well, correct the seasoning with salt and pepper to taste, and serve or store.

STORAGE NOTE   This sauce will keep in the refrigerator, in an airtight container, for up to 2 weeks. Pour the sauce into a jar, pour 2 tablespoons of olive oil over an inverted tablespoon to cover the surface, close the jar, and place in the refrigerator.

Salsa Cruda

Makes 3½ cups

This very refreshing sauce will keep in the refrigerator for about two days, but it is best when eaten on the day it is made.

1 or 2 jalapeño peppers, seeded and chopped
½-inch piece fresh ginger, peeled and chopped
1 large clove garlic, peeled and chopped (optional)
1 red bell pepper, seeded, deveined, and finely chopped (about 1 cup)
2 medium tomatoes, peeled, seeded, and finely chopped
1 large cucumber, peeled, seeded, and finely chopped (about 1 cup)
2 stalks celery, strings removed and finely chopped (about ½ cup)
4 scallions, white parts only, thinly sliced (about ½ cup)
2 tomatillos, hulled and finely chopped (optional)
¼ cup finely chopped fresh cilantro leaves
2 tablespoons finely chopped Italian parsley
2 teaspoons coarse salt
3 tablespoons olive oil
2 teaspoons raspberry vinegar or red-wine vinegar or lime
   or lemon juice

1. On a cutting board, mince together the hot pepper, ginger, and garlic, if using. Transfer this mixture to a bowl and add the bell pepper, tomatoes, cucumber, celery, scallions, and tomatillos, if using. Mix thoroughly.

2. Add the cilantro, parsley, salt, olive oil, and vinegar and mix well. Correct seasoning with salt and freshly ground black pepper to taste. The salsa is ready to serve.

Encurtido de Cebollas

Onion Relish

Serves 6 to 8

This relish is extremely versatile. It is perfect with ham, chicken, and turkey. It is also good with fried or baked fish, all types of baked squash, and other vegetable dishes. You can put it on sandwiches and use it to make appetizers. It should be made fresh, though it will keep for a day in the refrigerator.

4 large onions (about 3 pounds)
1 tablespoon coarse salt
1 or 2 fresh mirasol or jalapeño peppers, seeded and julienned
¼ cup pitted and sliced alfonso or Kalamata olives
¼ cup olive oil
¼ cup red-wine vinegar
Freshly ground white pepper

1. Peel the onions and cut them in half vertically. Remove and discard the roots. Place the onions cut side down on a board and thinly slice them into half-rings. Place them in a stainless-steel bowl, sprinkle with salt, and mix thoroughly. Let sit for 1 hour at room temperature. Transfer the onion rings to a strainer, rinse under cold running water, and drain well.

2. Return the onion rings to the stainless-steel bowl. Add the hot pepper, olives, and oil and toss well. Add the vinegar, toss, and correct the seasoning with salt and pepper to taste.

Mayonesa de Leche
Mayonnaise Made with Milk

—

Makes about 1 cup

This unusual mayonnaise has a delicate taste, a fine texture, and a stunning white color. Like egg mayonnaise, it can be flavored with different oils and seasonings.

Only the high speed of a blender can bind and emulsify the milk and oil. The oil must be added in a continuous extra-thin stream from start to finish. The ratio of milk to oil must be precise—a drop of oil too much and the mayonnaise will break immediately. Once the mayonnaise is thick and stiff and the blender starts burping, it is safe to stop the machine, even though there might still be a tablespoon or two of oil left. After you remove the mayonnaise from the blender jar, you can flavor and season it as you wish.

½ cup whole milk, at room temperature
½ teaspoon dry mustard
1 teaspoon coarse salt
1 cup light vegetable oil
1 or 2 teaspoons lemon or lime juice or white-wine vinegar
Ground white pepper

1. Place the milk, dry mustard, and salt in the jar of an electric blender. Cover and turn the motor on. Immediately remove the cap covering the opening in the lid or remove the lid altogether. With the motor running, start adding the oil in a steady, very thin stream. Continue adding the oil until it has been absorbed and the mayonnaise is thick and stiff. This should take about 8 minutes.

2. Transfer the mayonnaise to a bowl, beat in the lemon or lime juice, and correct the seasoning with salt and white pepper to taste.

BASIC TECHNIQUES

Asar Ajíes
Roasting Fresh Hot Peppers

—

To roast a fresh hot pepper, such as a jalapeño, mirasol, serrano, poblano, Anaheim, arbol, or ancho, hold it with a long fork over an open flame and turn until the skin is slightly charred all around. Rub the pepper with a damp cloth to remove the loose burnt skin. Remove the seeds. The pepper is ready to be used as an ingredient, garnish, or condiment or stored, tightly covered, in the refrigerator for up to 1 week.

NOTE You can also roast peppers in a preheated broiler. Place the peppers in a broiler pan as close to the heat source as possible. Turn until the skin is lightly charred all around. Remove from the heat and wipe with a damp cloth to remove the loose burnt skin. Remove the seeds and use as directed.

Asar Ajísecos
Roasting Dried Hot Peppers

—

To roast a dried hot pepper, hold it with tongs over an open flame and turn just long enough to char the edges of the pepper. The pepper is ready to be used.

Asar Pimientos
Roasting Bell Peppers

—

Preheat the oven to 450 degrees. If desired, rub the peppers with olive oil or vegetable oil. Arrange them in a roasting pan and roast for about 40 minutes, or until the peppers are soft and the skin is loose. When the peppers are cool enough to handle, gently peel off the loose skin and remove the seeds. The peppers are ready to be used or stored.

NOTE You can also roast the peppers in a preheated broiler. Broil them for about 25 minutes, turning frequently to brown them evenly all around and to loosen the skin. When the peppers are cool enough to handle, peel off the loose skin and remove the seeds.

STORAGE NOTE Roasted peppers can be stored in the refrigerator, barely covered with olive or vegetable oil, for up to 1 week.

Pelar Cebollas de Perla
Peeling Pearl Onions

—

Wash the onions and lightly trim the root ends; if the roots are clean and short, leave them as they are. To ensure that the onions do not fall apart during cooking, cut an X in the root ends, about ¼ inch or less deep. Drop the onions into rapidly boiling water and stir. Remove from the heat, cover, and let stand, undisturbed, for 1 or 2 minutes. Drain. When the onions are cool enough to handle, peel them and shave off the rest of the roots. Drop the onions into a bowl of ice-cold water until ready to use.

Asar Nueces
Roasting Nuts

Put the nuts in a heavy aluminum or cast-iron skillet, without any oil or butter. Roast over high heat while constantly shaking the pan, stirring and tossing the nuts, until slightly golden all around. Immediately remove them from the pan. They are ready to be used or stored.

NOTE   You can also roast nuts in the oven. Spread them on a baking tray and put it in a preheated 400-degree oven until golden. Keep a very close watch—nuts can burn in the blink of an eye.

STORAGE NOTE   Store roasted nuts in a tightly covered container, lined with brown paper, to keep them dry and crunchy. Keep them in a dry cool spot. Do not refrigerate them. For longer storage, freeze the nuts in a tightly covered container for up to 6 months.

Pelar Pistachos
Peeling Pistachios

Drop the pistachios into a pot of boiling water. Immediately remove from the heat and let the nuts soak for a few minutes to loosen the skins. Drain and spread out between two pieces of cloth. Gently rub the nuts against the cloth to remove the skins.

Limpieza de Mejillones
Cleaning Mussels

—

Scrub the mussels under cold running water with a brush or pot scrubber to remove all the sand and mud from the shells. Rinse them and place them in a bucket in a solution of ⅓ cup salt per gallon of water with 1 tablespoon baking soda or a sprinkling of flour or oatmeal. Leave to soak for about 2 hours. Discard any mussels that float or are broken or damaged. Rinse the remaining mussels and pull out and cut off the stringy beards. Drain and set aside until ready to use.

Limpieza de Almejas
Cleaning Clams

—

Scrub the clams and soak them for about 2 hours in a solution of ⅓ cup salt per gallon of water with a sprinkling of oatmeal or flour. Rinse under cold running water and drain. Shuck the clams, if desired. If there are traces of sand, place the shucked clams in a strainer and dip it into a bowl of ice-cold water. Shake to release the sand. Remove the strainer from the water and let the clams drain. Never rinse shucked clams under running water.

Limpieza de Calamares
Cleaning Squid

Place the squid on the work surface and peel off the spotted outer membrane. Pull the head, tentacles, and viscera out of the body. Remove the quill from the center of the body. Cut off and discard the head and viscera, saving the tentacles. Remove the beak from the tentacles. Rinse the body and tentacles thoroughly.

Sancochar Pulpo
Blanching Octopus

Unlike the large southern Pacific *pulpo,* the small octopus available in North America is easily tenderized by a relatively short period of cooking. After that, the octopus is ready to be used or stored in the refrigerator. One or two pieces of octopus in a fish stew or soup enriches the dish greatly.

1 fresh or frozen-and-thawed octopus
1 onion, unpeeled and quartered
6 peppercorns
6 juniper berries
1 head garlic, peeled and cut in half horizontally
1 bay leaf
1 tablespoon coarse salt

1. Cut off and discard the mouth part of the octopus, turn the head inside out, and remove and discard the viscera and ink sac. Rinse under cold running water and turn right side out again.

2. In a large saucepan, combine the remaining ingredients with 8 cups of water. Bring to a boil. Add the octopus, lower the heat, and simmer, uncovered, for 45 minutes.

(Continued)

3. Remove the pot from the heat and let the octopus sit in the hot liquid for 50 minutes. Drain, cool, and carefully peel off the purplish membranes from the head and the underside of the tentacles.

STORAGE NOTE   Blanched octopus will keep, tightly covered, in the refrigerator for up to 5 days.

Sasonar Vinagres
Flavored Vinegars

—

Flavored vinegars add a special touch to many dishes. They are easy to make at home. Simply let the flavoring—garlic, chili peppers, cinnamon, achiote, cloves, fennel, lemon or orange rind, flower petals, or whatever—steep in a good-quality white-wine vinegar for about two weeks. You can also steep herbs, such as thyme, tarragon, coriander, sage, rosemary, and mint, in white- or red-wine vinegar for one week. Decant flavored or herb vinegar into a clean jar after steeping.

Fruit vinegars are made by infusing soft fruits, such as currants, raspberries, blueberries, and so on, in red- or white-wine vinegar. Larger fruits like pears can also be used.

Combine about 2 pints of berries or 2 pounds of pears, quartered, with 3 cups of white- or red-wine vinegar in a glass or ceramic container. Stir with a wooden spoon, bruising the fruit, not mashing it. Cover and steep for 2 to 3 days. Transfer the mixture to an enameled or stainless-steel saucepan and heat just to the boiling point. Do not boil. Remove from the heat and strain through cheesecloth into a sterilized jar.

METRIC CONVERSION CHARTS

CONVERSIONS OF OUNCES TO GRAMS

Ounces (oz)	Grams (g)
1 oz	30 g*
2 oz	60 g
3 oz	85 g
4 oz	115 g
5 oz	140 g
6 oz	180 g
7 oz	200 g
8 oz	225 g
9 oz	250 g
10 oz	285 g
11 oz	300 g
12 oz	340 g
13 oz	370 g
14 oz	400 g
15 oz	425 g
16 oz	450 g
20 oz	565 g
24 oz	675 g
28 oz	800 g
32 oz	900 g

* Approximate. To convert ounces to grams, multiply number of ounces by 28.35.

CONVERSIONS OF POUNDS TO GRAMS AND KILOGRAMS

Pounds (lb)	Grams (g) Kilograms (kg)
1 lb	450 g*
1¼ lb	565 g
1½ lb	675 g
1¾ lb	800 g
2 lb	900 g
2½ lb	1,125 g; 1¼ kg
3 lb	1.350 g
3½ lb	1,500 g; 1½ kg
4 lb	1,800 g
4½ lb	2 kg
5 lb	2¼ kg
5½ lb	2½ kg
6 lb	2¾ kg
6½ lb	3 kg
7 lb	3¼ kg
7½ lb	3½ kg
8 lb	3¾ kg
9 lb	4 kg
10 lb	4½ kg

* Approximate. To convert pounds into grams, multiply number of pounds by 453.6.

CONVERSIONS OF FAHRENHEIT TO CELSIUS

Fahrenheit	Celsius
170°F	77°C*
180°F	82°C
190°F	88°C
200°F	95°C
225°F	110°C
250°F	120°C
275°F	135°C
300°F	150°C
325°F	165°C
350°F	180°C
375°F	190°C
400°F	205°C
425°F	220°C
450°F	230°C
475°F	245°C
500°F	260°C
525°F	275°C
550°F	290°C

* Approximate. To convert Fahrenheit into Celsius, subtract 32, multiply by 5, then divide by 9.

CONVERSIONS OF QUARTS TO LITERS

Quarts (qt)	Liters (L)
1 qt	1 L*
1½ qt	1½ L
2 qt	2 L
2½ qt	2½ L
3 qt	2¾ L
4 qt	3¾ L
5 qt	4¾ L
6 qt	5½ L
7 qt	6½ L
8 qt	7½ L
9 qt	8½ L
10 qt	9½ L

* Approximate. To convert quarts to liters, multiply number of quarts by .95.

INDEX

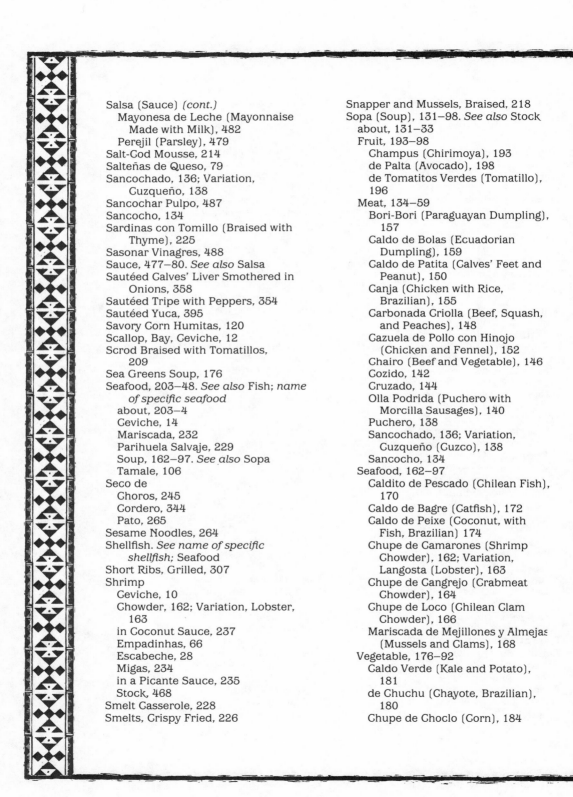